SHIN YOSHIDA

I always have a terrible time choosing Duel locations. They also influence how a Duel develops! Somebody take me to a world nobody's ever seen before and give me ideas to work with!

NAOHITO MIYOSHI

The *ARC-V* manga has entered its second half! What destinies await Yuya's and Eve's sides of the conflict? Is there any way to save all of them? No doubt their Duels will be the determining factor!

MASAHIRO HIKOKUBO

Attention all of you who have noticed differences in card values between the monthly chapters and graphic novels! You've got a sharp eye and can brag to your friends! What's that you say? You want me to stop making mistakes? Well, sorry! We'll do our best!!

5

YU-GI-OH! ARC-V

SHONEN JUMP MANGA EDITION

ORIGINAL CONCEPT BY
Kazuki Takahashi

PRODUCTION SUPPORT: **STUDIO DICE**

STORY BY
Shin Yoshida

ART BY
Naohito Miyoshi

DUEL COORDINATOR
Masahiro Hikokubo

TRANSLATION + ENGLISH ADAPTATION
Sarah Neufeld and John Werry, HC Language Solutions, Inc.

TOUCH-UP ART + LETTERING **John Hunt**

DESIGNER **Stacie Yamaki**

EDITOR **Mike Montesa**

Printed in the U.S.A.

Published by VIZ Media, LLC
P.O. Box 77010
San Francisco, CA 94107

10 9 8 7 6 5 4 3 2 1
First printing, March 2019

VIZ MEDIA
viz.com

SHONEN JUMP
shonenjump.com

ratings.viz.com RATED T TEEN

PARENTAL ADVISORY
YU-GI-OH! ARC-V is rated T for Teen and is recommended for ages 13 and up.

Yu-Gi-Oh! ARC-V

5

The Enemy's Hideout!!

ORIGINAL CONCEPT BY **Kazuki Takahashi**

PRODUCTION SUPPORT: **STUDIO DICE**

STORY BY **Shin Yoshida**

ART BY **Naohito Miyoshi**

DUEL COORDINATOR **Masahiro Hikokubo**

CHARACTERS

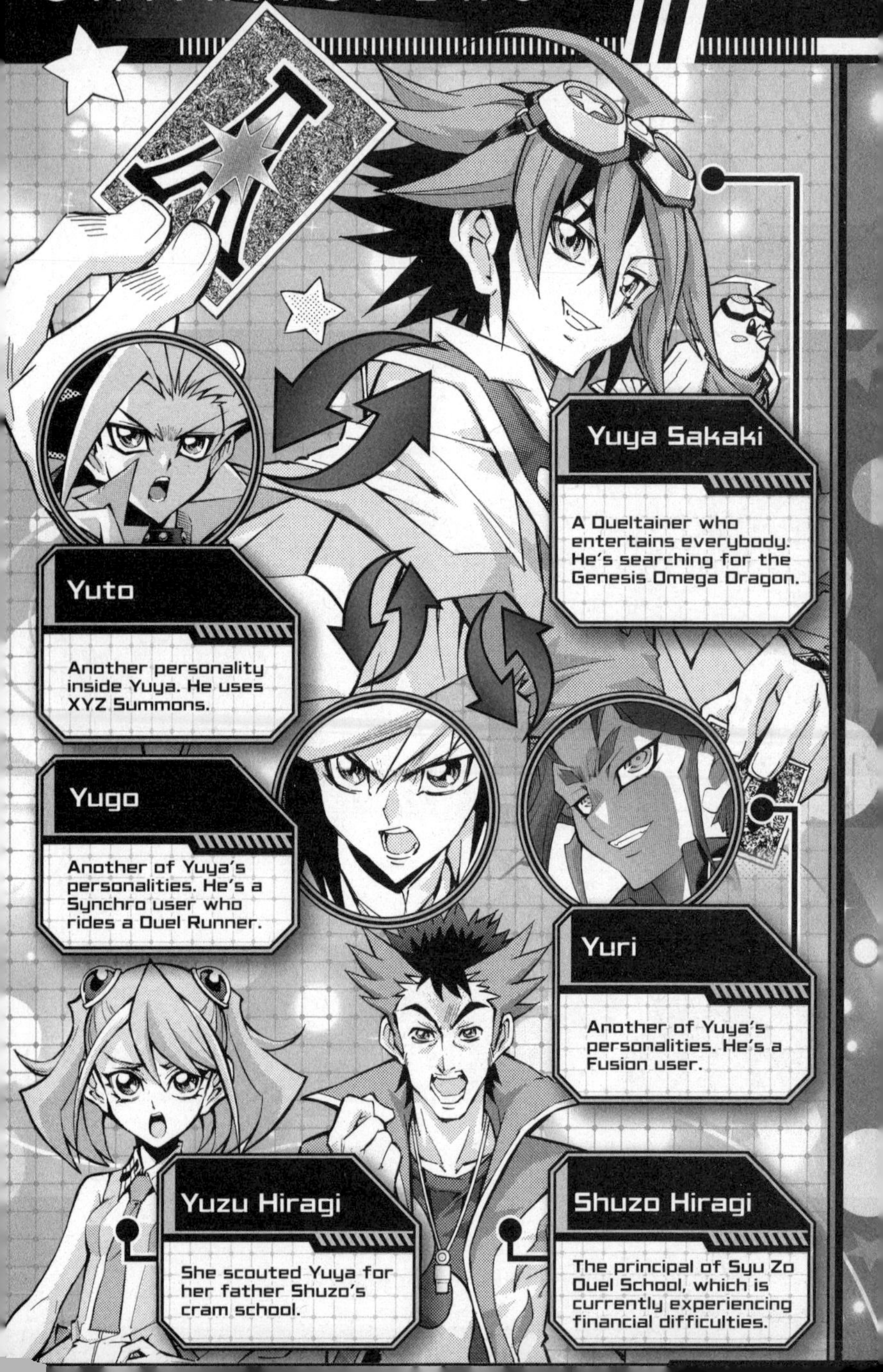
Yuya Sakaki
A Dueltainer who entertains everybody. He's searching for the Genesis Omega Dragon.
Yuto
Another personality inside Yuya. He uses XYZ Summons.
Yugo
Another of Yuya's personalities. He's a Synchro user who rides a Duel Runner.
Yuri
Another of Yuya's personalities. He's a Fusion user.
Yuzu Hiragi
She scouted Yuya for her father Shuzo's cram school.
Shuzo Hiragi
The principal of Syu Zo Duel School, which is currently experiencing financial difficulties.

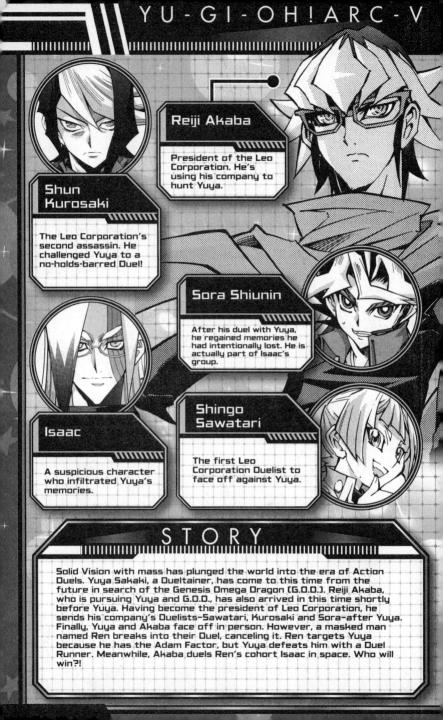

Reiji Akaba

President of the Leo Corporation. He's using his company to hunt Yuya.

Shun Kurosaki

The Leo Corporation's second assassin. He challenged Yuya to a no-holds-barred Duel!

Sora Shiunin

After his duel with Yuya, he regained memories he had intentionally lost. He is actually part of Isaac's group.

Isaac

A suspicious character who infiltrated Yuya's memories.

Shingo Sawatari

The first Leo Corporation Duelist to face off against Yuya.

STORY

Solid Vision with mass has plunged the world into the era of Action Duels. Yuya Sakaki, a Dueltainer, has come to this time from the future in search of the Genesis Omega Dragon (G.O.D.). Reiji Akaba, who is pursuing Yuya and G.O.D., has also arrived in this time shortly before Yuya. Having become the president of Leo Corporation, he sends his company's Duelists—Sawatari, Kurosaki and Sora—after Yuya. Finally, Yuya and Akaba face off in person. However, a masked man named Ren breaks into their Duel, canceling it. Ren targets Yuya because he has the Adam Factor, but Yuya defeats him with a Duel Runner. Meanwhile, Akaba duels Ren's cohort Isaac in space. Who will win?!

Yu-Gi-Oh! ARC-V

5 The Enemy's Hideout!!

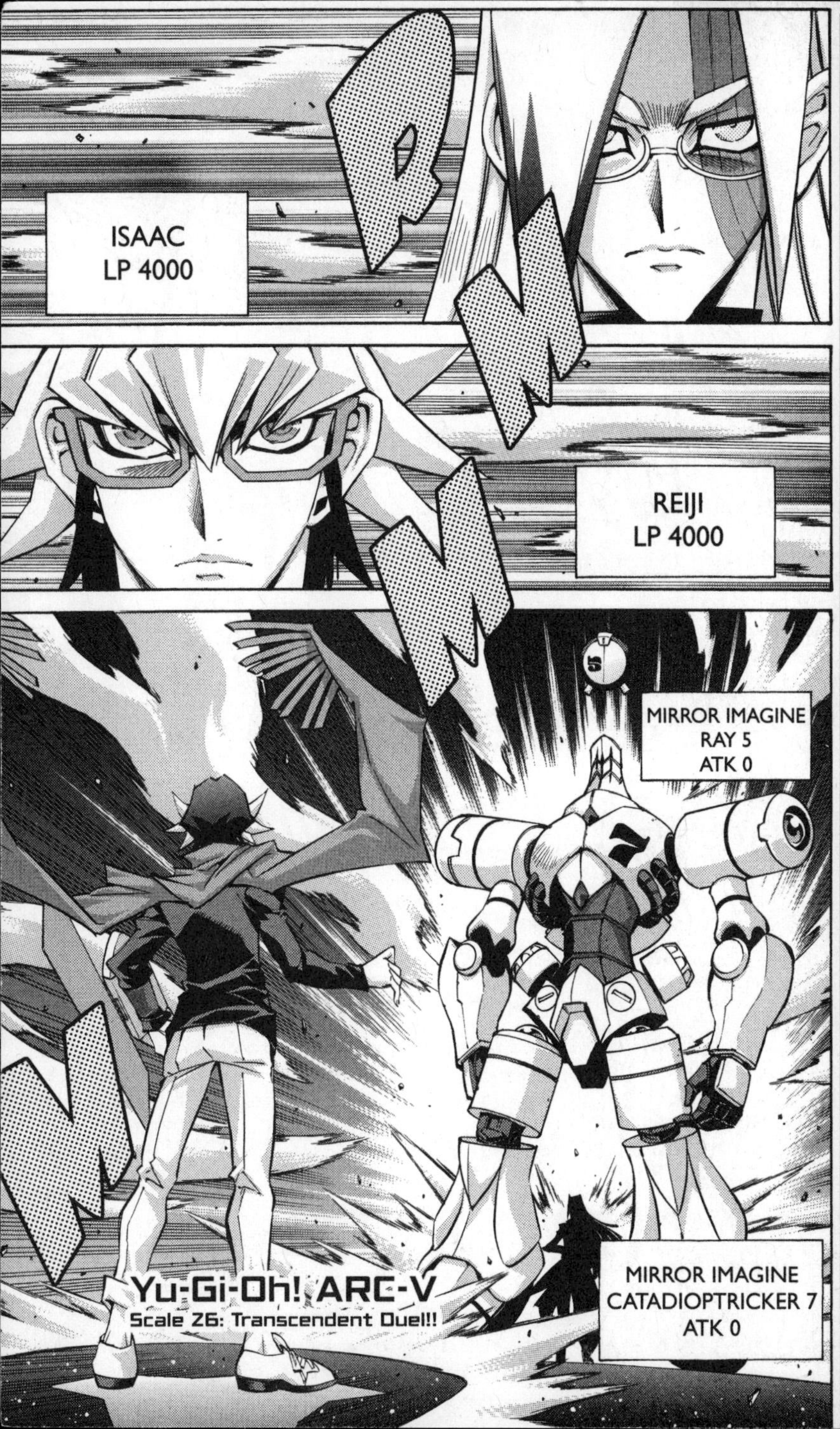
ISAAC
LP 4000
REIJI
LP 4000
MIRROR IMAGINE
RAY 5
ATK 0
MIRROR IMAGINE
CATADIOPTRICKER 7
ATK 0
Yu-Gi-Oh! ARC-V
Scale 26: Transcendent Duel!!

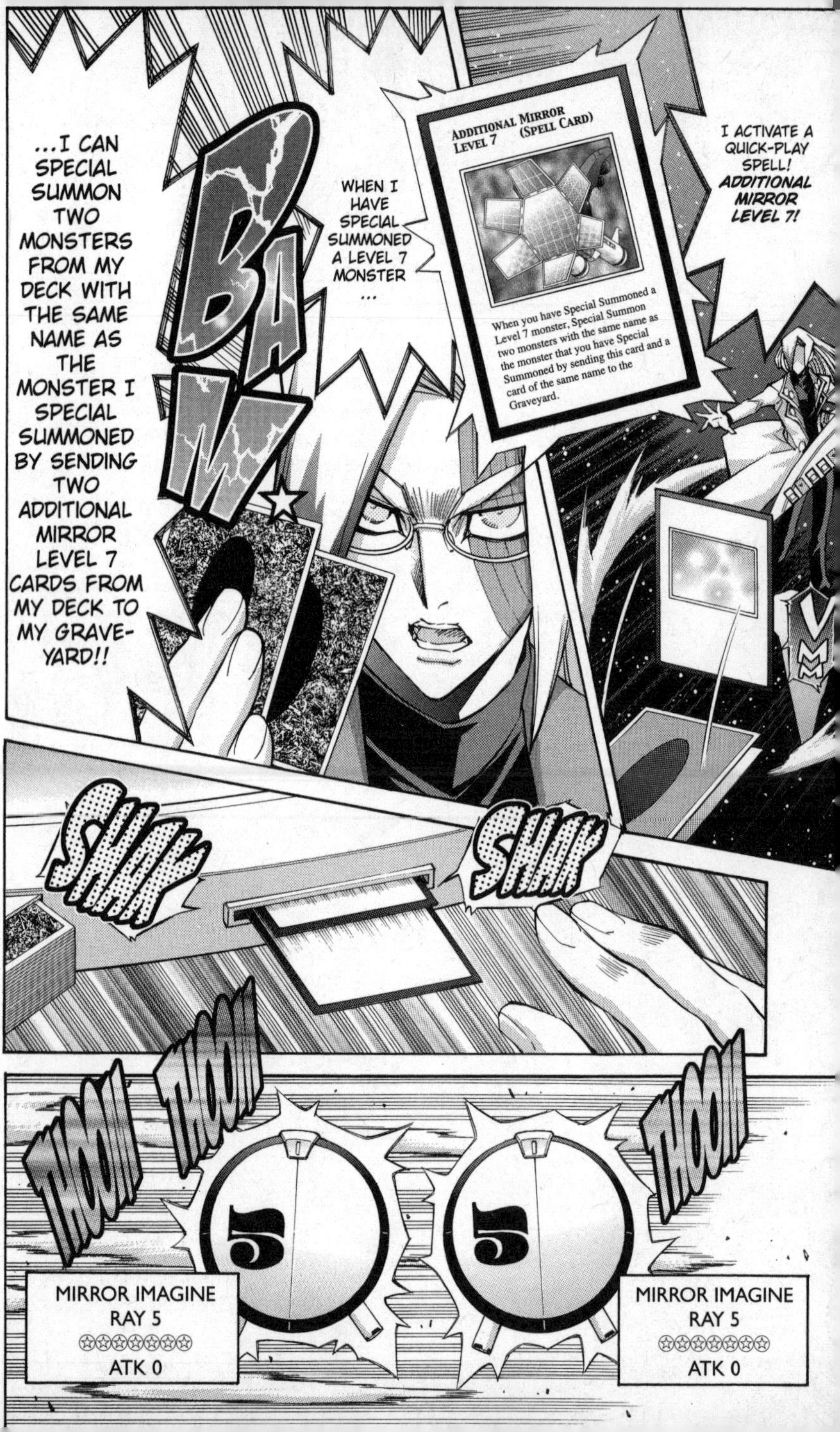
I ACTIVATE A QUICK-PLAY SPELL! ADDITIONAL MIRROR LEVEL 7!
ADDITIONAL MIRROR LEVEL 7 (SPELL CARD)
When you have Special Summoned a Level 7 monster, Special Summon two monsters with the same name as the monster that you have Special Summoned by sending this card and a card of the same name to the Graveyard.
WHEN I HAVE SPECIAL SUMMONED A LEVEL 7 MONSTER ...
BAM
...I CAN SPECIAL SUMMON TWO MONSTERS FROM MY DECK WITH THE SAME NAME AS THE MONSTER I SPECIAL SUMMONED BY SENDING TWO ADDITIONAL MIRROR LEVEL 7 CARDS FROM MY DECK TO MY GRAVEYARD!!
SHAK
SHAK
THOOM
THOOM
THOOM
5
5
MIRROR IMAGINE RAY 5
ATK 0
MIRROR IMAGINE RAY 5
ATK 0

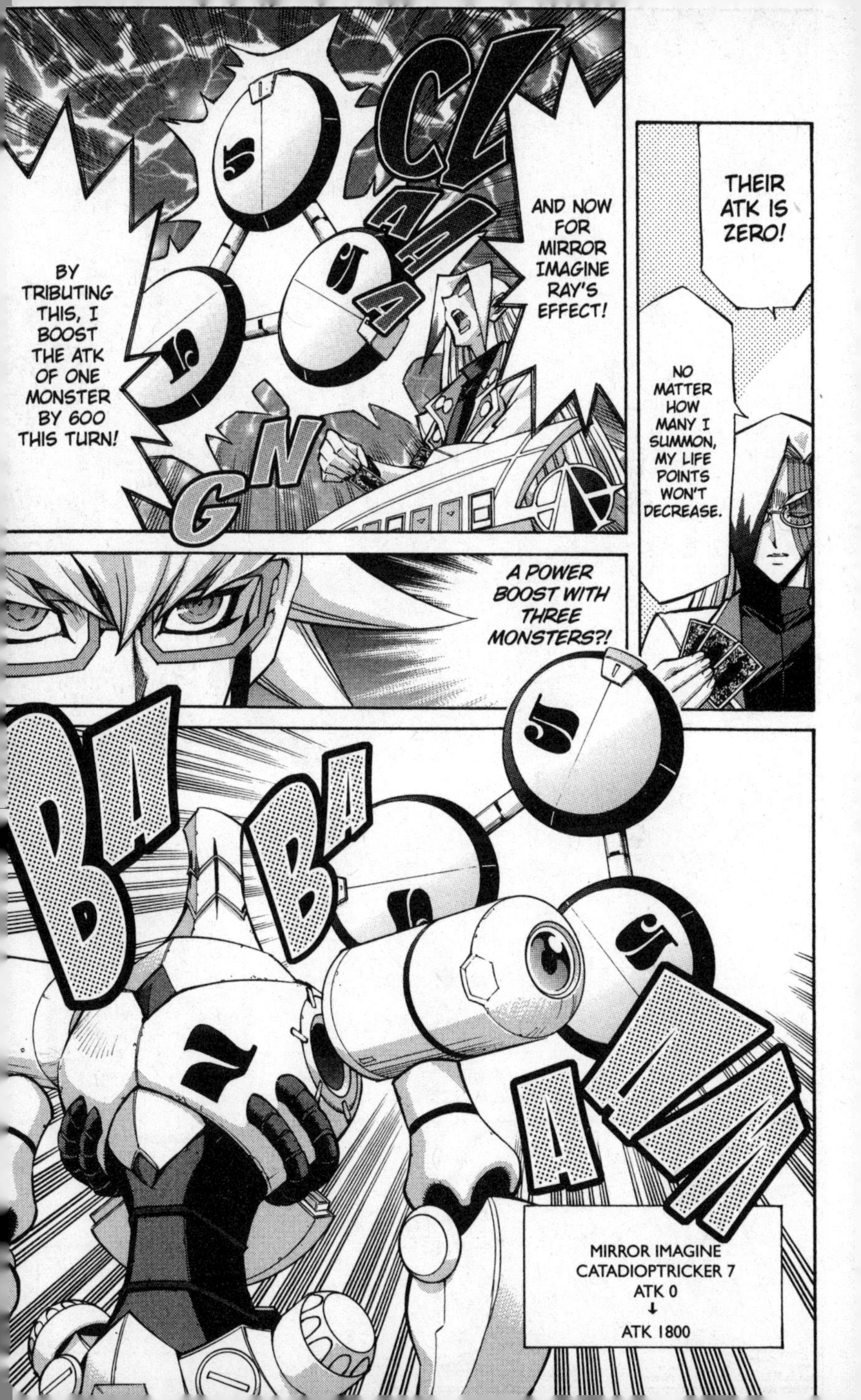
THEIR ATK IS ZERO!
NO MATTER HOW MANY I SUMMON, MY LIFE POINTS WON'T DECREASE.
AND NOW FOR MIRROR IMAGINE RAY'S EFFECT!
CLAAANG
BY TRIBUTING THIS, I BOOST THE ATK OF ONE MONSTER BY 600 THIS TURN!
A POWER BOOST WITH THREE MONSTERS?!
BABAAM
MIRROR IMAGINE CATADIOPTRICKER 7
ATK 0
↓
ATK 1800

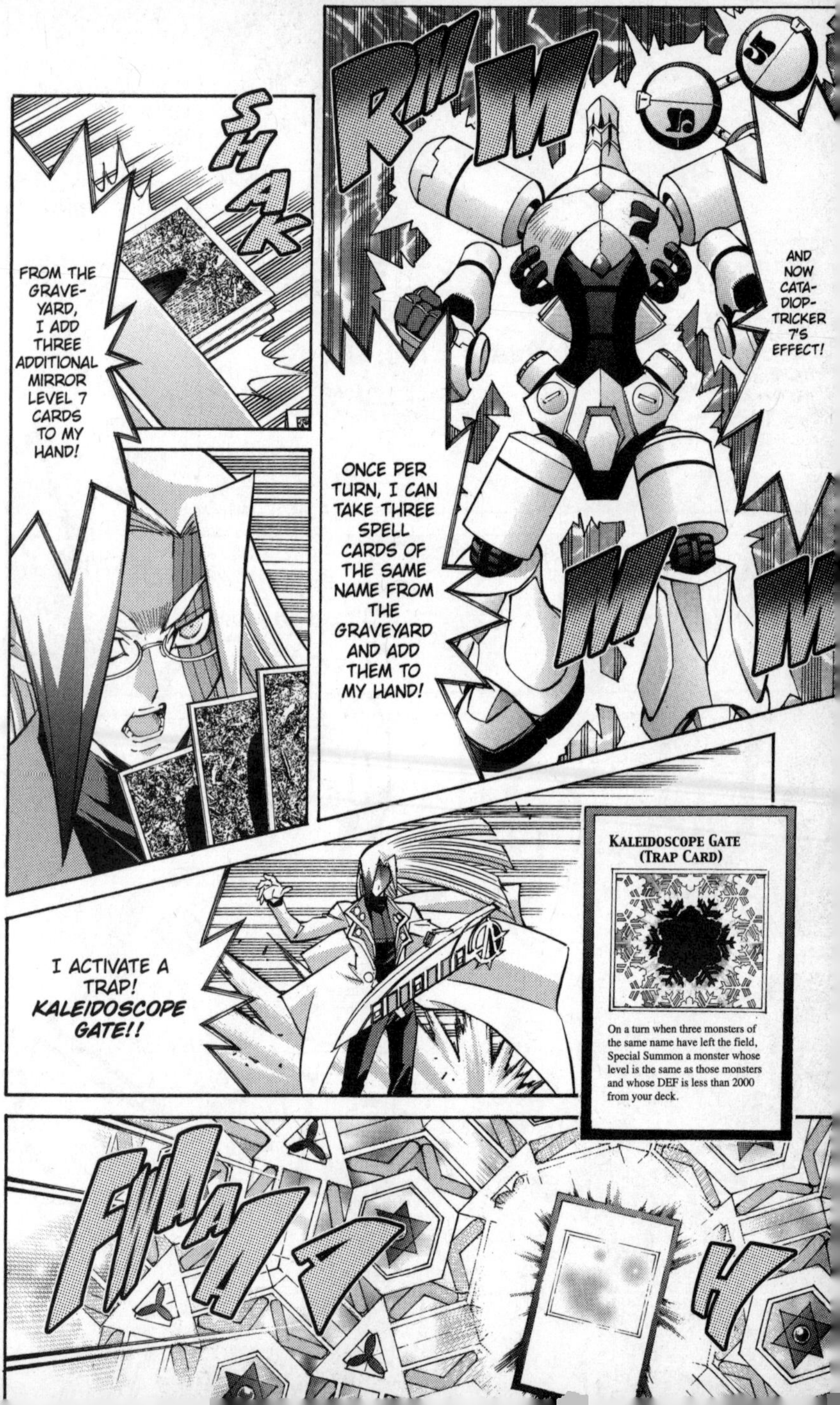
RMMM
AND NOW CATA-DIOP-TRICKER 7'S EFFECT!
ONCE PER TURN, I CAN TAKE THREE SPELL CARDS OF THE SAME NAME FROM THE GRAVEYARD AND ADD THEM TO MY HAND!
MM
SHAK
FROM THE GRAVE-YARD, I ADD THREE ADDITIONAL MIRROR LEVEL 7 CARDS TO MY HAND!
KALEIDOSCOPE GATE (TRAP CARD)
On a turn when three monsters of the same name have left the field, Special Summon a monster whose level is the same as those monsters and whose DEF is less than 2000 from your deck.
I ACTIVATE A TRAP! KALEIDOSCOPE GATE!!
FWAAAAH

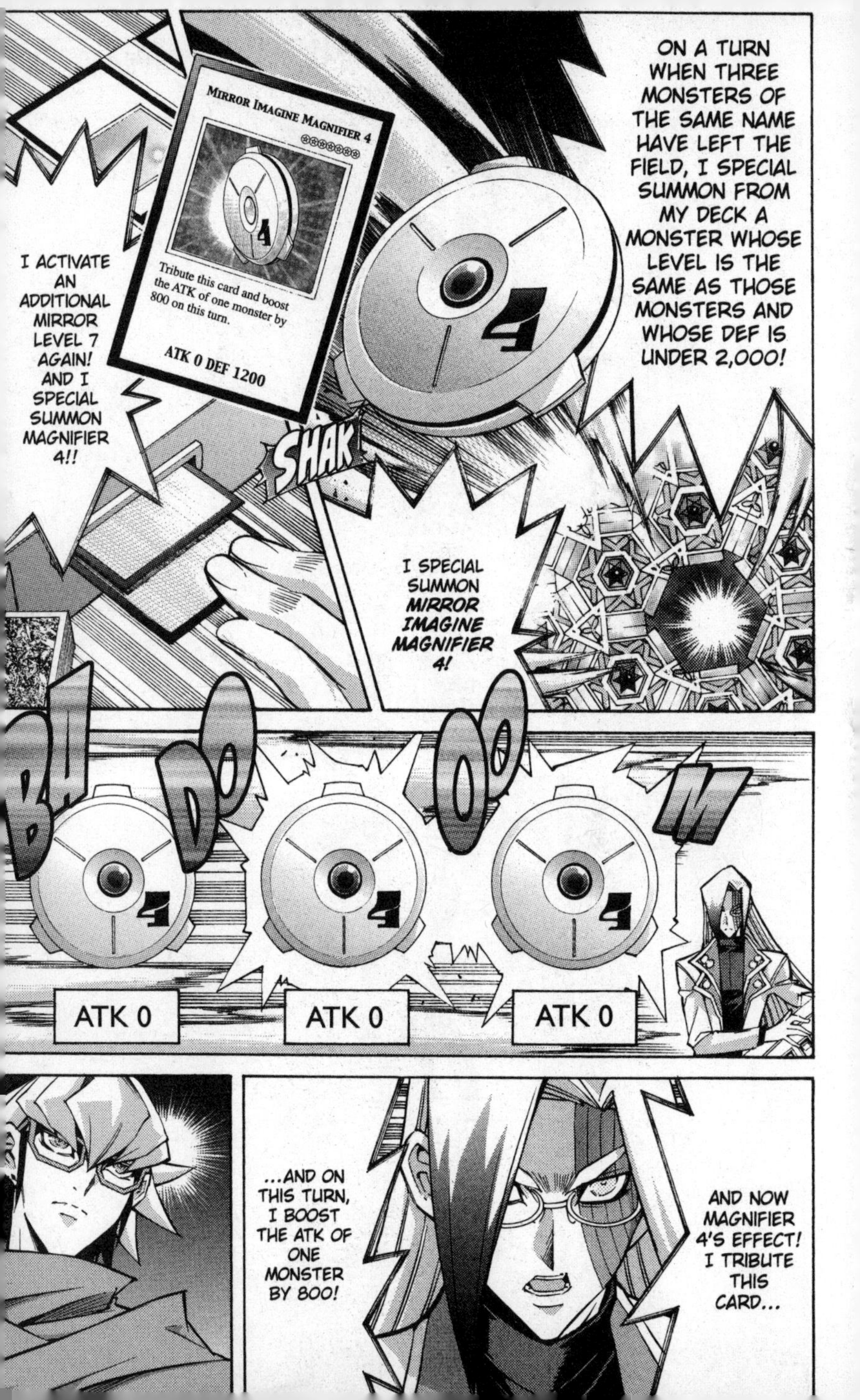
ON A TURN WHEN THREE MONSTERS OF THE SAME NAME HAVE LEFT THE FIELD, I SPECIAL SUMMON FROM MY DECK A MONSTER WHOSE LEVEL IS THE SAME AS THOSE MONSTERS AND WHOSE DEF IS UNDER 2,000!
I ACTIVATE AN ADDITIONAL MIRROR LEVEL 7 AGAIN! AND I SPECIAL SUMMON MAGNIFIER 4!!
MIRROR IMAGINE MAGNIFIER 4
Tribute this card and boost the ATK of one monster by 800 on this turn.
ATK 0 DEF 1200
SHAK
I SPECIAL SUMMON MIRROR IMAGINE MAGNIFIER 4!
BADOOOM
ATK 0
ATK 0
ATK 0
AND NOW MAGNIFIER 4'S EFFECT! I TRIBUTE THIS CARD...
...AND ON THIS TURN, I BOOST THE ATK OF ONE MONSTER BY 800!

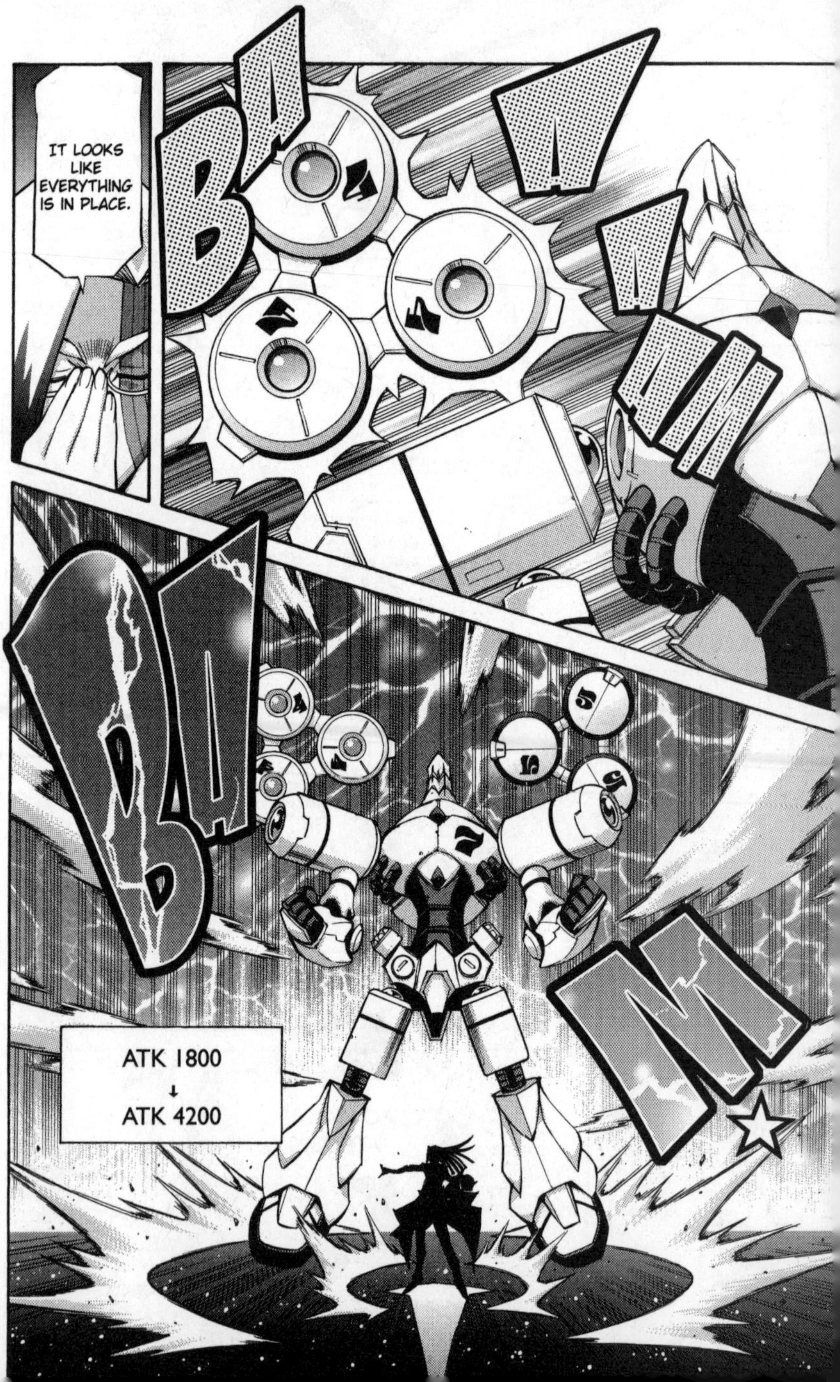
IT LOOKS LIKE EVERYTHING IS IN PLACE.
BAM
ATK 1800
↓
ATK 4200

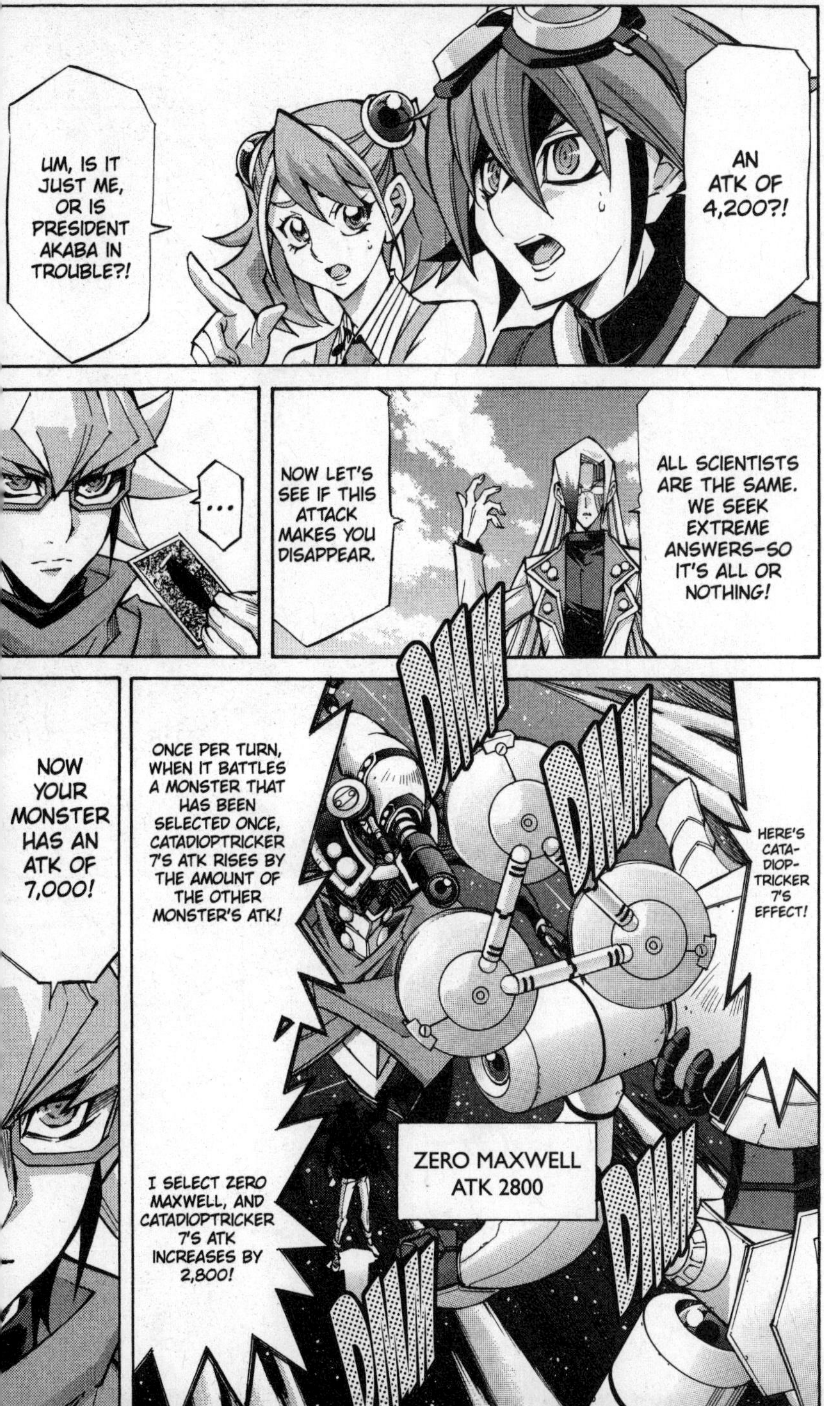
AN ATK OF 4,200?!
UM, IS IT JUST ME, OR IS PRESIDENT AKABA IN TROUBLE?!
ALL SCIENTISTS ARE THE SAME. WE SEEK EXTREME ANSWERS—SO IT'S ALL OR NOTHING!
NOW LET'S SEE IF THIS ATTACK MAKES YOU DISAPPEAR.
...
HERE'S CATA-DIOP-TRICKER 7'S EFFECT!
ONCE PER TURN, WHEN IT BATTLES A MONSTER THAT HAS BEEN SELECTED ONCE, CATADIOPTRICKER 7'S ATK RISES BY THE AMOUNT OF THE OTHER MONSTER'S ATK!
ZERO MAXWELL ATK 2800
I SELECT ZERO MAXWELL, AND CATADIOPTRICKER 7'S ATK INCREASES BY 2,800!
NOW YOUR MONSTER HAS AN ATK OF 7,000!

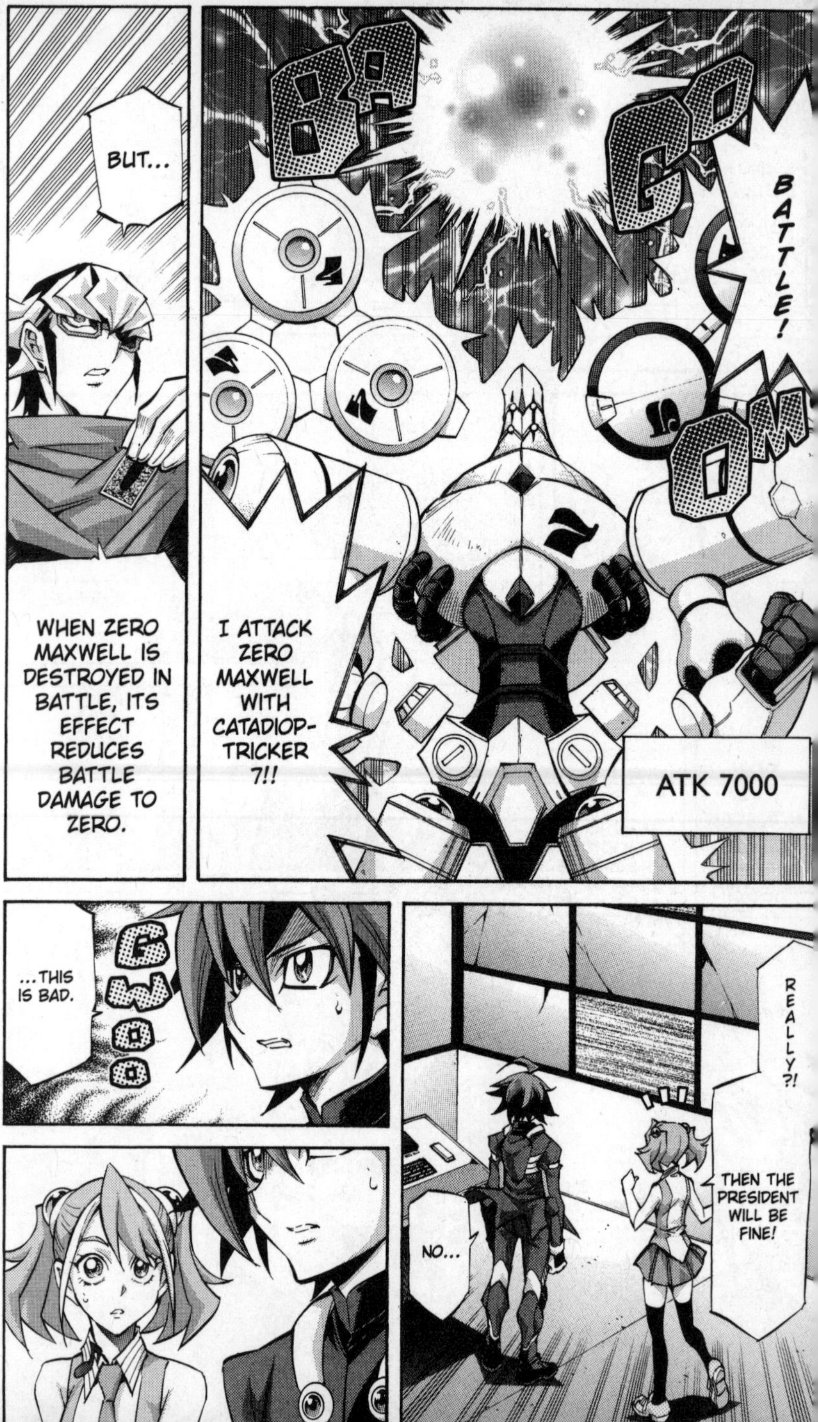
BAGOOM
BATTLE!
ATK 7000
I ATTACK ZERO MAXWELL WITH CATADIOP-TRICKER 7!!
BUT...
WHEN ZERO MAXWELL IS DESTROYED IN BATTLE, ITS EFFECT REDUCES BATTLE DAMAGE TO ZERO.
REALLY?!
THEN THE PRESIDENT WILL BE FINE!
NO...
GWOOO
...THIS IS BAD.

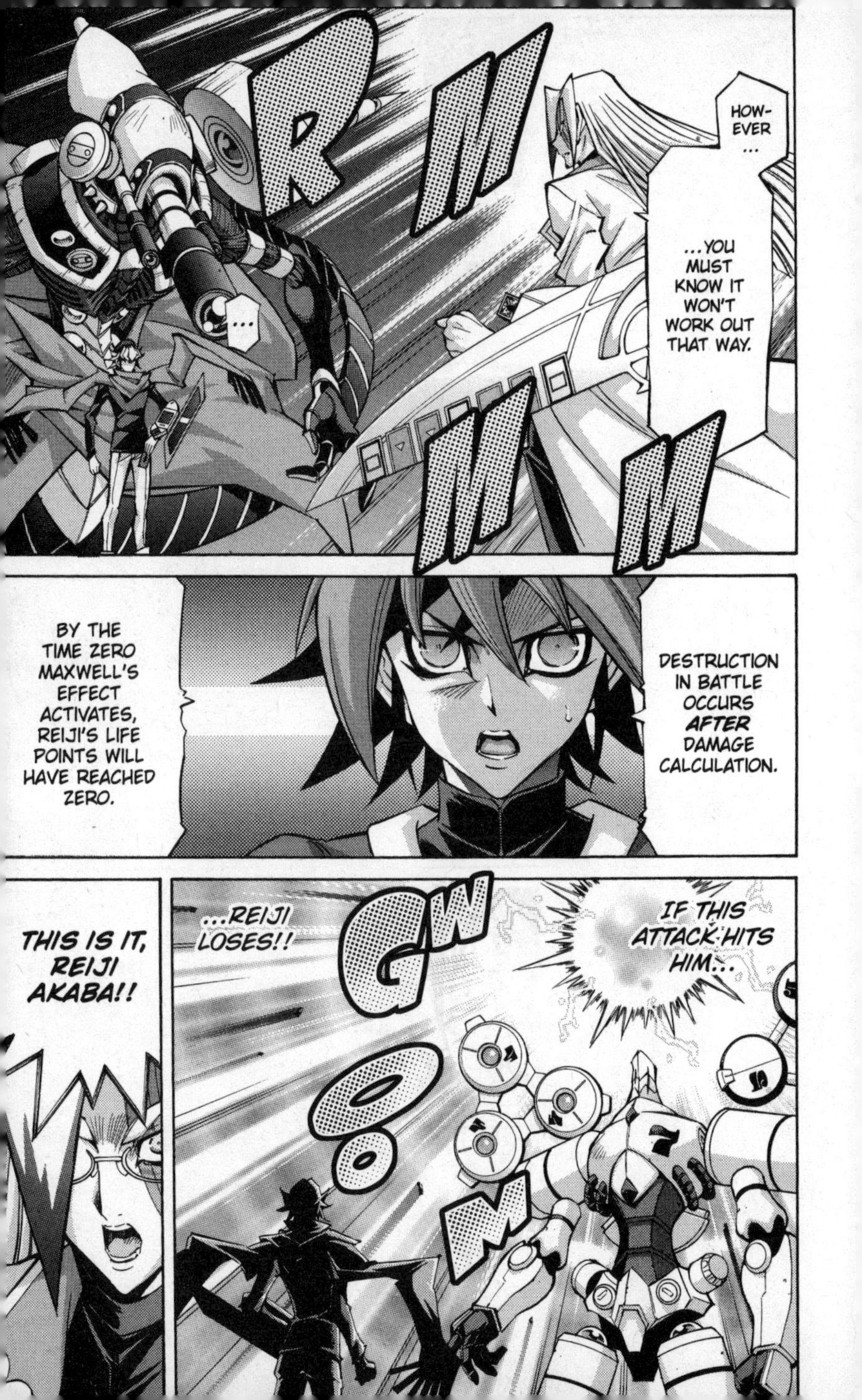
HOW-EVER ...
RMMM
...
...YOU MUST KNOW IT WON'T WORK OUT THAT WAY.
DESTRUCTION IN BATTLE OCCURS AFTER DAMAGE CALCULATION.
BY THE TIME ZERO MAXWELL'S EFFECT ACTIVATES, REIJI'S LIFE POINTS WILL HAVE REACHED ZERO.
IF THIS ATTACK HITS HIM...
GWOOOM
...REIJI LOSES!!
THIS IS IT, REIJI AKABA!!

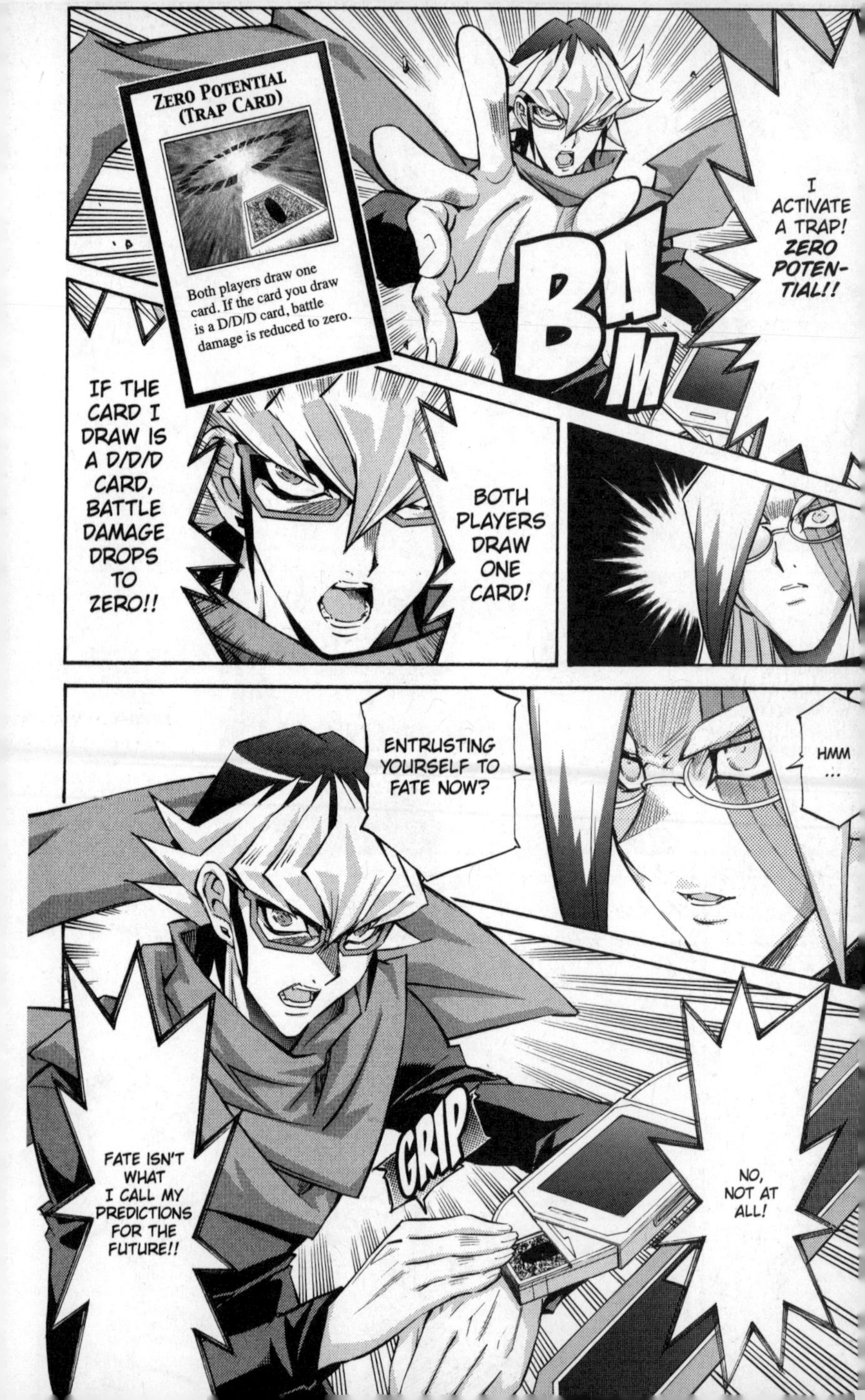
I ACTIVATE A TRAP! ZERO POTENTIAL!!
BAM
ZERO POTENTIAL (TRAP CARD)
Both players draw one card. If the card you draw is a D/D/D card, battle damage is reduced to zero.
BOTH PLAYERS DRAW ONE CARD!
IF THE CARD I DRAW IS A D/D/D CARD, BATTLE DAMAGE DROPS TO ZERO!!
HMM...
ENTRUSTING YOURSELF TO FATE NOW?
NO, NOT AT ALL!
GRIP
FATE ISN'T WHAT I CALL MY PREDICTIONS FOR THE FUTURE!!

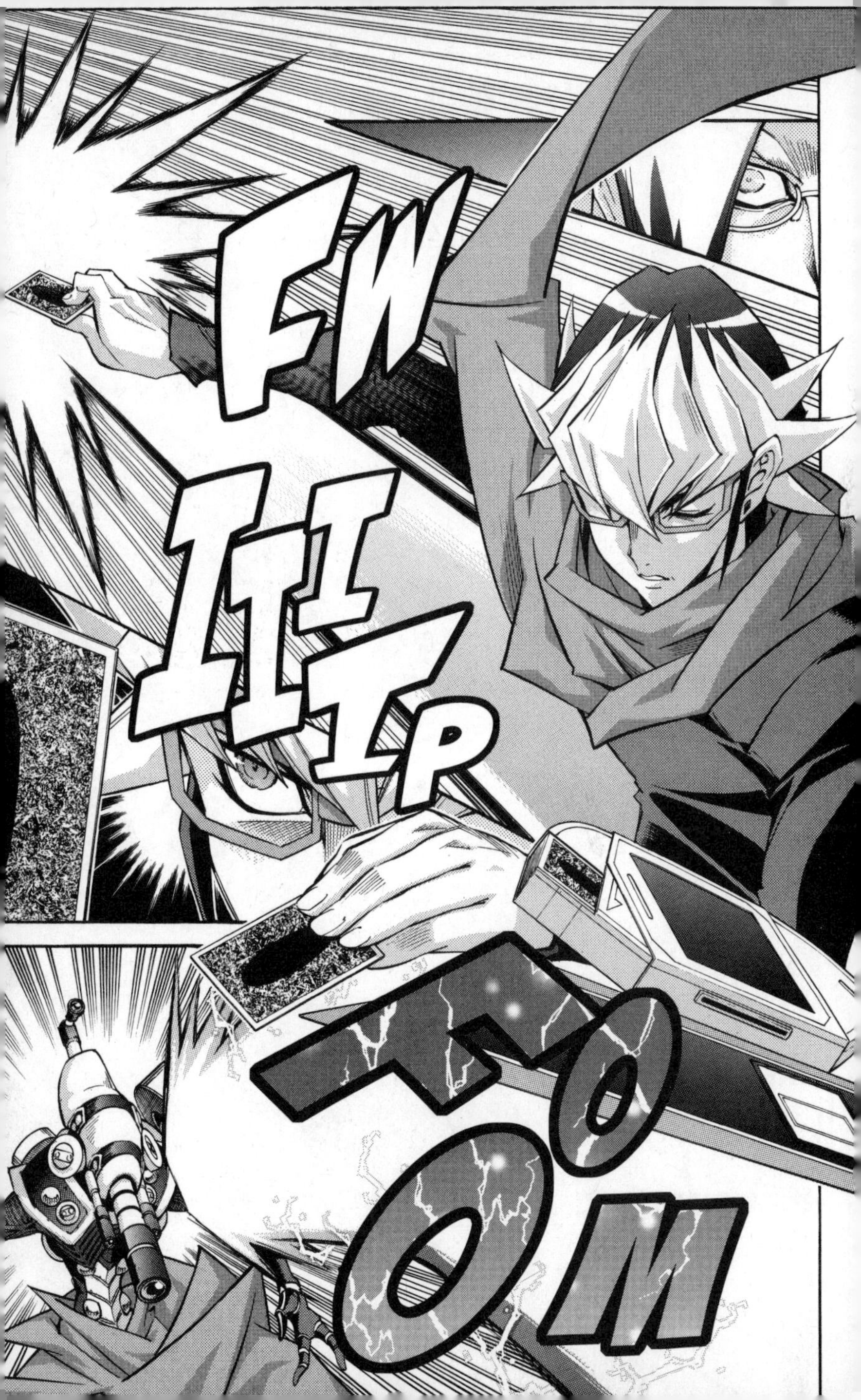
FWIIIP
FOOM

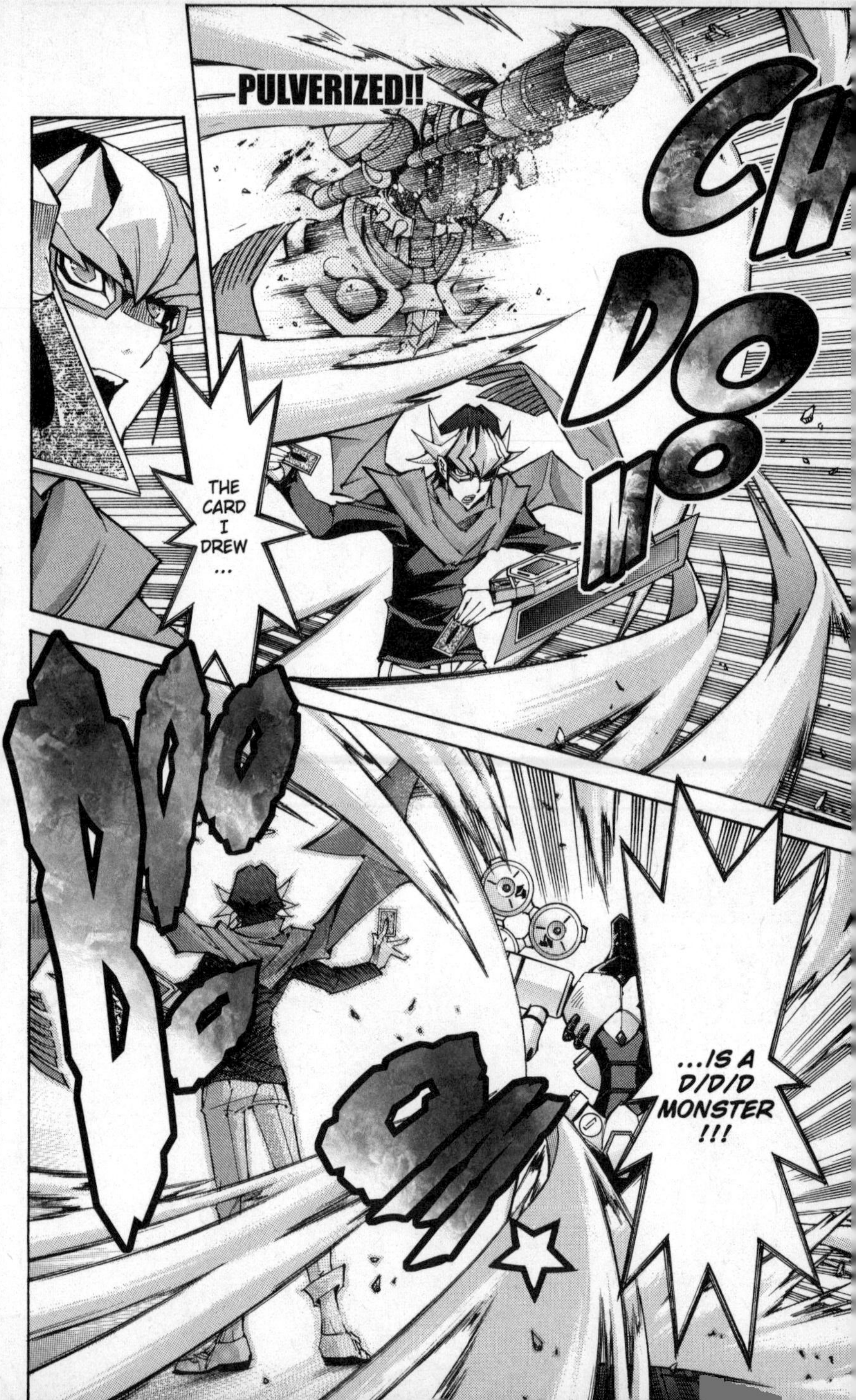
CHDOOM
PULVERIZED!!
THE CARD I DREW ...
DOOOM
...IS A D/D/D MONSTER !!!

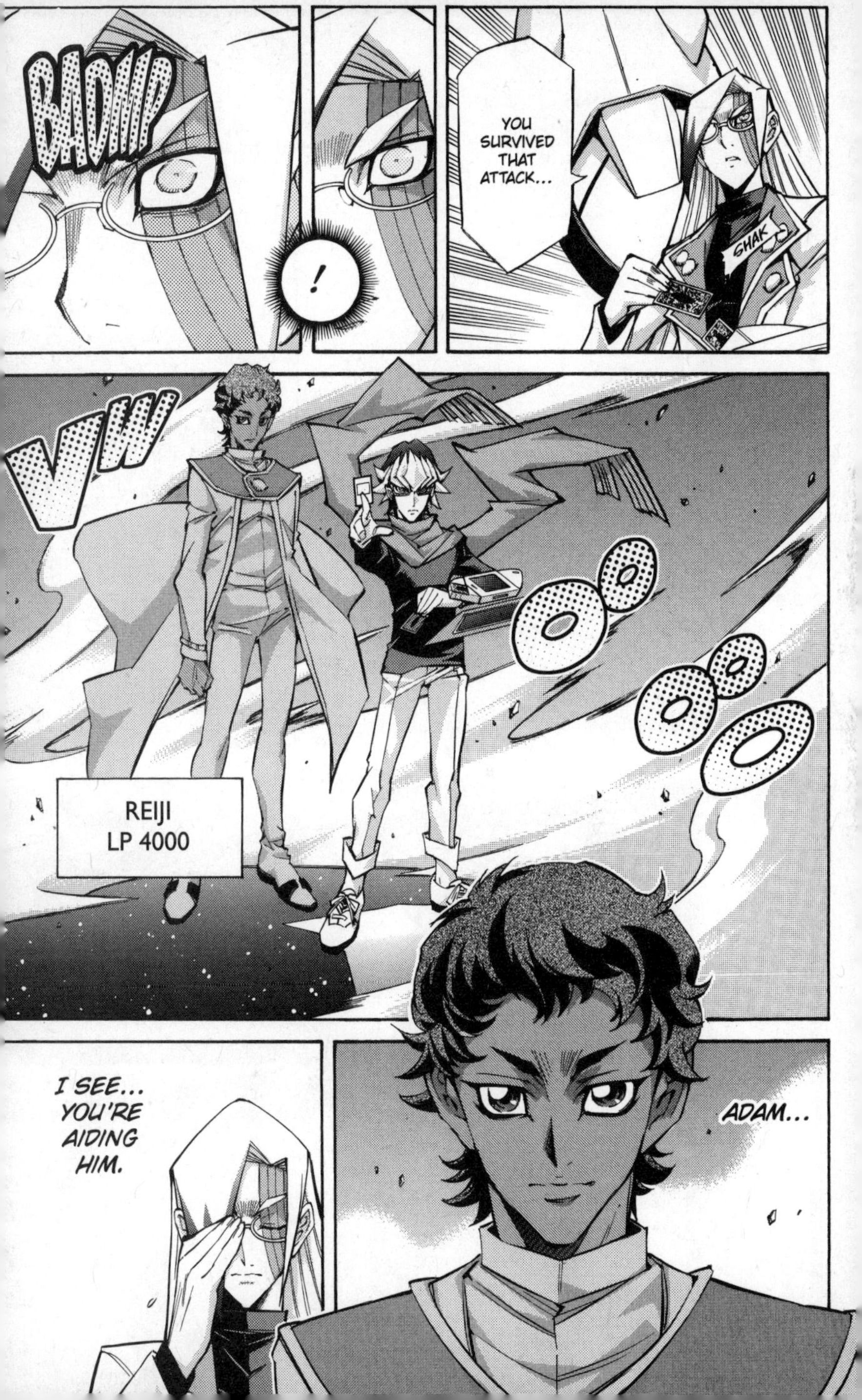
YOU SURVIVED THAT ATTACK...
SHAK
!
BADMP
VW
REIJI
LP 4000
ADAM...
I SEE... YOU'RE AIDING HIM.

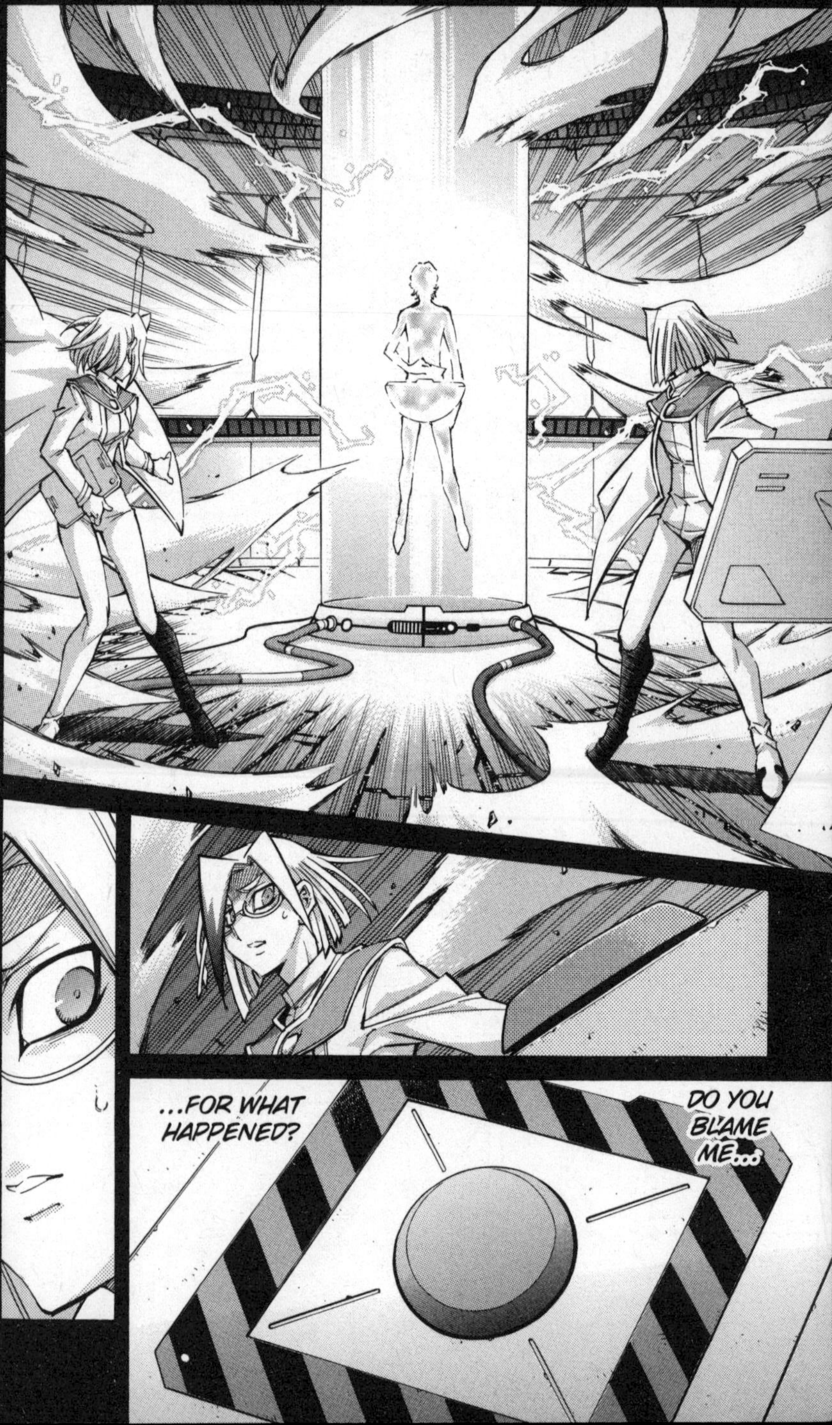
DO YOU BLAME ME...
...FOR WHAT HAPPENED?

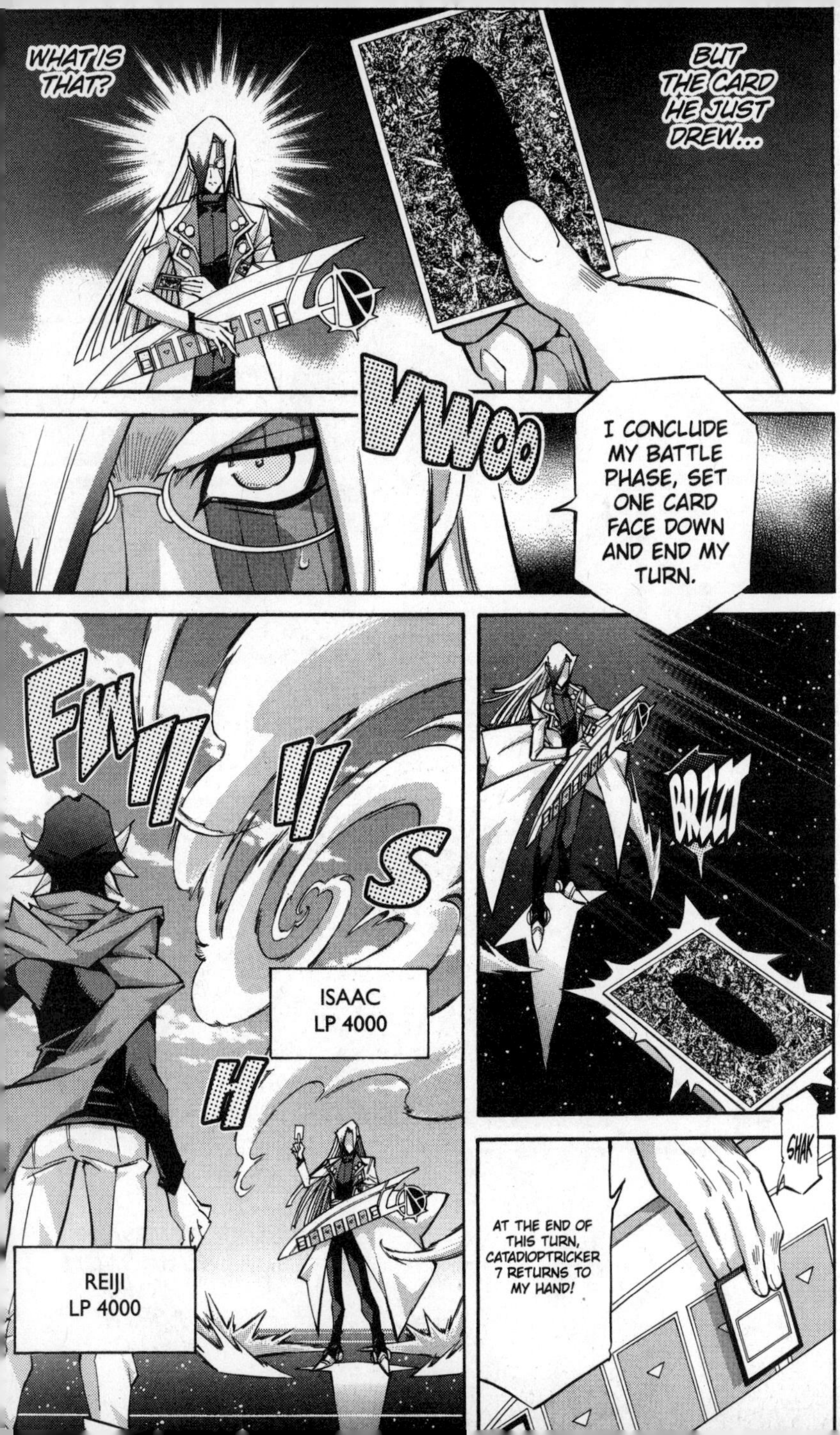
BUT THE CARD HE JUST DREW...
WHAT IS THAT?
VWOO
I CONCLUDE MY BATTLE PHASE, SET ONE CARD FACE DOWN AND END MY TURN.
BRZZT
SHAK
AT THE END OF THIS TURN, CATADIOPTRICKER 7 RETURNS TO MY HAND!
FWIIIISSH
ISAAC LP 4000
REIJI LP 4000

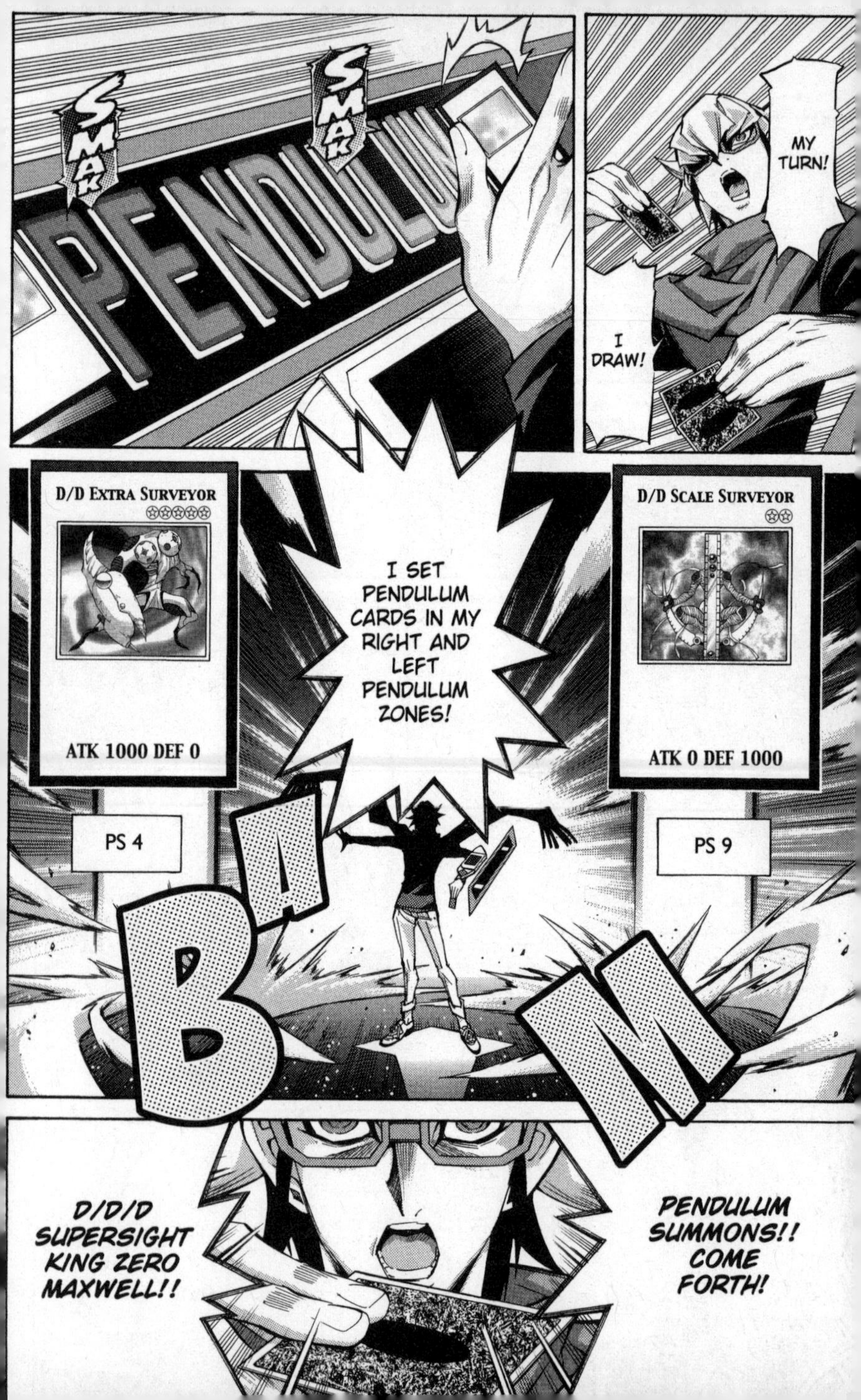
MY TURN!
I DRAW!
SMAK
SMAK
PENDULU
D/D Scale Surveyor
ATK 0 DEF 1000
PS 9
I SET PENDULUM CARDS IN MY RIGHT AND LEFT PENDULUM ZONES!
D/D Extra Surveyor
ATK 1000 DEF 0
PS 4
BAM
PENDULUM SUMMONS!! COME FORTH!
D/D/D SUPERSIGHT KING ZERO MAXWELL!!

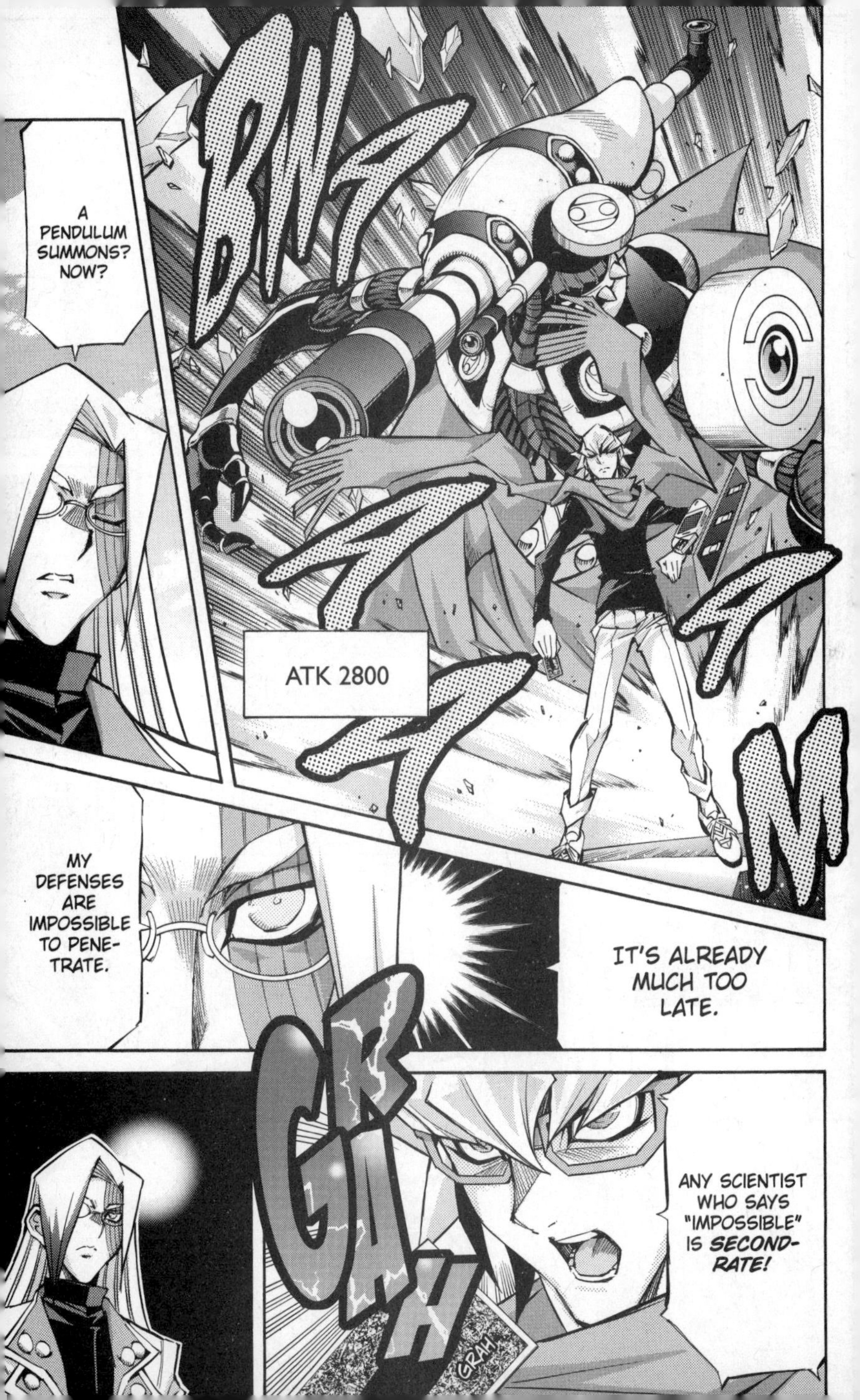
ATK 2800
A PENDULUM SUMMONS? NOW?
MY DEFENSES ARE IMPOSSIBLE TO PENE-TRATE.
IT'S ALREADY MUCH TOO LATE.
ANY SCIENTIST WHO SAYS "IMPOSSIBLE" IS *SECOND-RATE!*
GRAH

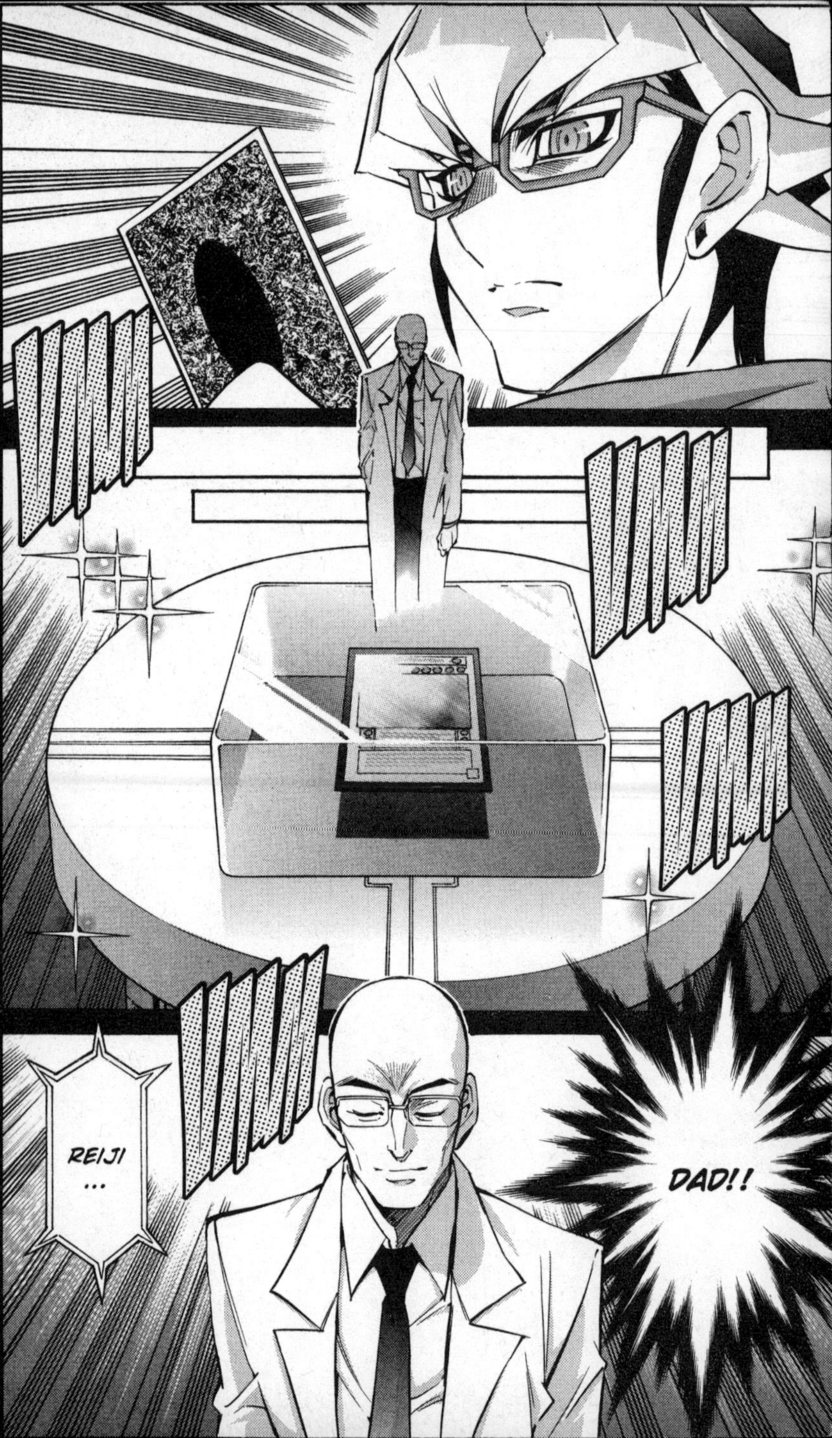
DAD!!
REIJI ...

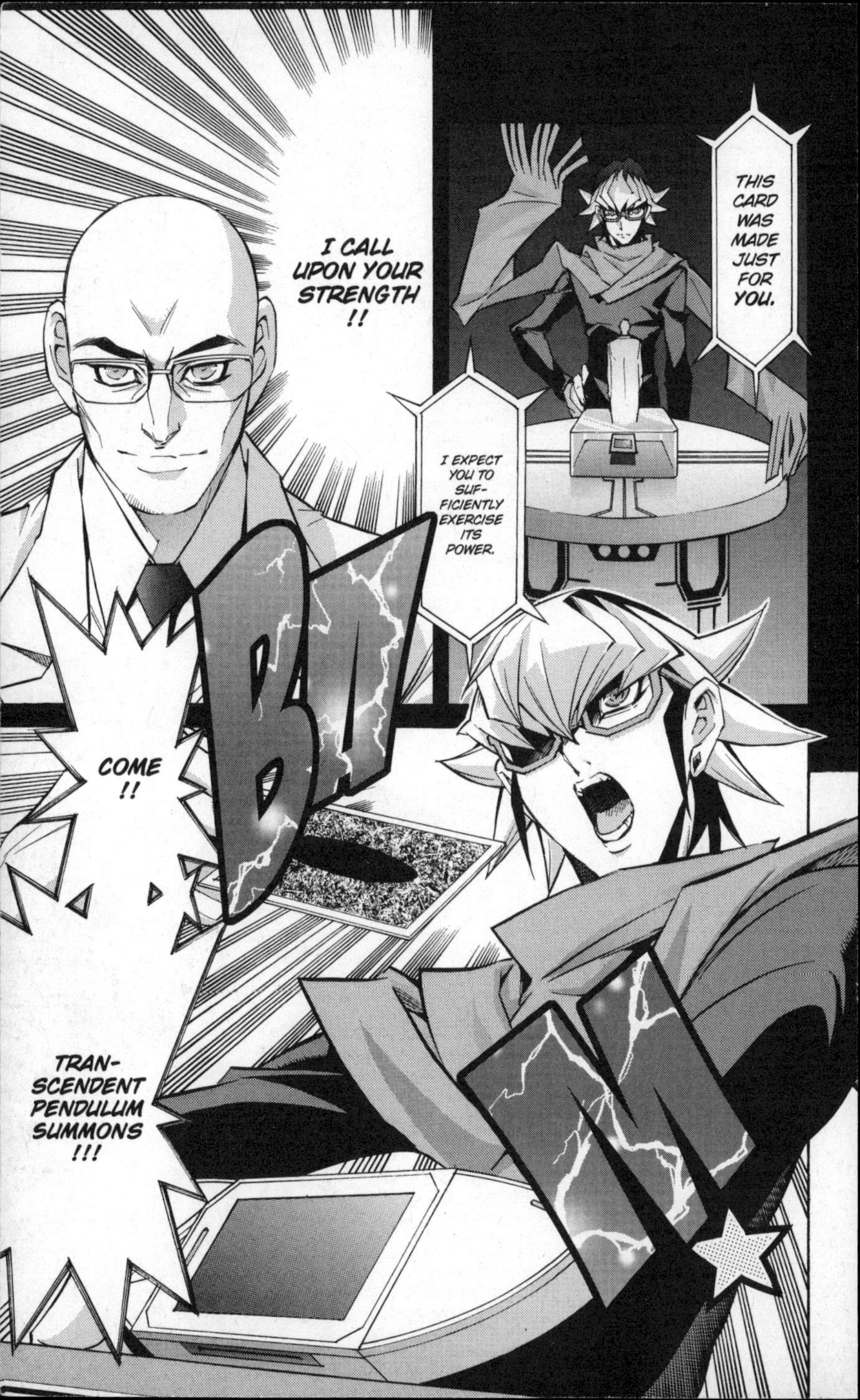
THIS CARD WAS MADE JUST FOR YOU.
I EXPECT YOU TO SUF-FICIENTLY EXERCISE ITS POWER.
I CALL UPON YOUR STRENGTH !!
COME !!
TRAN-SCENDENT PENDULUM SUMMONS !!!

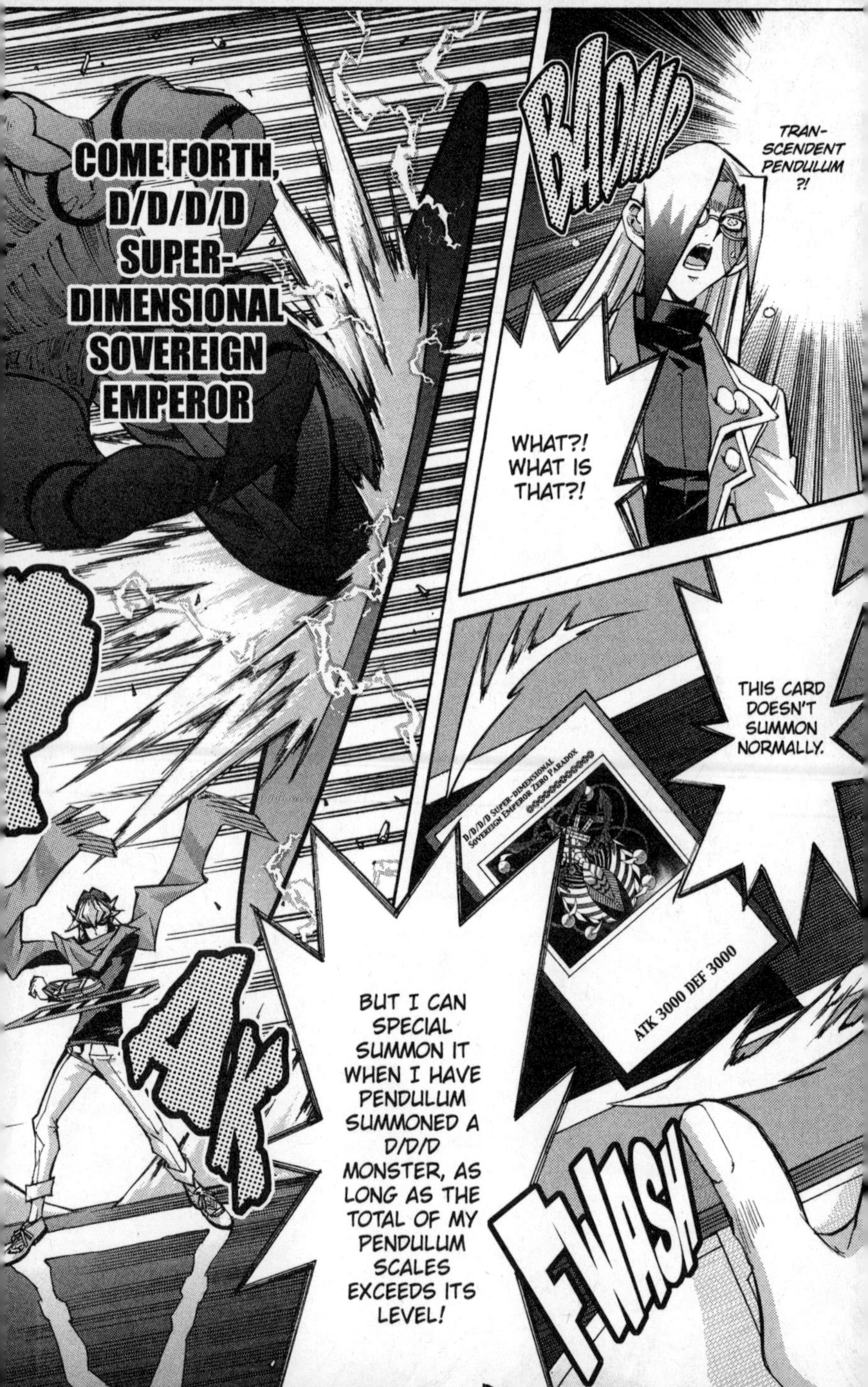
TRANSCENDENT PENDULUM?!
WHAT?! WHAT IS THAT?!
THIS CARD DOESN'T SUMMON NORMALLY.
D/D/D/D SUPER-DIMENSIONAL SOVEREIGN EMPEROR ZERO PARADOX
ATK 3000 DEF 3000
BUT I CAN SPECIAL SUMMON IT WHEN I HAVE PENDULUM SUMMONED A D/D/D MONSTER, AS LONG AS THE TOTAL OF MY PENDULUM SCALES EXCEEDS ITS LEVEL!
COME FORTH, D/D/D/D SUPER-DIMENSIONAL SOVEREIGN EMPEROR

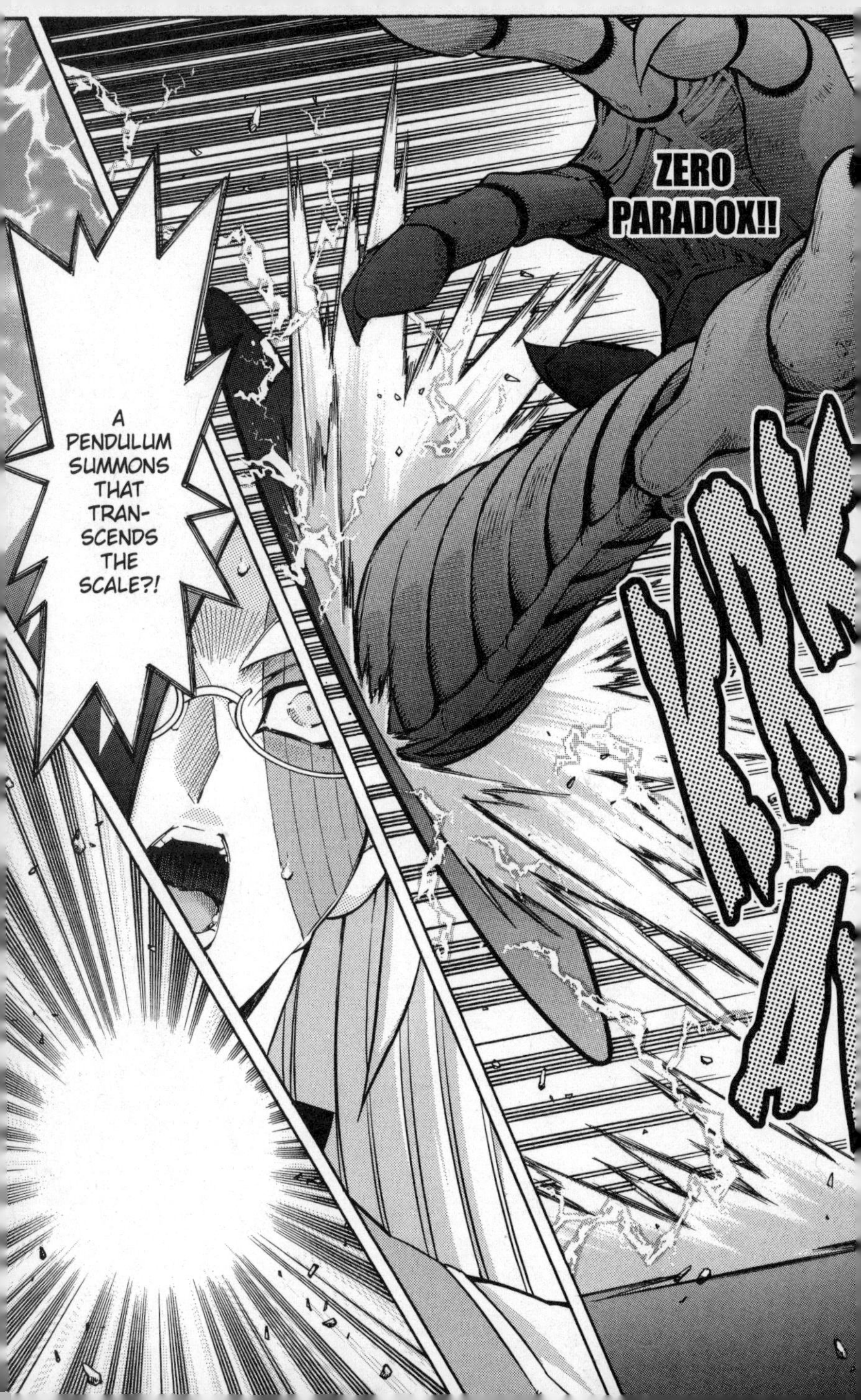
ZERO PARADOX!!
A PENDULUM SUMMONS THAT TRAN- SCENDS THE SCALE?!

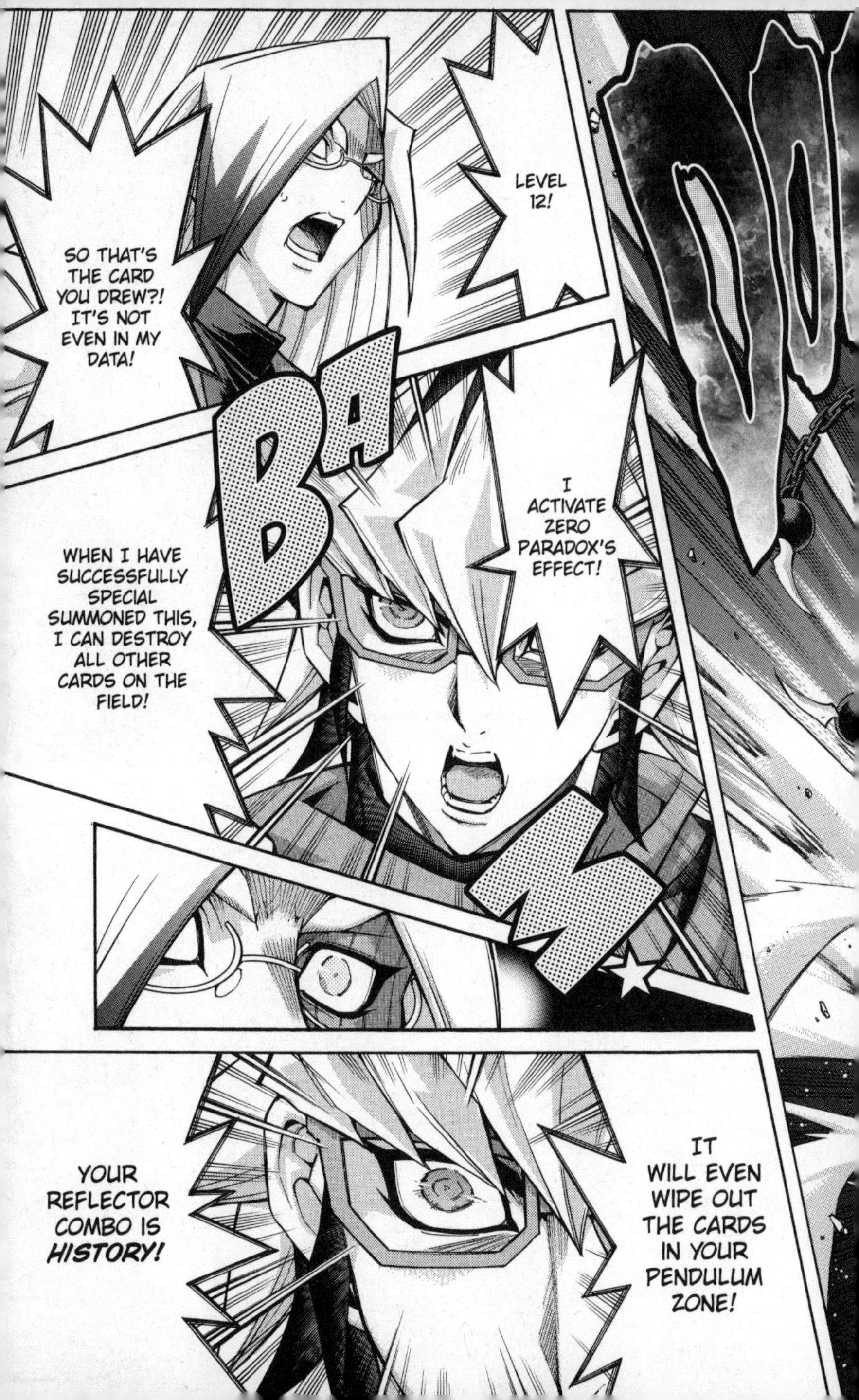

LEVEL 12!
SO THAT'S THE CARD YOU DREW?! IT'S NOT EVEN IN MY DATA!
BAM
I ACTIVATE ZERO PARADOX'S EFFECT!
WHEN I HAVE SUCCESSFULLY SPECIAL SUMMONED THIS, I CAN DESTROY ALL OTHER CARDS ON THE FIELD!
IT WILL EVEN WIPE OUT THE CARDS IN YOUR PENDULUM ZONE!
YOUR REFLECTOR COMBO IS ***HISTORY!***

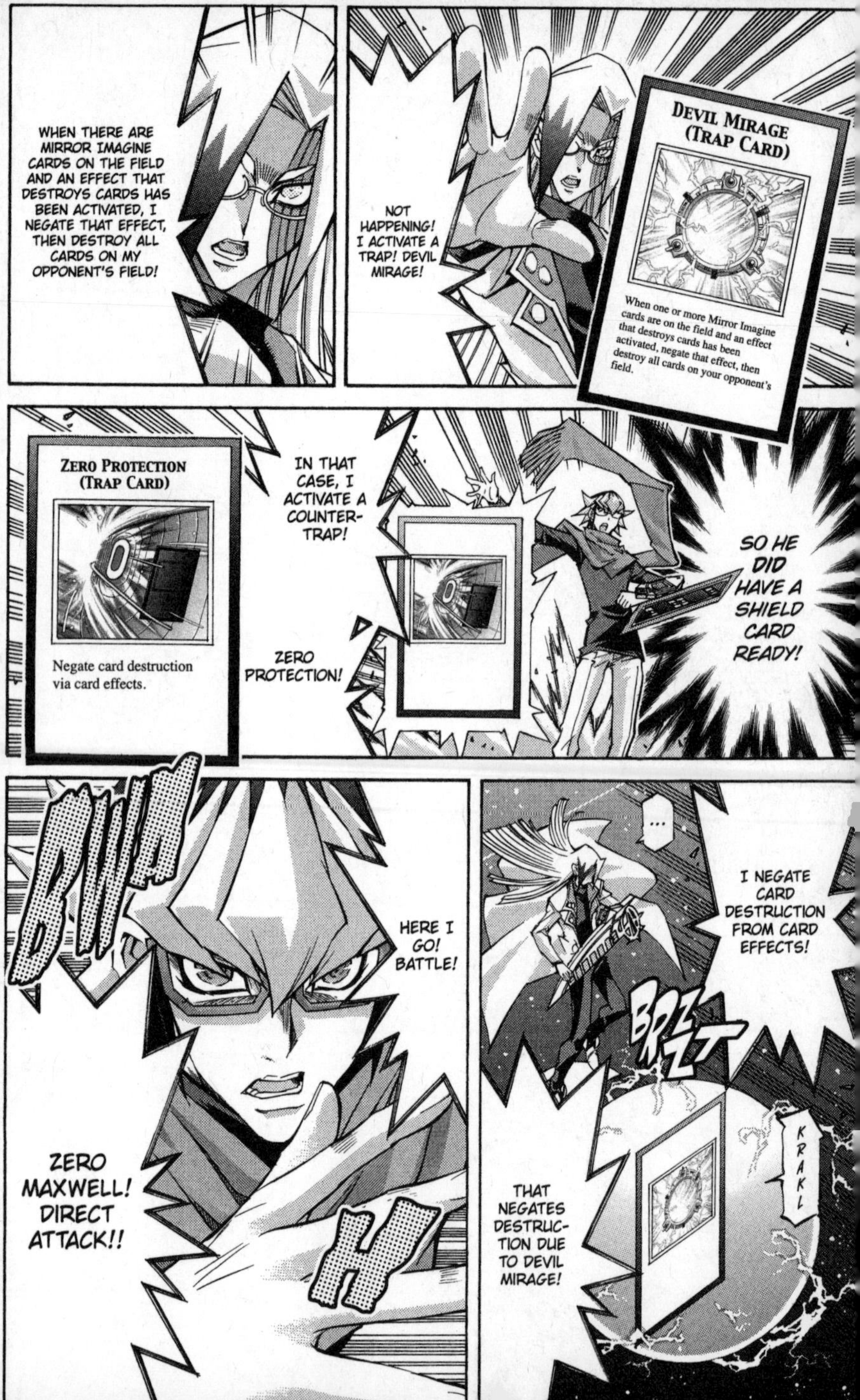
DEVIL MIRAGE
(TRAP CARD)
When one or more Mirror Imagine cards are on the field and an effect that destroys cards has been activated, negate that effect, then destroy all cards on your opponent's field.
NOT HAPPENING! I ACTIVATE A TRAP! DEVIL MIRAGE!
WHEN THERE ARE MIRROR IMAGINE CARDS ON THE FIELD AND AN EFFECT THAT DESTROYS CARDS HAS BEEN ACTIVATED, I NEGATE THAT EFFECT, THEN DESTROY ALL CARDS ON MY OPPONENT'S FIELD!
SO HE DID HAVE A SHIELD CARD READY!
IN THAT CASE, I ACTIVATE A COUNTER-TRAP!
ZERO PROTECTION!
ZERO PROTECTION
(TRAP CARD)
Negate card destruction via card effects.
...
I NEGATE CARD DESTRUCTION FROM CARD EFFECTS!
BRZZT
KRAKL
THAT NEGATES DESTRUCTION DUE TO DEVIL MIRAGE!
BWAH
HERE I GO! BATTLE!
ZERO MAXWELL! DIRECT ATTACK!!

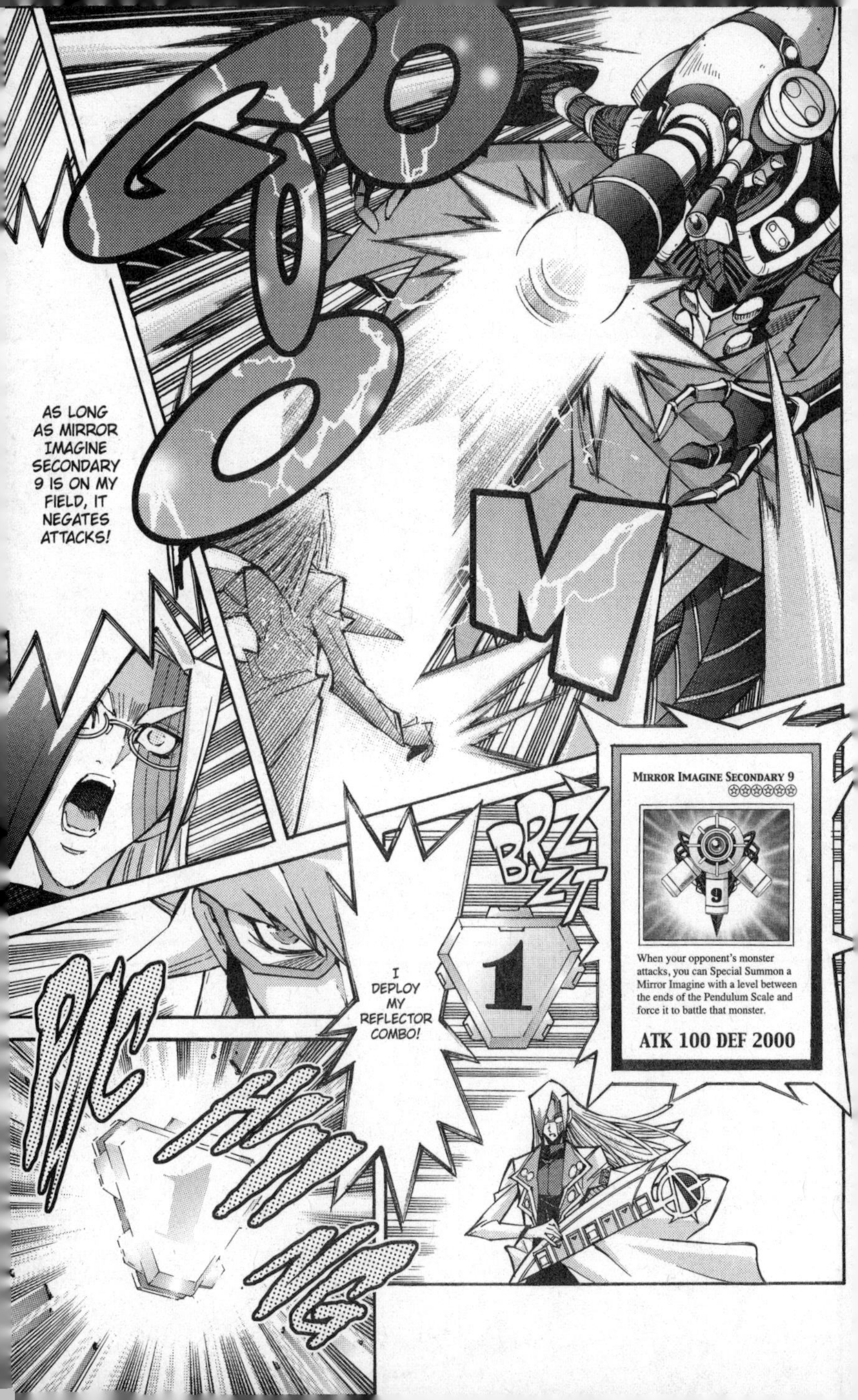
AS LONG AS MIRROR IMAGINE SECONDARY 9 IS ON MY FIELD, IT NEGATES ATTACKS!
Mirror Imagine Secondary 9
9
When your opponent's monster attacks, you can Special Summon a Mirror Imagine with a level between the ends of the Pendulum Scale and force it to battle that monster.
ATK 100 DEF 2000
BRZZT
1
I DEPLOY MY REFLECTOR COMBO!

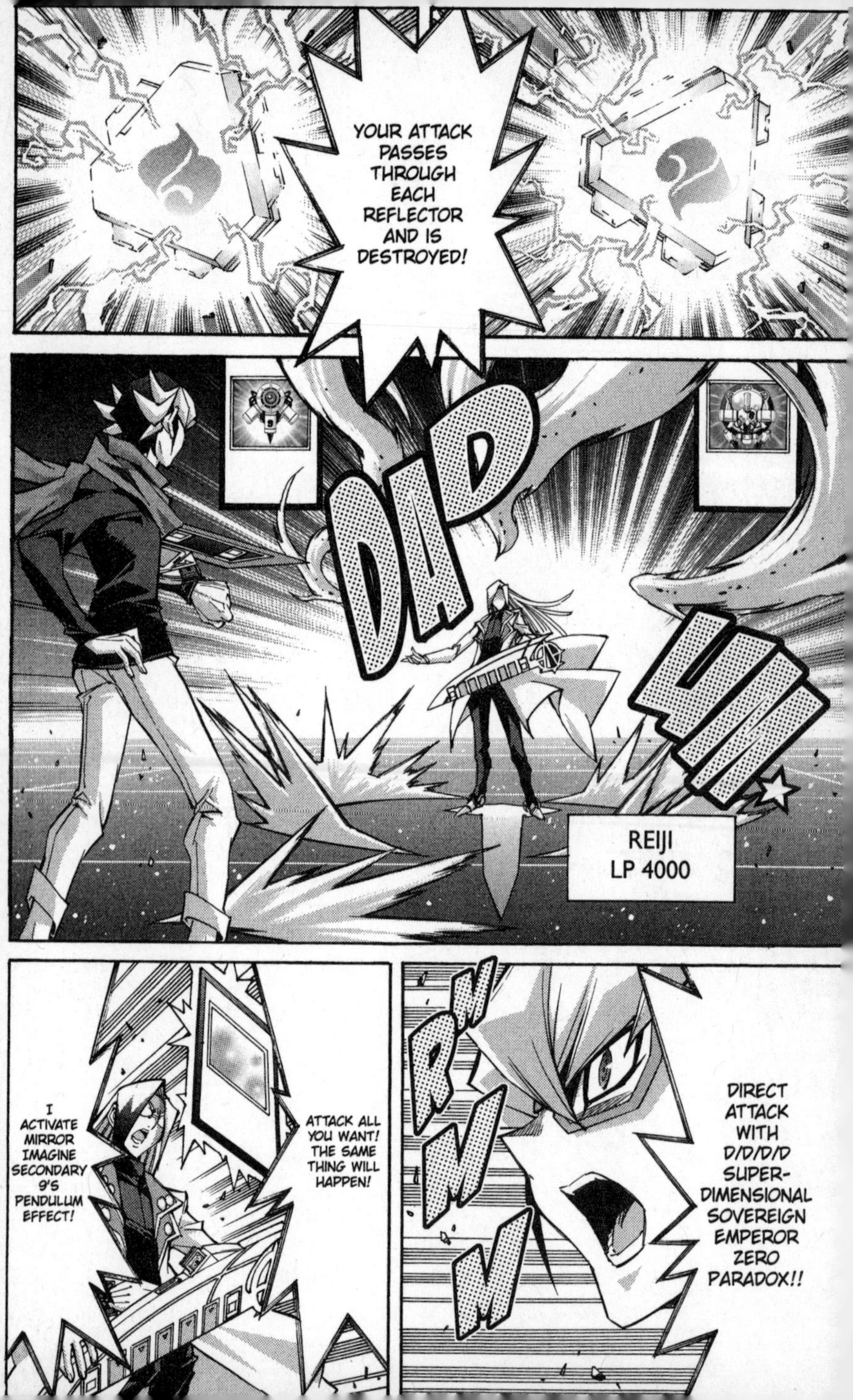
YOUR ATTACK PASSES THROUGH EACH REFLECTOR AND IS DESTROYED!
DAP
WHIP
REIJI LP 4000
DIRECT ATTACK WITH D/D/D/D SUPER-DIMENSIONAL SOVEREIGN EMPEROR ZERO PARADOX!!
RMMM
ATTACK ALL YOU WANT! THE SAME THING WILL HAPPEN!
I ACTIVATE MIRROR IMAGINE SECONDARY 9'S PENDULUM EFFECT!

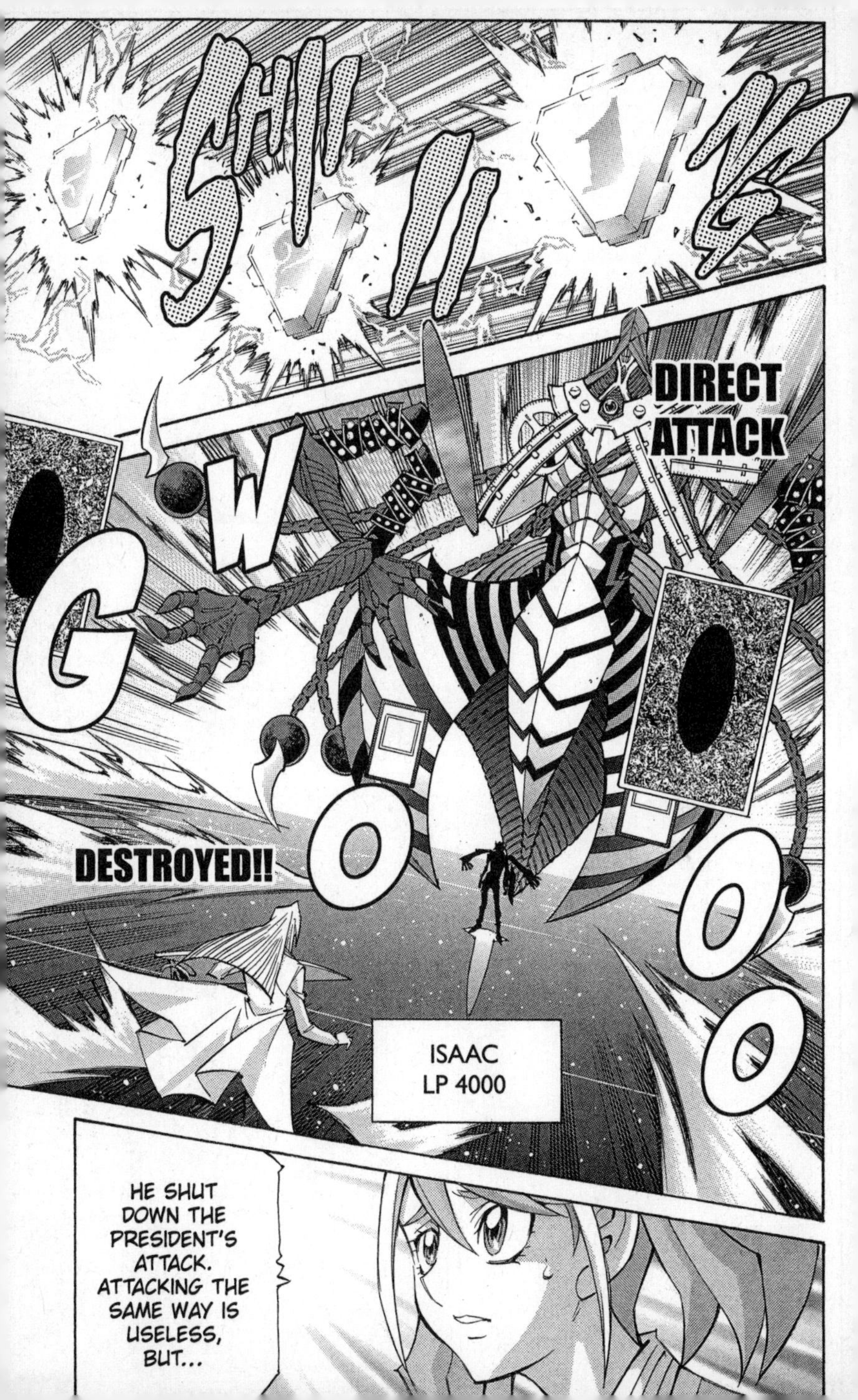
DIRECT ATTACK
GWOOOO
DESTROYED!!
ISAAC
LP 4000
HE SHUT DOWN THE PRESIDENT'S ATTACK. ATTACKING THE SAME WAY IS USELESS, BUT...

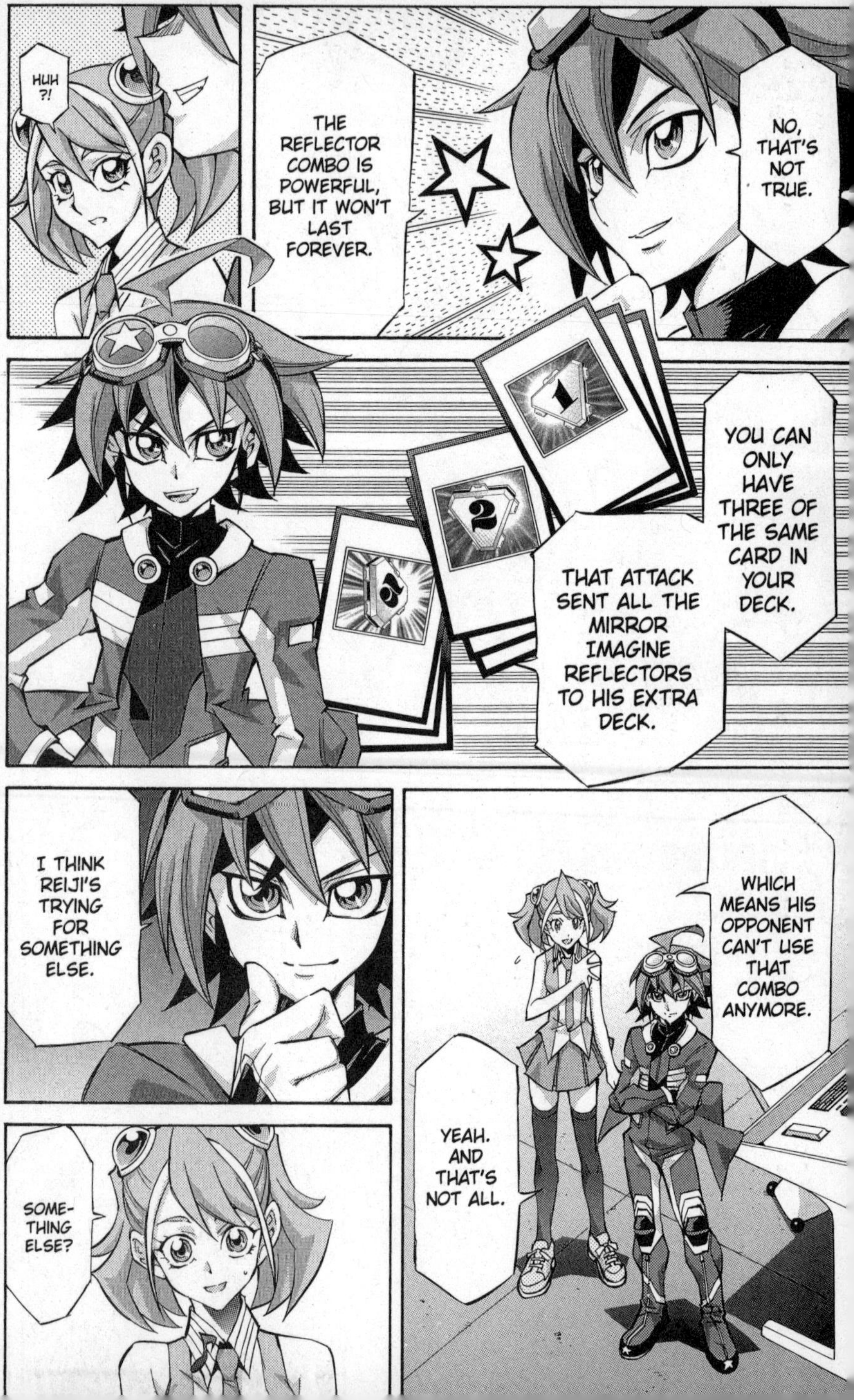
NO, THAT'S NOT TRUE.
THE REFLECTOR COMBO IS POWERFUL, BUT IT WON'T LAST FOREVER.
HUH ?!
YOU CAN ONLY HAVE THREE OF THE SAME CARD IN YOUR DECK.
THAT ATTACK SENT ALL THE MIRROR IMAGINE REFLECTORS TO HIS EXTRA DECK.
WHICH MEANS HIS OPPONENT CAN'T USE THAT COMBO ANYMORE.
YEAH. AND THAT'S NOT ALL.
I THINK REIJI'S TRYING FOR SOMETHING ELSE.
SOME-THING ELSE?

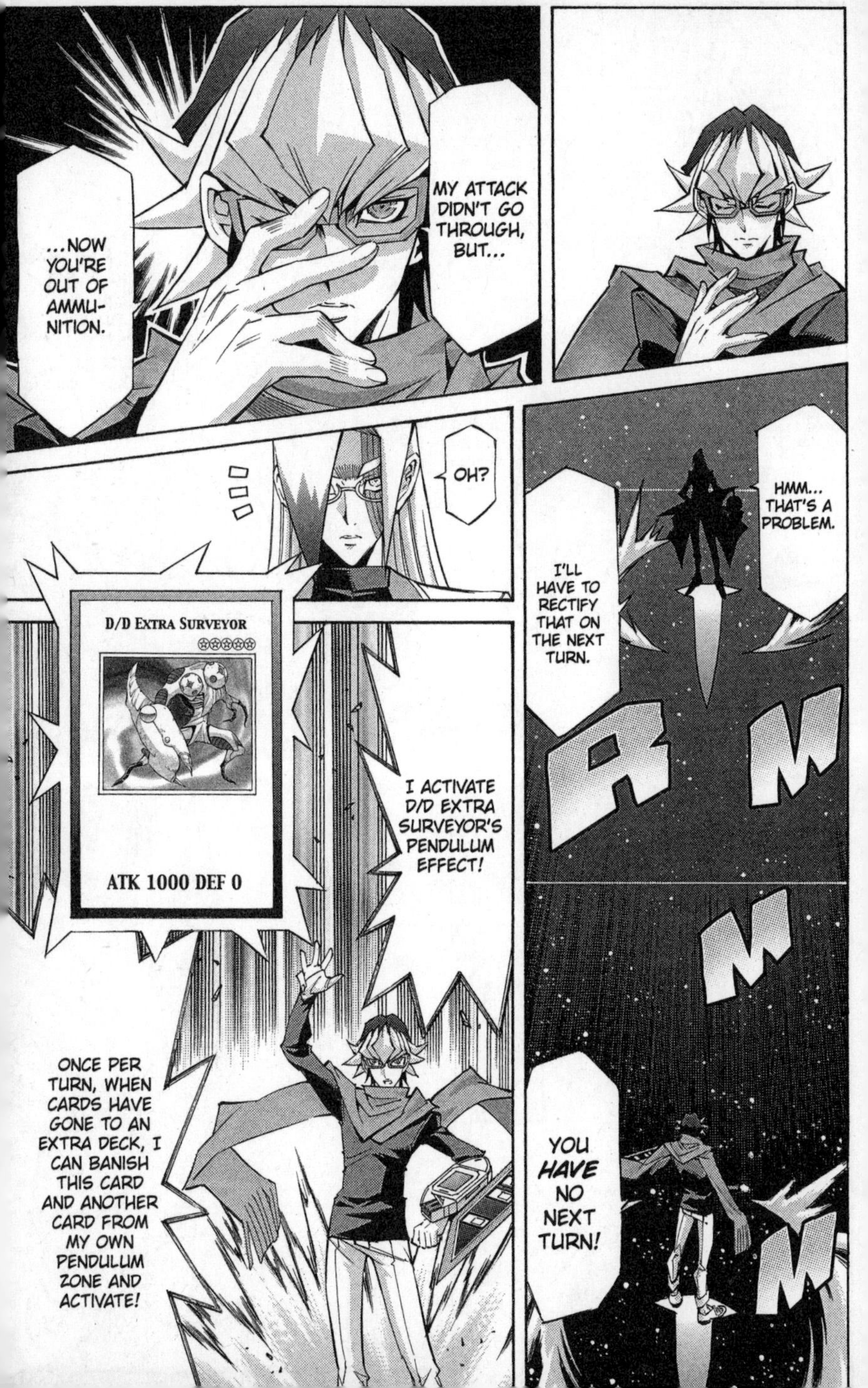

MY ATTACK DIDN'T GO THROUGH, BUT...
...NOW YOU'RE OUT OF AMMUNITION.
HMM... THAT'S A PROBLEM.
I'LL HAVE TO RECTIFY THAT ON THE NEXT TURN.
RAMMM
YOU *HAVE* NO NEXT TURN!
OH?
D/D EXTRA SURVEYOR
ATK 1000 DEF 0
I ACTIVATE D/D EXTRA SURVEYOR'S PENDULUM EFFECT!
ONCE PER TURN, WHEN CARDS HAVE GONE TO AN EXTRA DECK, I CAN BANISH THIS CARD AND ANOTHER CARD FROM MY OWN PENDULUM ZONE AND ACTIVATE!

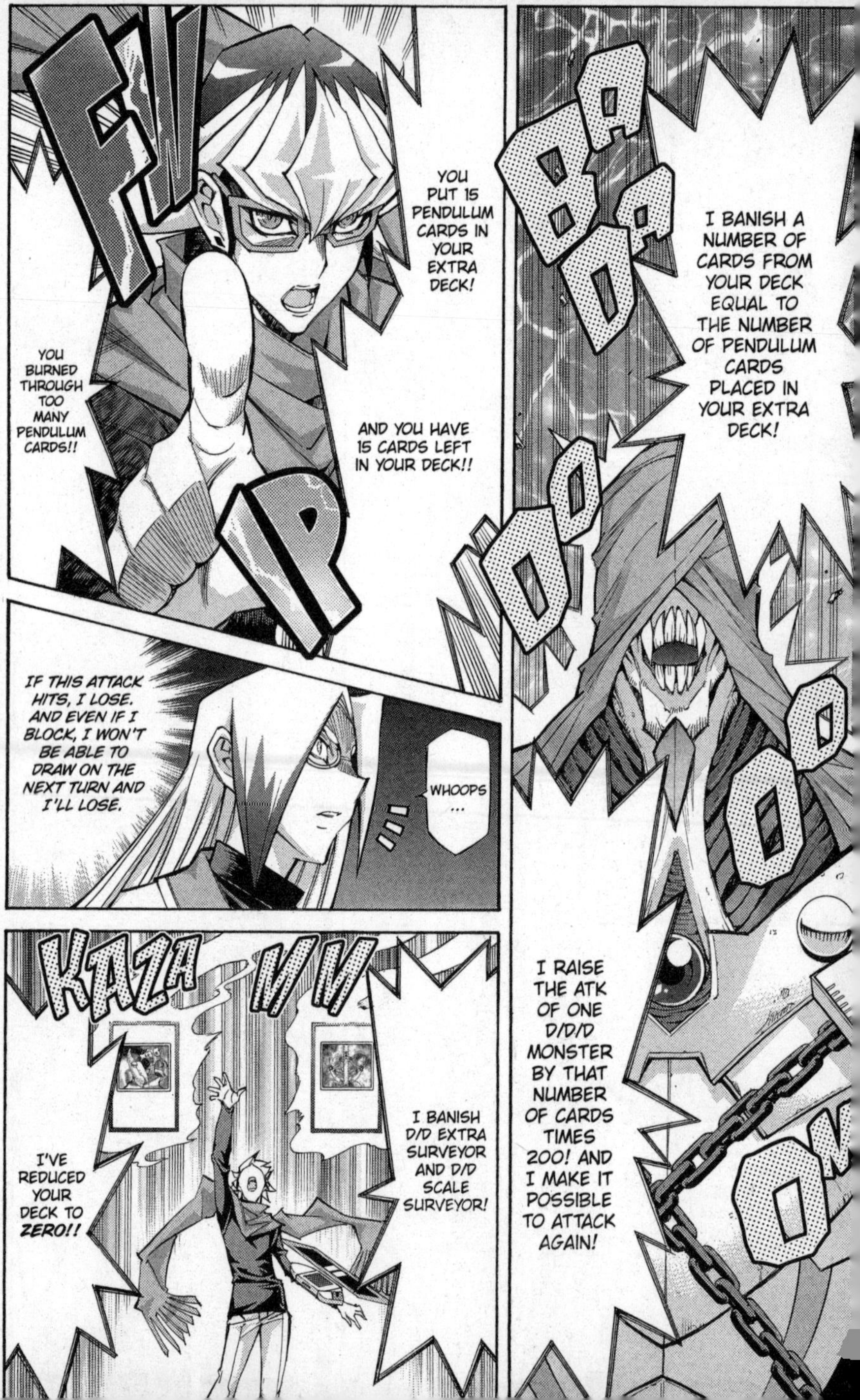
I BANISH A NUMBER OF CARDS FROM YOUR DECK EQUAL TO THE NUMBER OF PENDULUM CARDS PLACED IN YOUR EXTRA DECK!
I RAISE THE ATK OF ONE D/D/D MONSTER BY THAT NUMBER OF CARDS TIMES 200! AND I MAKE IT POSSIBLE TO ATTACK AGAIN!
YOU PUT 15 PENDULUM CARDS IN YOUR EXTRA DECK!
AND YOU HAVE 15 CARDS LEFT IN YOUR DECK!!
YOU BURNED THROUGH TOO MANY PENDULUM CARDS!!
WHOOPS ...
IF THIS ATTACK HITS, I LOSE. AND EVEN IF I BLOCK, I WON'T BE ABLE TO DRAW ON THE NEXT TURN AND I'LL LOSE.
KAZA
I BANISH D/D EXTRA SURVEYOR AND D/D SCALE SURVEYOR!
I'VE REDUCED YOUR DECK TO ZERO!!

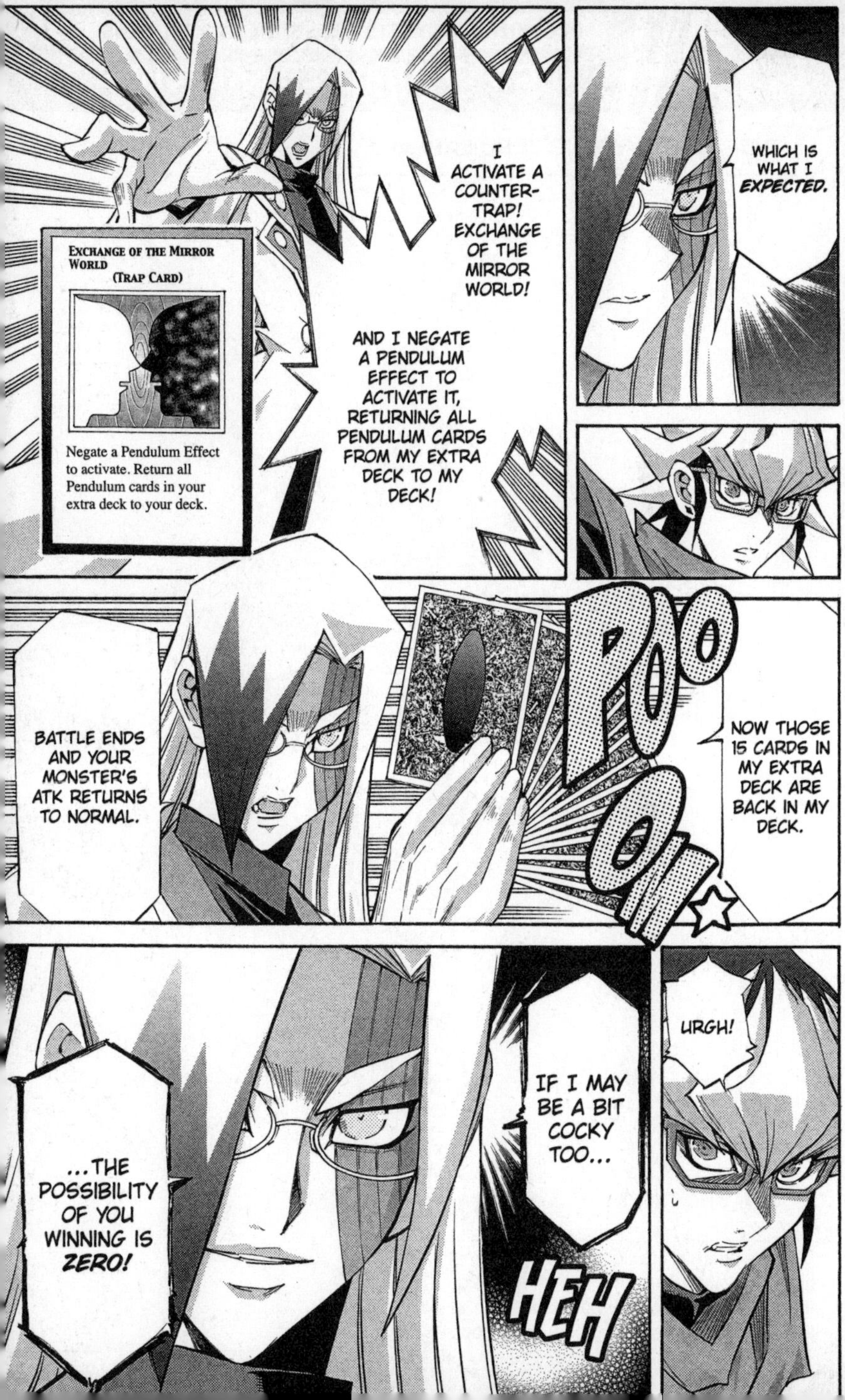
WHICH IS WHAT I EXPECTED.
I ACTIVATE A COUNTER-TRAP! EXCHANGE OF THE MIRROR WORLD!
AND I NEGATE A PENDULUM EFFECT TO ACTIVATE IT, RETURNING ALL PENDULUM CARDS FROM MY EXTRA DECK TO MY DECK!
EXCHANGE OF THE MIRROR WORLD
(TRAP CARD)
Negate a Pendulum Effect to activate. Return all Pendulum cards in your extra deck to your deck.
NOW THOSE 15 CARDS IN MY EXTRA DECK ARE BACK IN MY DECK.
POOOM
BATTLE ENDS AND YOUR MONSTER'S ATK RETURNS TO NORMAL.
URGH!
IF I MAY BE A BIT COCKY TOO...
HEH
...THE POSSIBILITY OF YOU WINNING IS ZERO!

D/D/D DESTINY KING ZERO LAPLACE

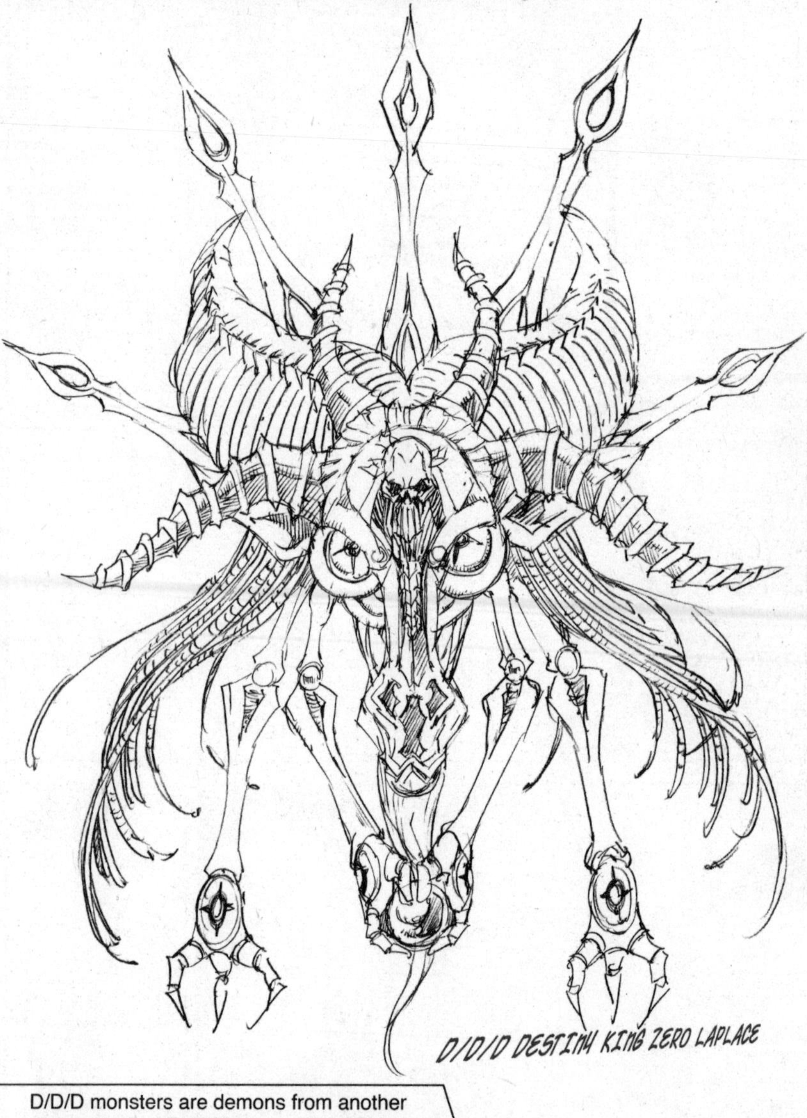
D/D/D DESTINY KING ZERO LAPLACE

D/D/D monsters are demons from another dimension that Reiji Akaba controls! This monster has a distinctive design featuring skull and goat elements emerging from a clock motif!

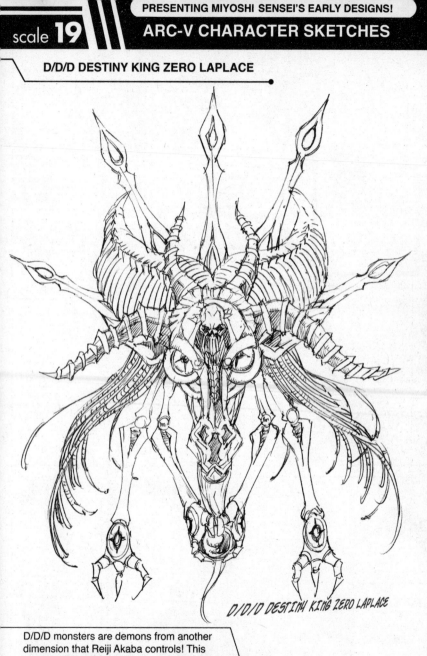

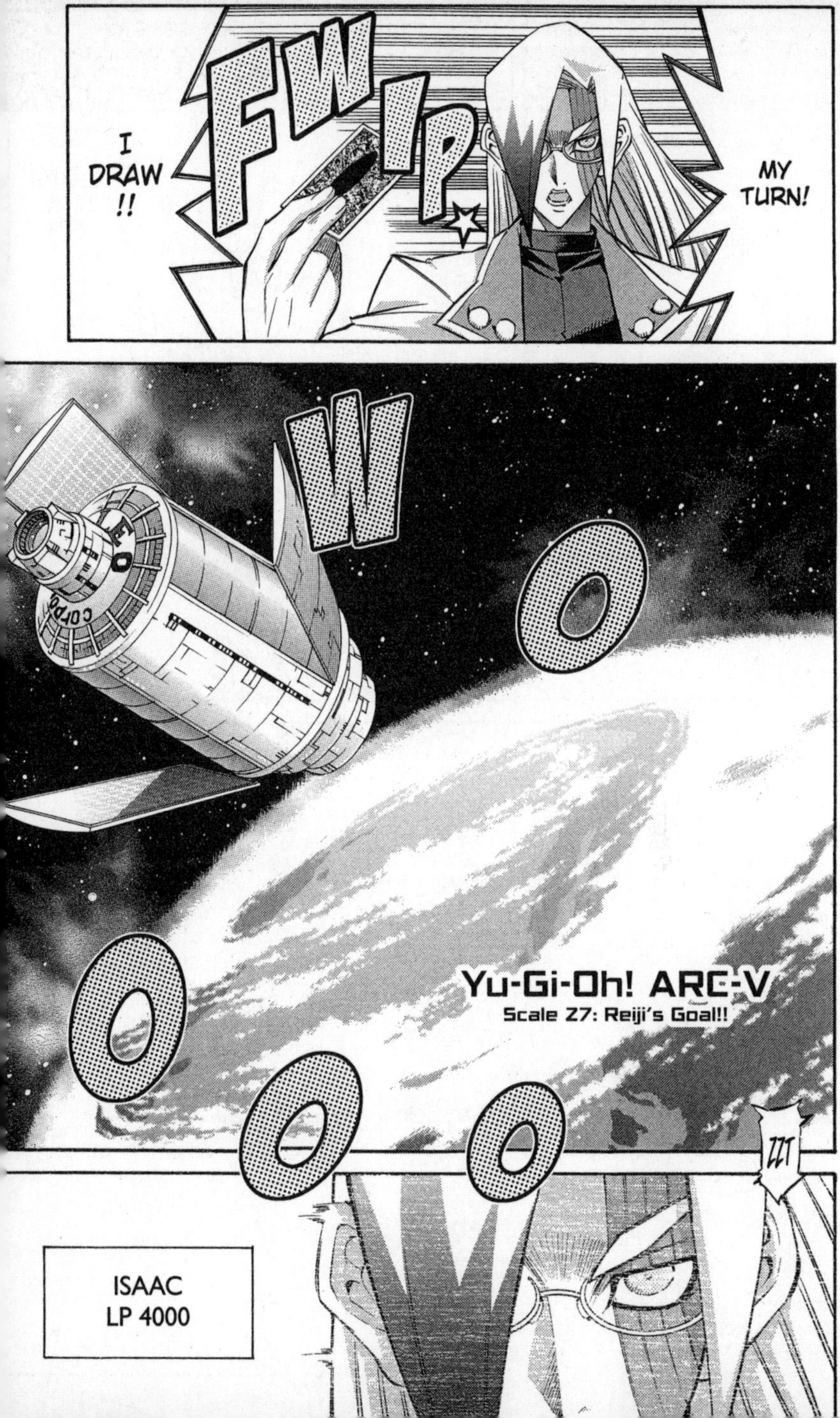
MY TURN!
FWIP
I DRAW!!
FWOOOOO
Yu-Gi-Oh! ARC-V
Scale 27: Reiji's Goal!!
ZZT
ISAAC
LP 4000

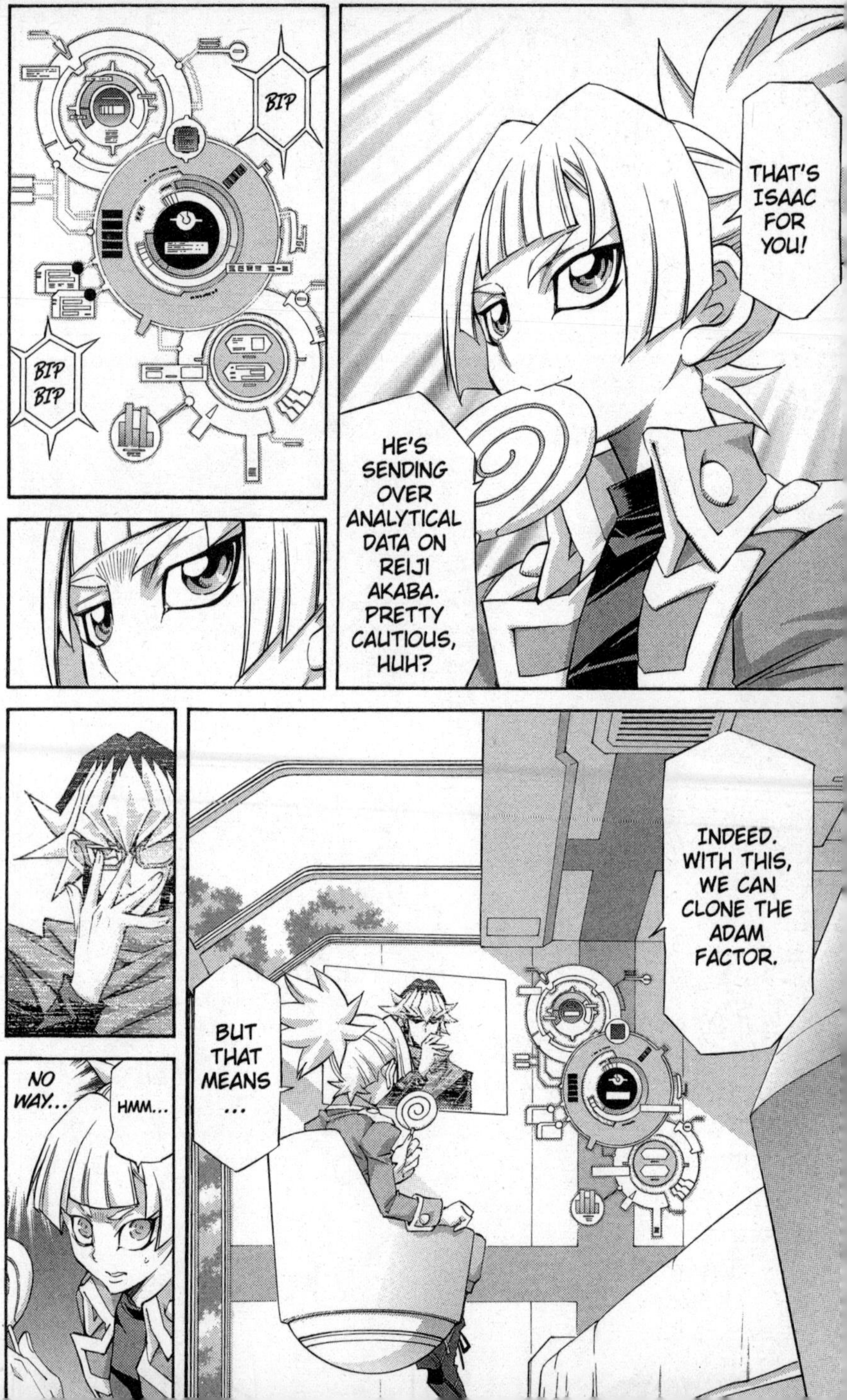
THAT'S ISAAC FOR YOU!
HE'S SENDING OVER ANALYTICAL DATA ON REIJI AKABA. PRETTY CAUTIOUS, HUH?
BIP
BIP BIP
INDEED. WITH THIS, WE CAN CLONE THE ADAM FACTOR.
BUT THAT MEANS ...
HMM...
NO WAY...

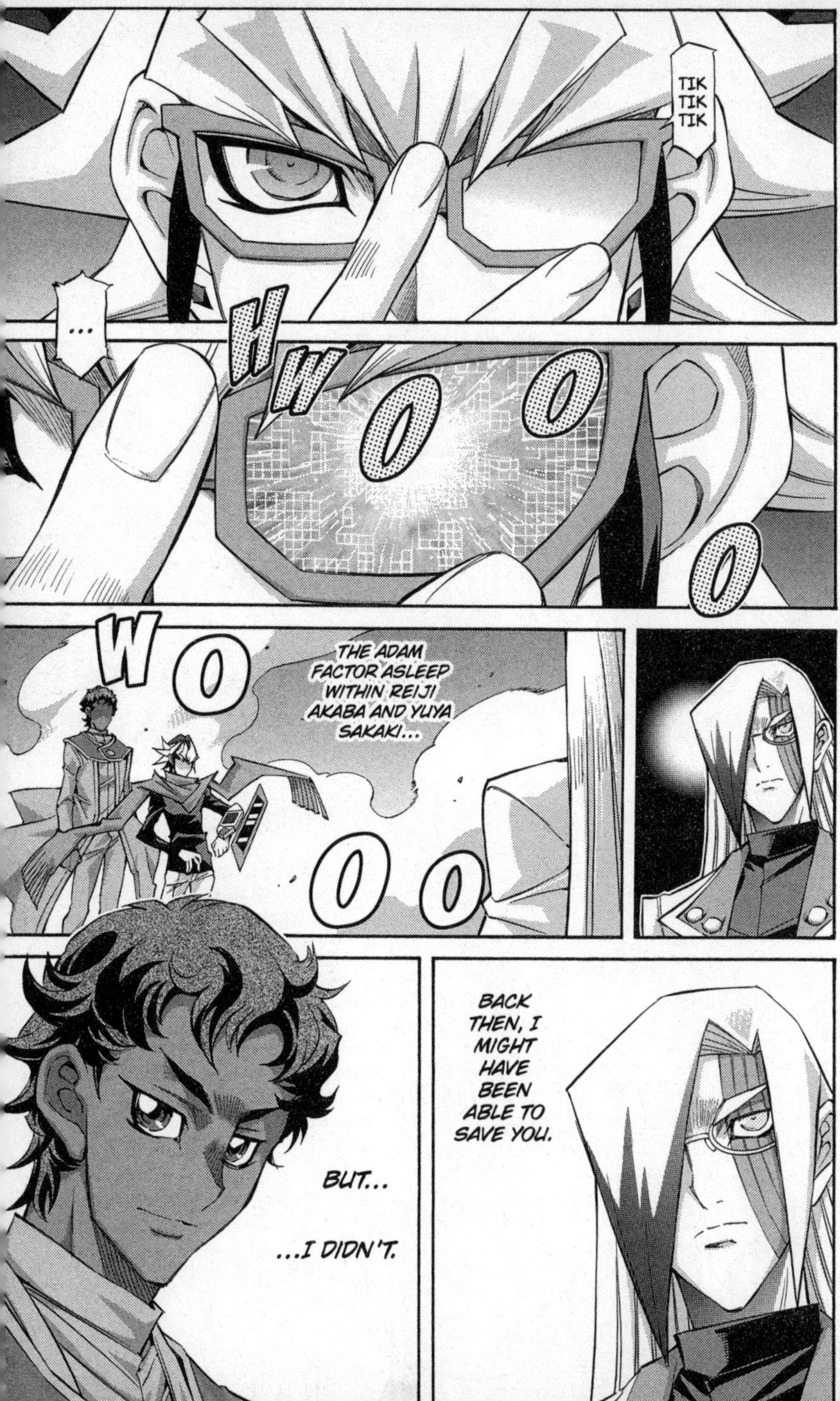
TIK TIK TIK
...
HWOOO
WOOOO
THE ADAM FACTOR ASLEEP WITHIN REIJI AKABA AND YUYA SAKAKI...
BACK THEN, I MIGHT HAVE BEEN ABLE TO SAVE YOU.
BUT...
...I DIDN'T.

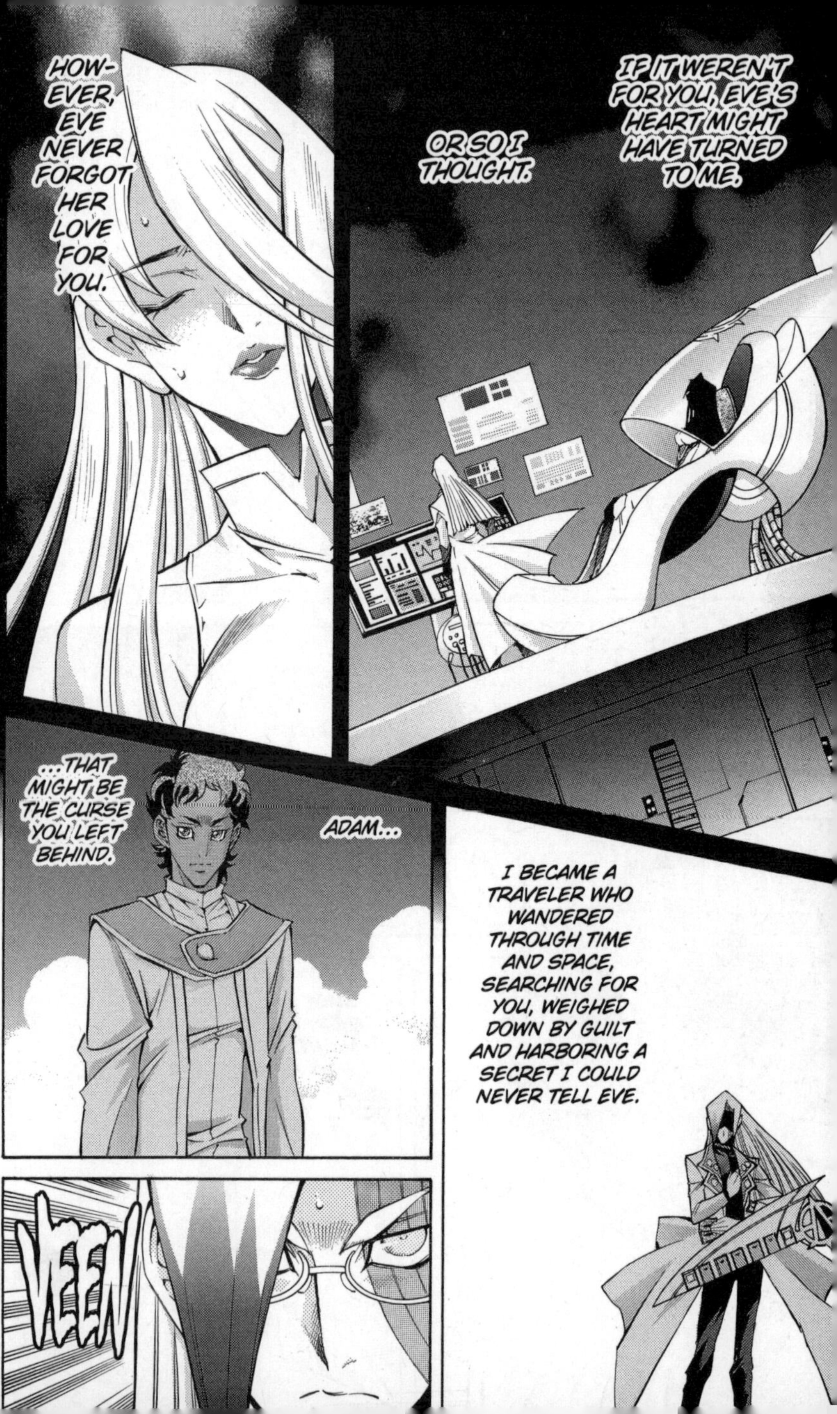
IF IT WEREN'T FOR YOU, EVE'S HEART MIGHT HAVE TURNED TO ME.
OR SO I THOUGHT.
HOW-EVER, EVE NEVER FORGOT HER LOVE FOR YOU.
I BECAME A TRAVELER WHO WANDERED THROUGH TIME AND SPACE, SEARCHING FOR YOU, WEIGHED DOWN BY GUILT AND HARBORING A SECRET I COULD NEVER TELL EVE.
ADAM...
...THAT MIGHT BE THE CURSE YOU LEFT BEHIND.
VEEEN

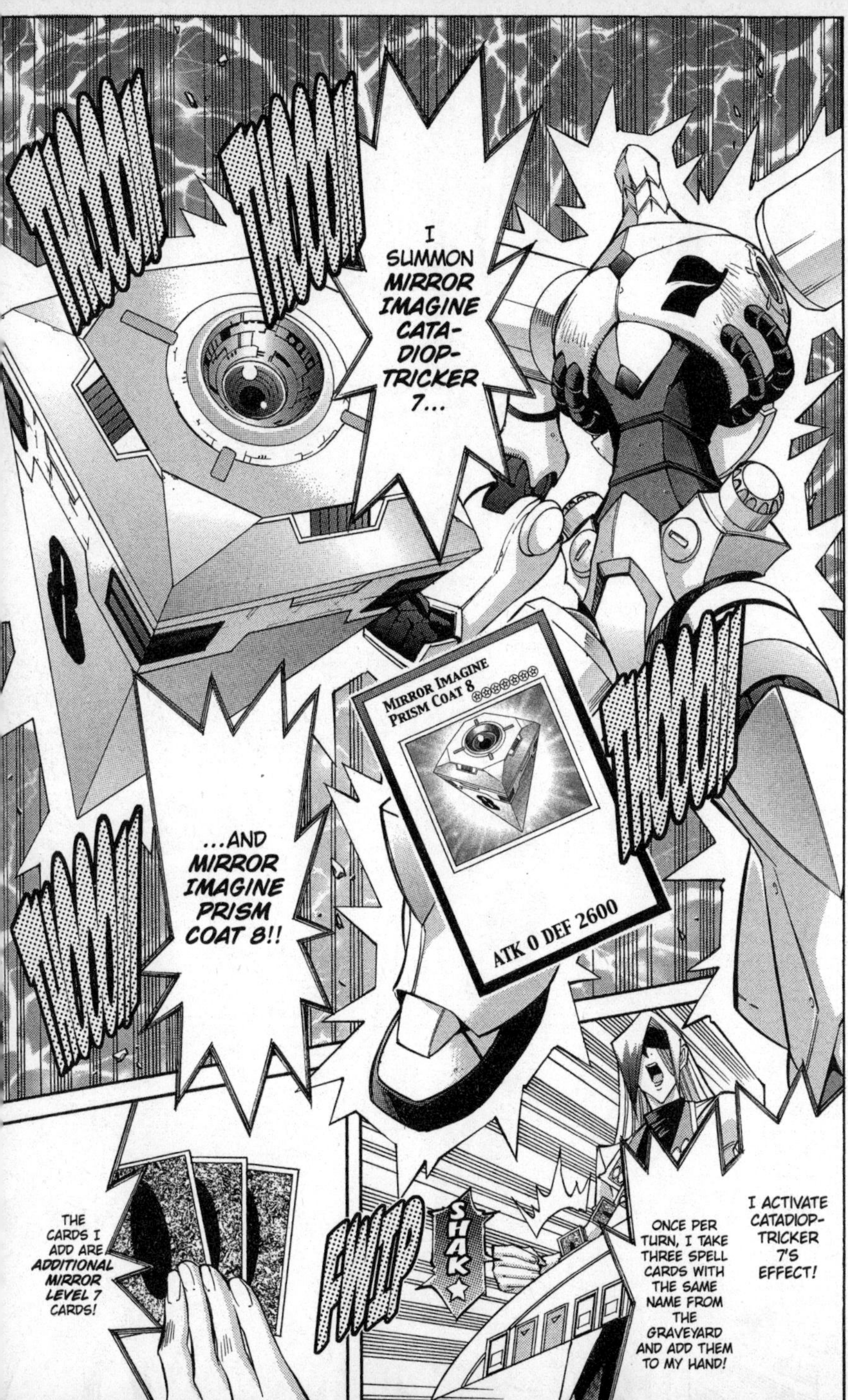
I SUMMON MIRROR IMAGINE CATA-DIOP-TRICKER 7...
...AND MIRROR IMAGINE PRISM COAT 8!!
MIRROR IMAGINE PRISM COAT 8
ATK 0 DEF 2600
I ACTIVATE CATADIOP-TRICKER 7'S EFFECT!
ONCE PER TURN, I TAKE THREE SPELL CARDS WITH THE SAME NAME FROM THE GRAVEYARD AND ADD THEM TO MY HAND!
SHAK
THE CARDS I ADD ARE ADDITIONAL MIRROR LEVEL 7 CARDS!

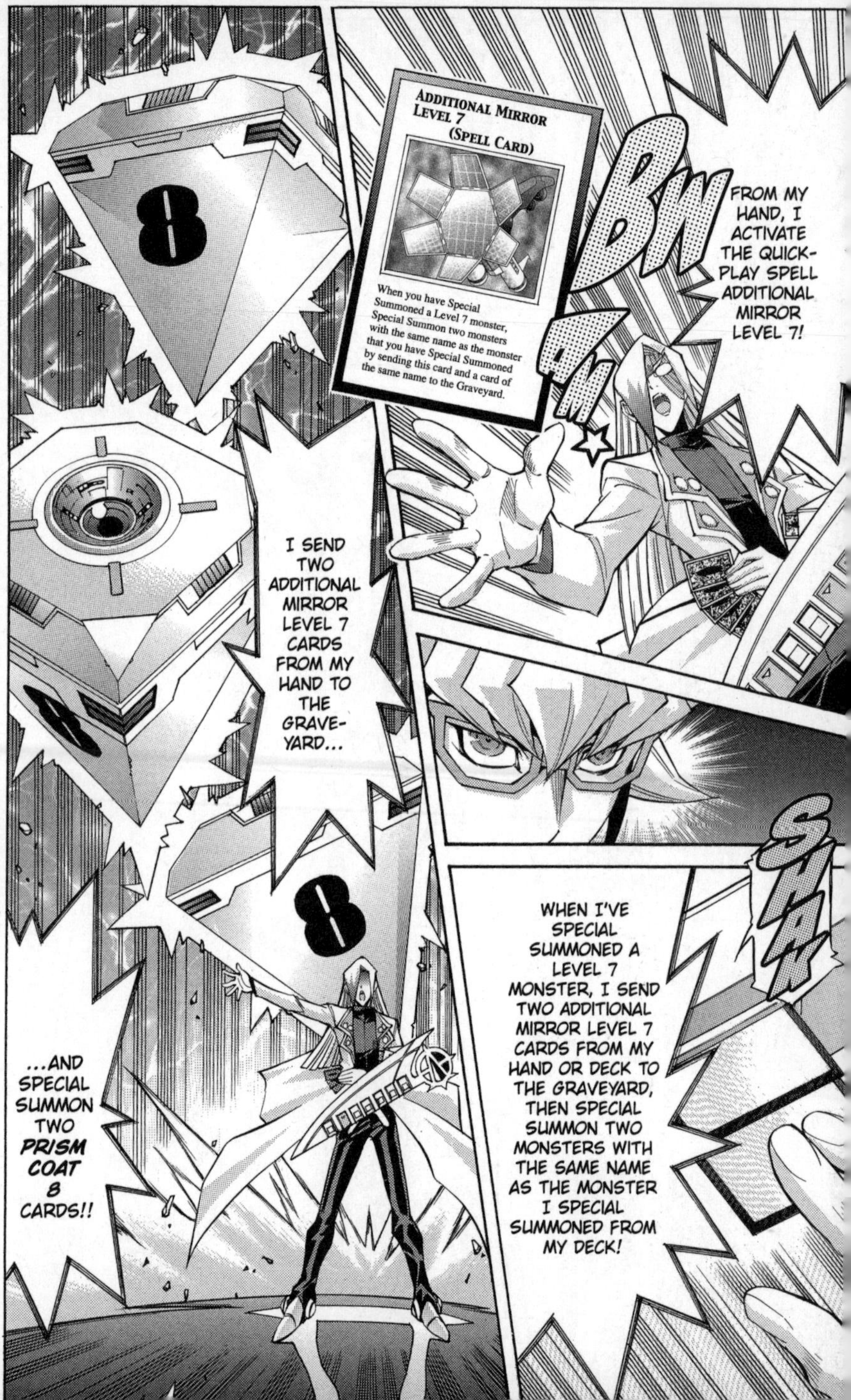
BWAM
FROM MY HAND, I ACTIVATE THE QUICK-PLAY SPELL ADDITIONAL MIRROR LEVEL 7!
ADDITIONAL MIRROR LEVEL 7
(SPELL CARD)
When you have Special Summoned a Level 7 monster, Special Summon two monsters with the same name as the monster that you have Special Summoned by sending this card and a card of the same name to the Graveyard.
SHAK
WHEN I'VE SPECIAL SUMMONED A LEVEL 7 MONSTER, I SEND TWO ADDITIONAL MIRROR LEVEL 7 CARDS FROM MY HAND OR DECK TO THE GRAVEYARD, THEN SPECIAL SUMMON TWO MONSTERS WITH THE SAME NAME AS THE MONSTER I SPECIAL SUMMONED FROM MY DECK!
I SEND TWO ADDITIONAL MIRROR LEVEL 7 CARDS FROM MY HAND TO THE GRAVEYARD...
...AND SPECIAL SUMMON TWO PRISM COAT 8 CARDS!!

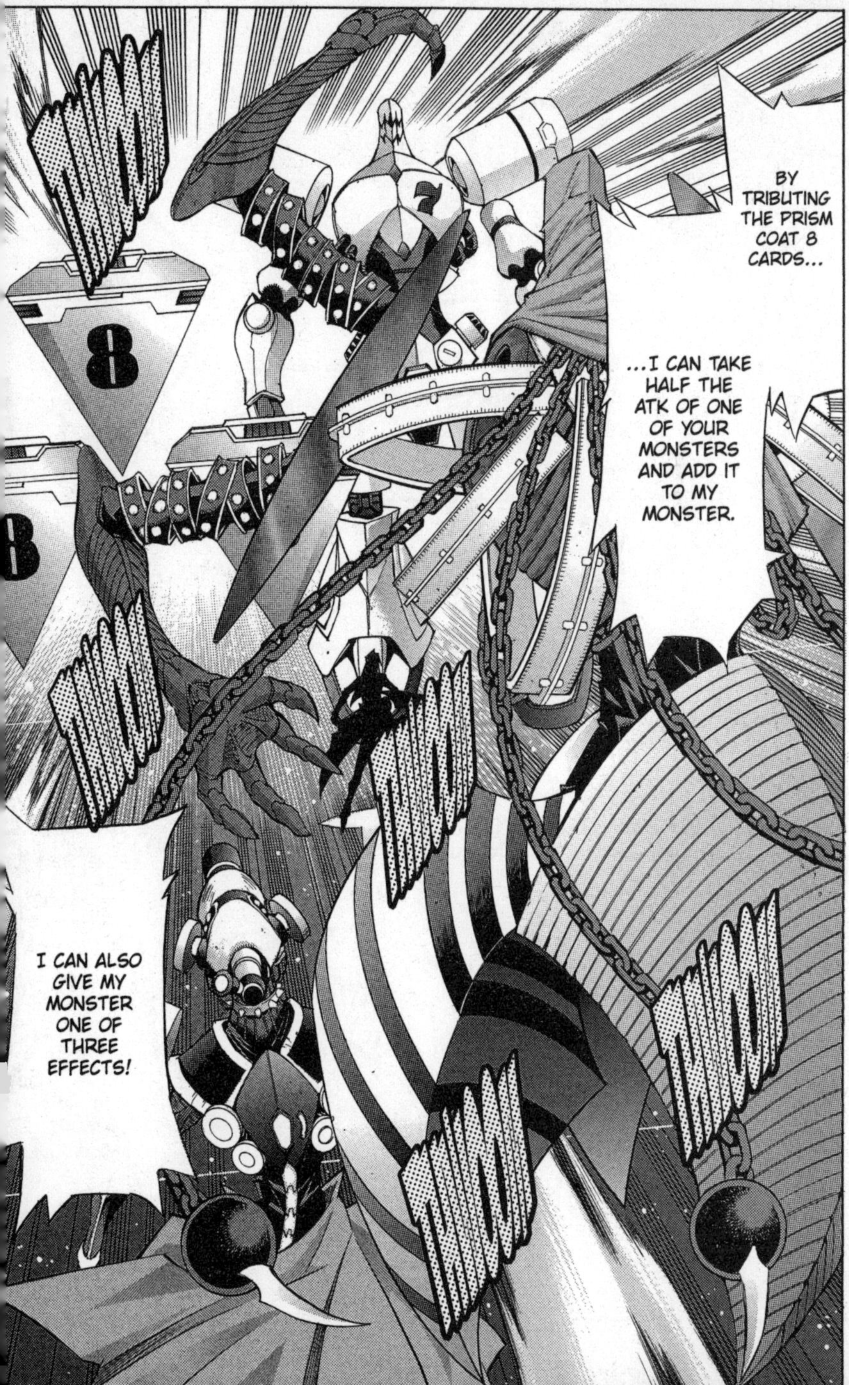
THMM
BY TRIBUTING THE PRISM COAT 8 CARDS...
...I CAN TAKE HALF THE ATK OF ONE OF YOUR MONSTERS AND ADD IT TO MY MONSTER.
THMM
THMM
THMM
THMM
I CAN ALSO GIVE MY MONSTER ONE OF THREE EFFECTS!

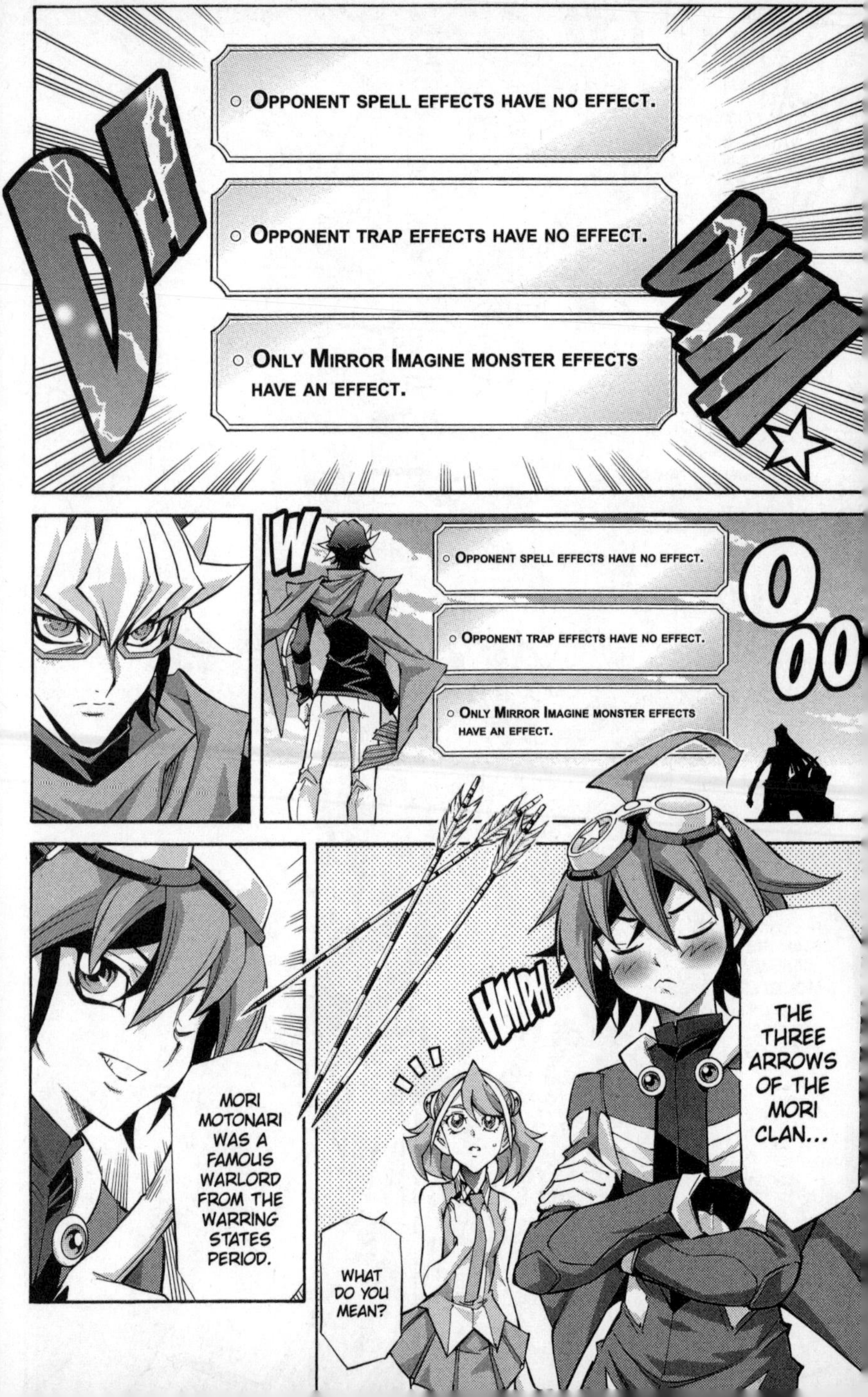
○ Opponent spell effects have no effect.
○ Opponent trap effects have no effect.
○ Only Mirror Imagine monster effects have an effect.
WOOO
○ Opponent spell effects have no effect.
○ Opponent trap effects have no effect.
○ Only Mirror Imagine monster effects have an effect.
THE THREE ARROWS OF THE MORI CLAN...
HMPH
...
WHAT DO YOU MEAN?
MORI MOTONARI WAS A FAMOUS WARLORD FROM THE WARRING STATES PERIOD.

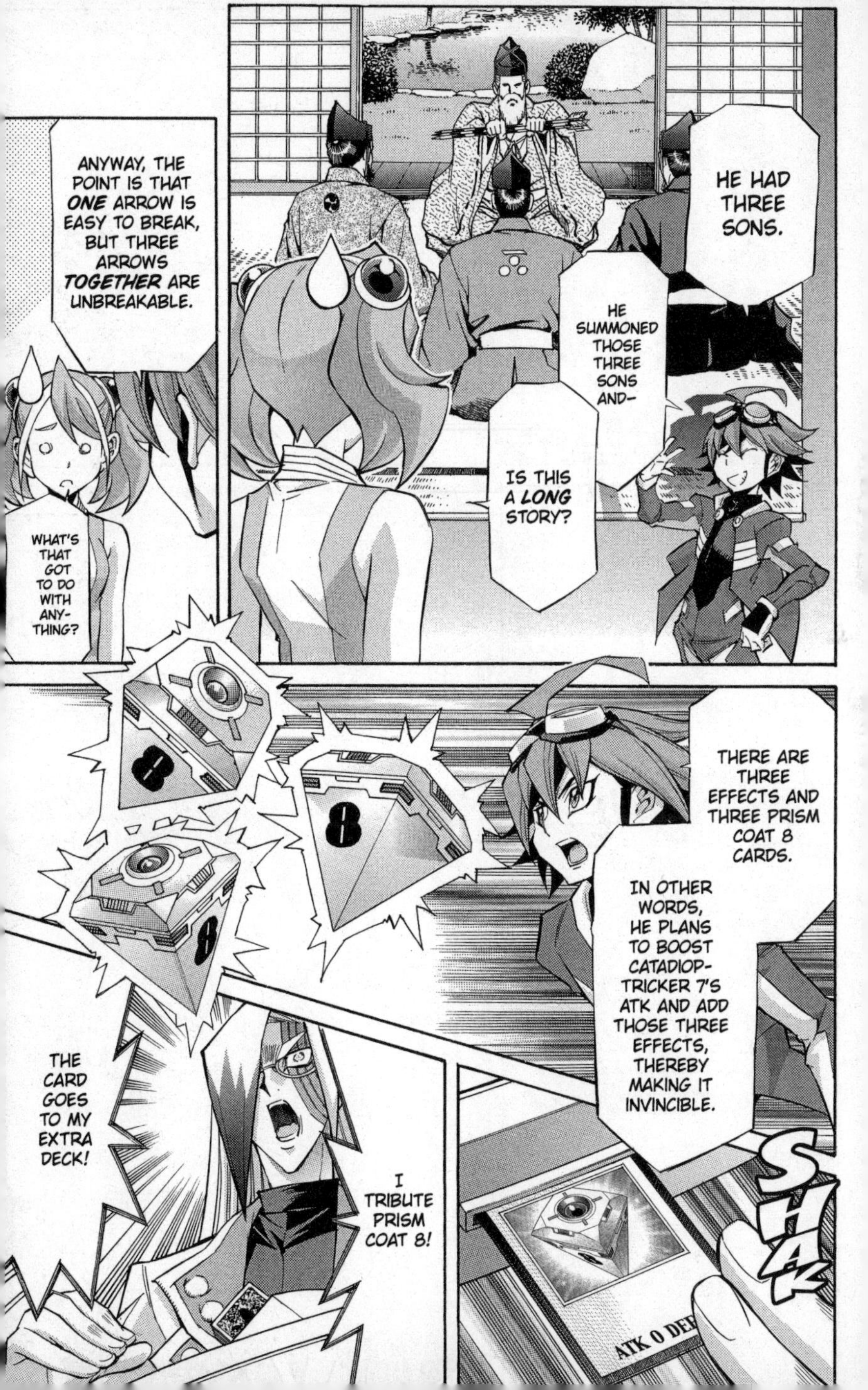
HE HAD THREE SONS.
HE SUMMONED THOSE THREE SONS AND–
IS THIS A LONG STORY?
ANYWAY, THE POINT IS THAT ONE ARROW IS EASY TO BREAK, BUT THREE ARROWS TOGETHER ARE UNBREAKABLE.
WHAT'S THAT GOT TO DO WITH ANYTHING?
THERE ARE THREE EFFECTS AND THREE PRISM COAT 8 CARDS.
IN OTHER WORDS, HE PLANS TO BOOST CATADIOPTRICKER 7'S ATK AND ADD THOSE THREE EFFECTS, THEREBY MAKING IT INVINCIBLE.
SHAK
I TRIBUTE PRISM COAT 8!
THE CARD GOES TO MY EXTRA DECK!

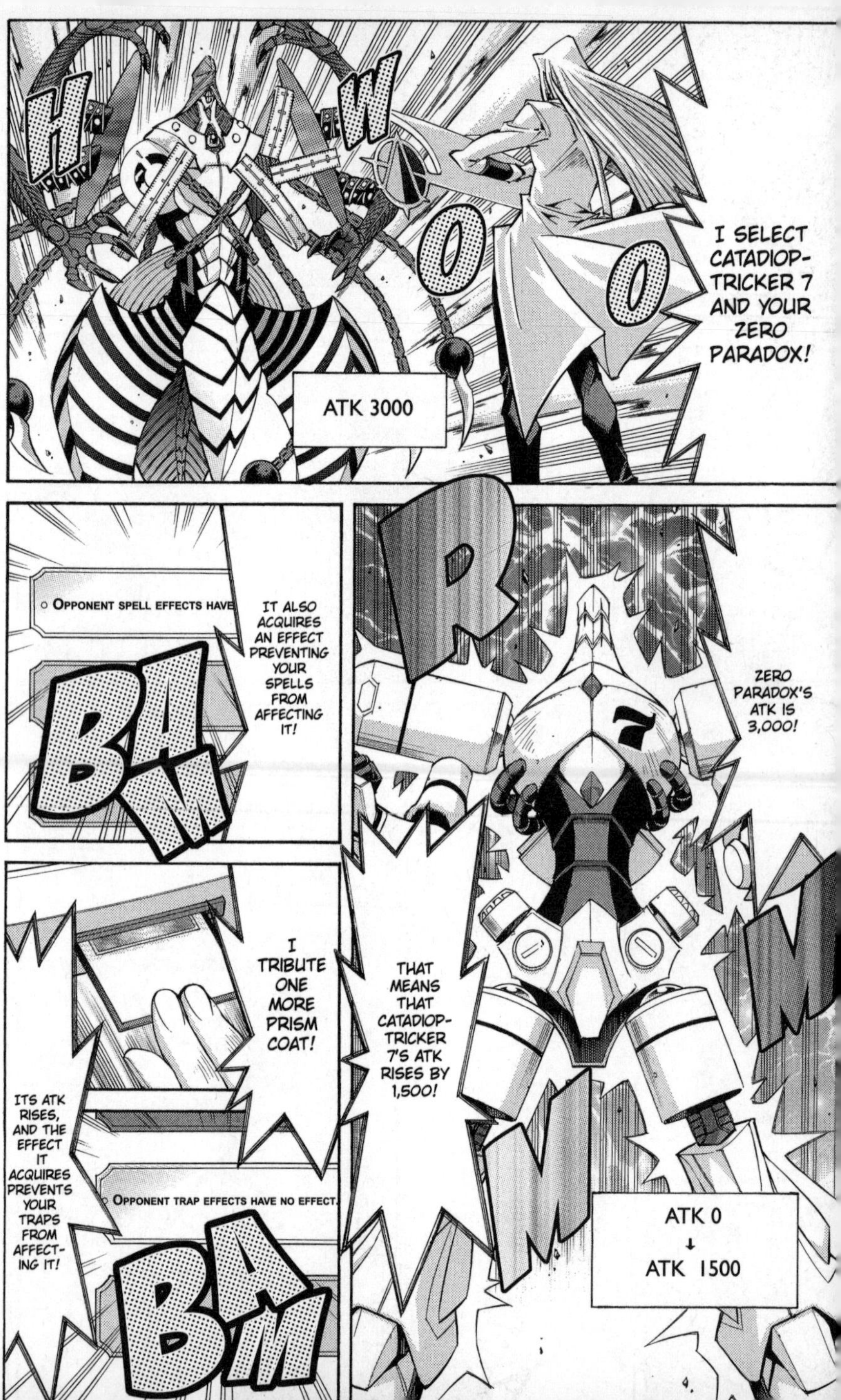
HWOO
I SELECT CATADIOP-TRICKER 7 AND YOUR ZERO PARADOX!
ATK 3000
RMM
ZERO PARADOX'S ATK IS 3,000!
THAT MEANS THAT CATADIOP-TRICKER 7'S ATK RISES BY 1,500!
ATK 0
↓
ATK 1500
Opponent spell effects have
IT ALSO ACQUIRES AN EFFECT PREVENTING YOUR SPELLS FROM AFFECTING IT!
BAM
I TRIBUTE ONE MORE PRISM COAT!
ITS ATK RISES, AND THE EFFECT IT ACQUIRES PREVENTS YOUR TRAPS FROM AFFECTING IT!
Opponent trap effects have no effect.
BAM

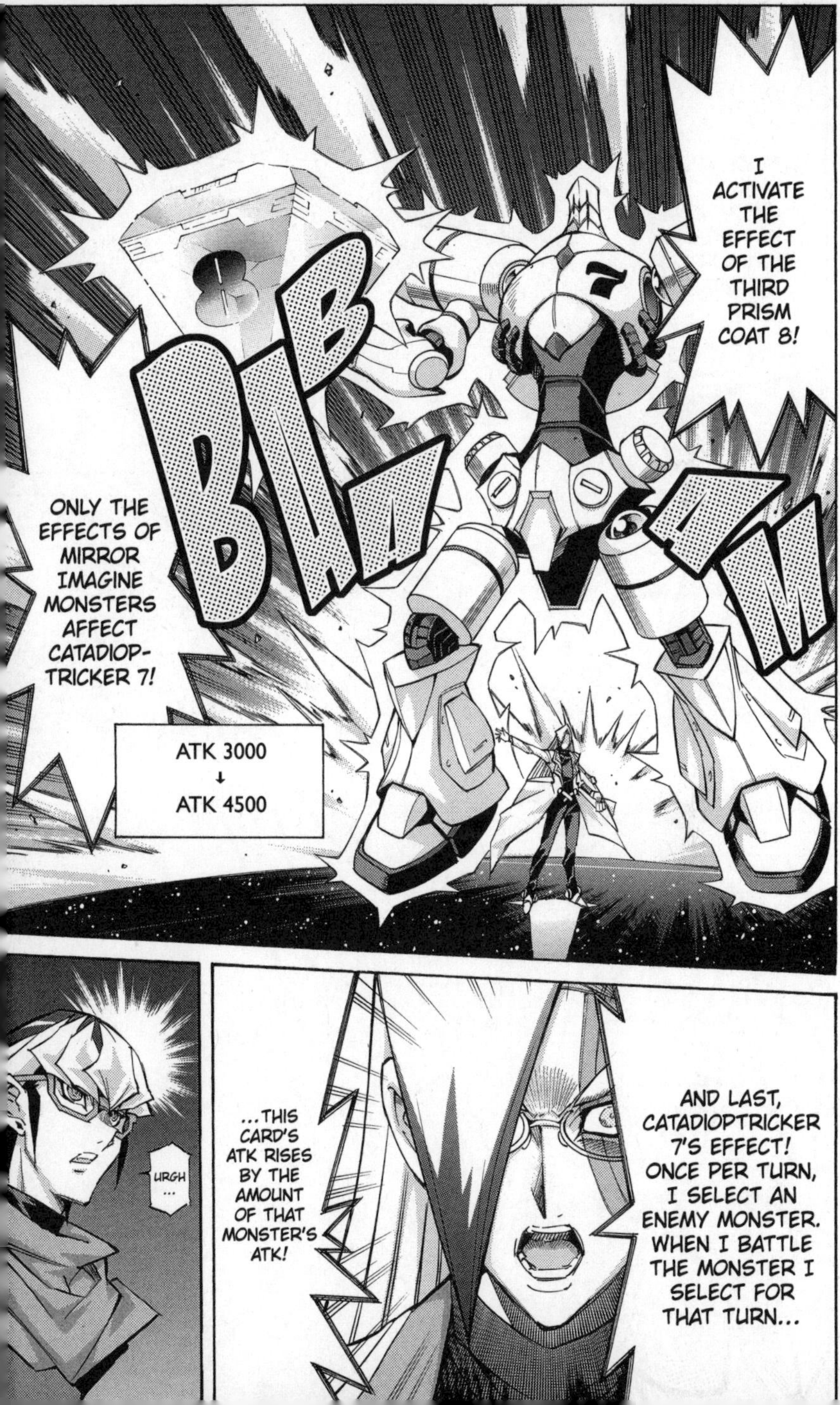
I ACTIVATE THE EFFECT OF THE THIRD PRISM COAT 8!
ONLY THE EFFECTS OF MIRROR IMAGINE MONSTERS AFFECT CATADIOP-TRICKER 7!
ATK 3000 ↓ ATK 4500
AND LAST, CATADIOPTRICKER 7'S EFFECT! ONCE PER TURN, I SELECT AN ENEMY MONSTER. WHEN I BATTLE THE MONSTER I SELECT FOR THAT TURN...
...THIS CARD'S ATK RISES BY THE AMOUNT OF THAT MONSTER'S ATK!
URGH ...

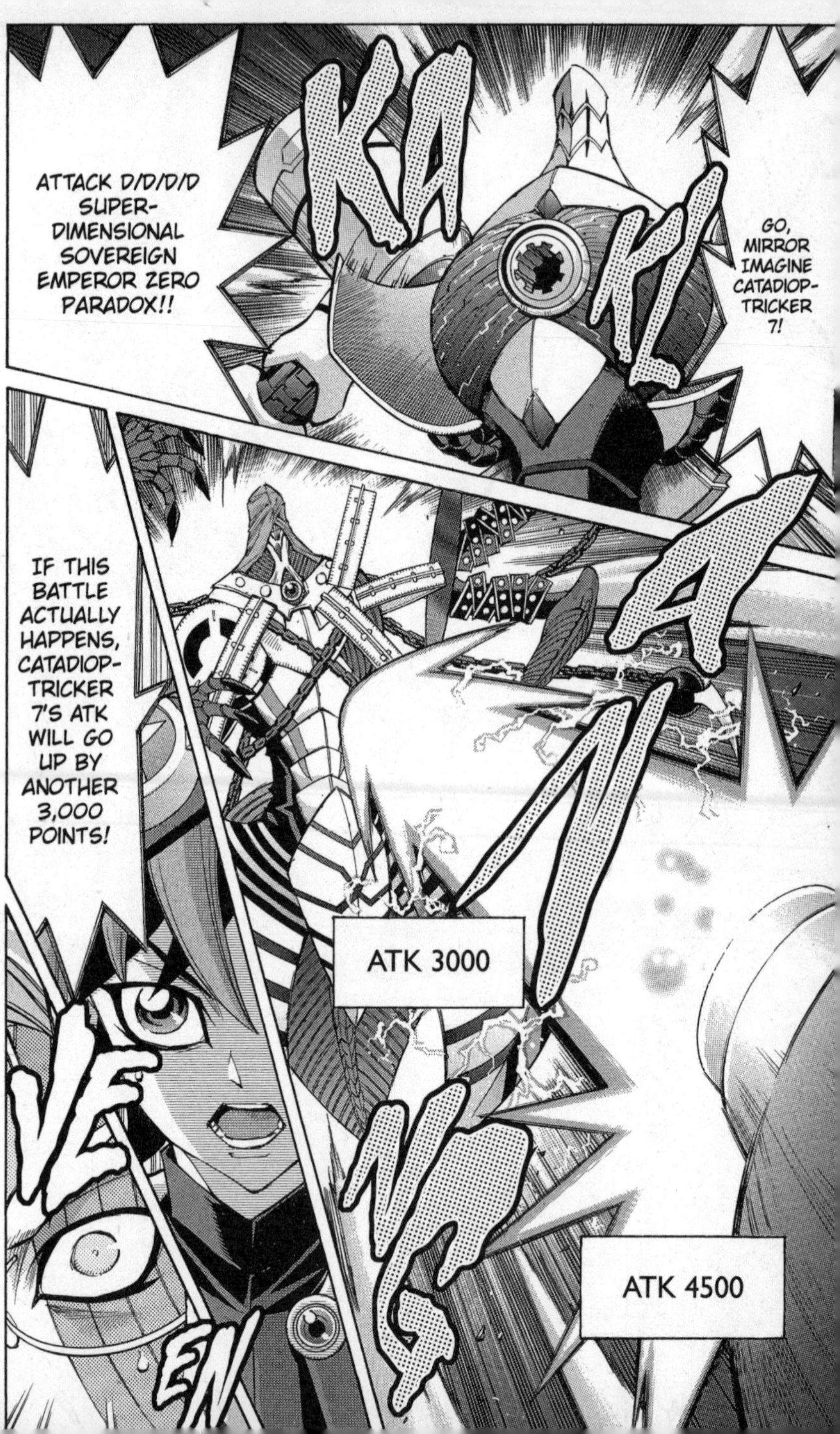
GO, MIRROR IMAGINE CATADIOP-TRICKER 7!
ATTACK D/D/D/D SUPER-DIMENSIONAL SOVEREIGN EMPEROR ZERO PARADOX!!
KA KI!
ATK 4500
ATK 3000
IF THIS BATTLE ACTUALLY HAPPENS, CATADIOP-TRICKER 7'S ATK WILL GO UP BY ANOTHER 3,000 POINTS!

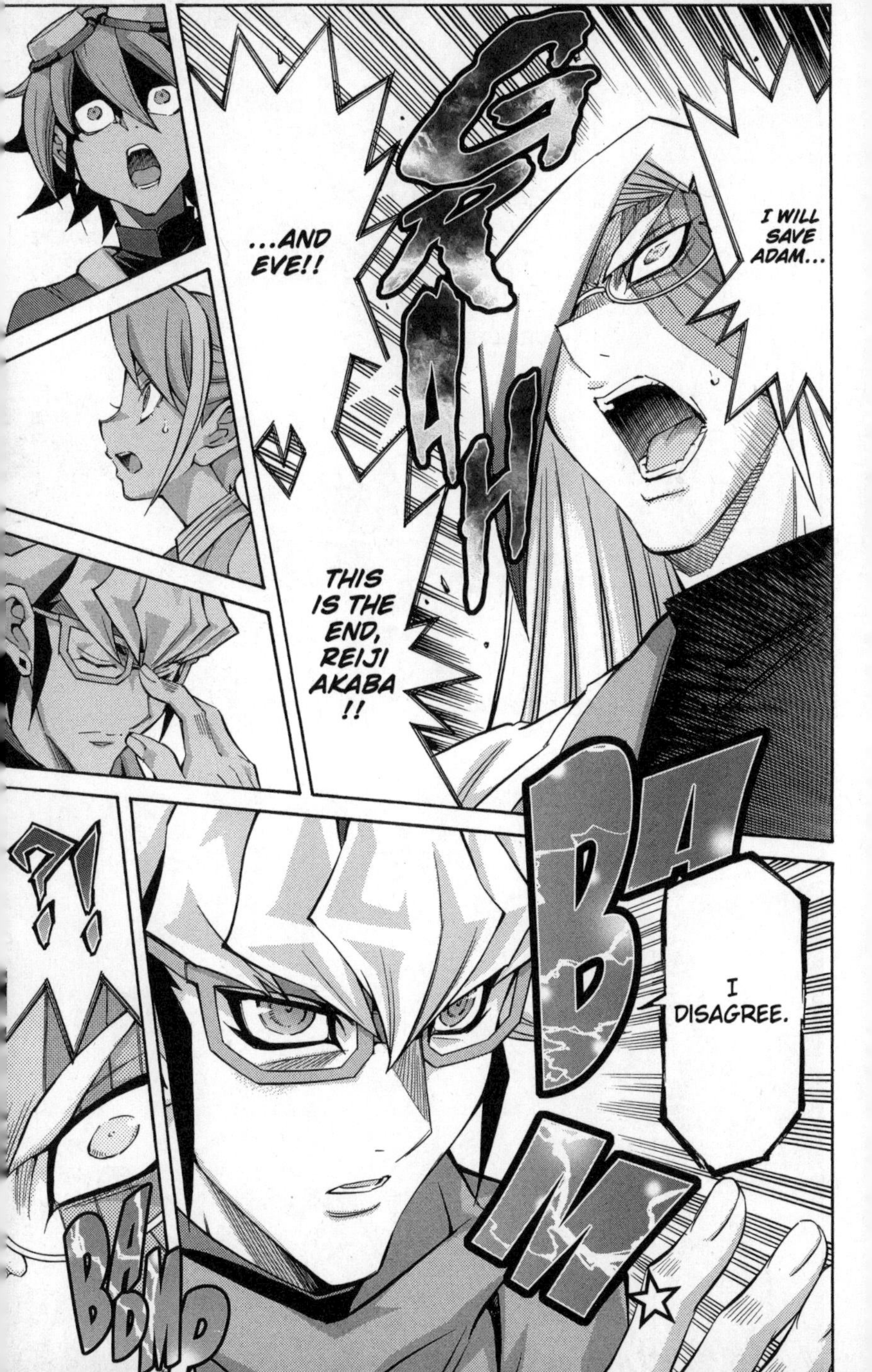
I WILL SAVE ADAM...
...AND EVE!!
THIS IS THE END, REIJI AKABA!!
I DISAGREE.
?!

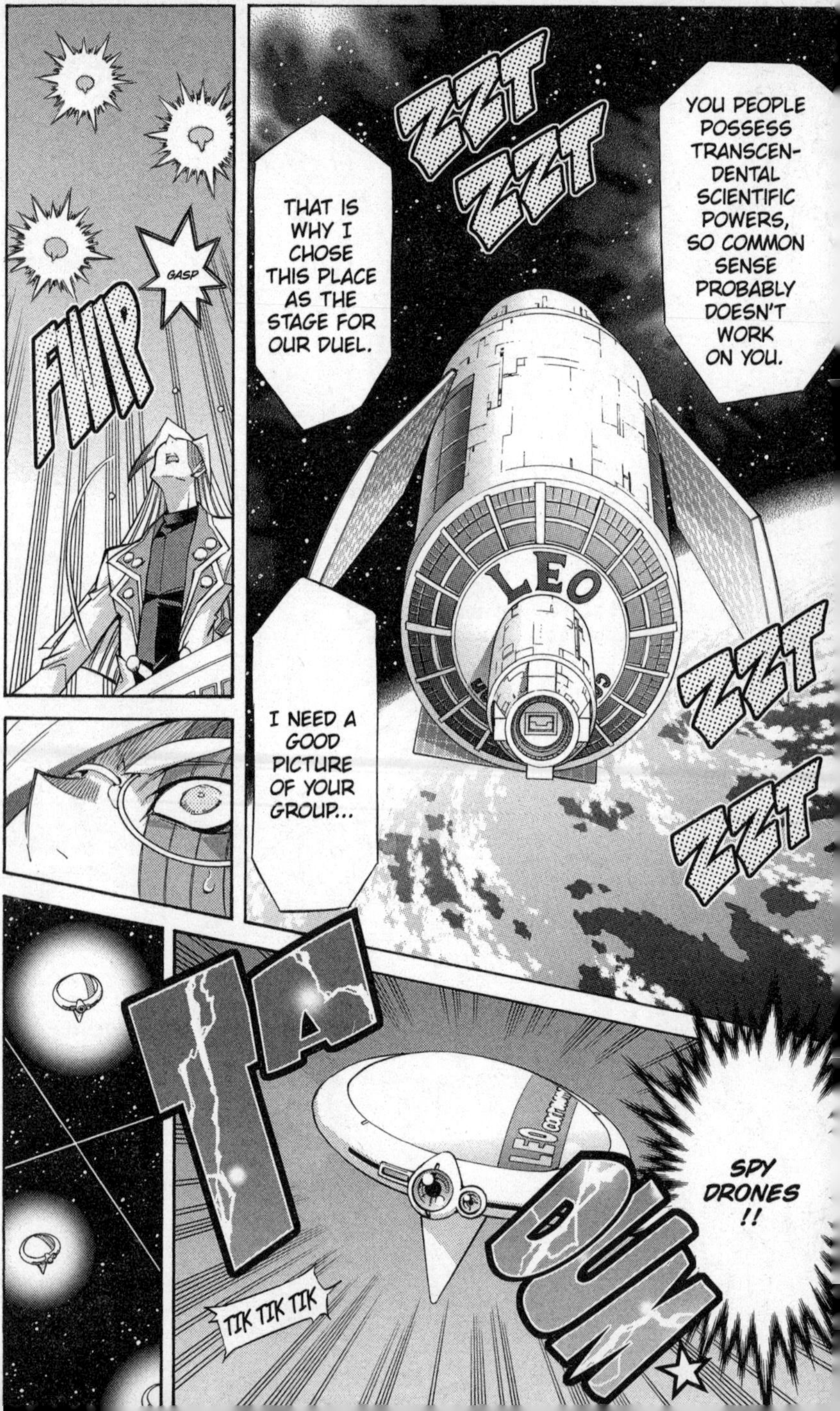
ZZT ZZT
YOU PEOPLE POSSESS TRANSCEN-DENTAL SCIENTIFIC POWERS, SO COMMON SENSE PROBABLY DOESN'T WORK ON YOU.
THAT IS WHY I CHOSE THIS PLACE AS THE STAGE FOR OUR DUEL.
LEO
ZZT ZZT
I NEED A GOOD PICTURE OF YOUR GROUP...
GASP
FWIP
TA-DUM
SPY DRONES !!
TIK TIK TIK

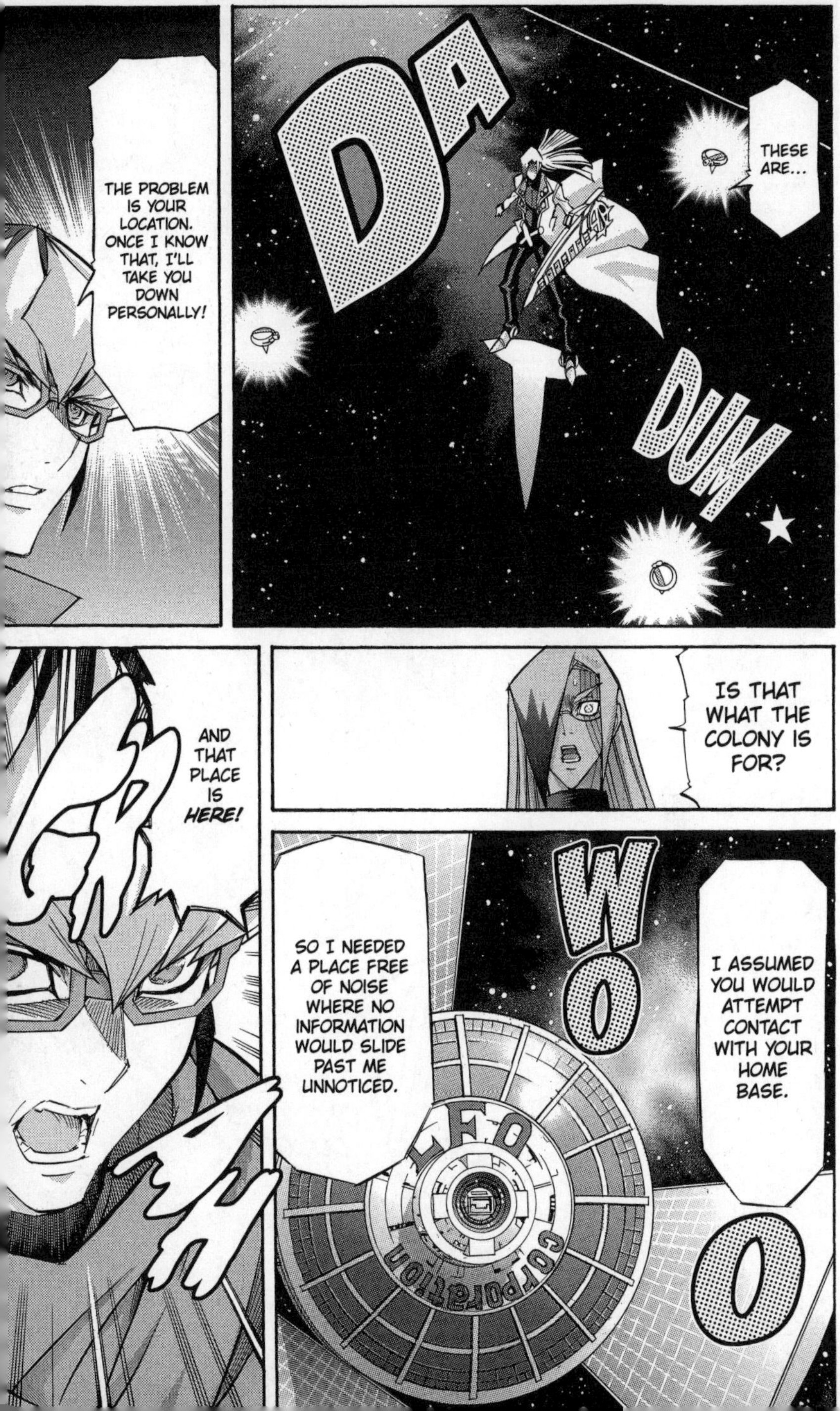
THESE ARE...
DA
DUM
THE PROBLEM IS YOUR LOCATION. ONCE I KNOW THAT, I'LL TAKE YOU DOWN PERSONALLY!
IS THAT WHAT THE COLONY IS FOR?
I ASSUMED YOU WOULD ATTEMPT CONTACT WITH YOUR HOME BASE.
WOO
SO I NEEDED A PLACE FREE OF NOISE WHERE NO INFORMATION WOULD SLIDE PAST ME UNNOTICED.
LEO Corporation
AND THAT PLACE IS *HERE!*

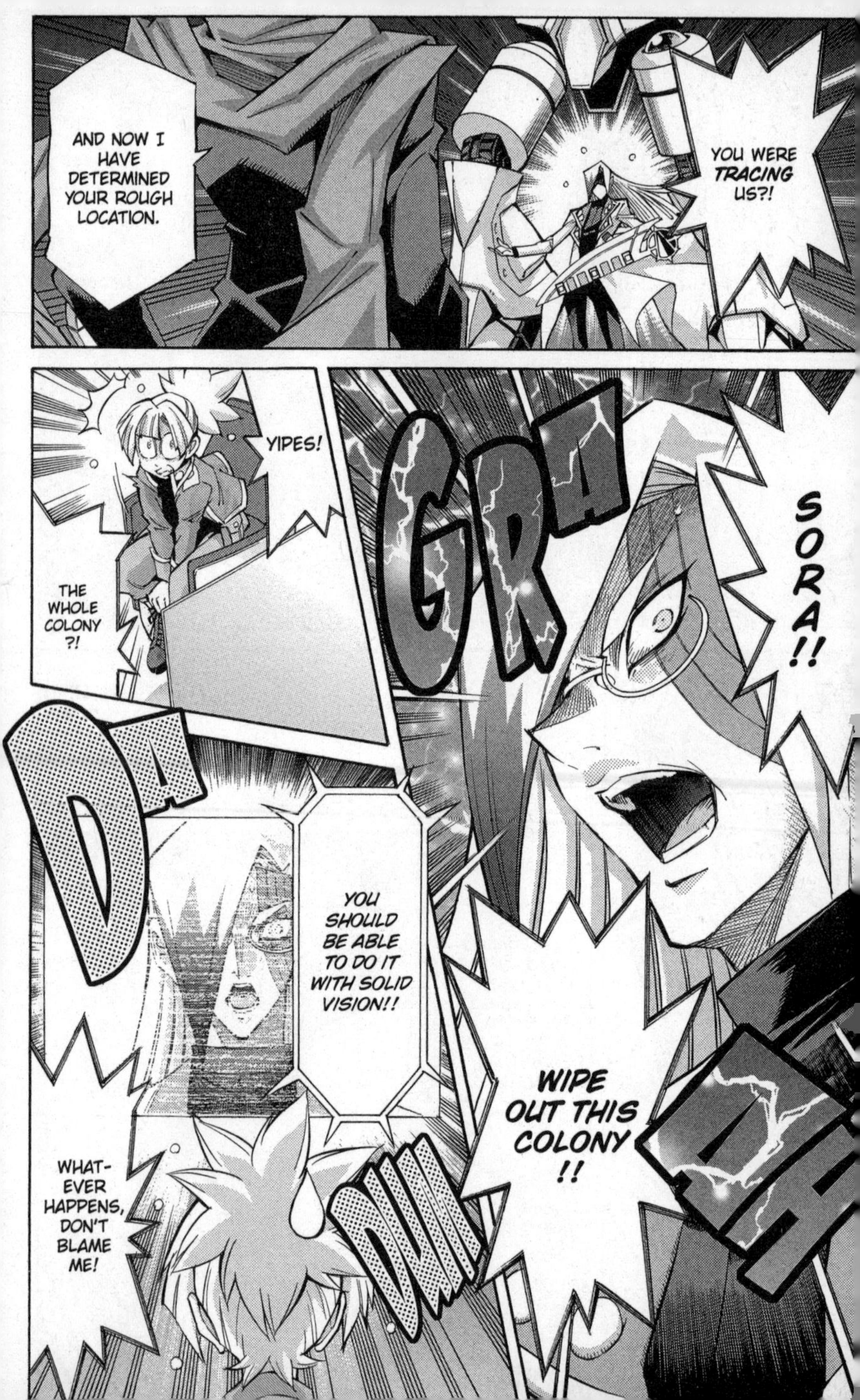

YOU WERE TRACING US?!
AND NOW I HAVE DETERMINED YOUR ROUGH LOCATION.
GRA
SORA!!
WIPE OUT THIS COLONY!!
YIPES!
THE WHOLE COLONY?!
DA
YOU SHOULD BE ABLE TO DO IT WITH SOLID VISION!!
WHAT-EVER HAPPENS, DON'T BLAME ME!

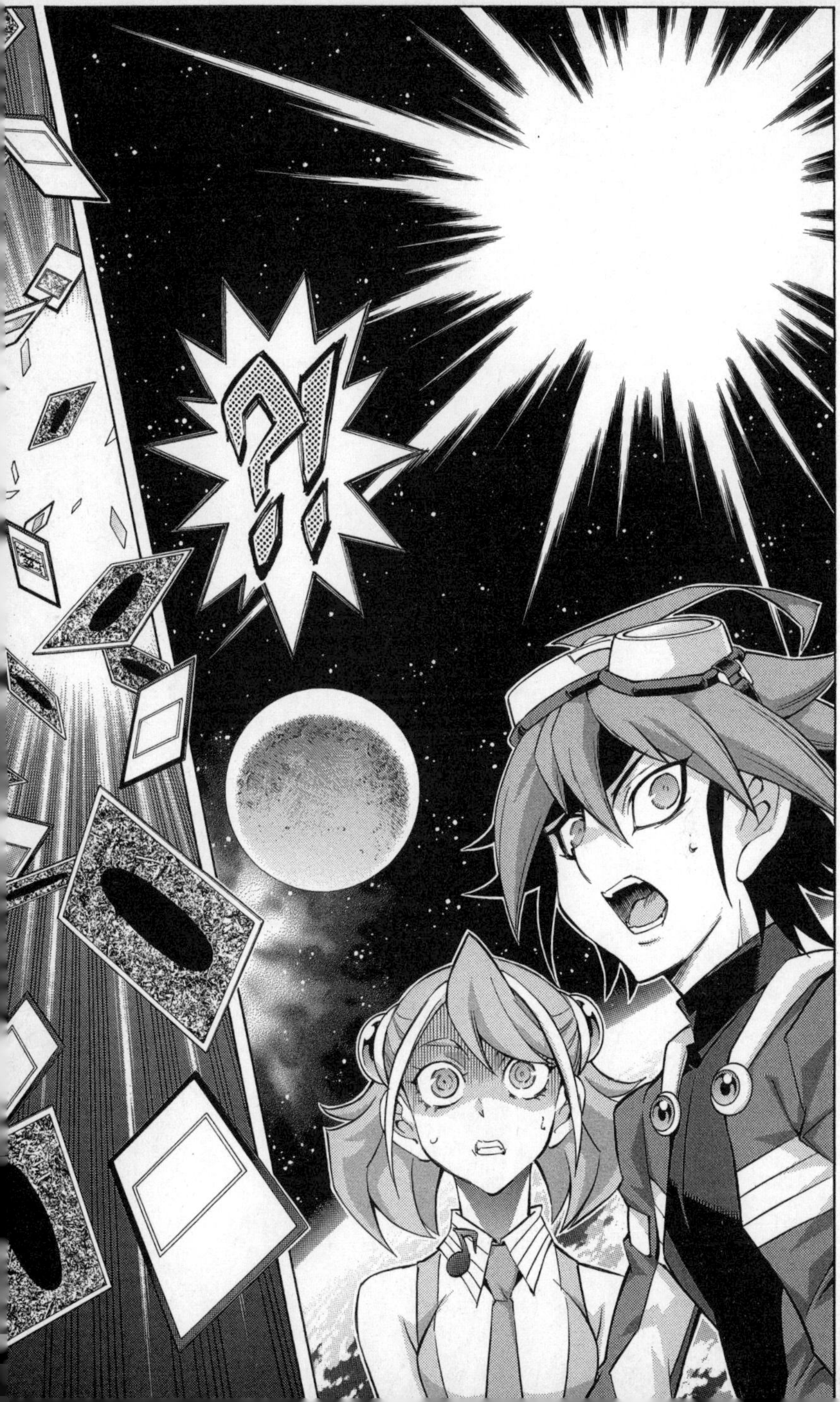
?!

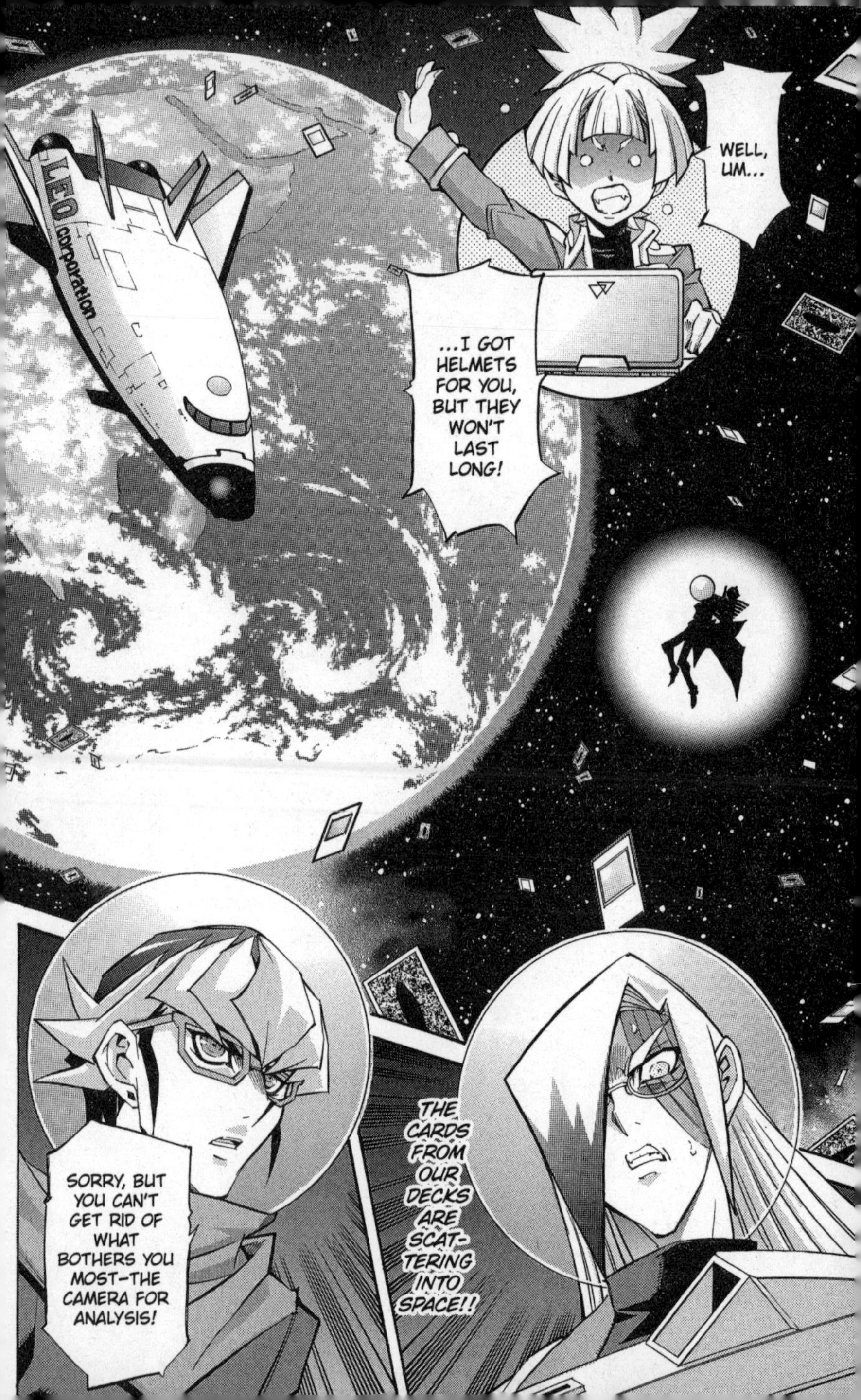
WELL, UM...
...I GOT HELMETS FOR YOU, BUT THEY WON'T LAST LONG!
LEO corporation
THE CARDS FROM OUR DECKS ARE SCAT-TERING INTO SPACE!!
SORRY, BUT YOU CAN'T GET RID OF WHAT BOTHERS YOU MOST—THE CAMERA FOR ANALYSIS!

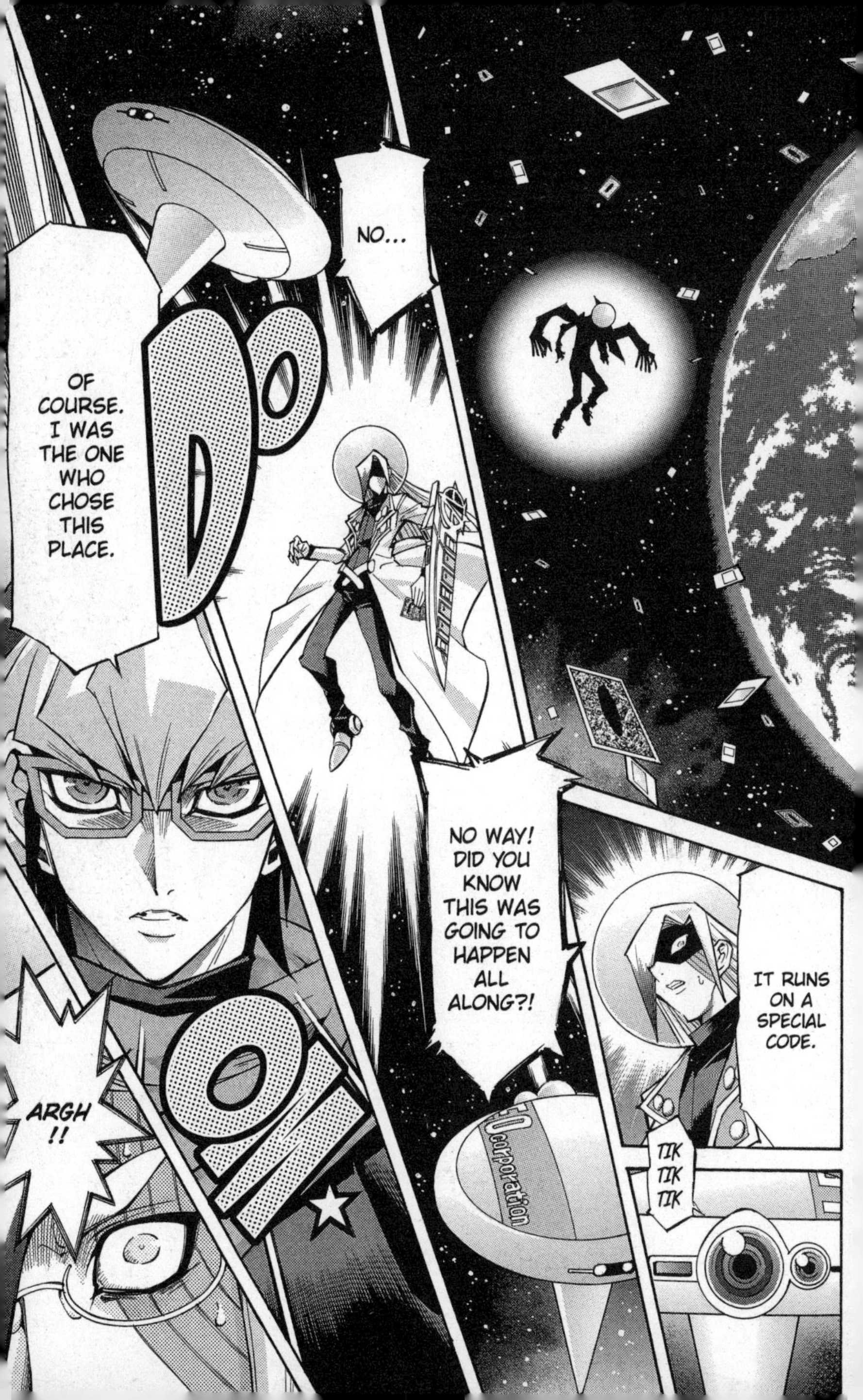
NO...
NO WAY! DID YOU KNOW THIS WAS GOING TO HAPPEN ALL ALONG?!
IT RUNS ON A SPECIAL CODE.
TIK TIK TIK
OF COURSE. I WAS THE ONE WHO CHOSE THIS PLACE.
ARGH!!

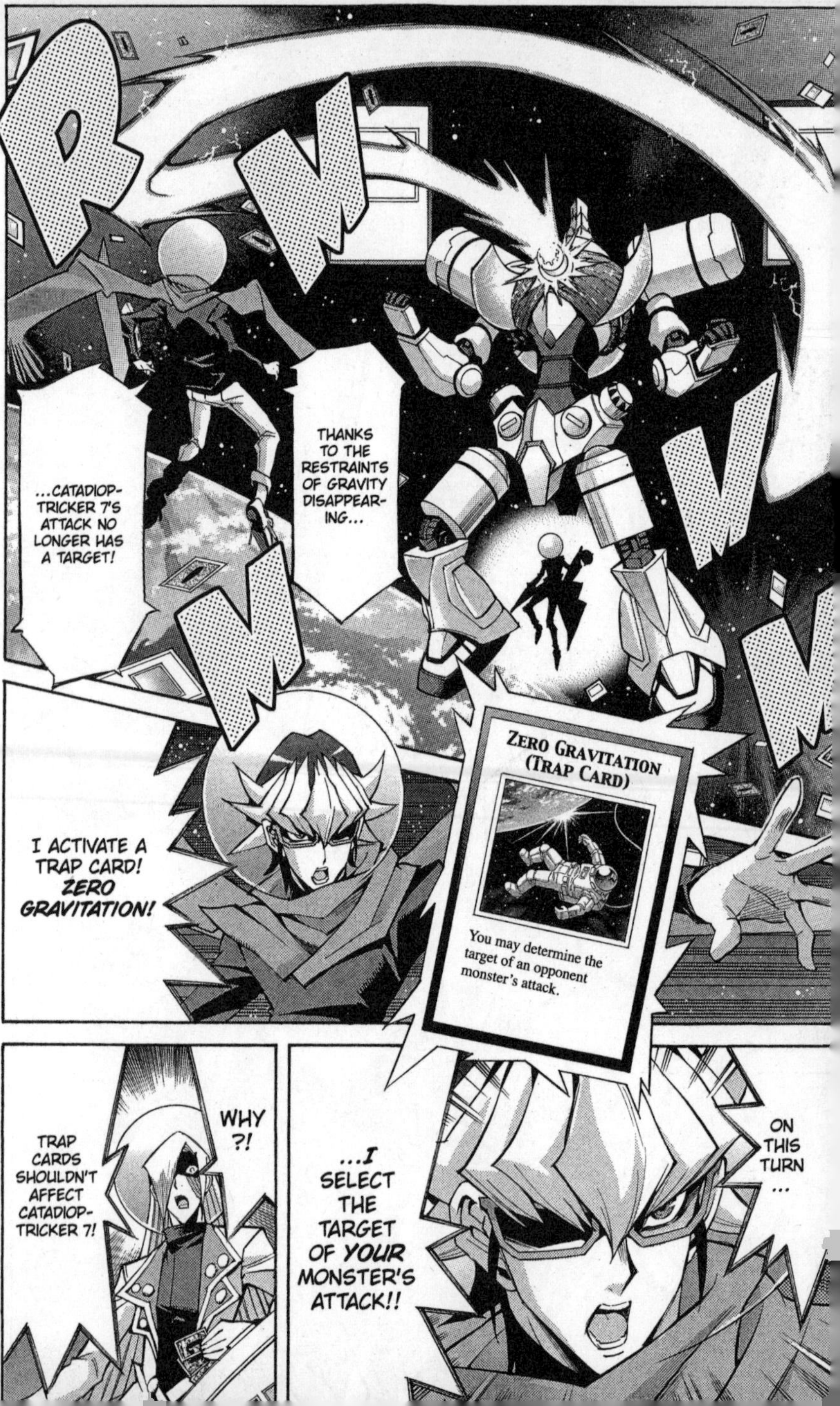
THANKS TO THE RESTRAINTS OF GRAVITY DISAPPEARING...
...CATADIOP-TRICKER 7'S ATTACK NO LONGER HAS A TARGET!
ZERO GRAVITATION (TRAP CARD)
You may determine the target of an opponent monster's attack.
I ACTIVATE A TRAP CARD! ZERO GRAVITATION!
ON THIS TURN...
...I SELECT THE TARGET OF YOUR MONSTER'S ATTACK!!
WHY?!
TRAP CARDS SHOULDN'T AFFECT CATADIOP-TRICKER 7!

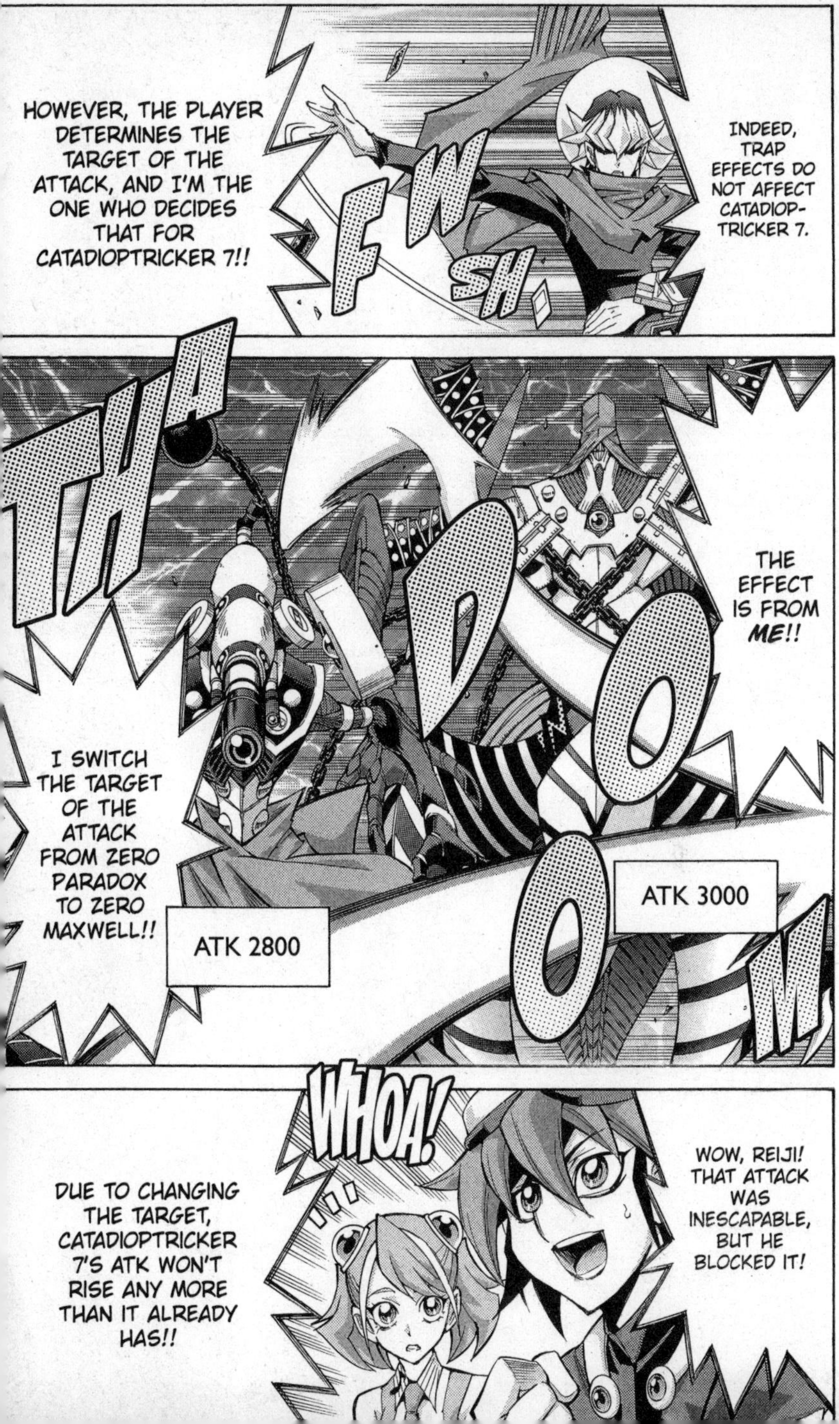
INDEED, TRAP EFFECTS DO NOT AFFECT CATADIOP-TRICKER 7.
FWSH
HOWEVER, THE PLAYER DETERMINES THE TARGET OF THE ATTACK, AND I'M THE ONE WHO DECIDES THAT FOR CATADIOPTRICKER 7!!
THE EFFECT IS FROM *ME*!!
DOOOM
ATK 3000
THA
ATK 2800
I SWITCH THE TARGET OF THE ATTACK FROM ZERO PARADOX TO ZERO MAXWELL!!
WHOA!
WOW, REIJI! THAT ATTACK WAS INESCAPABLE, BUT HE BLOCKED IT!
DUE TO CHANGING THE TARGET, CATADIOPTRICKER 7'S ATK WON'T RISE ANY MORE THAN IT ALREADY HAS!!

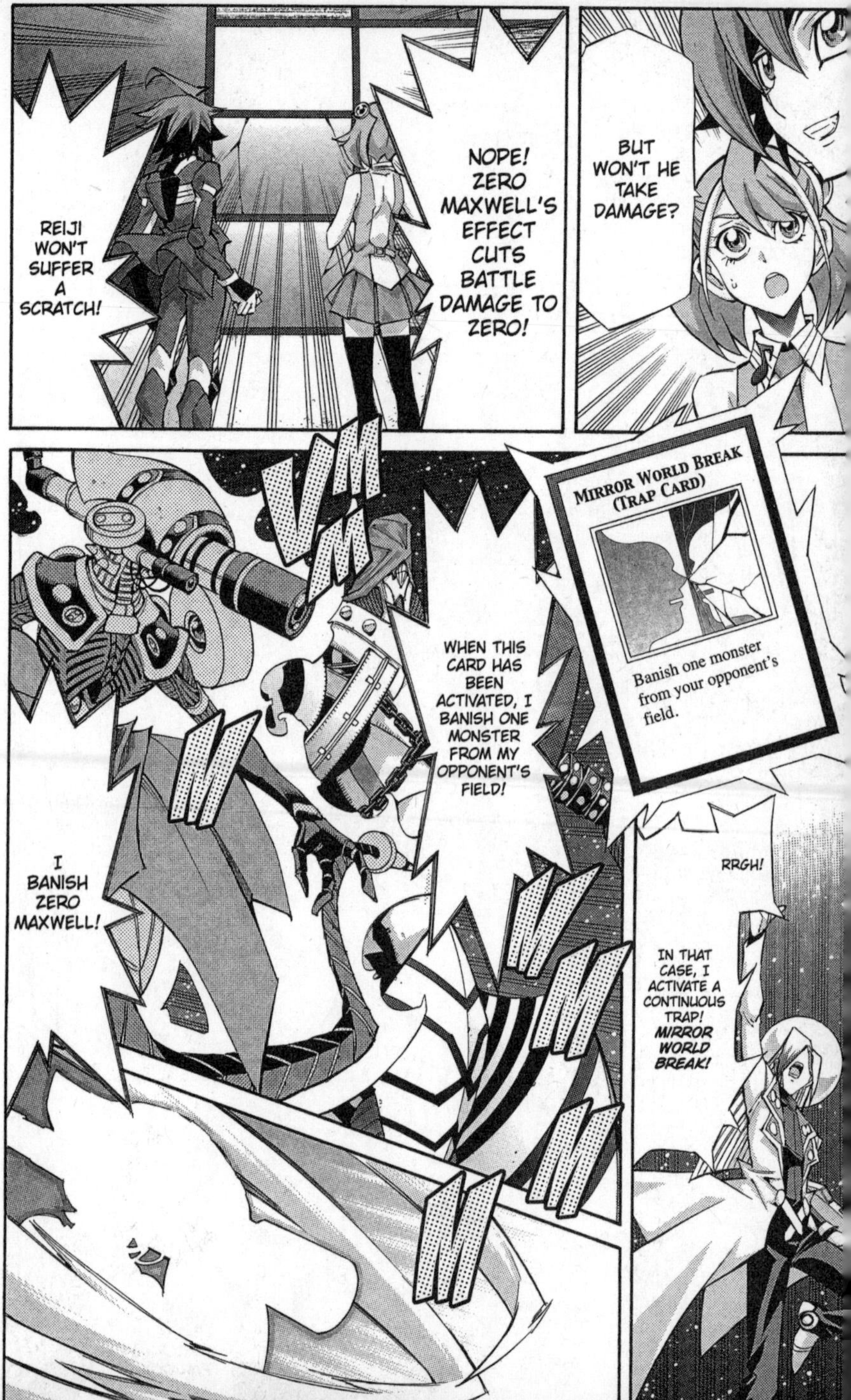
BUT WON'T HE TAKE DAMAGE?
NOPE! ZERO MAXWELL'S EFFECT CUTS BATTLE DAMAGE TO ZERO!
REIJI WON'T SUFFER A SCRATCH!
RRGH!
IN THAT CASE, I ACTIVATE A CONTINUOUS TRAP! MIRROR WORLD BREAK!
MIRROR WORLD BREAK (TRAP CARD)
Banish one monster from your opponent's field.
WHEN THIS CARD HAS BEEN ACTIVATED, I BANISH ONE MONSTER FROM MY OPPONENT'S FIELD!
I BANISH ZERO MAXWELL!
VM VM
M M M M M M

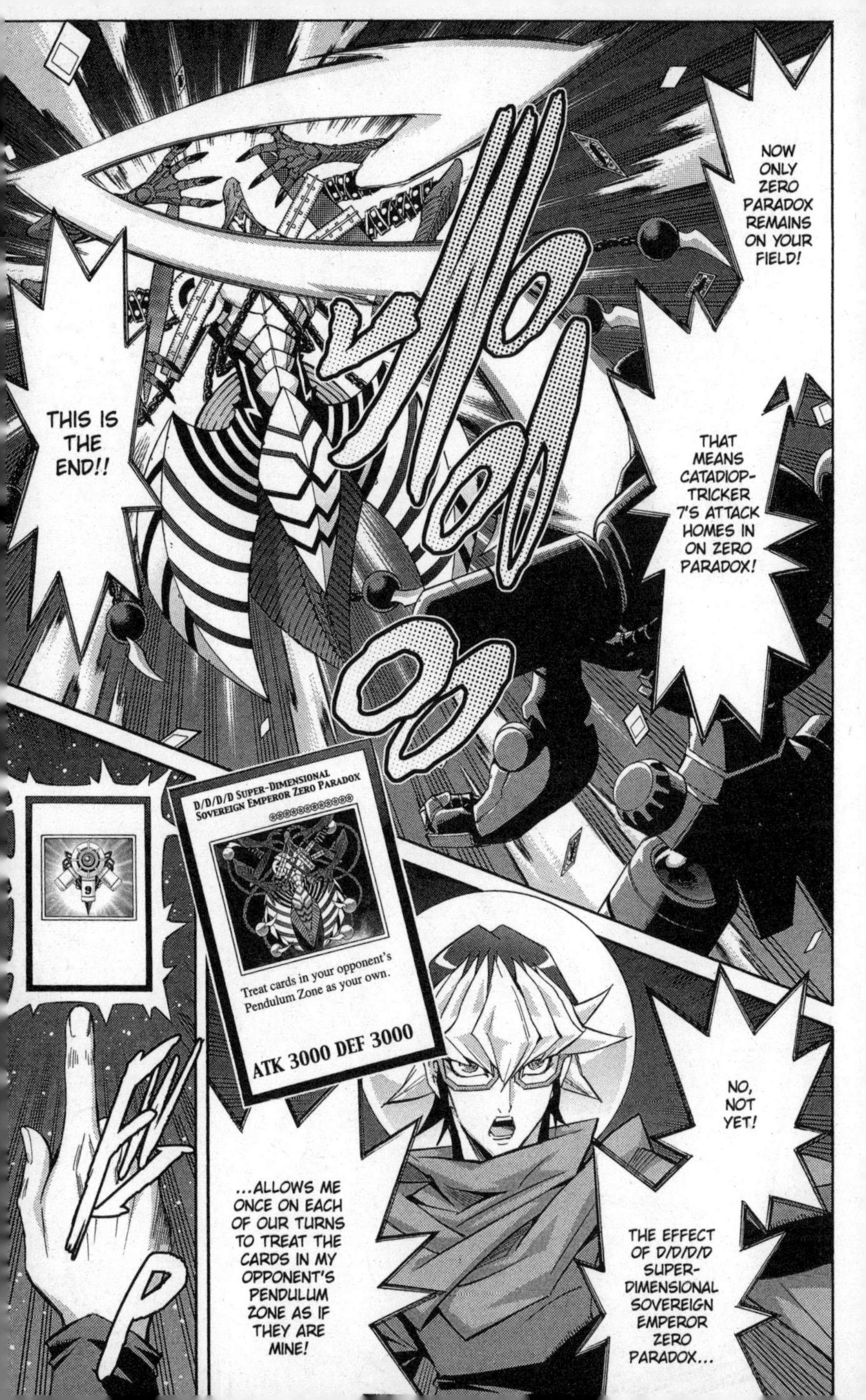
NOW ONLY ZERO PARADOX REMAINS ON YOUR FIELD!
THAT MEANS CATADIOP-TRICKER 7'S ATTACK HOMES IN ON ZERO PARADOX!
THIS IS THE END!!
NO, NOT YET!
THE EFFECT OF D/D/D/D SUPER-DIMENSIONAL SOVEREIGN EMPEROR ZERO PARADOX...
D/D/D/D SUPER-DIMENSIONAL SOVEREIGN EMPEROR ZERO PARADOX
Treat cards in your opponent's Pendulum Zone as your own.
ATK 3000 DEF 3000
...ALLOWS ME ONCE ON EACH OF OUR TURNS TO TREAT THE CARDS IN MY OPPONENT'S PENDULUM ZONE AS IF THEY ARE MINE!

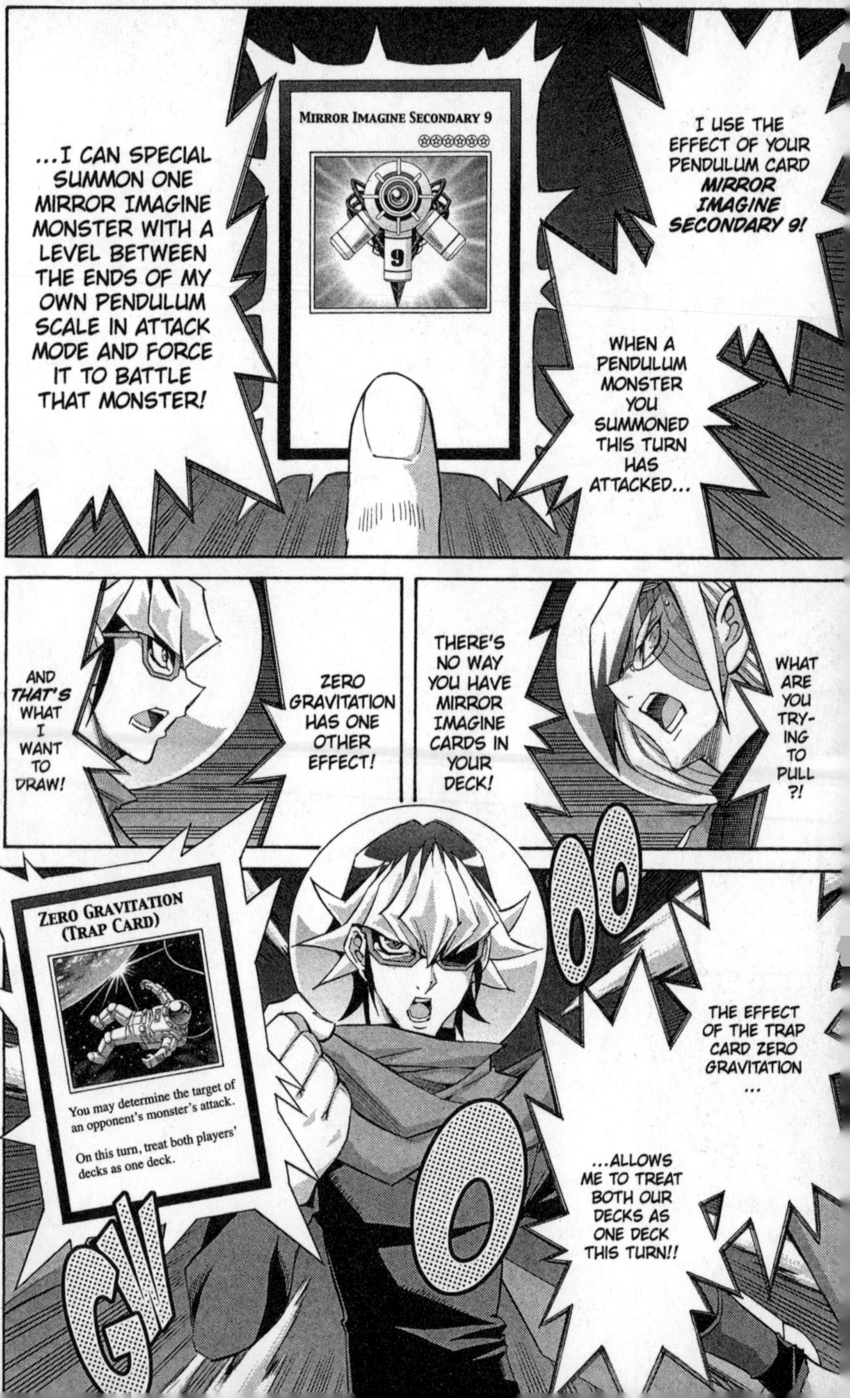
I USE THE EFFECT OF YOUR PENDULUM CARD *MIRROR IMAGINE SECONDARY 9!*
WHEN A PENDULUM MONSTER YOU SUMMONED THIS TURN HAS ATTACKED...
MIRROR IMAGINE SECONDARY 9
...I CAN SPECIAL SUMMON ONE MIRROR IMAGINE MONSTER WITH A LEVEL BETWEEN THE ENDS OF MY OWN PENDULUM SCALE IN ATTACK MODE AND FORCE IT TO BATTLE THAT MONSTER!
WHAT ARE YOU TRYING TO PULL?!
THERE'S NO WAY YOU HAVE MIRROR IMAGINE CARDS IN YOUR DECK!
ZERO GRAVITATION HAS ONE OTHER EFFECT!
AND *THAT'S* WHAT I WANT TO DRAW!
THE EFFECT OF THE TRAP CARD ZERO GRAVITATION ...
...ALLOWS ME TO TREAT BOTH OUR DECKS AS ONE DECK THIS TURN!!
ZERO GRAVITATION (TRAP CARD)
You may determine the target of an opponent's monster's attack.
On this turn, treat both players' decks as one deck.

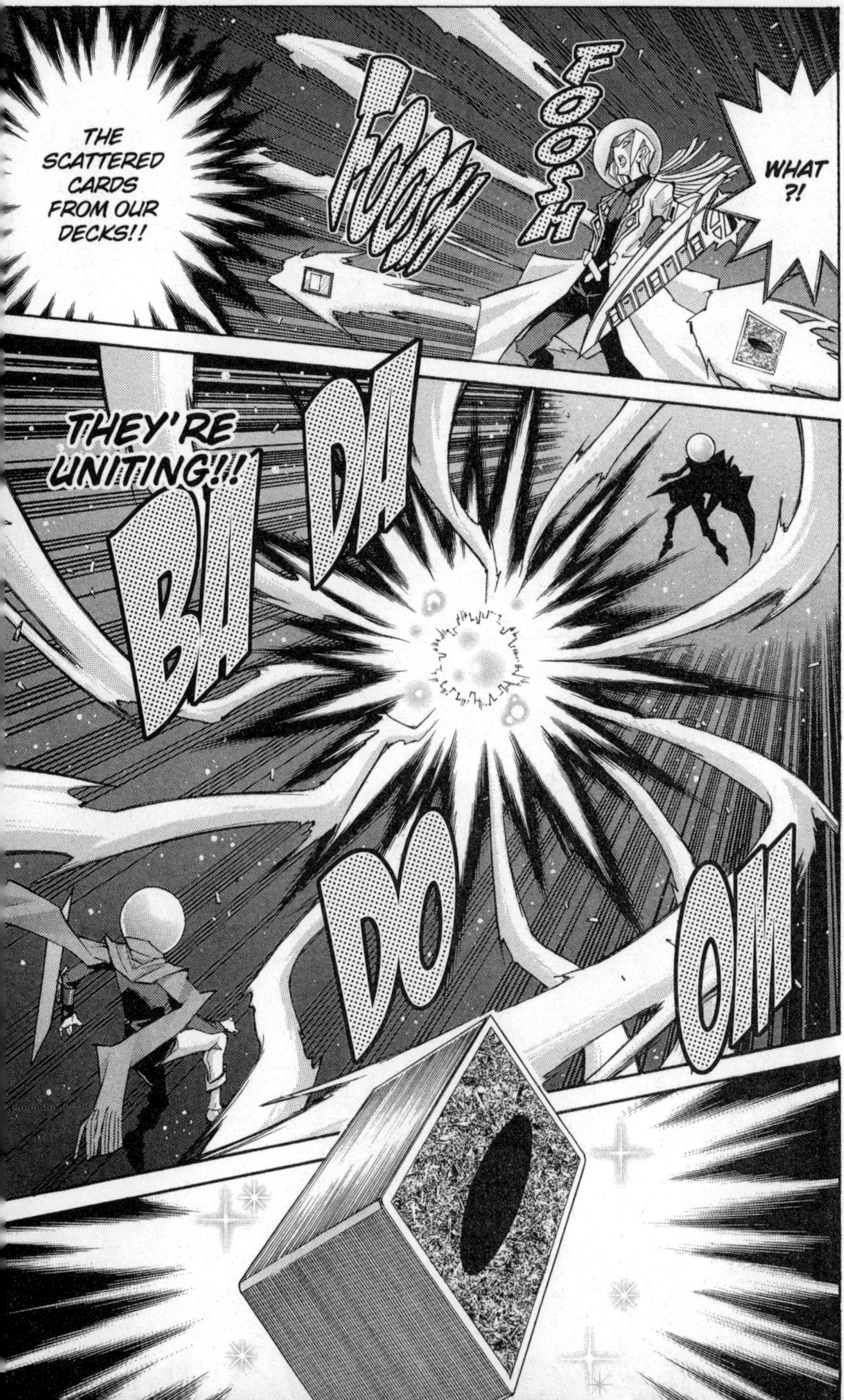
WHAT ?!
FOOOSH
THE SCATTERED CARDS FROM OUR DECKS!!
THEY'RE UNITING!!
BA DA
DO OM

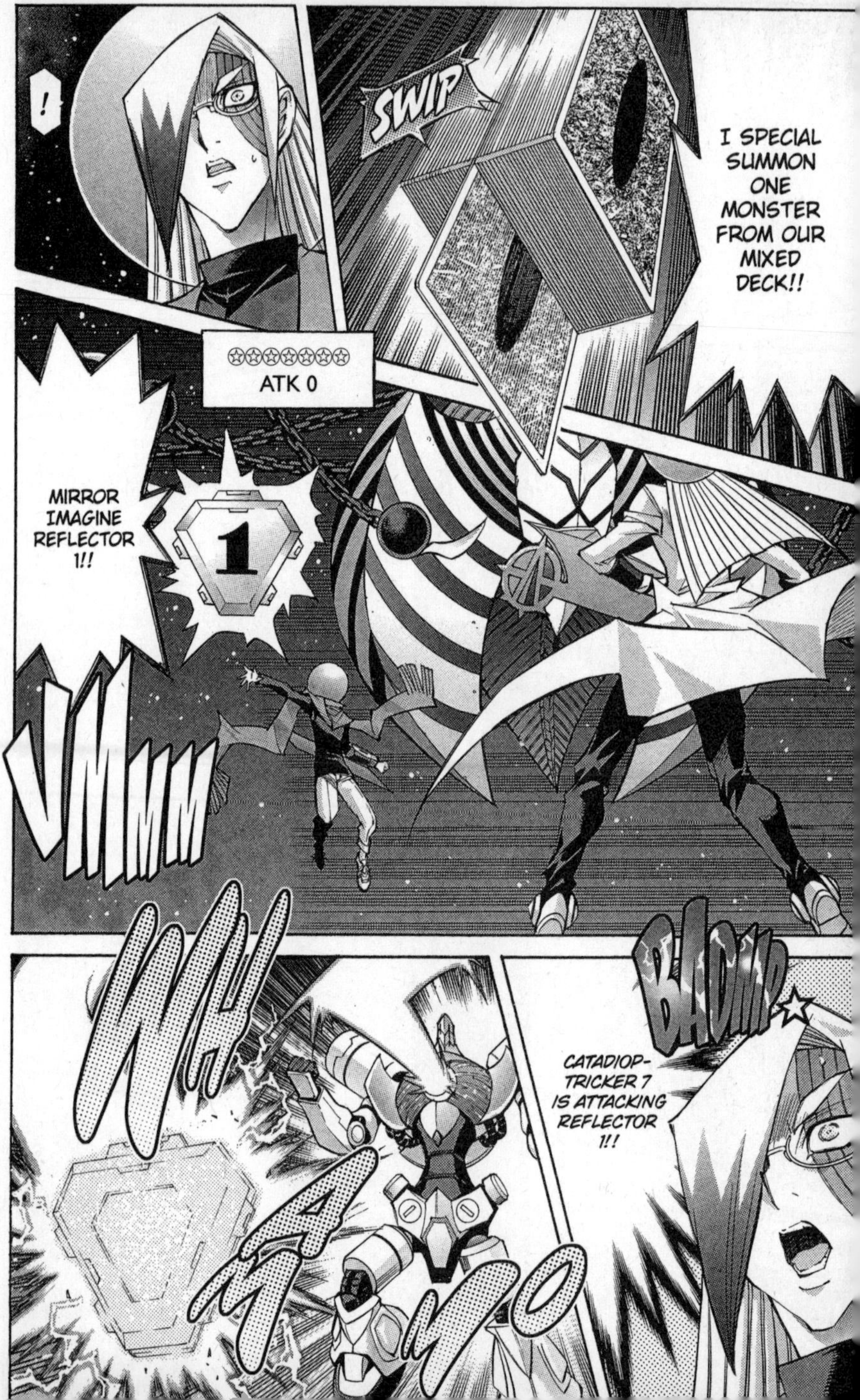
I SPECIAL SUMMON ONE MONSTER FROM OUR MIXED DECK!!
SWIP
!
☆☆☆☆☆☆☆
ATK 0
MIRROR IMAGINE REFLECTOR 1!!
1
JMMMM
BADMP
CATADIOP-TRICKER 7 IS ATTACKING REFLECTOR 1!!

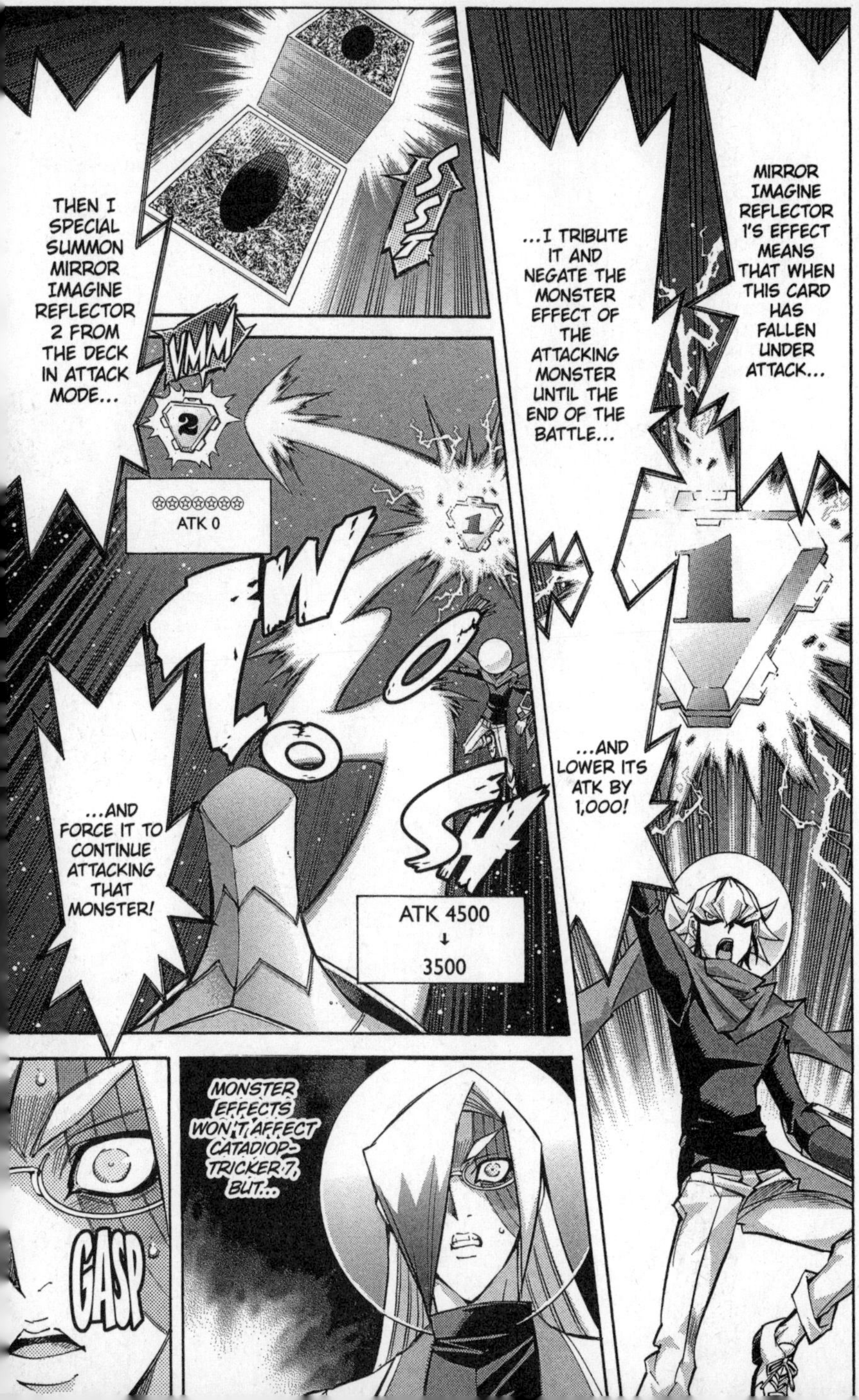
MIRROR IMAGINE REFLECTOR 1'S EFFECT MEANS THAT WHEN THIS CARD HAS FALLEN UNDER ATTACK...
...I TRIBUTE IT AND NEGATE THE MONSTER EFFECT OF THE ATTACKING MONSTER UNTIL THE END OF THE BATTLE...
...AND LOWER ITS ATK BY 1,000!
THEN I SPECIAL SUMMON MIRROR IMAGINE REFLECTOR 2 FROM THE DECK IN ATTACK MODE...
VMM
☆☆☆☆☆☆☆
ATK 0
WOOSH
ATK 4500 ↓ 3500
...AND FORCE IT TO CONTINUE ATTACKING THAT MONSTER!
MONSTER EFFECTS WON'T AFFECT CATADIOP-TRICKER 7, BUT...
GASP

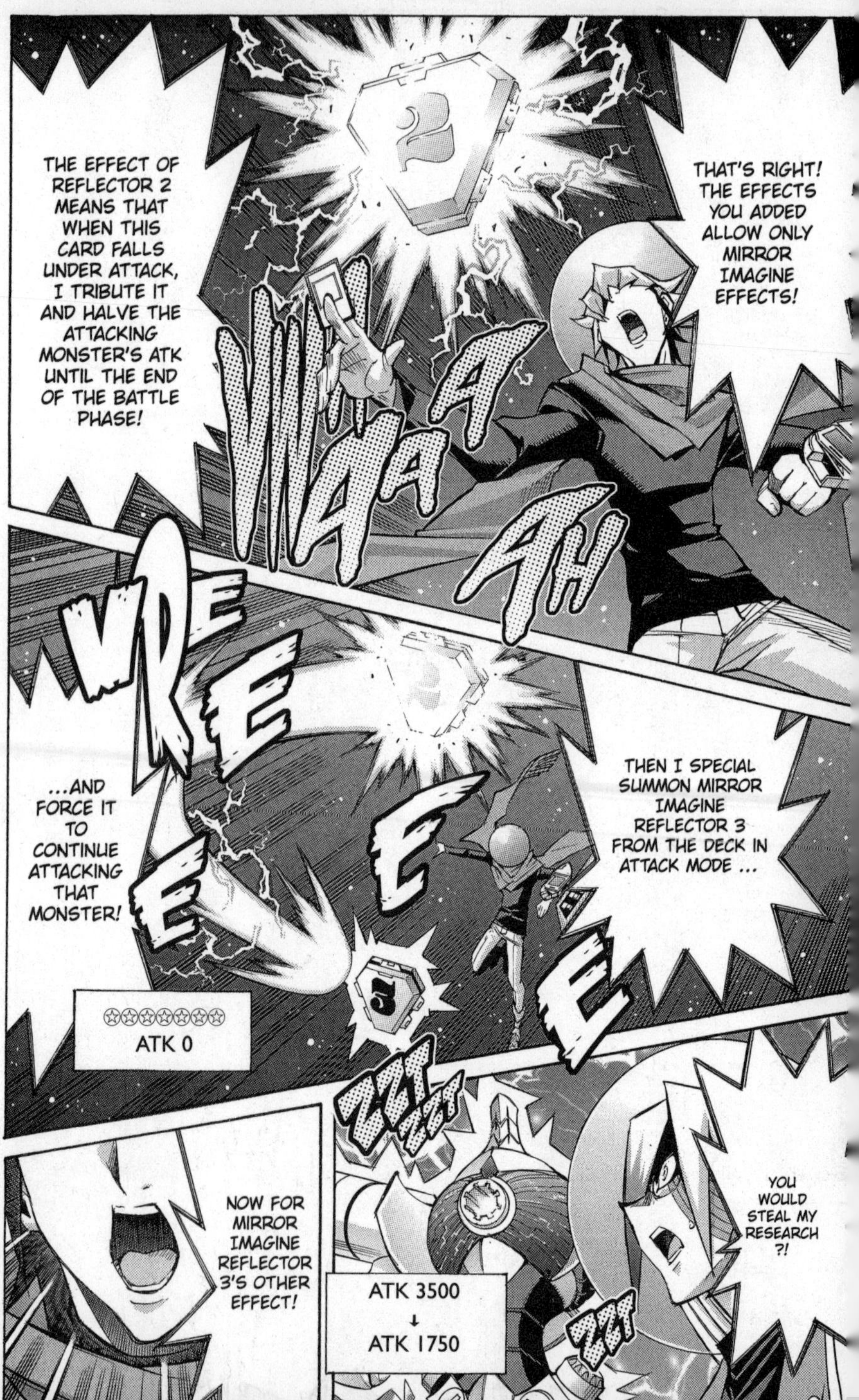
THAT'S RIGHT! THE EFFECTS YOU ADDED ALLOW ONLY MIRROR IMAGINE EFFECTS!
VWAAAAH
THE EFFECT OF REFLECTOR 2 MEANS THAT WHEN THIS CARD FALLS UNDER ATTACK, I TRIBUTE IT AND HALVE THE ATTACKING MONSTER'S ATK UNTIL THE END OF THE BATTLE PHASE!
THEN I SPECIAL SUMMON MIRROR IMAGINE REFLECTOR 3 FROM THE DECK IN ATTACK MODE ...
VREEEEE
...AND FORCE IT TO CONTINUE ATTACKING THAT MONSTER!
☆☆☆☆☆☆☆
ATK 0
ZZT ZZT
YOU WOULD STEAL MY RESEARCH ?!
ZZT
ATK 3500
↓
ATK 1750
NOW FOR MIRROR IMAGINE REFLECTOR 3'S OTHER EFFECT!

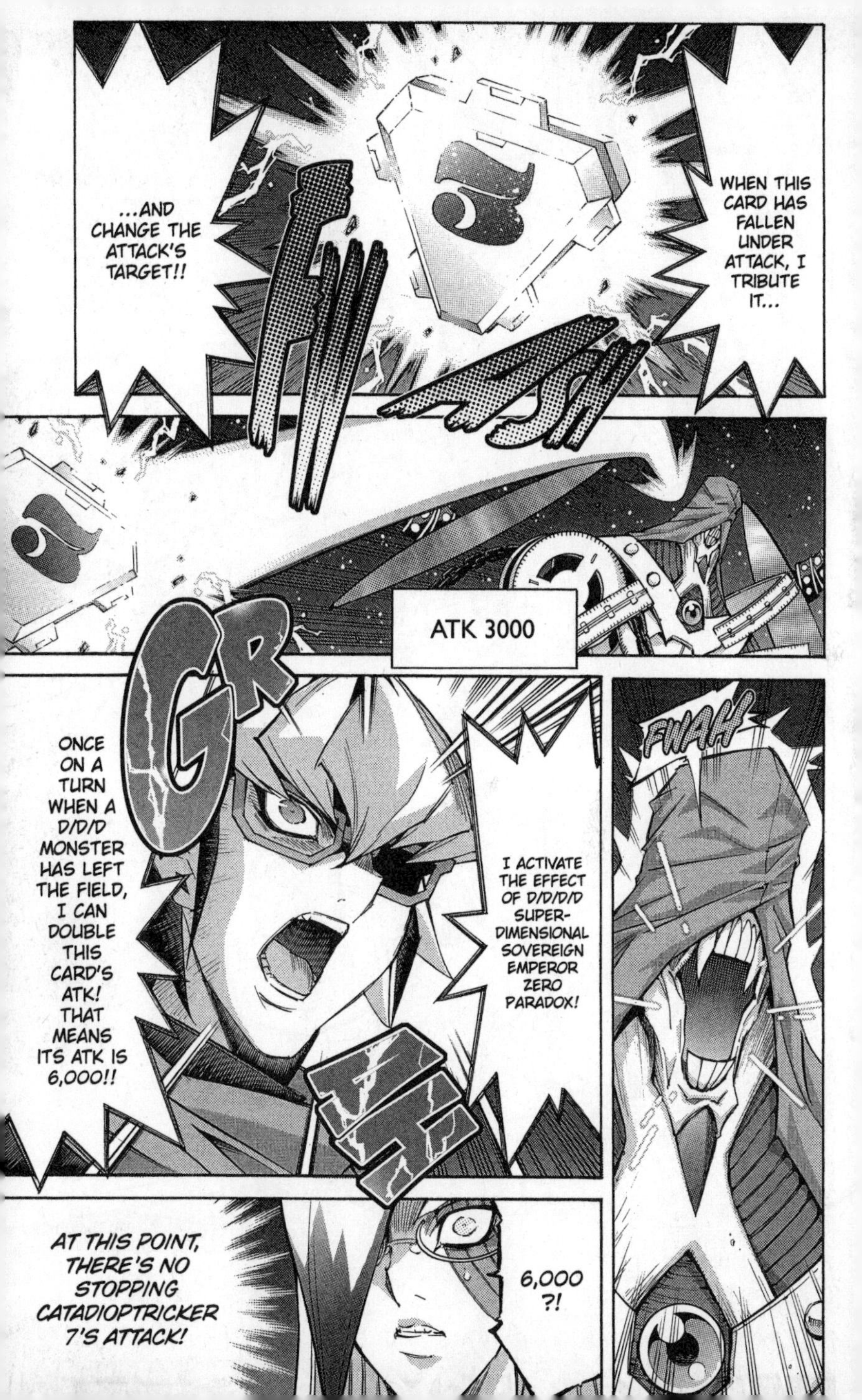
WHEN THIS CARD HAS FALLEN UNDER ATTACK, I TRIBUTE IT...
...AND CHANGE THE ATTACK'S TARGET!!
FWASH
ATK 3000
FWAH
I ACTIVATE THE EFFECT OF D/D/D/D SUPER-DIMENSIONAL SOVEREIGN EMPEROR ZERO PARADOX!
ONCE ON A TURN WHEN A D/D/D MONSTER HAS LEFT THE FIELD, I CAN DOUBLE THIS CARD'S ATK! THAT MEANS ITS ATK IS 6,000!!
GR
6,000 ?!
AT THIS POINT, THERE'S NO STOPPING CATADIOPTRICKER 7'S ATTACK!

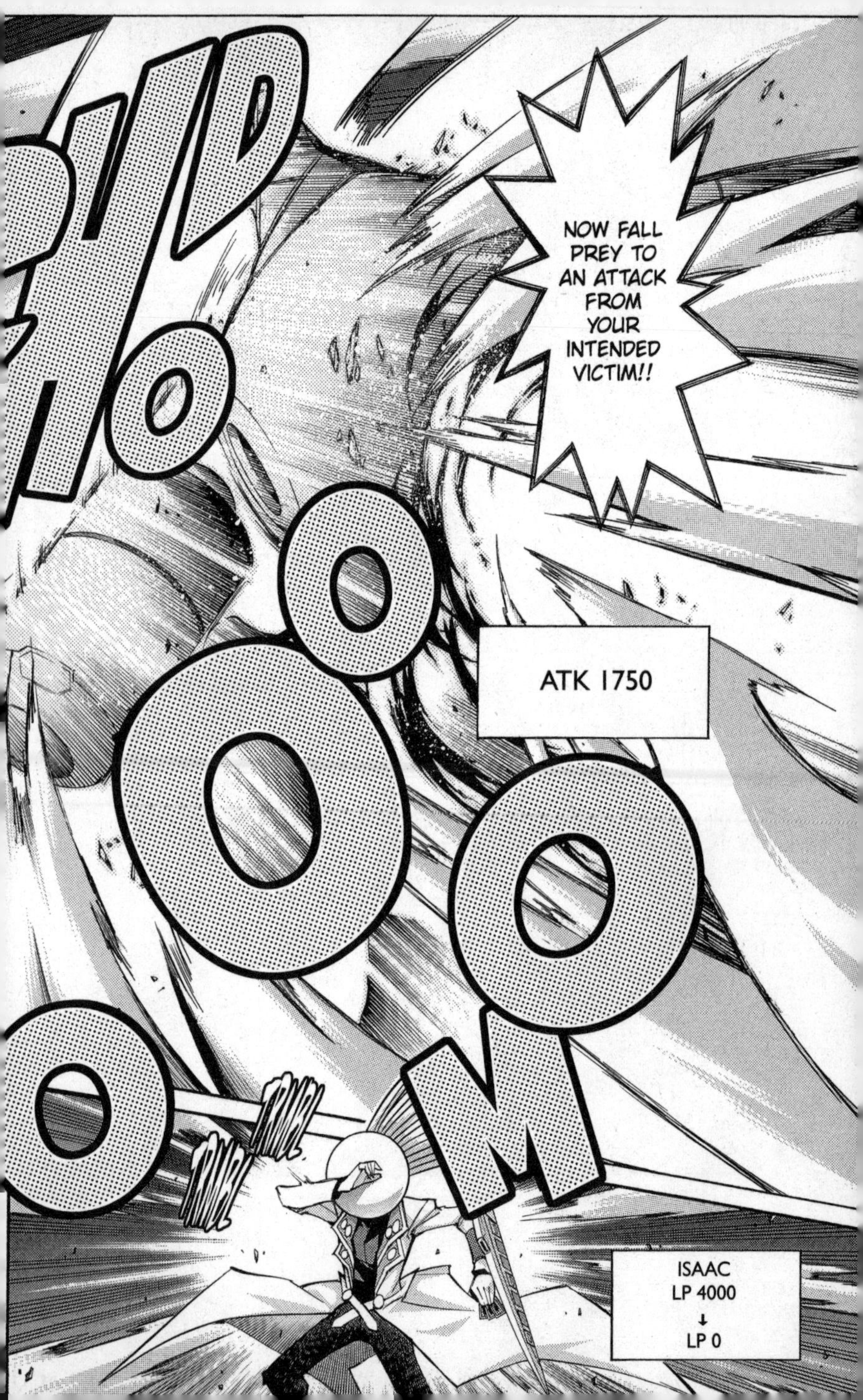
NOW FALL PREY TO AN ATTACK FROM YOUR INTENDED VICTIM!!
ATK 1750
ISAAC LP 4000 ↓ LP 0

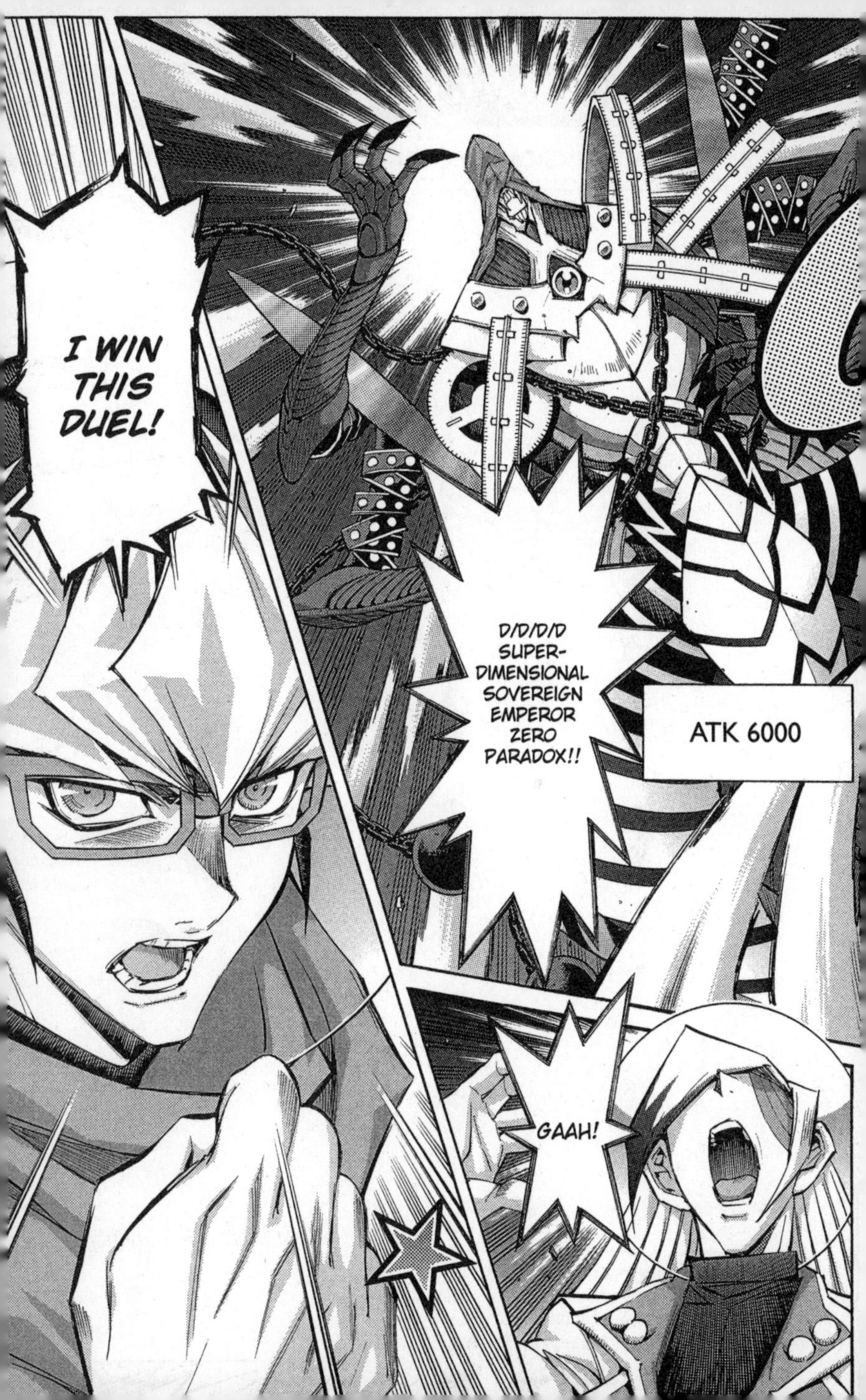
D/D/D/D SUPER-DIMENSIONAL SOVEREIGN EMPEROR ZERO PARADOX!!
ATK 6000
GAAH!
I WIN THIS DUEL!

PRESENTING MIYOSHI SENSEI'S EARLY DESIGNS!

ARC-V CHARACTER SKETCHES

D/D/D/D SUPERDIMENSIONAL SOVEREIGN EMPEROR ZERO PARADOX

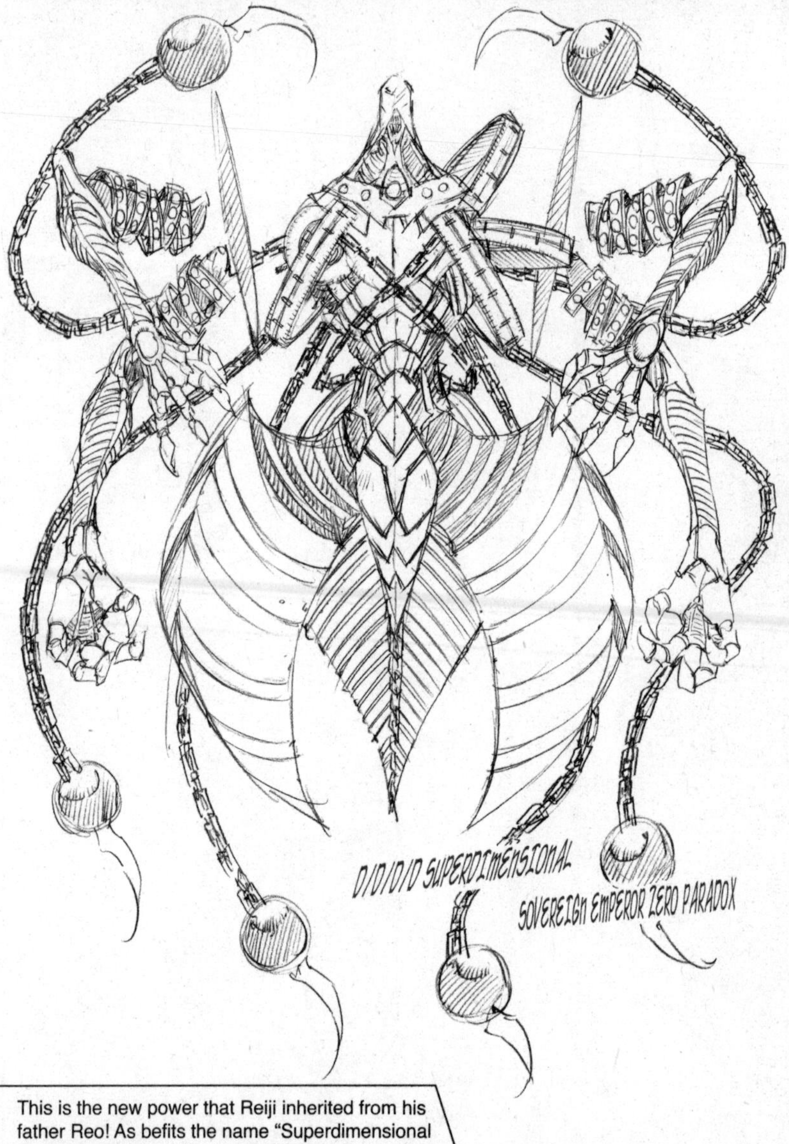
D/D/D/D SUPERDIMENSIONAL
SOVEREIGN EMPEROR ZERO PARADOX

This is the new power that Reiji inherited from his father Reo! As befits the name "Superdimensional Sovereign Emperor," it descends to the field with a Pendulum Summons that transcends the scale!

Scale 28: The Enemy's Hideout!!

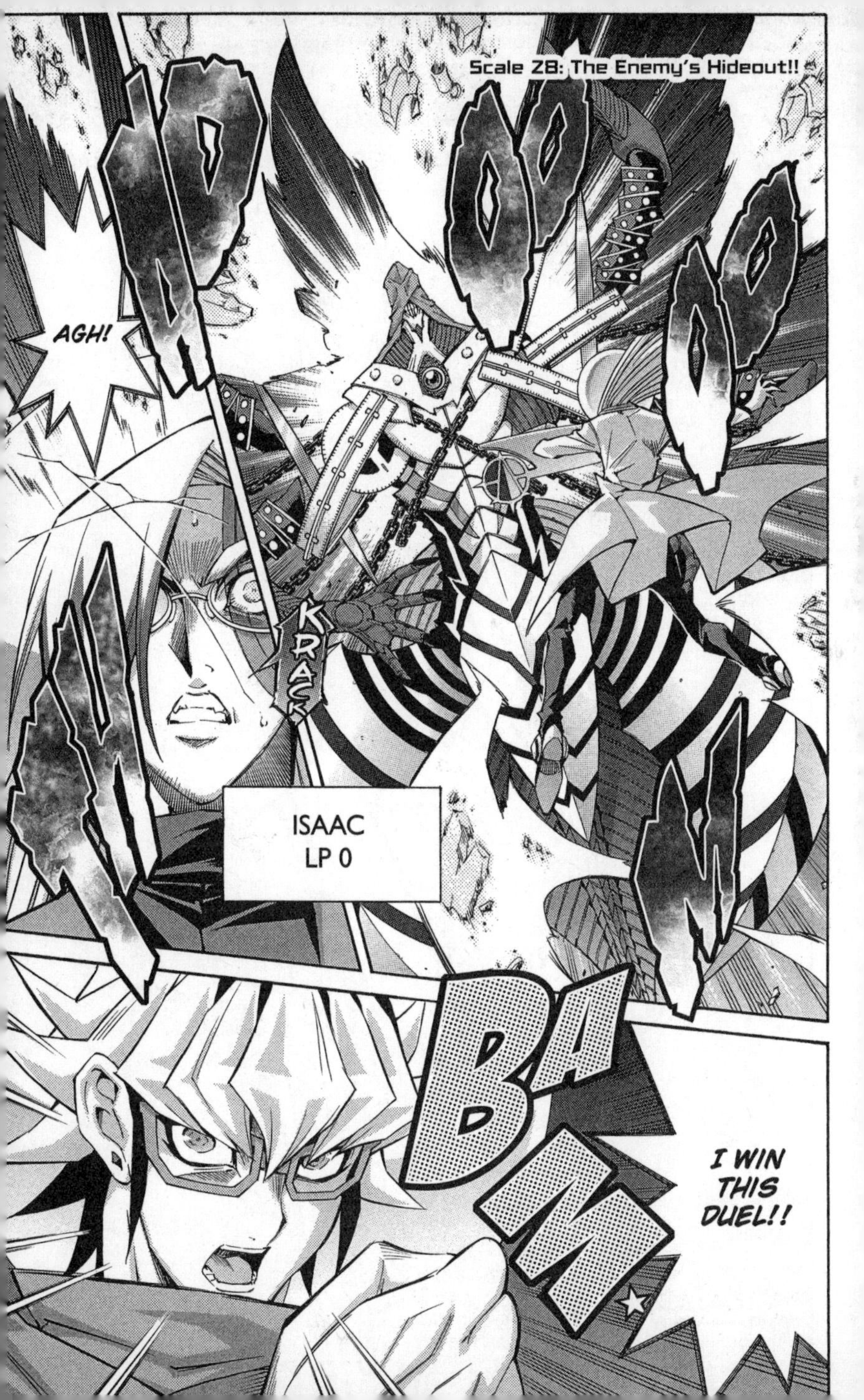
AGH!
KRACK
ISAAC
LP 0
I WIN THIS DUEL!!
BAM

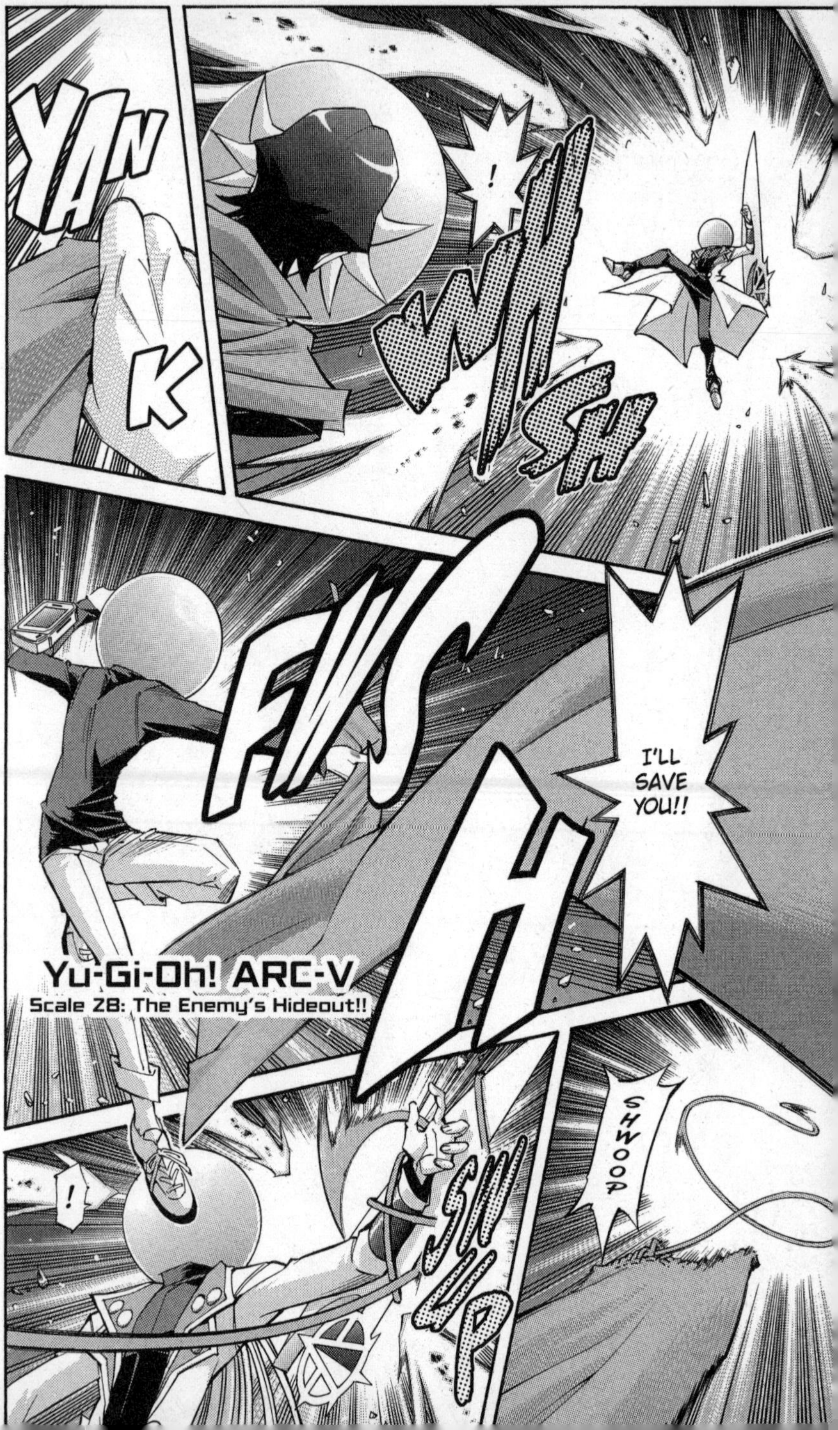
YANK
!
I'LL SAVE YOU!!
Yu-Gi-Oh! ARC-V
Scale 28: The Enemy's Hideout!!
SHWOOP
!

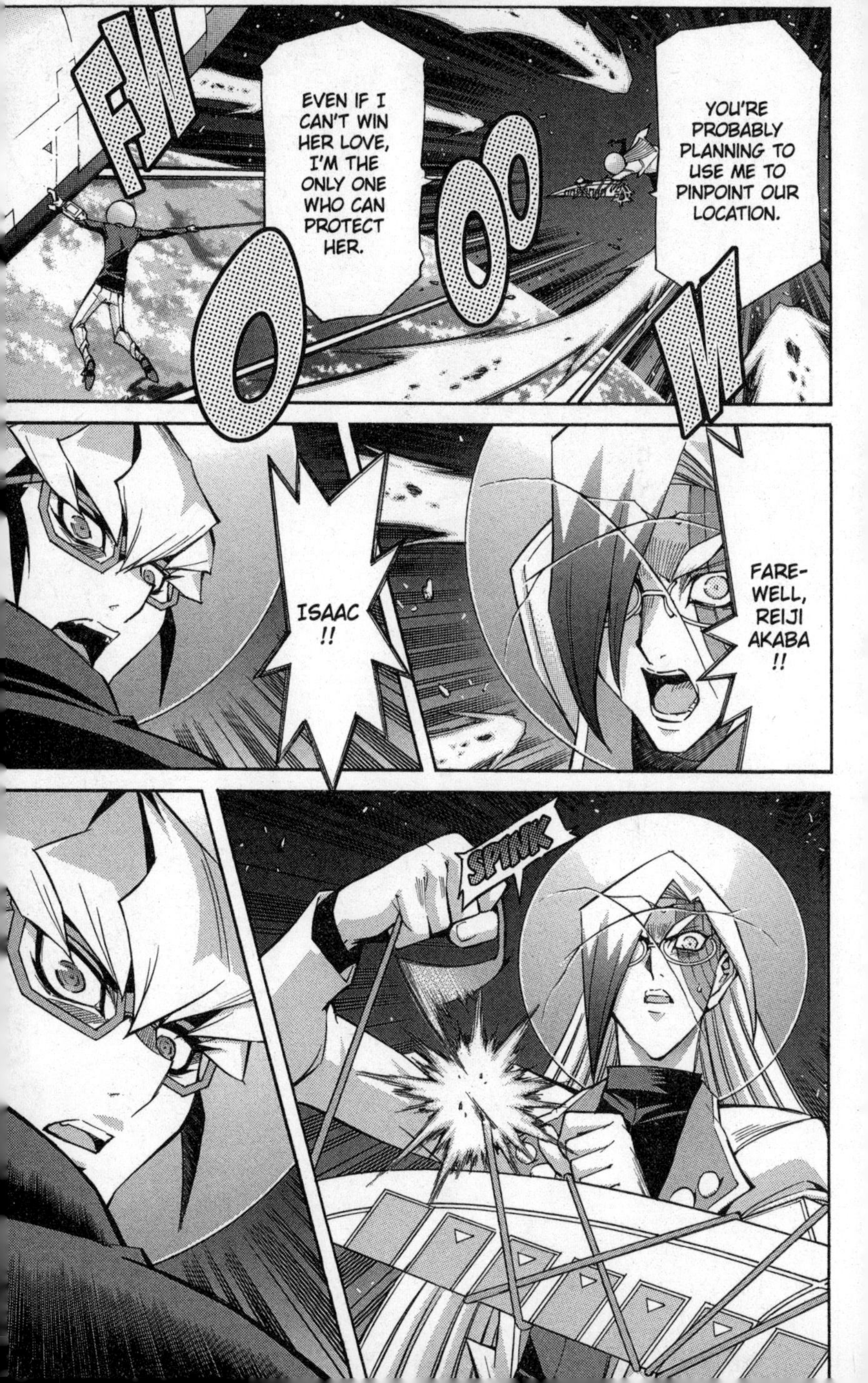

YOU'RE PROBABLY PLANNING TO USE ME TO PINPOINT OUR LOCATION.
EVEN IF I CAN'T WIN HER LOVE, I'M THE ONLY ONE WHO CAN PROTECT HER.
FWOOOM
FARE-WELL, REIJI AKABA!!
ISAAC!!
SPINK

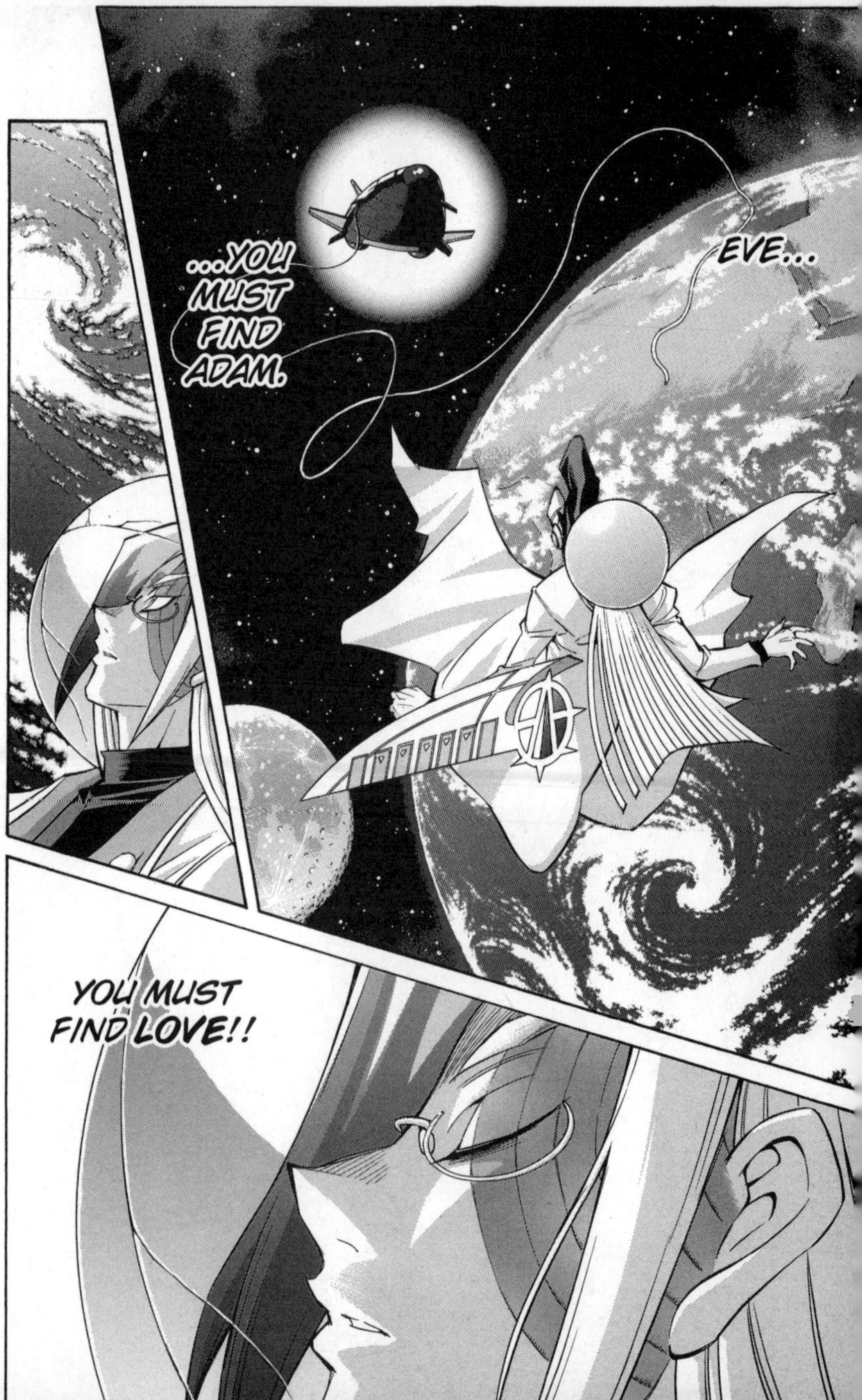
EVE...
...YOU MUST FIND ADAM.
YOU MUST FIND LOVE!!

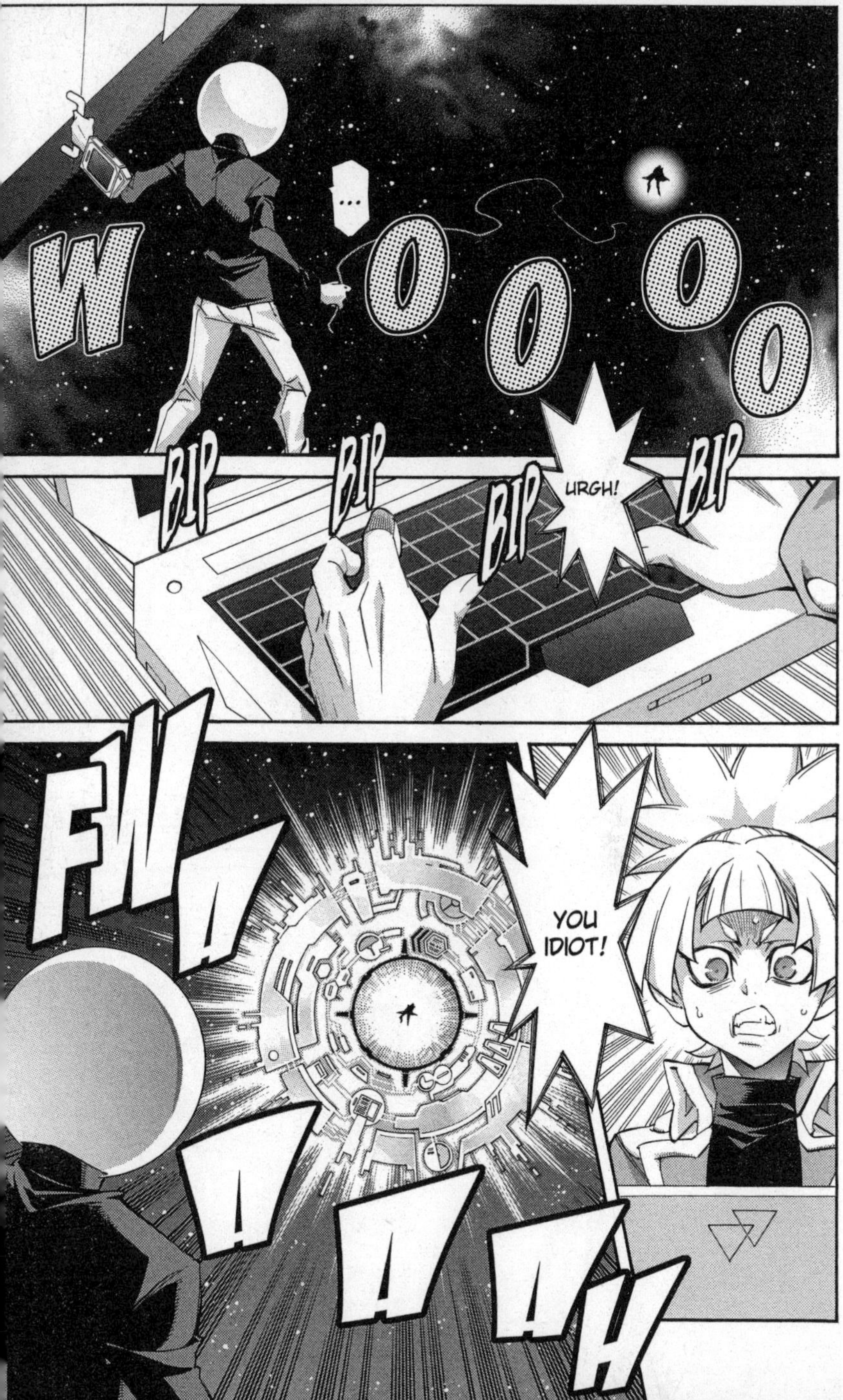
...
WOOOOOO
BIP
URGH!
BIP
BIP
BIP
YOU IDIOT!
FWAAAAH

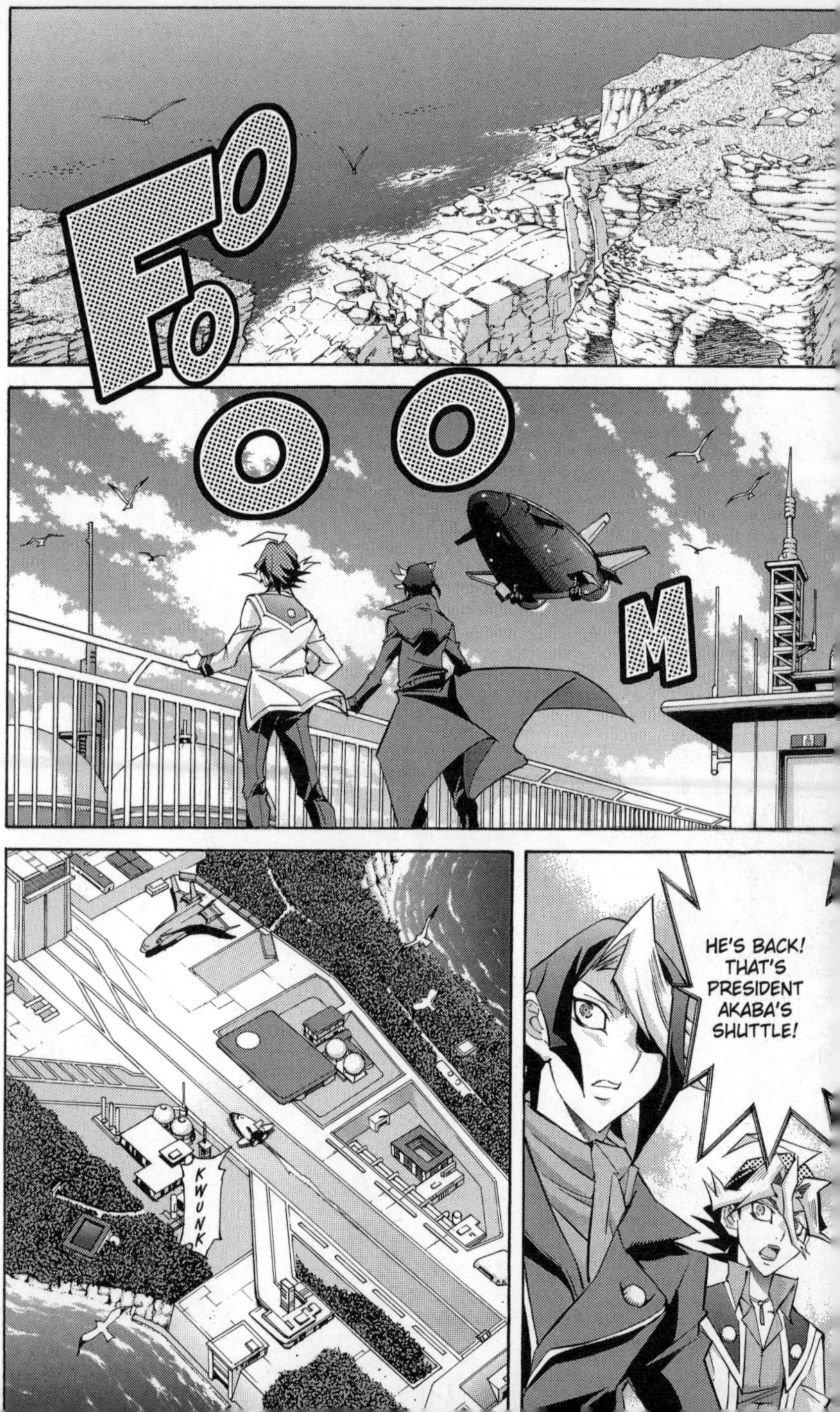
FOOOOOM
HE'S BACK! THAT'S PRESIDENT AKABA'S SHUTTLE!
KWUNK

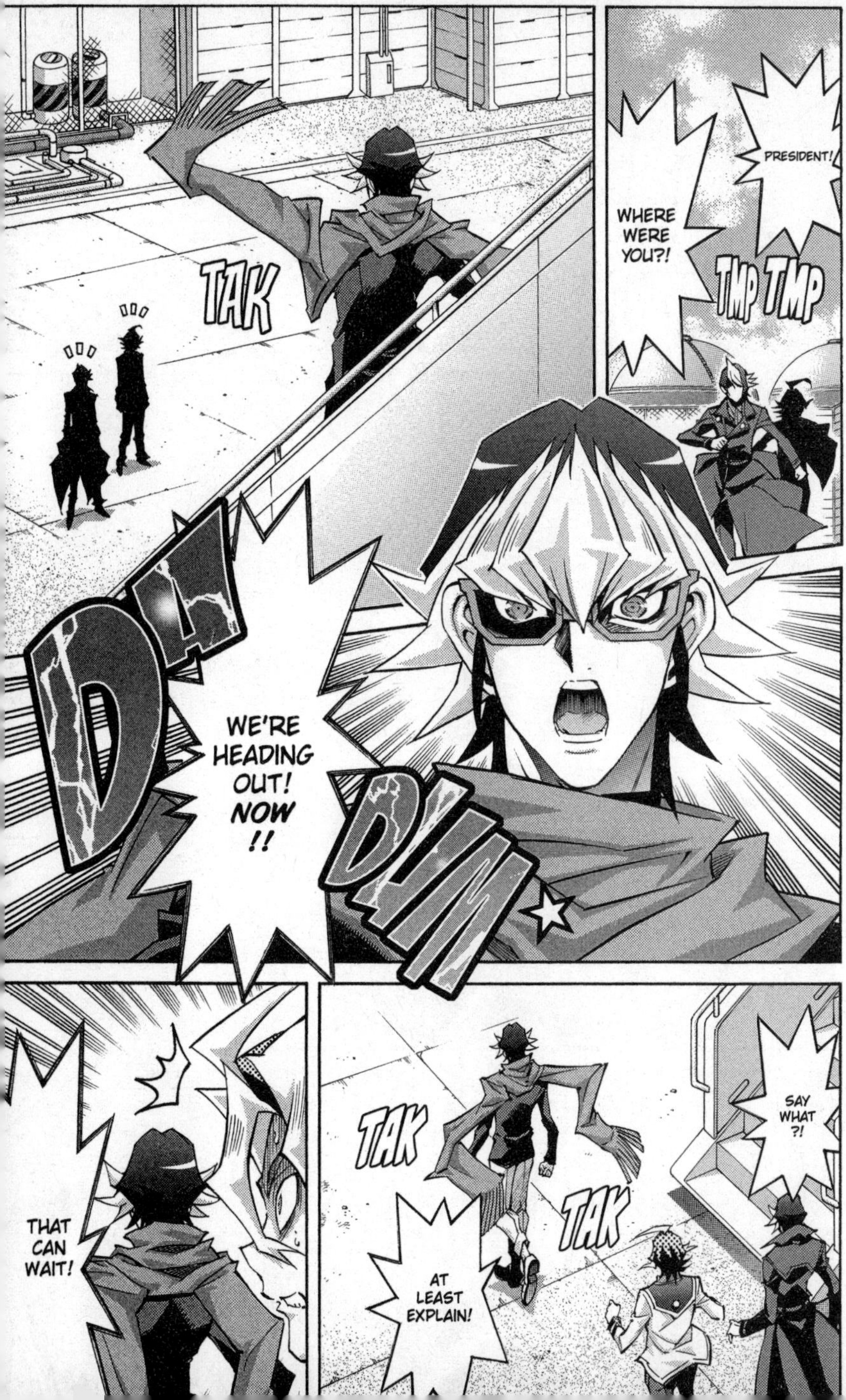
PRESIDENT!
WHERE WERE YOU?!
TMP TMP
TAK
WE'RE HEADING OUT! NOW!!
DA
DUM
SAY WHAT?!
TAK
TAK
AT LEAST EXPLAIN!
THAT CAN WAIT!

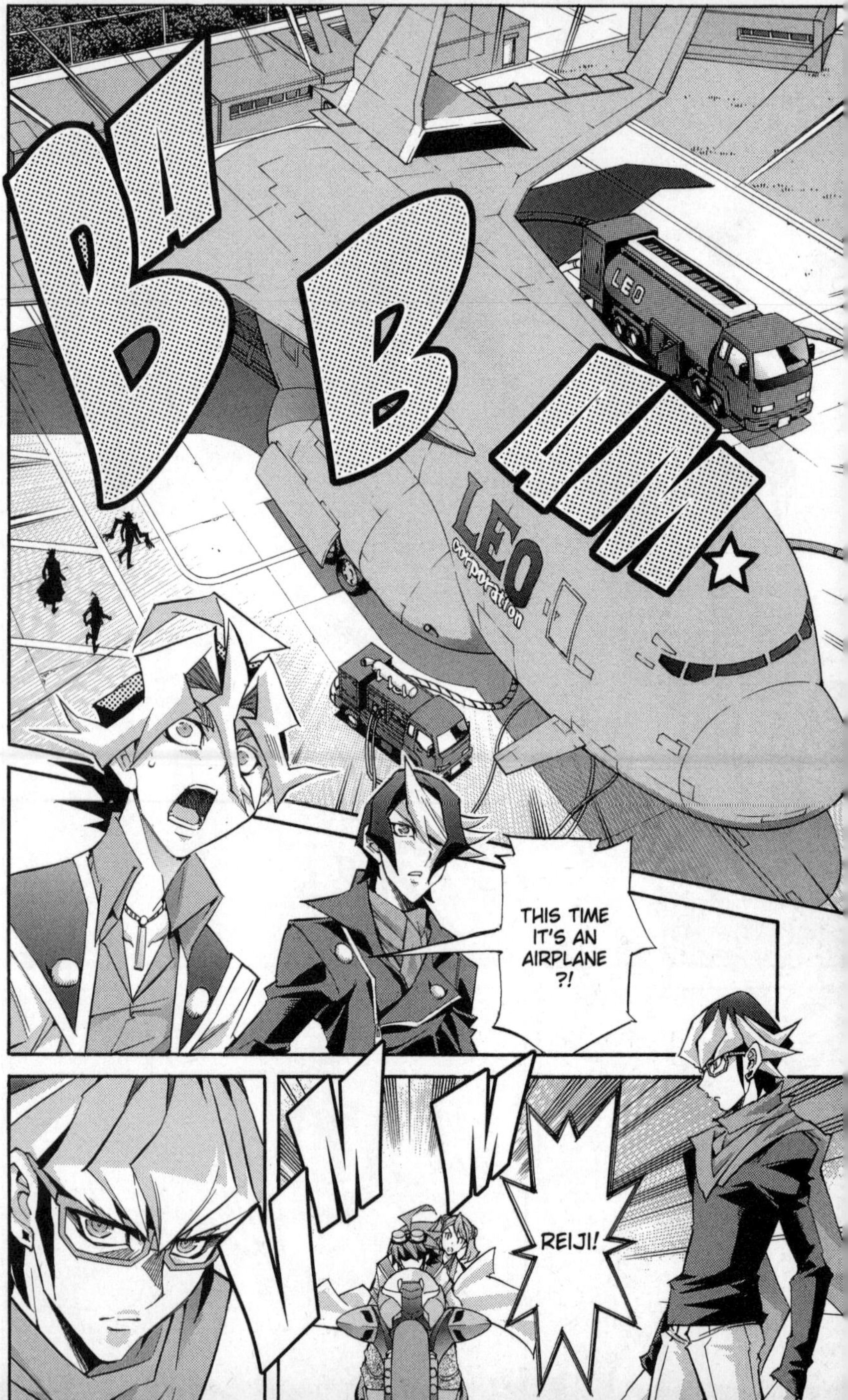
LEO
LEO corporation
THIS TIME IT'S AN AIRPLANE ?!
REIJI!

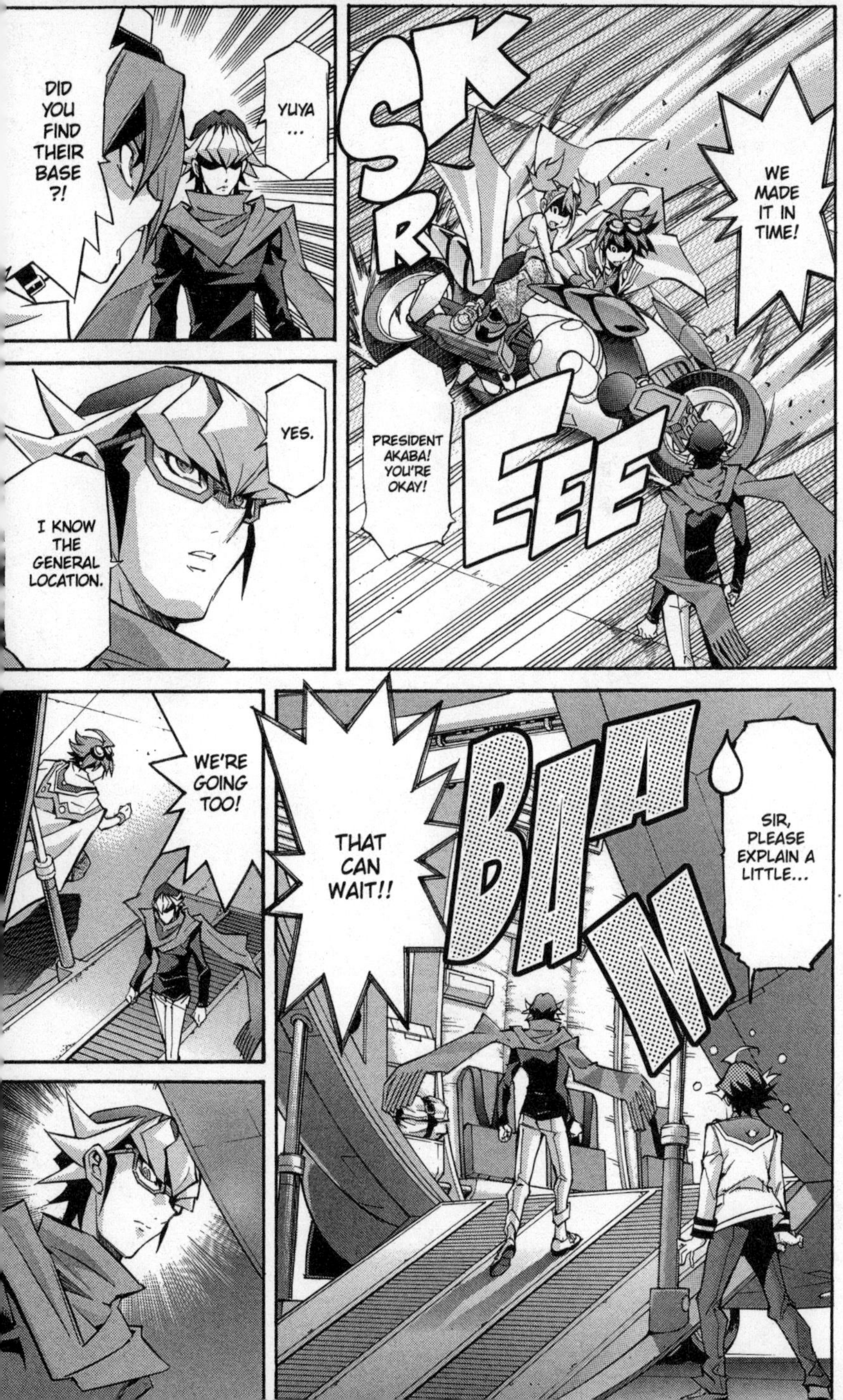
SKREEE
WE MADE IT IN TIME!
PRESIDENT AKABA! YOU'RE OKAY!
YUYA...
DID YOU FIND THEIR BASE?!
YES.
I KNOW THE GENERAL LOCATION.
BAAM
SIR, PLEASE EXPLAIN A LITTLE...
THAT CAN WAIT!!
WE'RE GOING TOO!

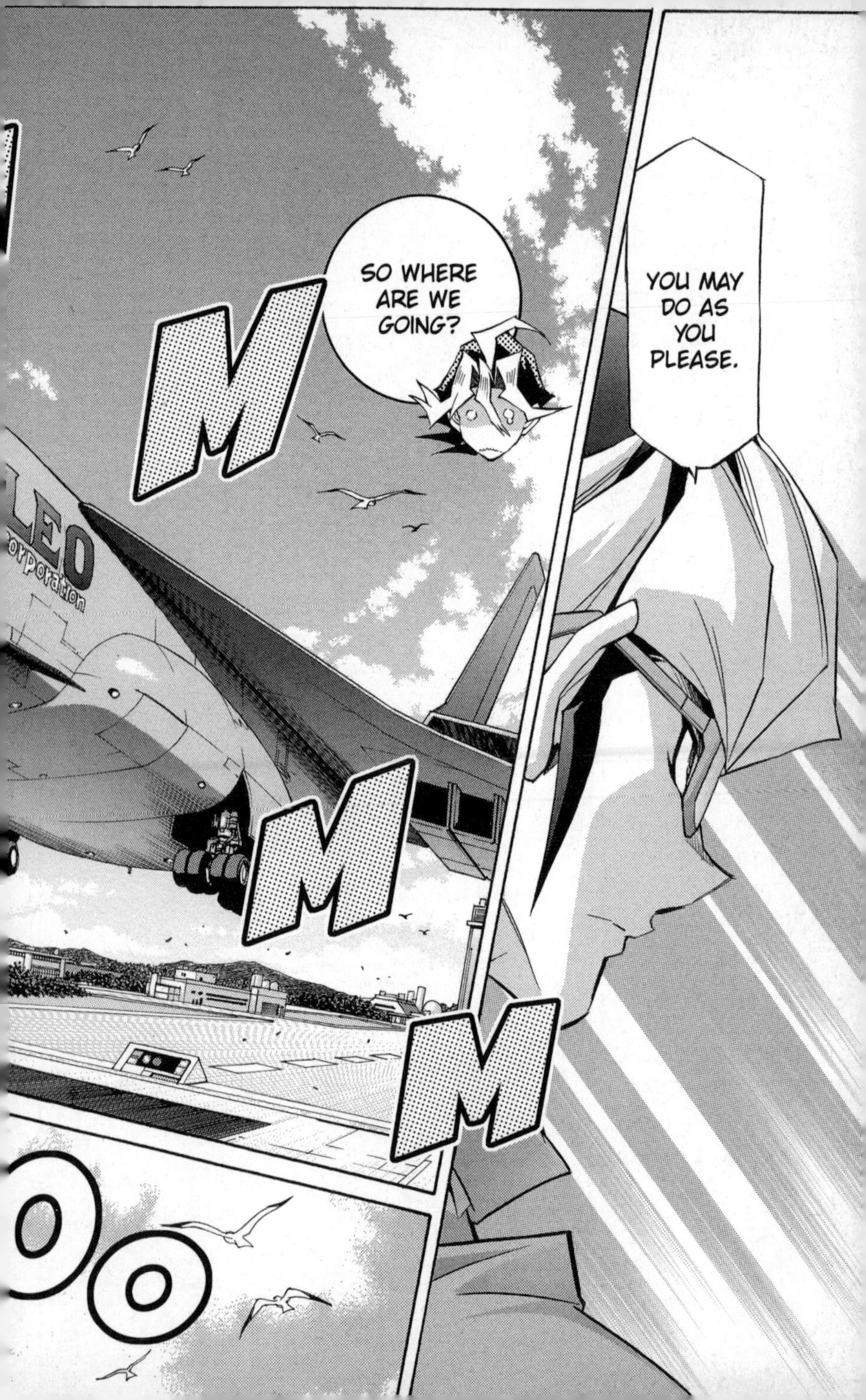
YOU MAY DO AS YOU PLEASE.
SO WHERE ARE WE GOING?
MMM
LEO Corporation
OO

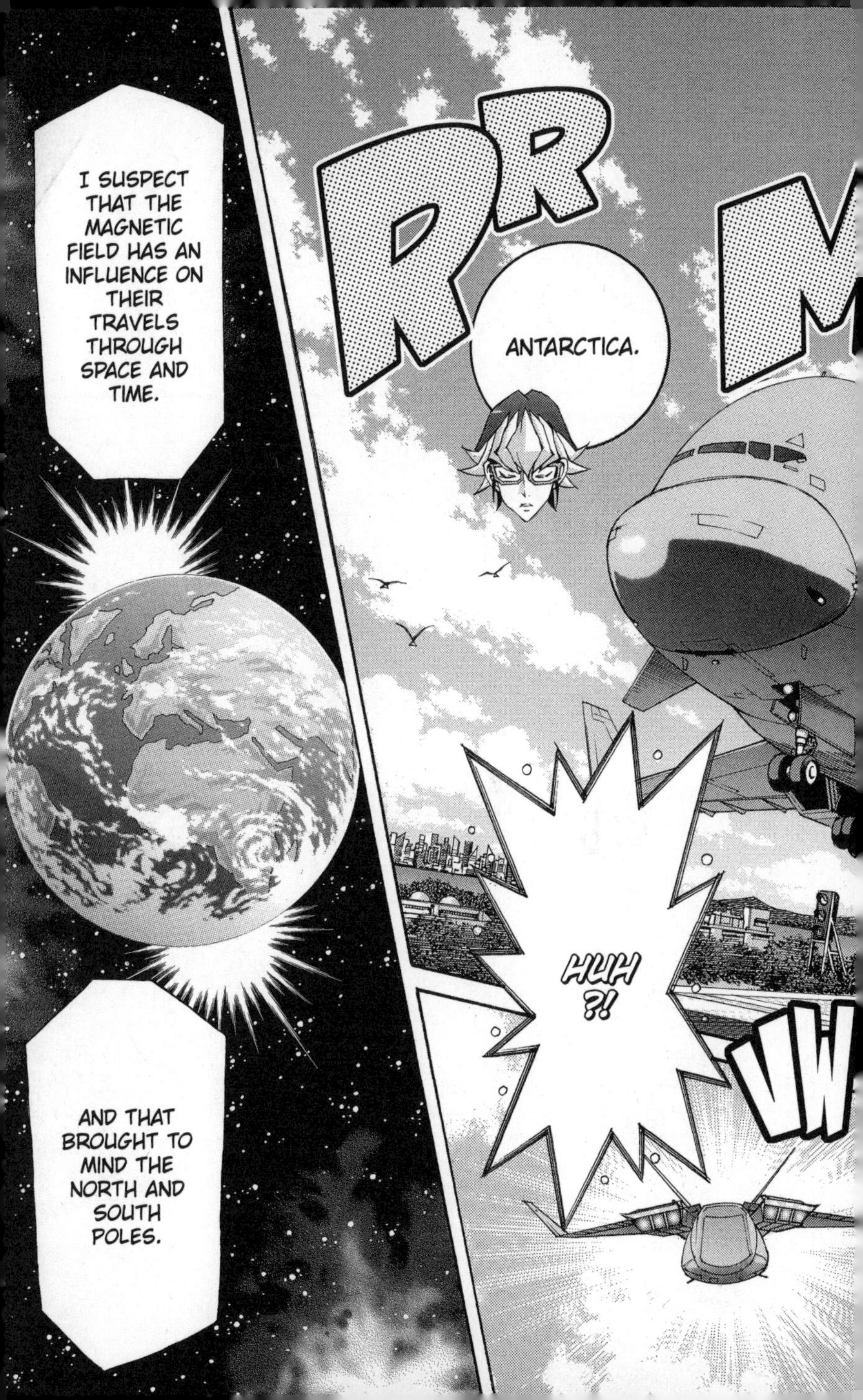
I SUSPECT THAT THE MAGNETIC FIELD HAS AN INFLUENCE ON THEIR TRAVELS THROUGH SPACE AND TIME.
AND THAT BROUGHT TO MIND THE NORTH AND SOUTH POLES.
ANTARCTICA.
HUH ?!

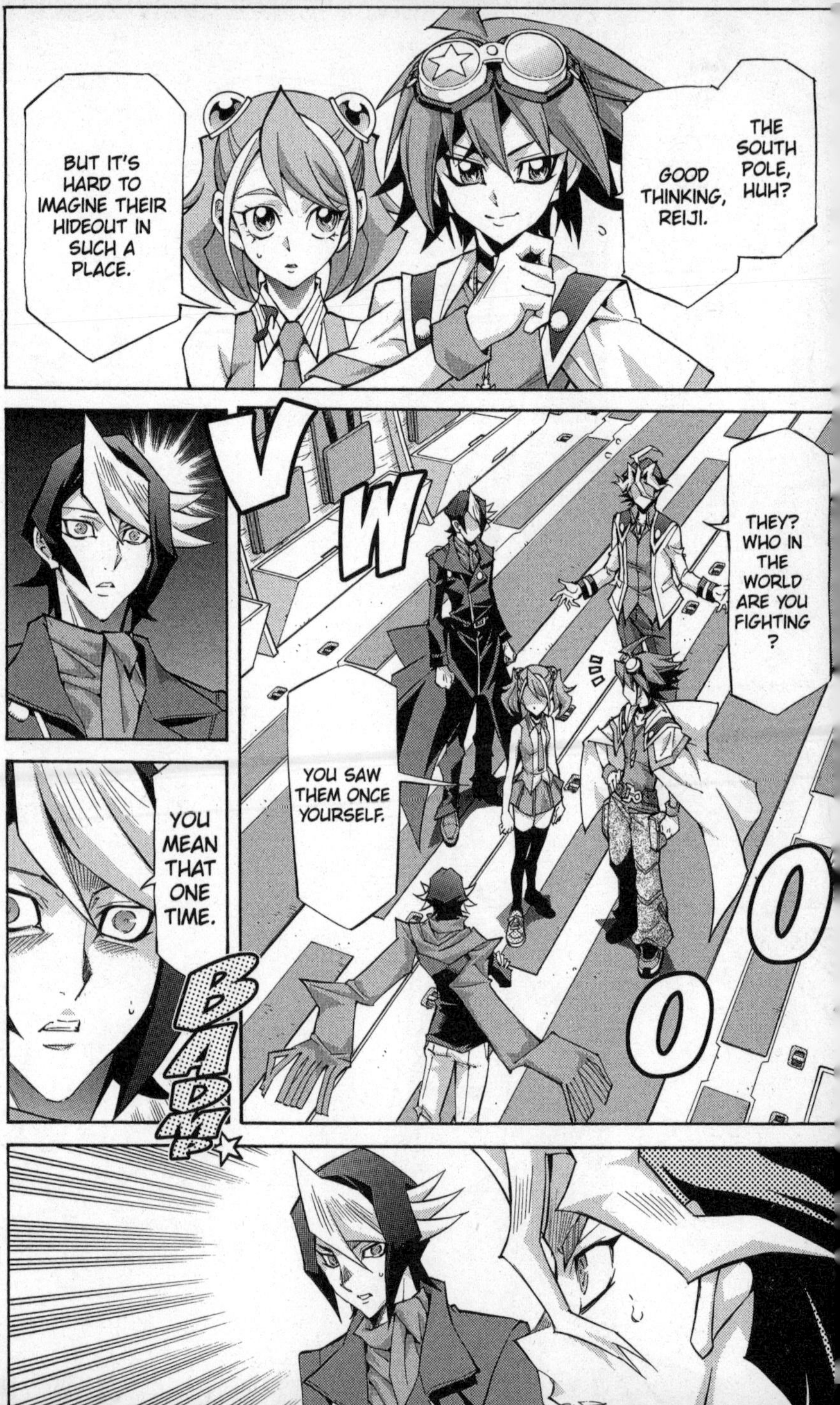
THE SOUTH POLE, HUH?
GOOD THINKING, REIJI.
BUT IT'S HARD TO IMAGINE THEIR HIDEOUT IN SUCH A PLACE.
THEY? WHO IN THE WORLD ARE YOU FIGHTING?
OOOO
YOU SAW THEM ONCE YOURSELF.
VW
YOU MEAN THAT ONE TIME.
BADMP

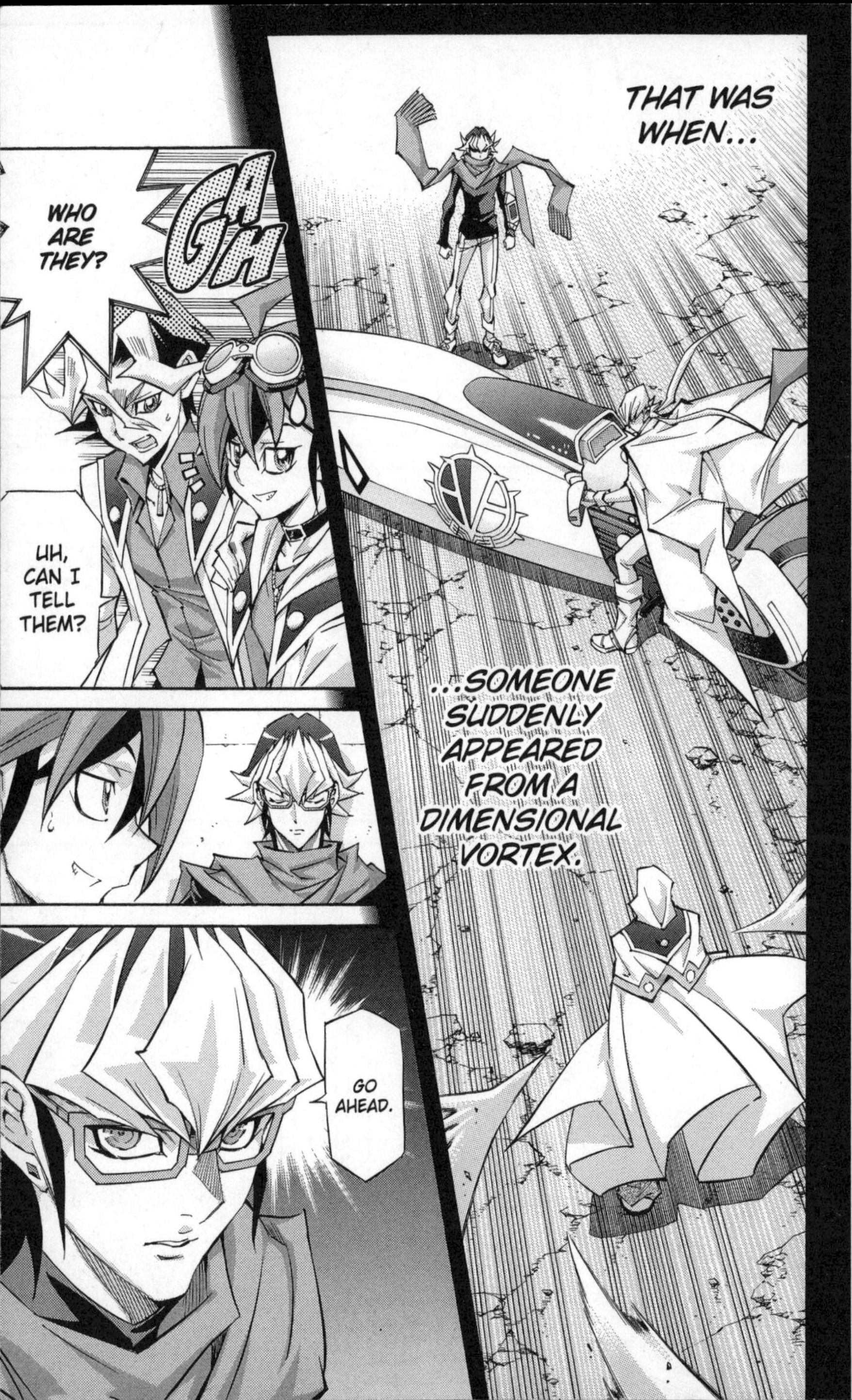
THAT WAS WHEN...
...SOMEONE SUDDENLY APPEARED FROM A DIMENSIONAL VORTEX.
GAGH
WHO ARE THEY?
UH, CAN I TELL THEM?
GO AHEAD.

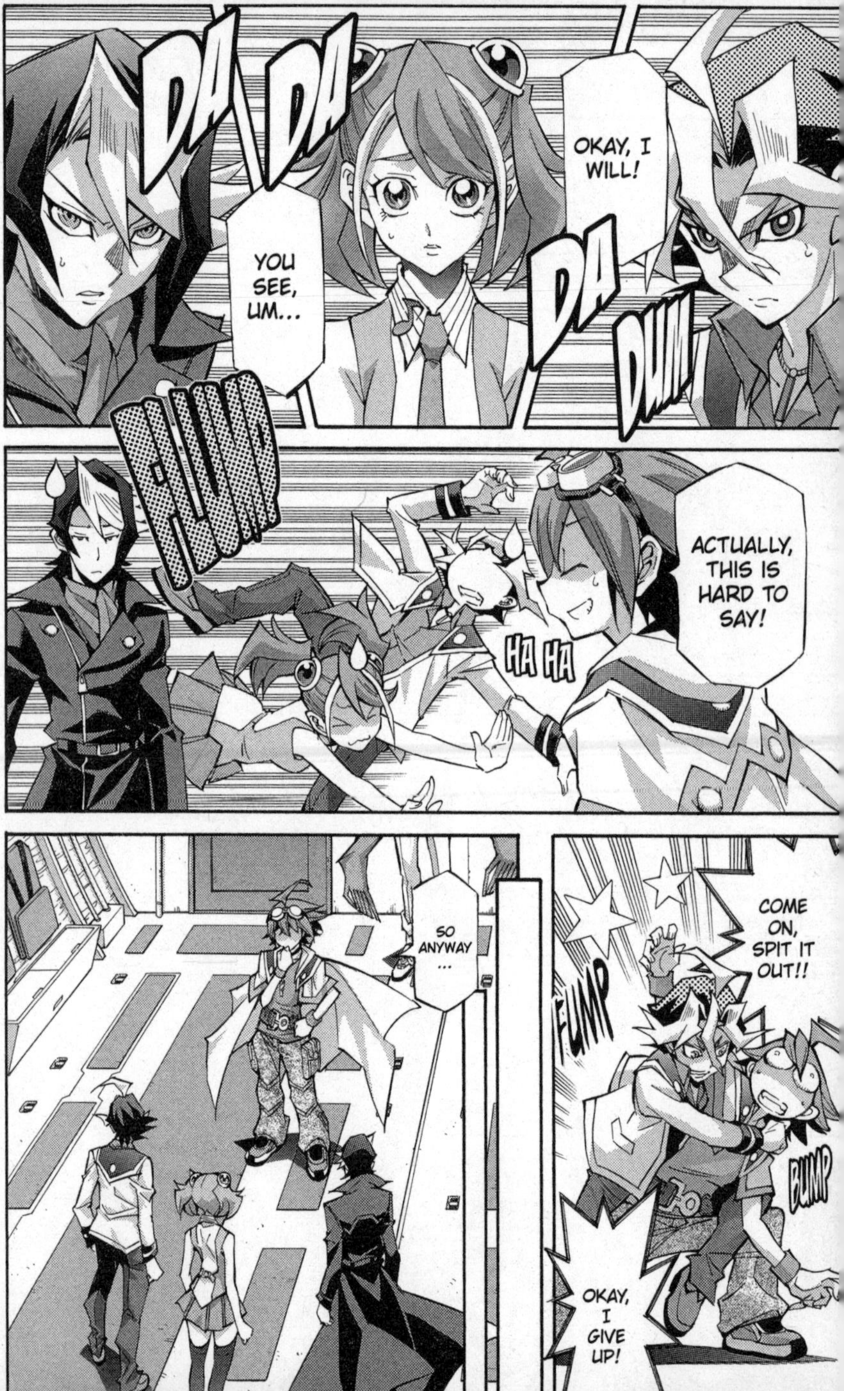
OKAY, I WILL!
DA DA
YOU SEE, UM...
DA DUM
ACTUALLY, THIS IS HARD TO SAY!
FUMP
HA HA
COME ON, SPIT IT OUT!!
FUMP
BUMP
OKAY, I GIVE UP!
SO ANYWAY ...

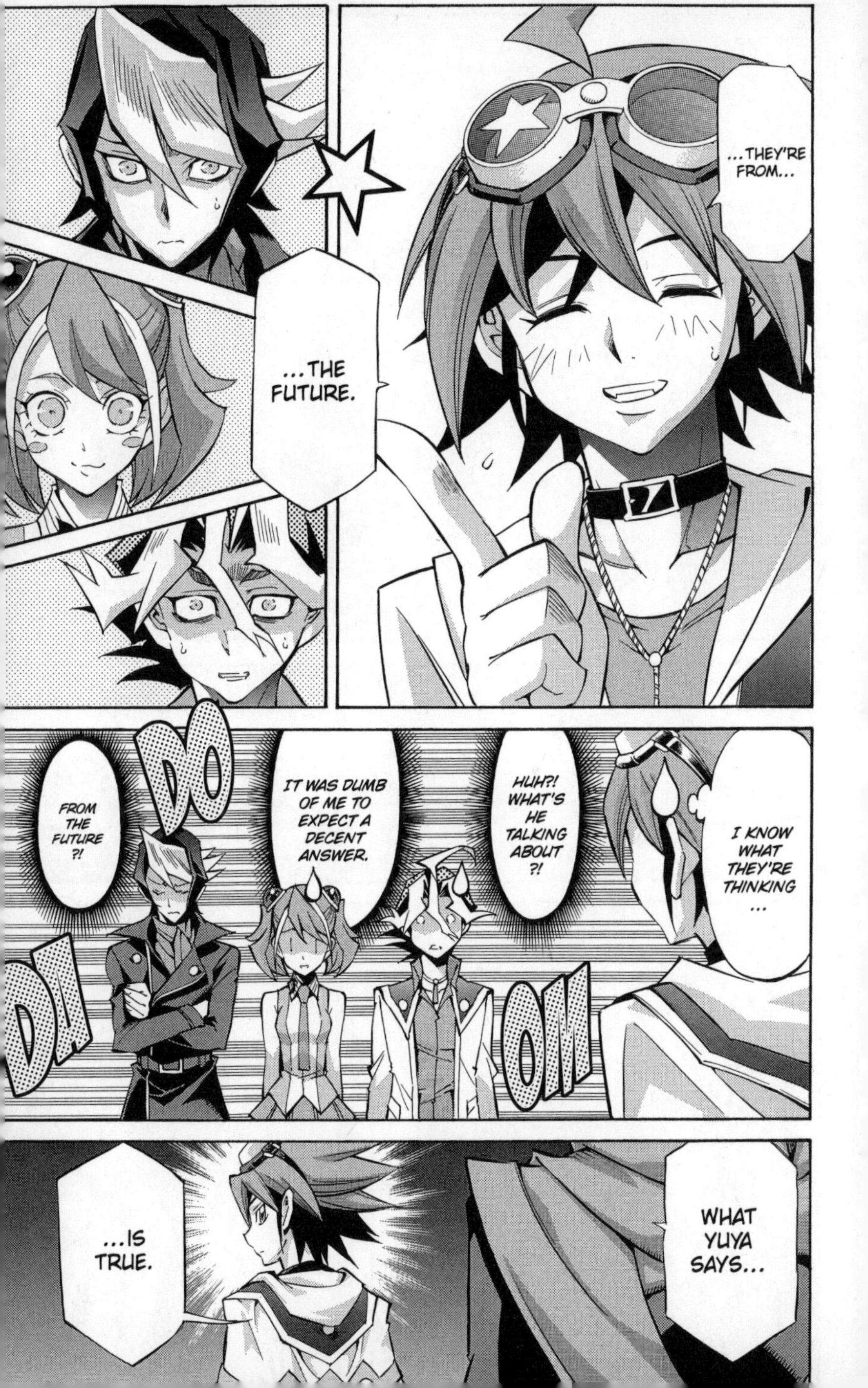
...THEY'RE FROM...
...THE FUTURE.
I KNOW WHAT THEY'RE THINKING...
HUH?! WHAT'S HE TALKING ABOUT?!
OM
IT WAS DUMB OF ME TO EXPECT A DECENT ANSWER.
DO
FROM THE FUTURE?!
DA
WHAT YUYA SAYS...
...IS TRUE.

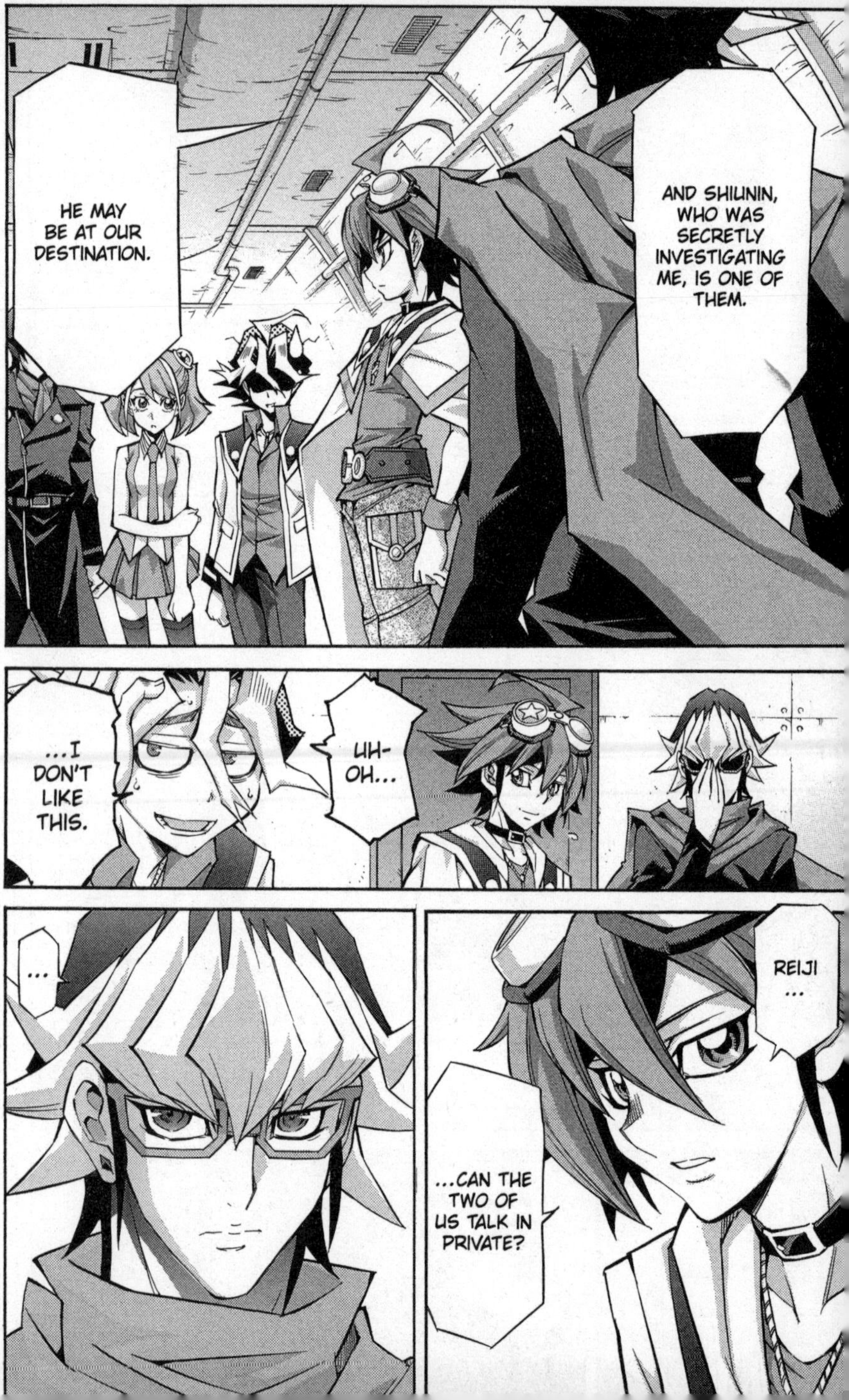
AND SHIUNIN, WHO WAS SECRETLY INVESTIGATING ME, IS ONE OF THEM.
HE MAY BE AT OUR DESTINATION.
UH-OH...
...I DON'T LIKE THIS.
REIJI ...
...CAN THE TWO OF US TALK IN PRIVATE?
...

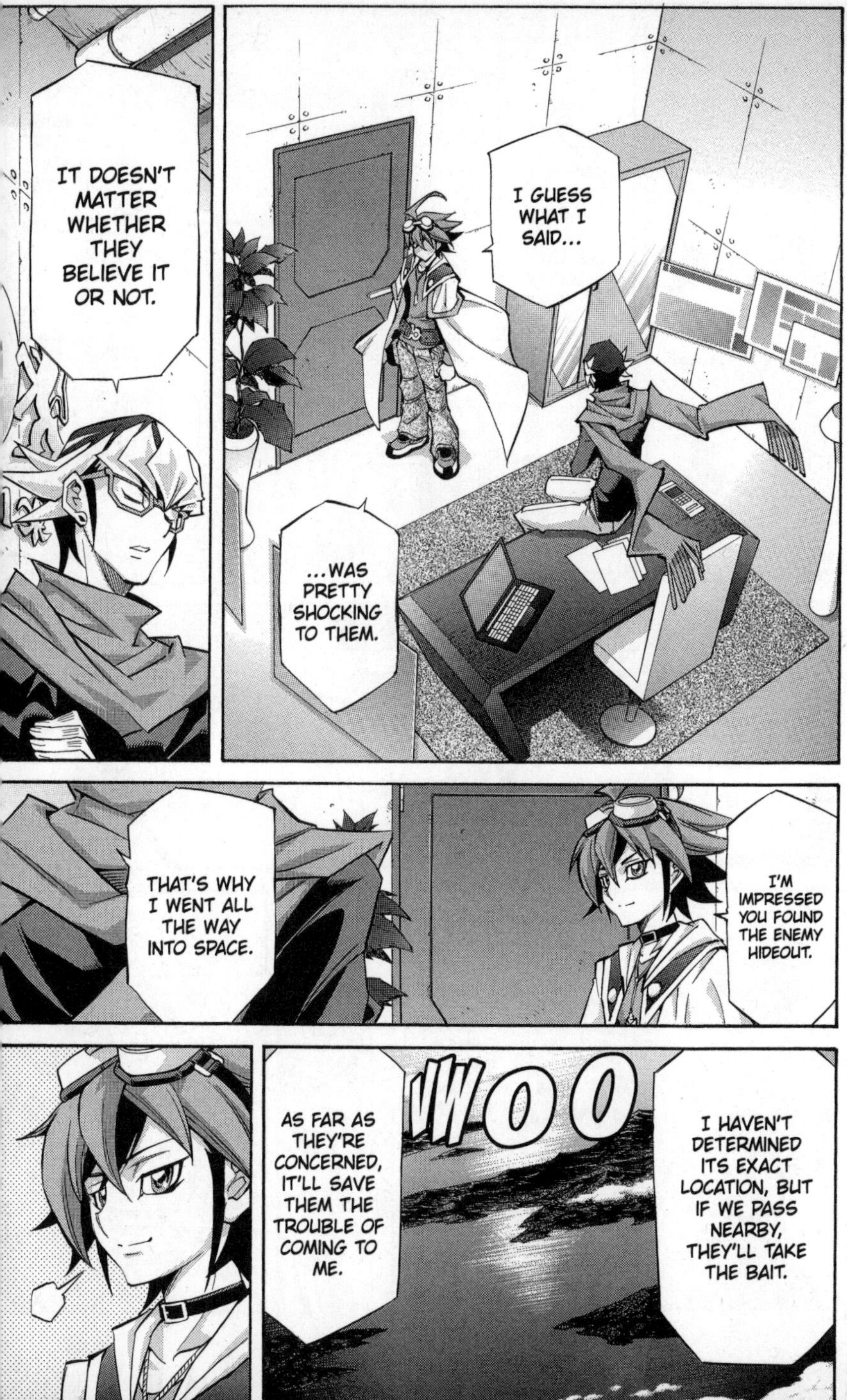
I GUESS WHAT I SAID...
...WAS PRETTY SHOCKING TO THEM.
IT DOESN'T MATTER WHETHER THEY BELIEVE IT OR NOT.
I'M IMPRESSED YOU FOUND THE ENEMY HIDEOUT.
THAT'S WHY I WENT ALL THE WAY INTO SPACE.
I HAVEN'T DETERMINED ITS EXACT LOCATION, BUT IF WE PASS NEARBY, THEY'LL TAKE THE BAIT.
VWOO
AS FAR AS THEY'RE CONCERNED, IT'LL SAVE THEM THE TROUBLE OF COMING TO ME.

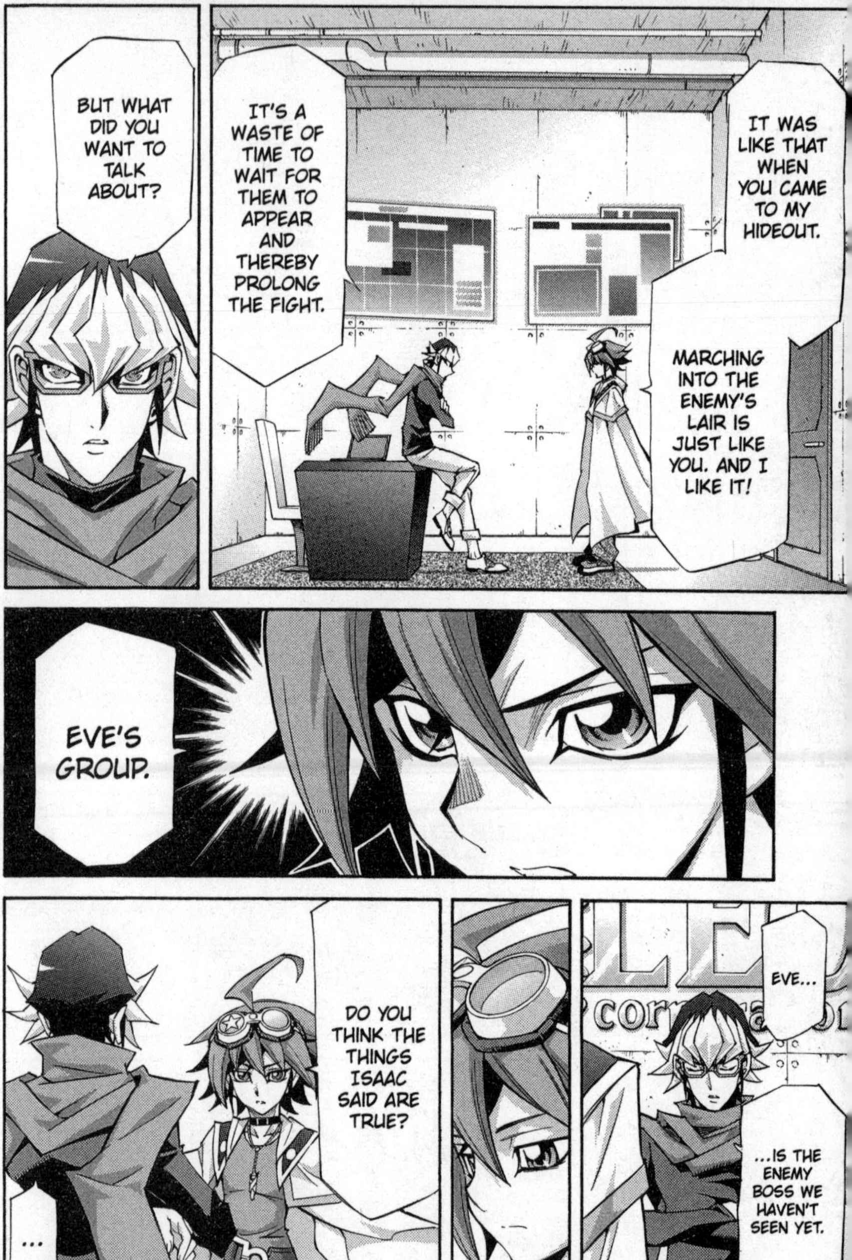
IT'S A WASTE OF TIME TO WAIT FOR THEM TO APPEAR AND THEREBY PROLONG THE FIGHT.
IT WAS LIKE THAT WHEN YOU CAME TO MY HIDEOUT.
MARCHING INTO THE ENEMY'S LAIR IS JUST LIKE YOU. AND I LIKE IT!
BUT WHAT DID YOU WANT TO TALK ABOUT?
EVE'S GROUP.
EVE...
...IS THE ENEMY BOSS WE HAVEN'T SEEN YET.
DO YOU THINK THE THINGS ISAAC SAID ARE TRUE?
...

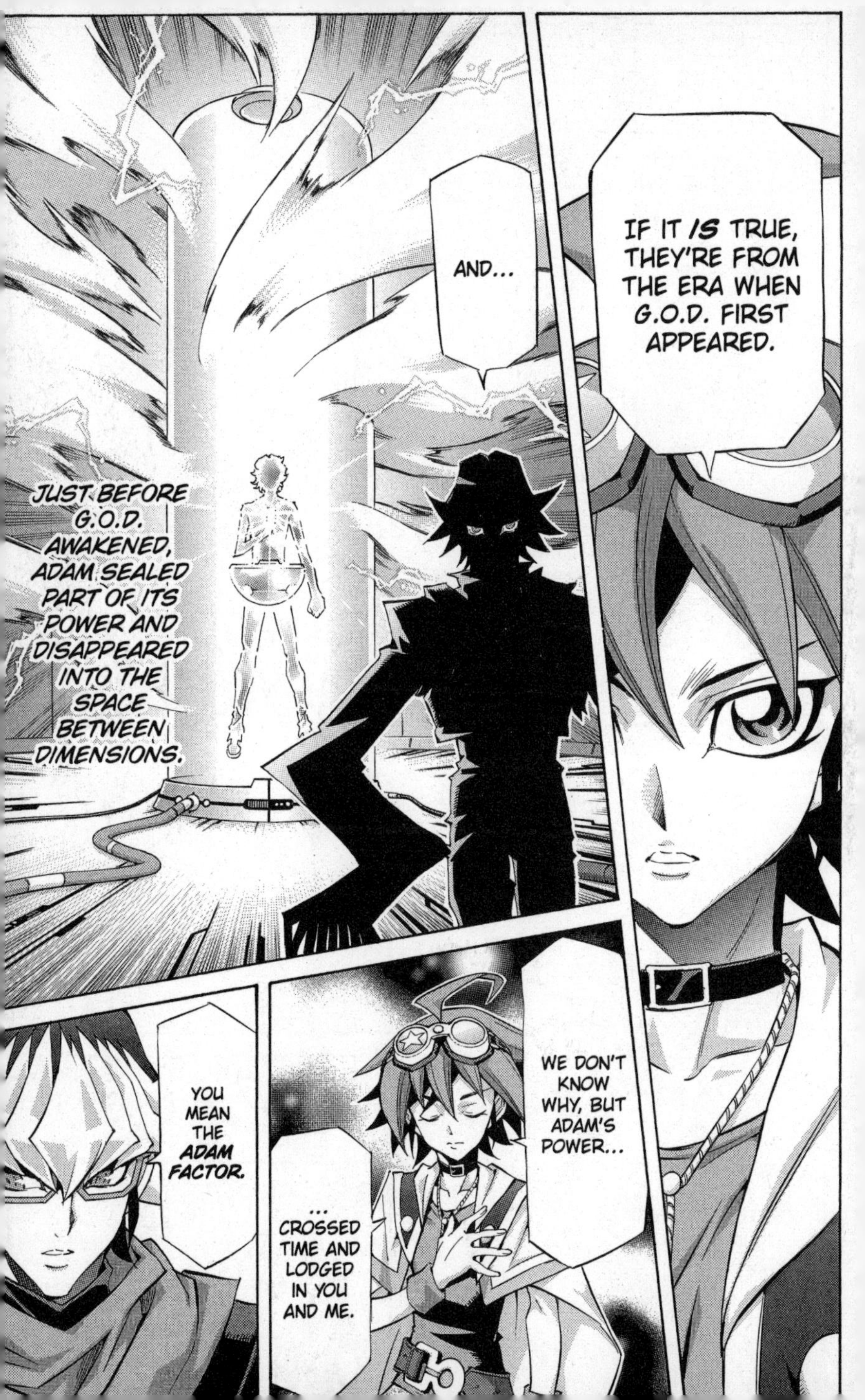
IF IT *IS* TRUE, THEY'RE FROM THE ERA WHEN G.O.D. FIRST APPEARED.
AND...
JUST BEFORE G.O.D. AWAKENED, ADAM SEALED PART OF ITS POWER AND DISAPPEARED INTO THE SPACE BETWEEN DIMENSIONS.
WE DON'T KNOW WHY, BUT ADAM'S POWER...
...CROSSED TIME AND LODGED IN YOU AND ME.
YOU MEAN THE *ADAM FACTOR.*

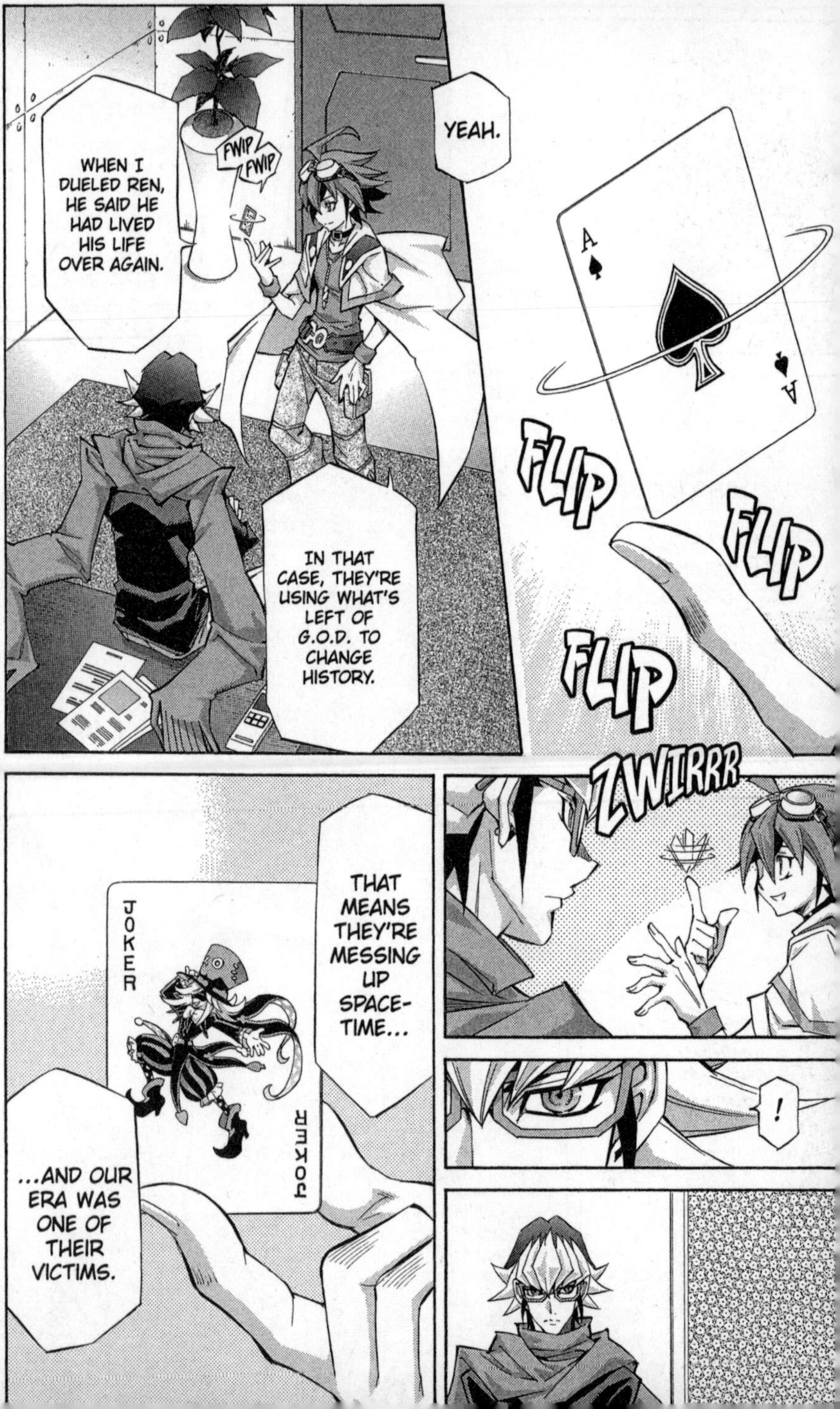
FLIP
FLIP
FLIP
A
A
YEAH.
FWIP FWIP
WHEN I DUELED REN, HE SAID HE HAD LIVED HIS LIFE OVER AGAIN.
IN THAT CASE, THEY'RE USING WHAT'S LEFT OF G.O.D. TO CHANGE HISTORY.
ZWIRRR
!
THAT MEANS THEY'RE MESSING UP SPACE-TIME...
JOKER
...AND OUR ERA WAS ONE OF THEIR VICTIMS.

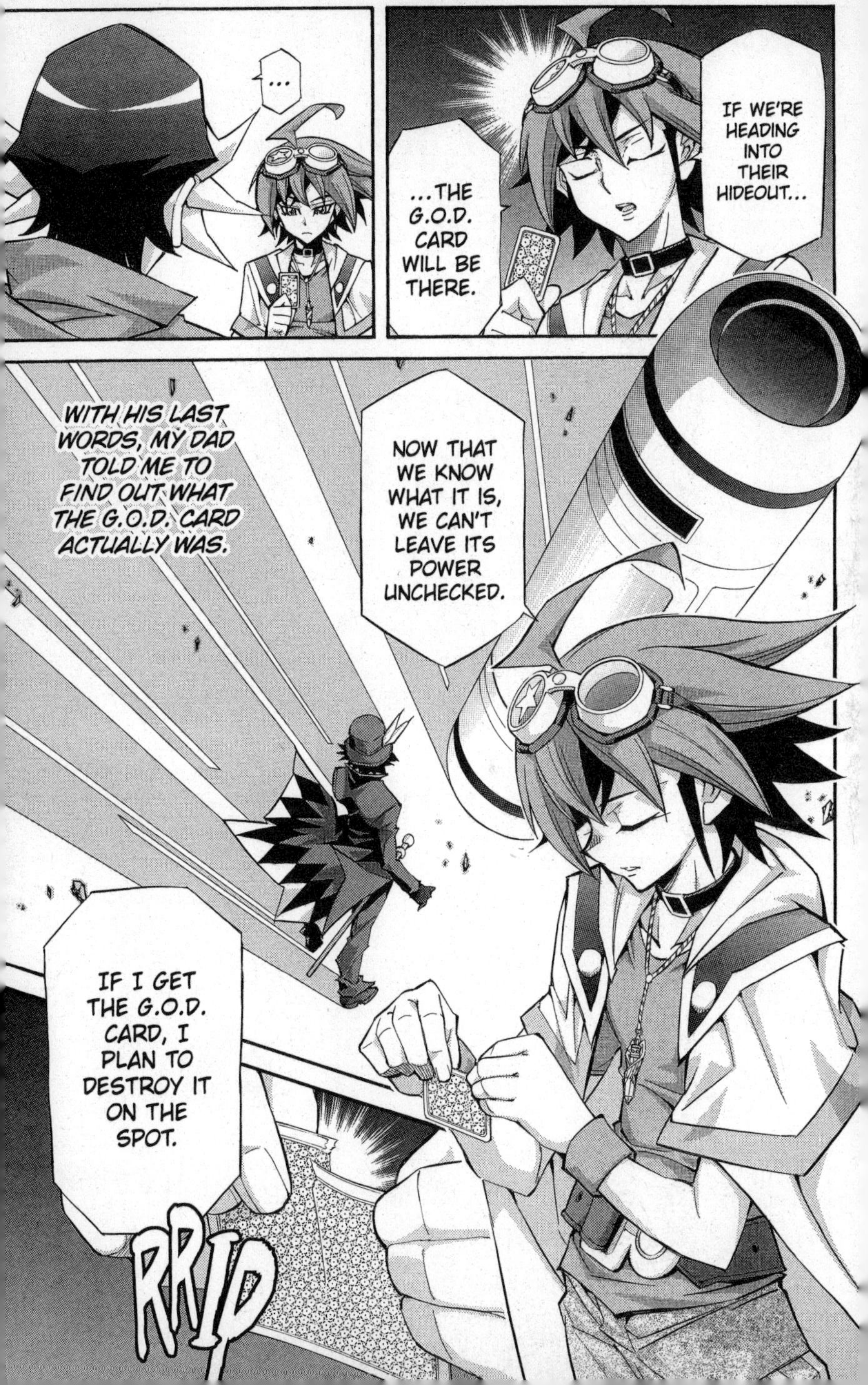
IF WE'RE HEADING INTO THEIR HIDEOUT...
...THE G.O.D. CARD WILL BE THERE.
...
NOW THAT WE KNOW WHAT IT IS, WE CAN'T LEAVE ITS POWER UNCHECKED.
WITH HIS LAST WORDS, MY DAD TOLD ME TO FIND OUT WHAT THE G.O.D. CARD ACTUALLY WAS.
IF I GET THE G.O.D. CARD, I PLAN TO DESTROY IT ON THE SPOT.
RRIP

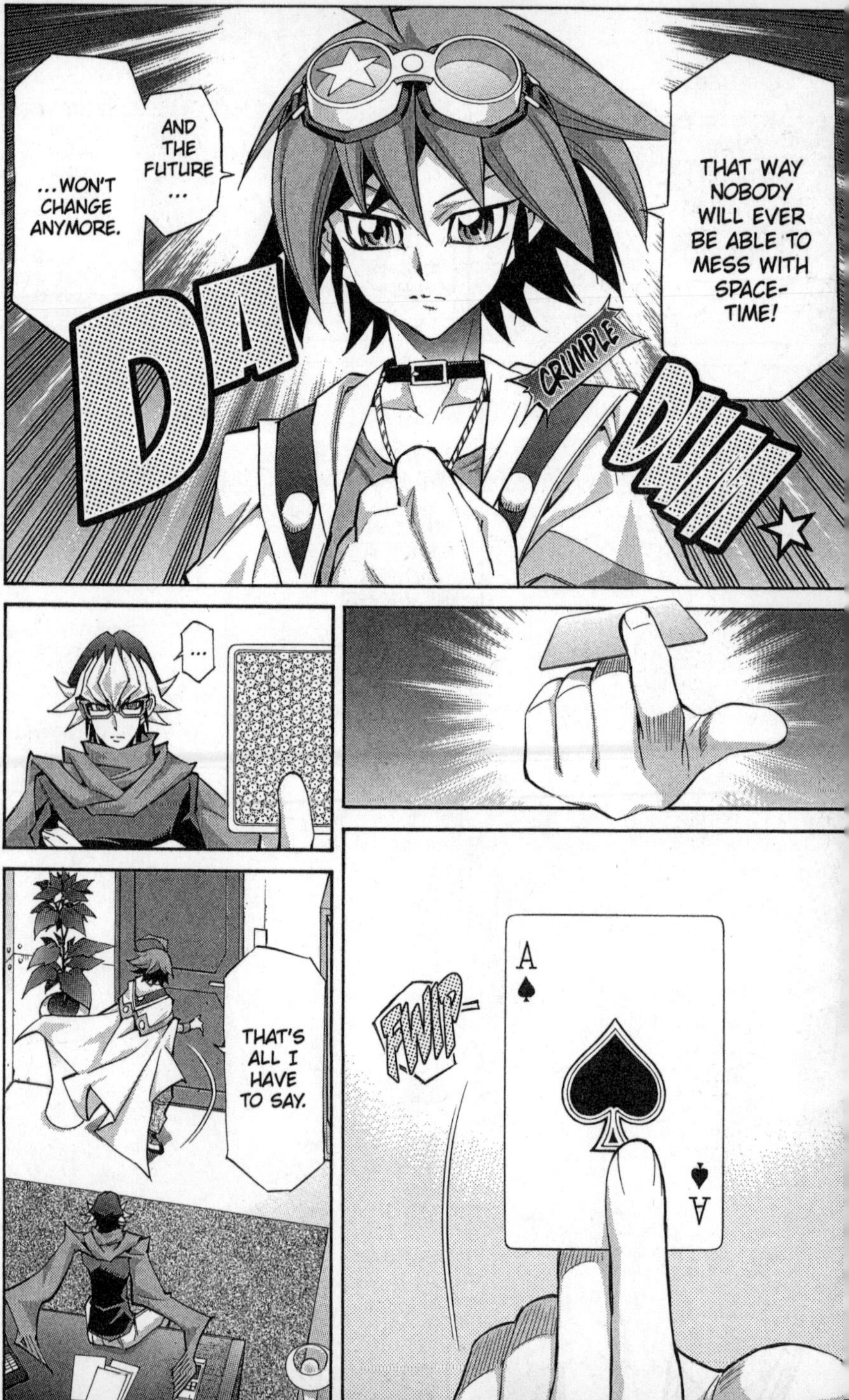
THAT WAY NOBODY WILL EVER BE ABLE TO MESS WITH SPACE-TIME!
AND THE FUTURE ...
...WON'T CHANGE ANYMORE.
CRUMPLE
DA
DUM
...
FWIP
THAT'S ALL I HAVE TO SAY.

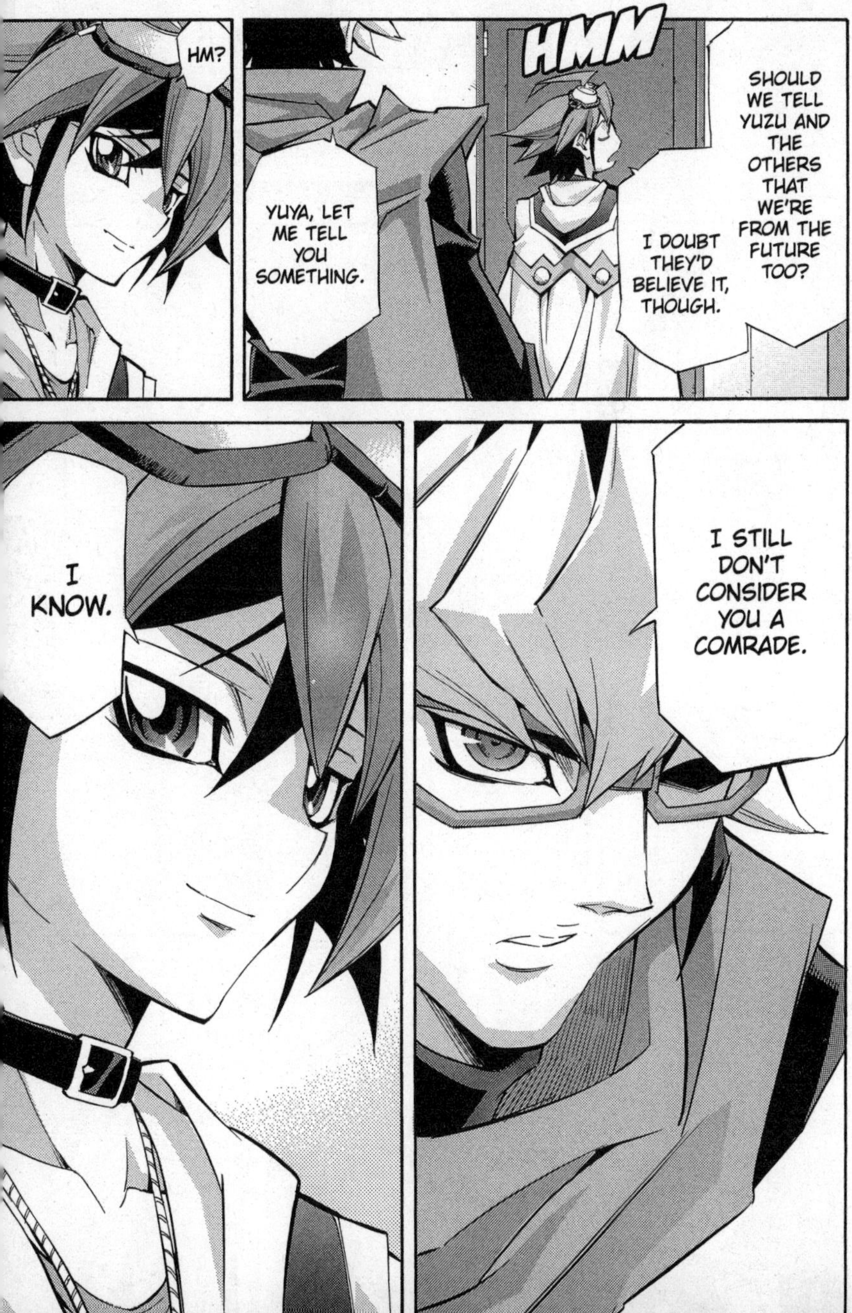
SHOULD WE TELL YUZU AND THE OTHERS THAT WE'RE FROM THE FUTURE TOO?
HMM
I DOUBT THEY'D BELIEVE IT, THOUGH.
YUYA, LET ME TELL YOU SOMETHING.
HM?
I STILL DON'T CONSIDER YOU A COMRADE.
I KNOW.

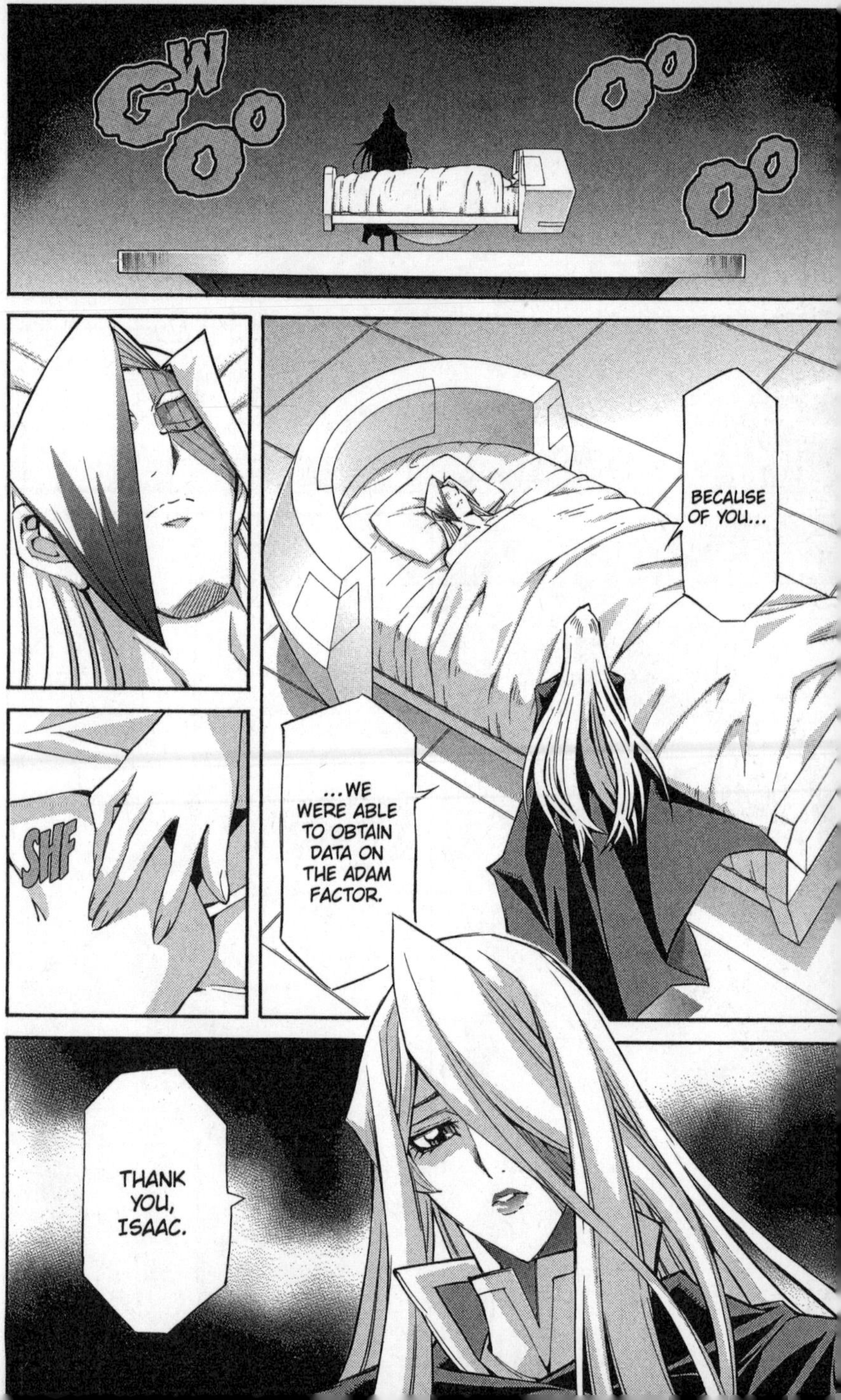
GWOOOO
OOOO
BECAUSE OF YOU...
...WE WERE ABLE TO OBTAIN DATA ON THE ADAM FACTOR.
SHF
THANK YOU, ISAAC.

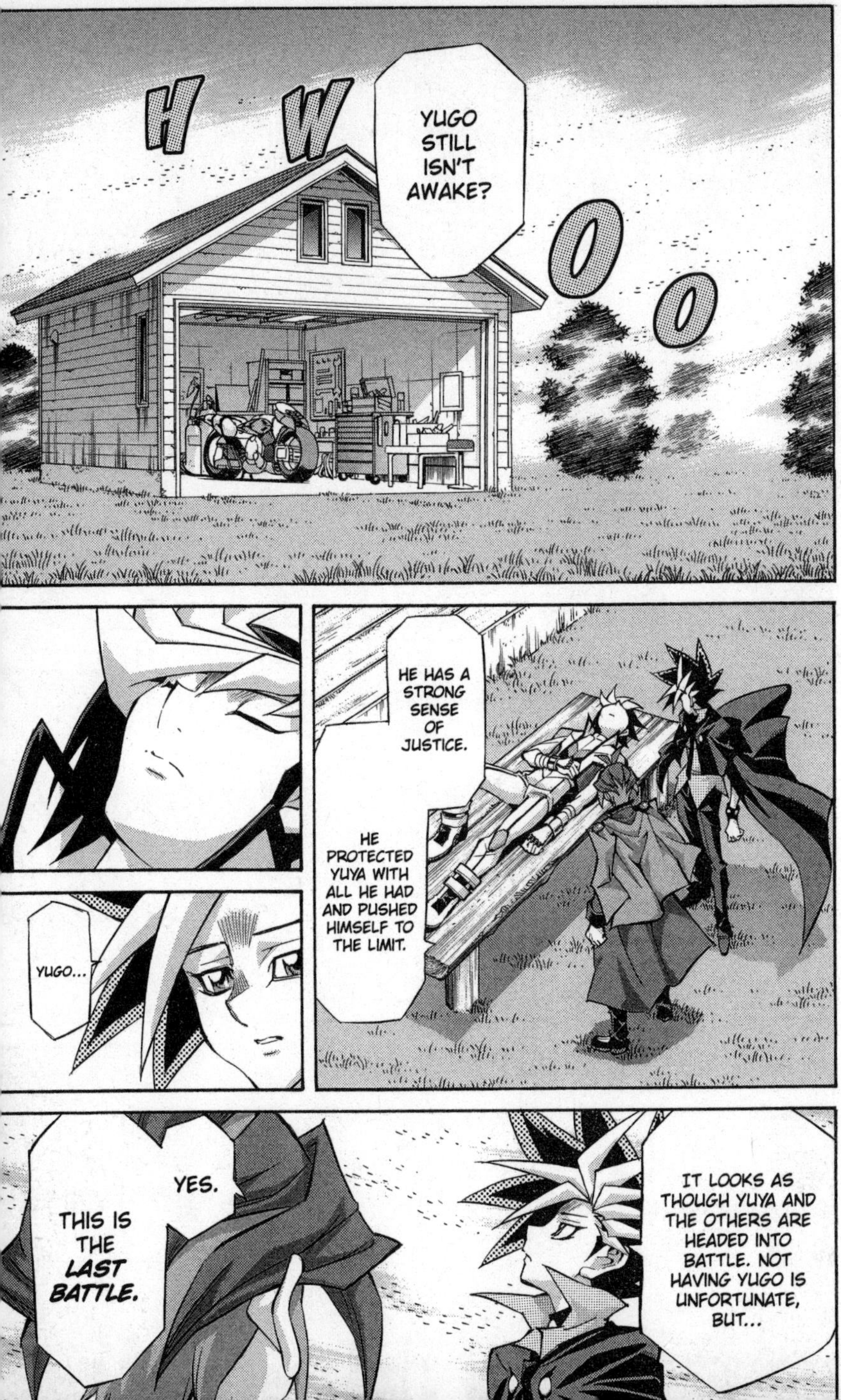
HWOO
YUGO STILL ISN'T AWAKE?
HE HAS A STRONG SENSE OF JUSTICE.
HE PROTECTED YUYA WITH ALL HE HAD AND PUSHED HIMSELF TO THE LIMIT.
YUGO...
IT LOOKS AS THOUGH YUYA AND THE OTHERS ARE HEADED INTO BATTLE. NOT HAVING YUGO IS UNFORTUNATE, BUT...
YES.
THIS IS THE *LAST BATTLE.*

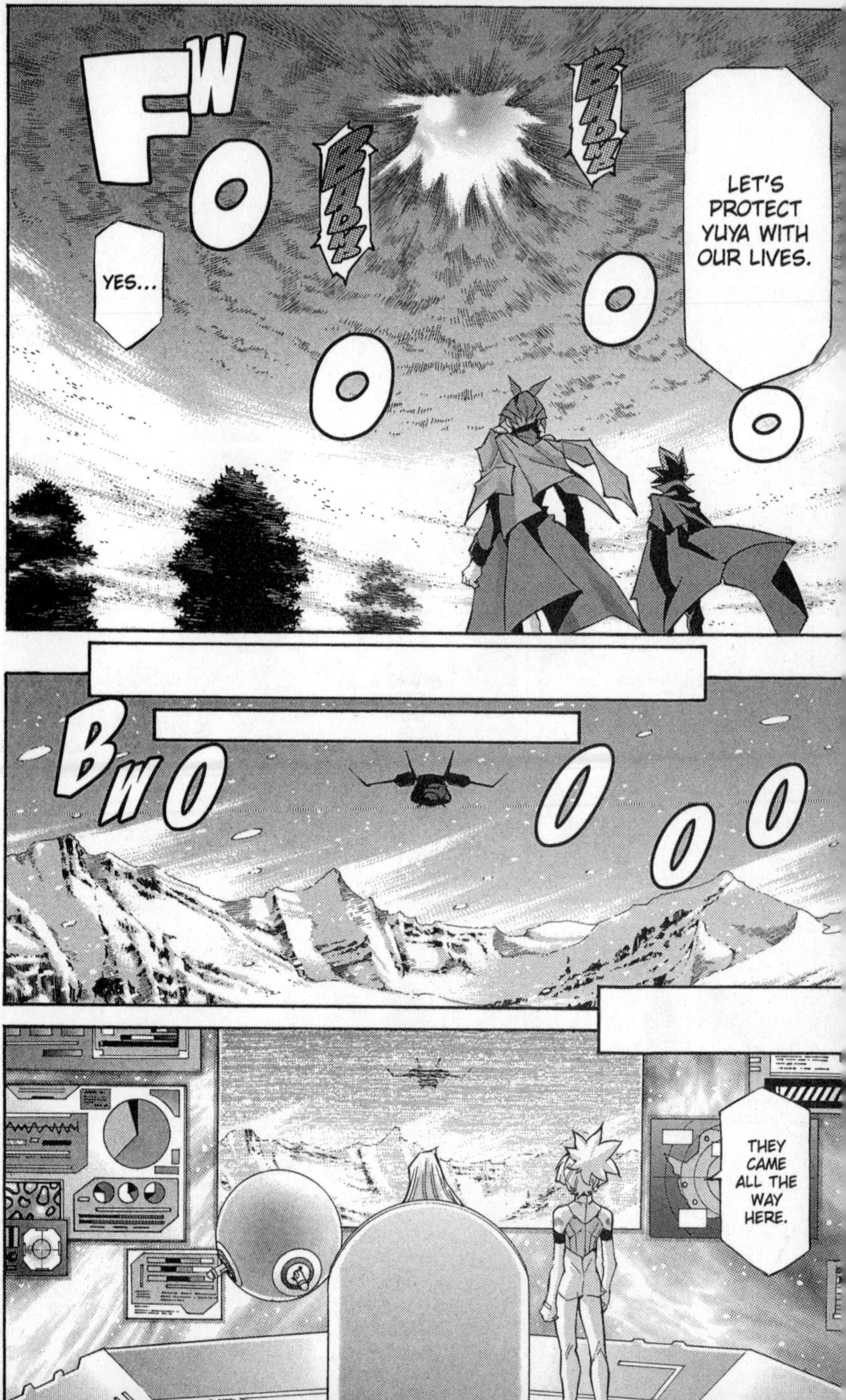
LET'S PROTECT YUYA WITH OUR LIVES.
FWOOOO
YES...
BWOOOOO
THEY CAME ALL THE WAY HERE.

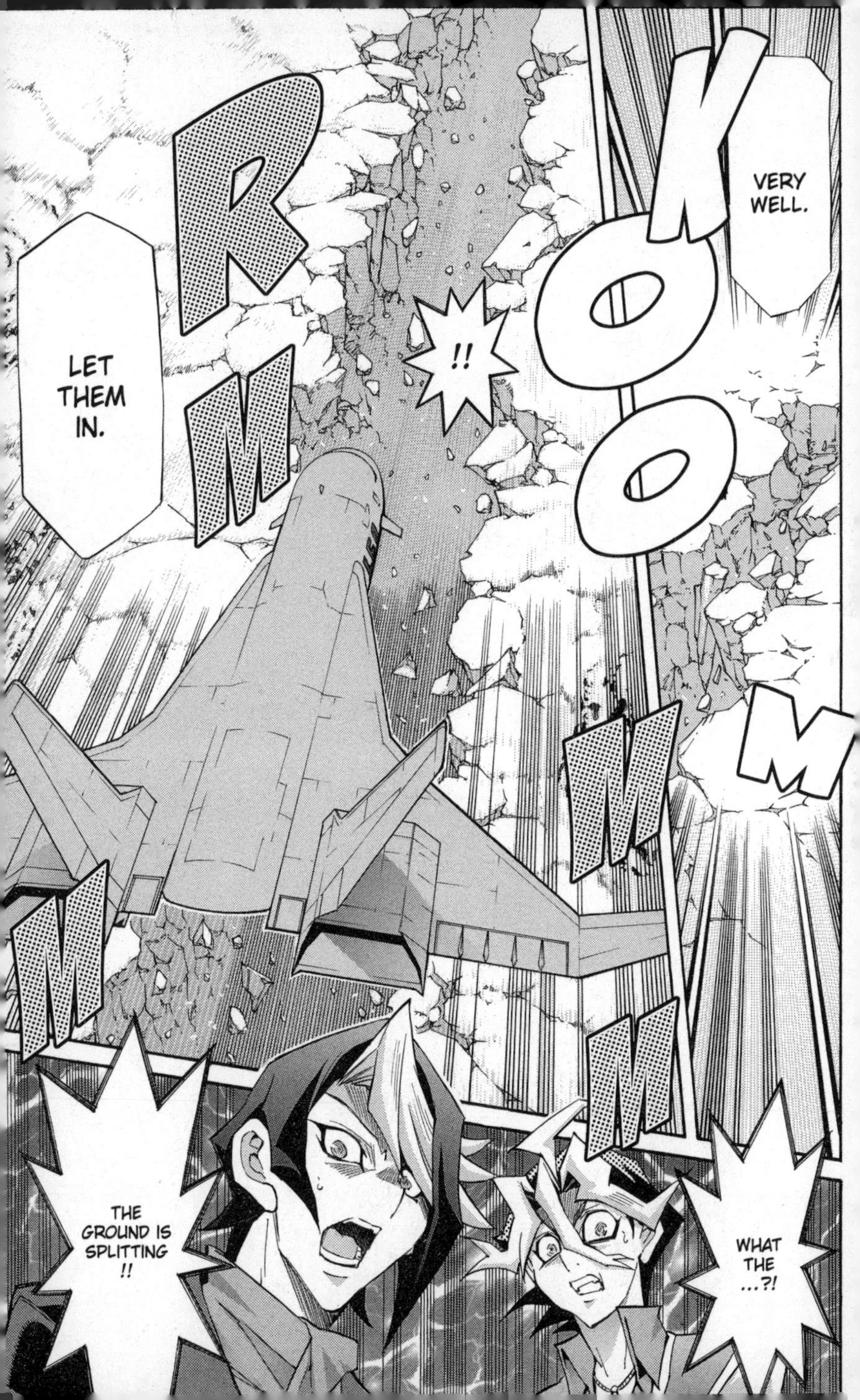
VERY WELL.
KOOMMM
LET THEM IN.
RMMM
!!
WHAT THE ...?!
THE GROUND IS SPLITTING !!

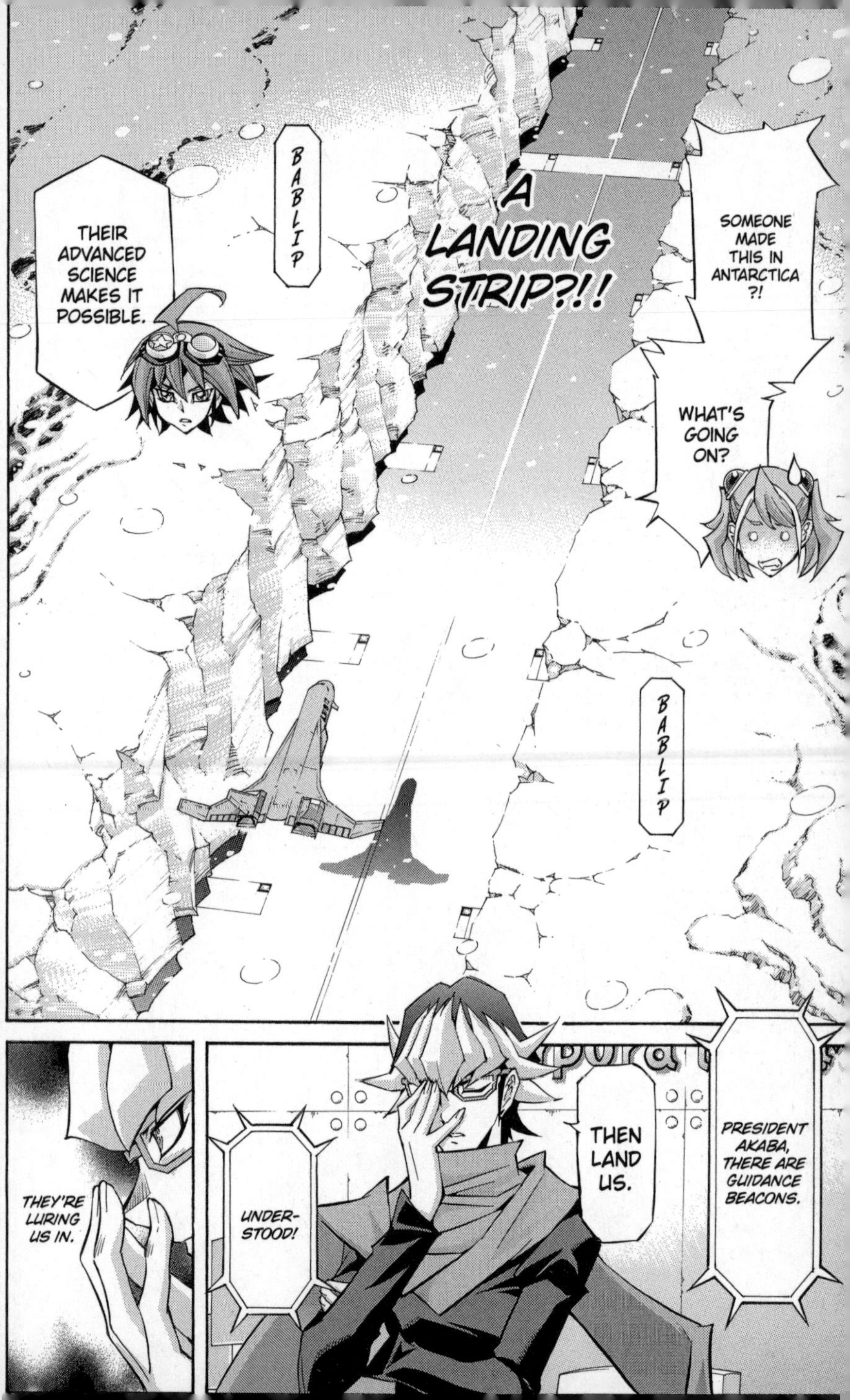
SOMEONE MADE THIS IN ANTARCTICA ?!
A LANDING STRIP?!!
BABLIP
THEIR ADVANCED SCIENCE MAKES IT POSSIBLE.
WHAT'S GOING ON?
BABLIP
PRESIDENT AKABA, THERE ARE GUIDANCE BEACONS.
THEN LAND US.
UNDER-STOOD!
THEY'RE LURING US IN.

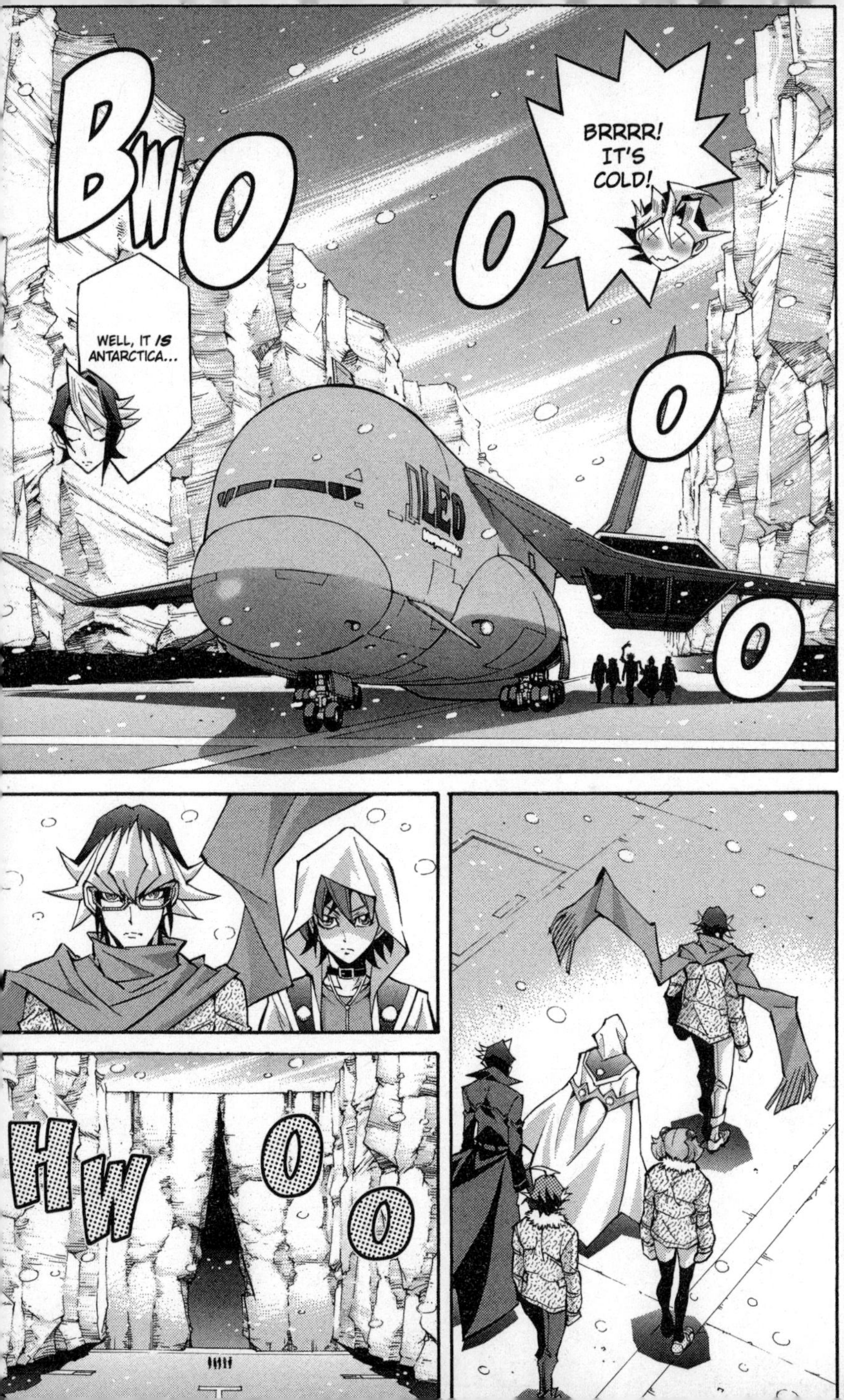
BWOOOOO
BRRRR! IT'S COLD!
WELL, IT *IS* ANTARCTICA...
HWOOO

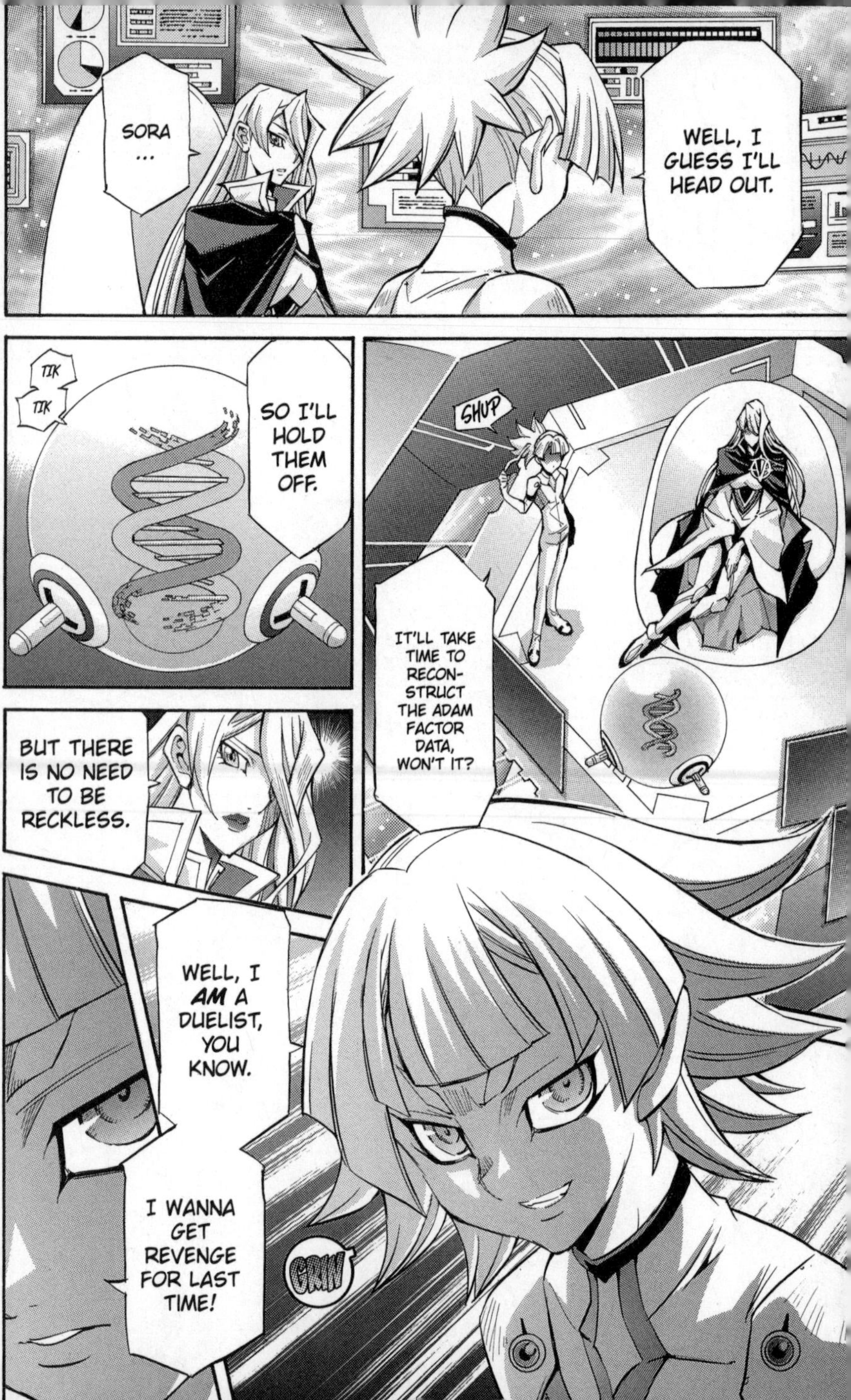
WELL, I GUESS I'LL HEAD OUT.
SORA ...
SHUP
IT'LL TAKE TIME TO RECON-STRUCT THE ADAM FACTOR DATA, WON'T IT?
SO I'LL HOLD THEM OFF.
TIK
TIK
BUT THERE IS NO NEED TO BE RECKLESS.
WELL, I AM A DUELIST, YOU KNOW.
I WANNA GET REVENGE FOR LAST TIME!
GRIN

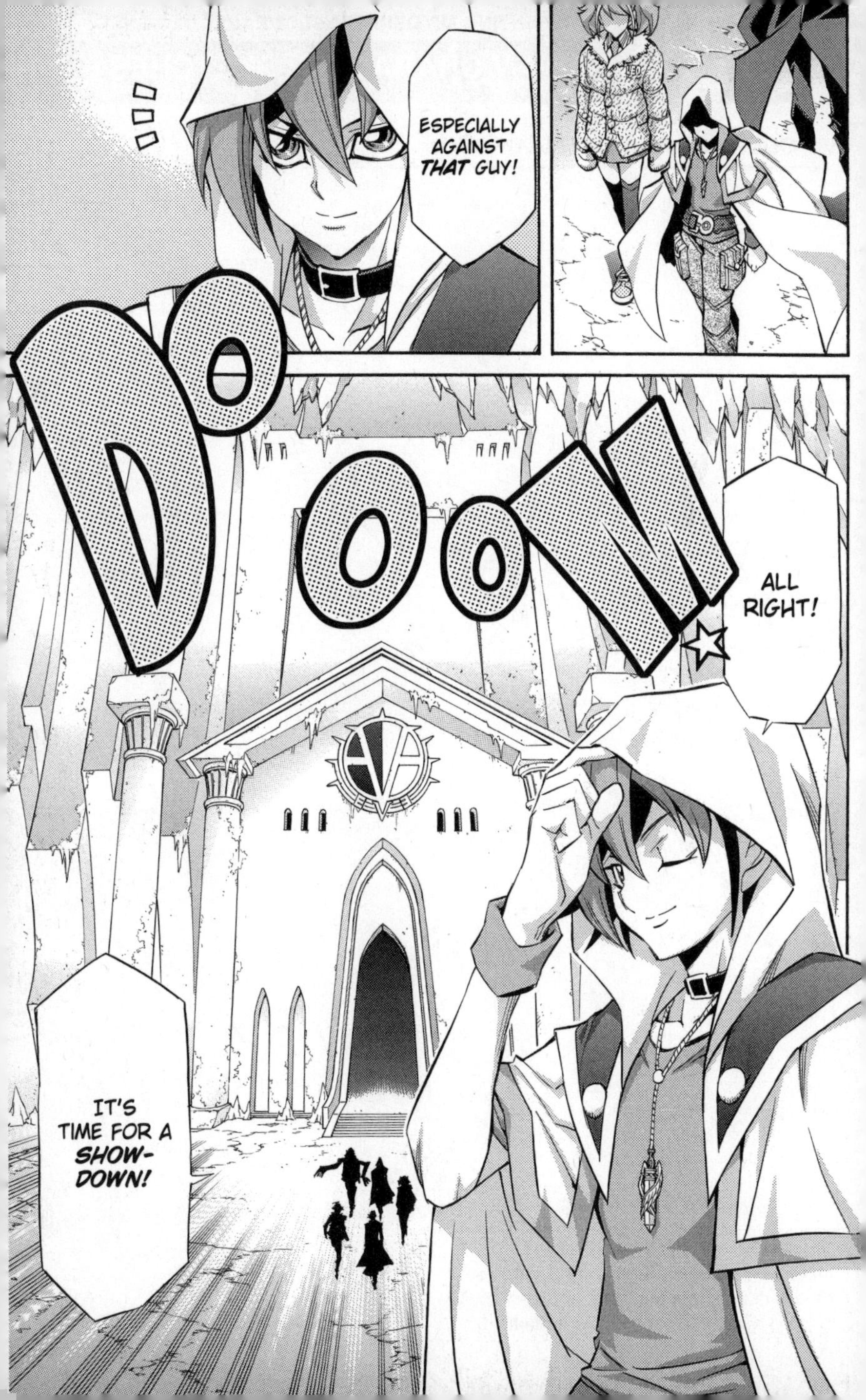
ESPECIALLY AGAINST THAT GUY!
DOOOM
ALL RIGHT!
IT'S TIME FOR A SHOW-DOWN!

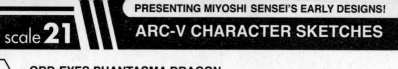
ODD-EYES PHANTASMA DRAGON

ODD-EYES PHANTASMA DRAGON

The product of Yuya's off-the-charts imagination, this elusive monster ignores the Pendulum Scale when it appears! Its shining wings slice across the battlefield!

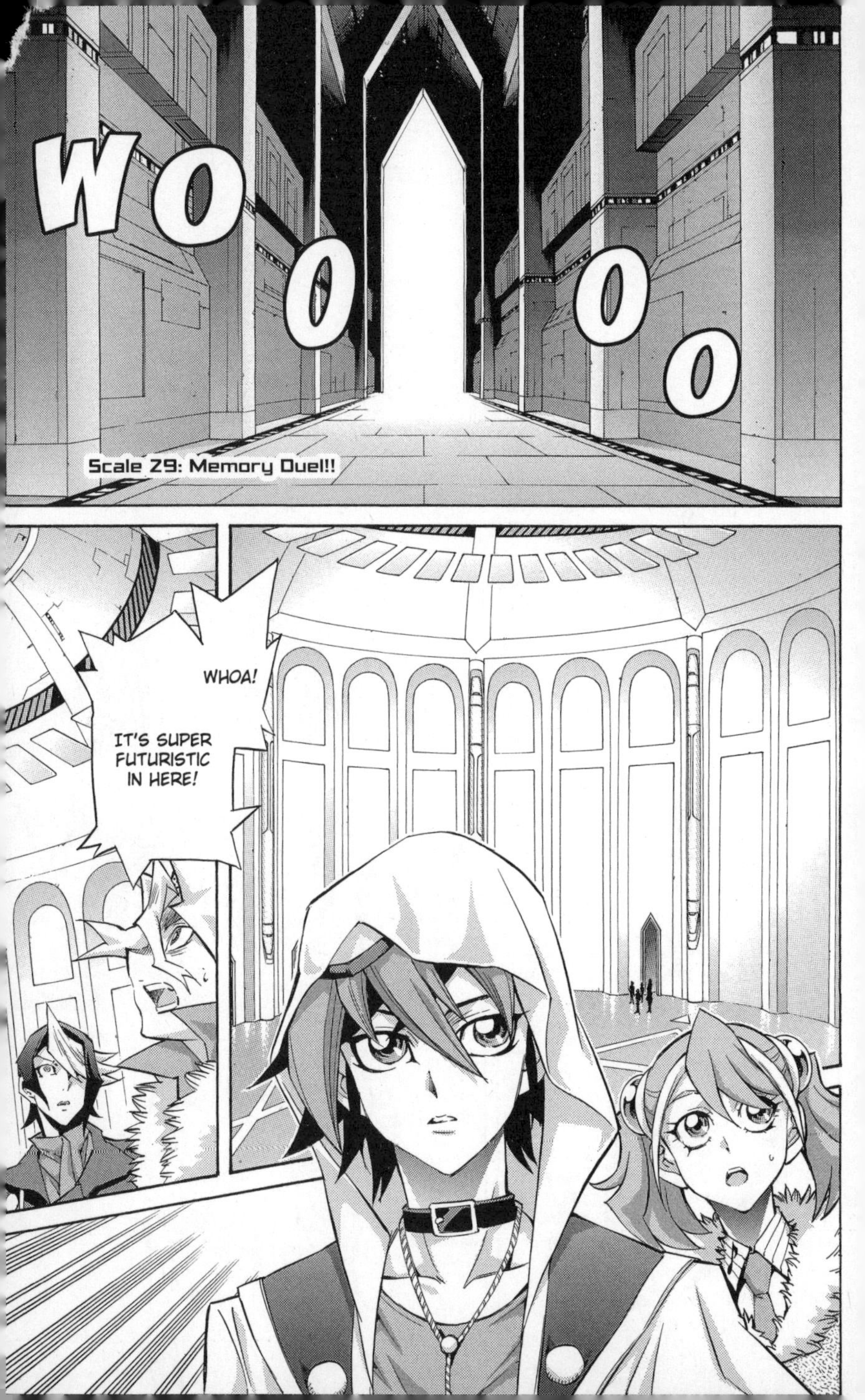
WOOOO
Scale 29: Memory Duel!!
WHOA!
IT'S SUPER FUTURISTIC IN HERE!

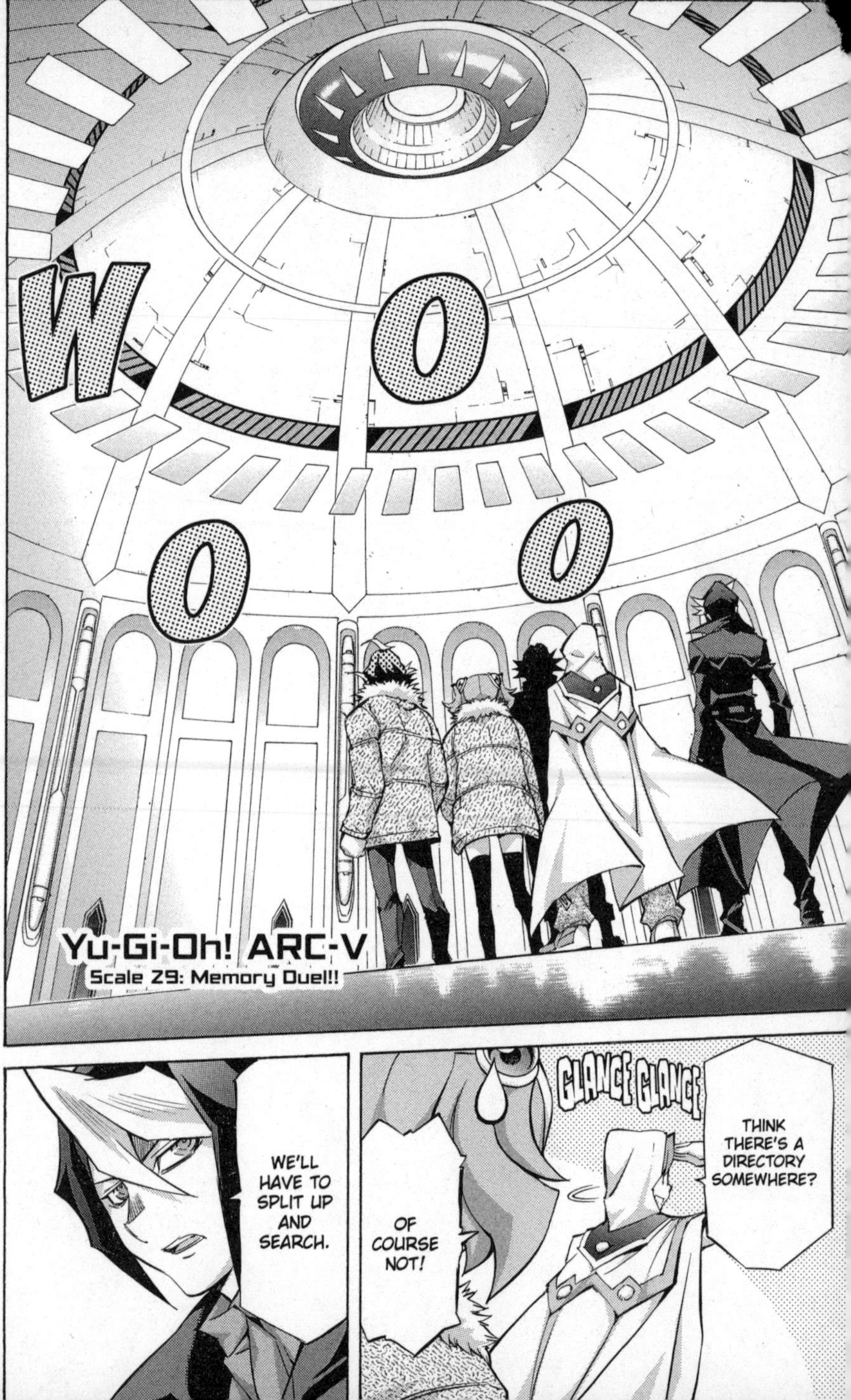
WOOOO
Yu-Gi-Oh! ARC-V
Scale 29: Memory Duel!!
GLANCE GLANCE
THINK THERE'S A DIRECTORY SOMEWHERE?
OF COURSE NOT!
WE'LL HAVE TO SPLIT UP AND SEARCH.

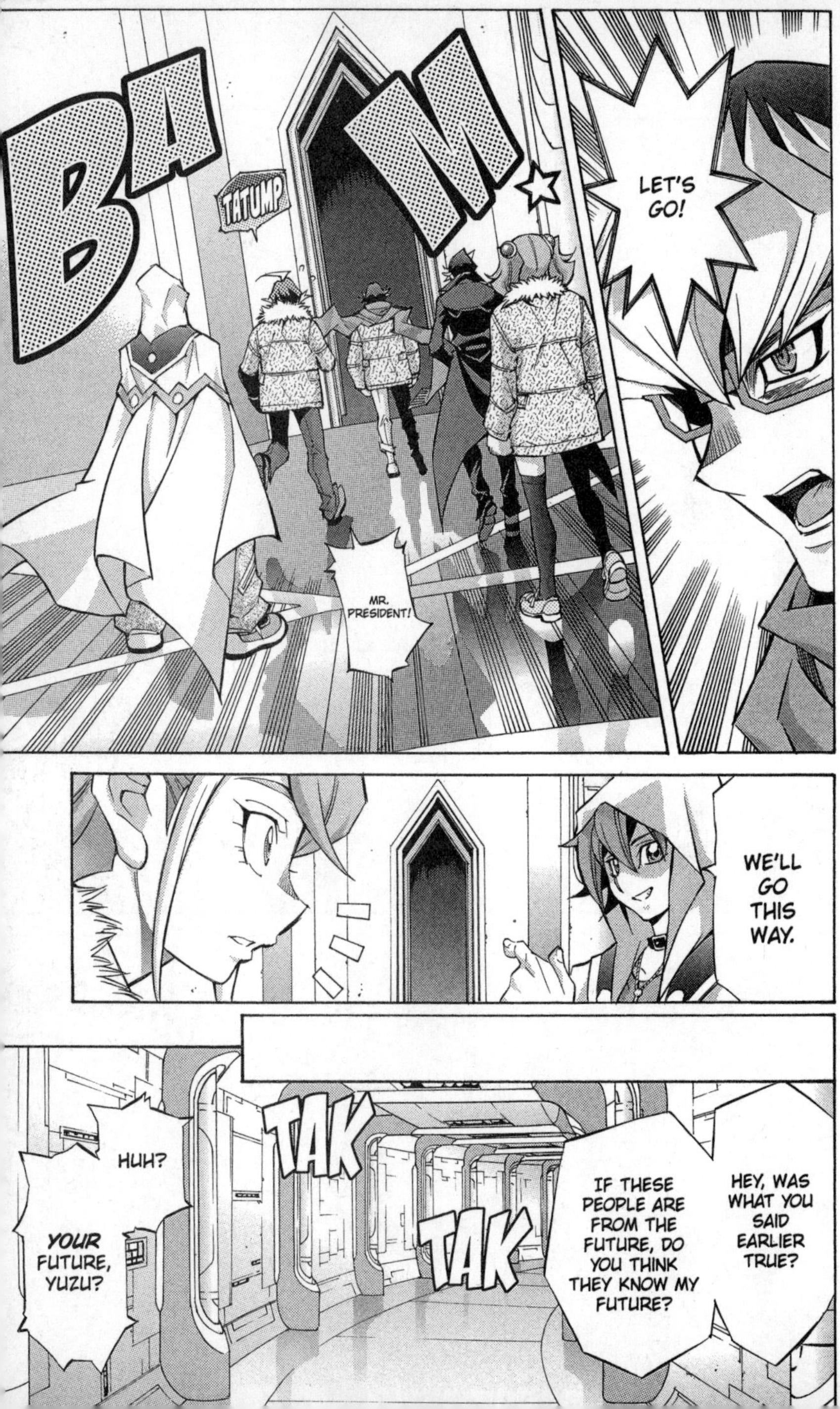
LET'S GO!
BAM
TATUMP
MR. PRESIDENT!
WE'LL GO THIS WAY.
HEY, WAS WHAT YOU SAID EARLIER TRUE?
IF THESE PEOPLE ARE FROM THE FUTURE, DO YOU THINK THEY KNOW MY FUTURE?
TAK
TAK
HUH?
YOUR FUTURE, YUZU?

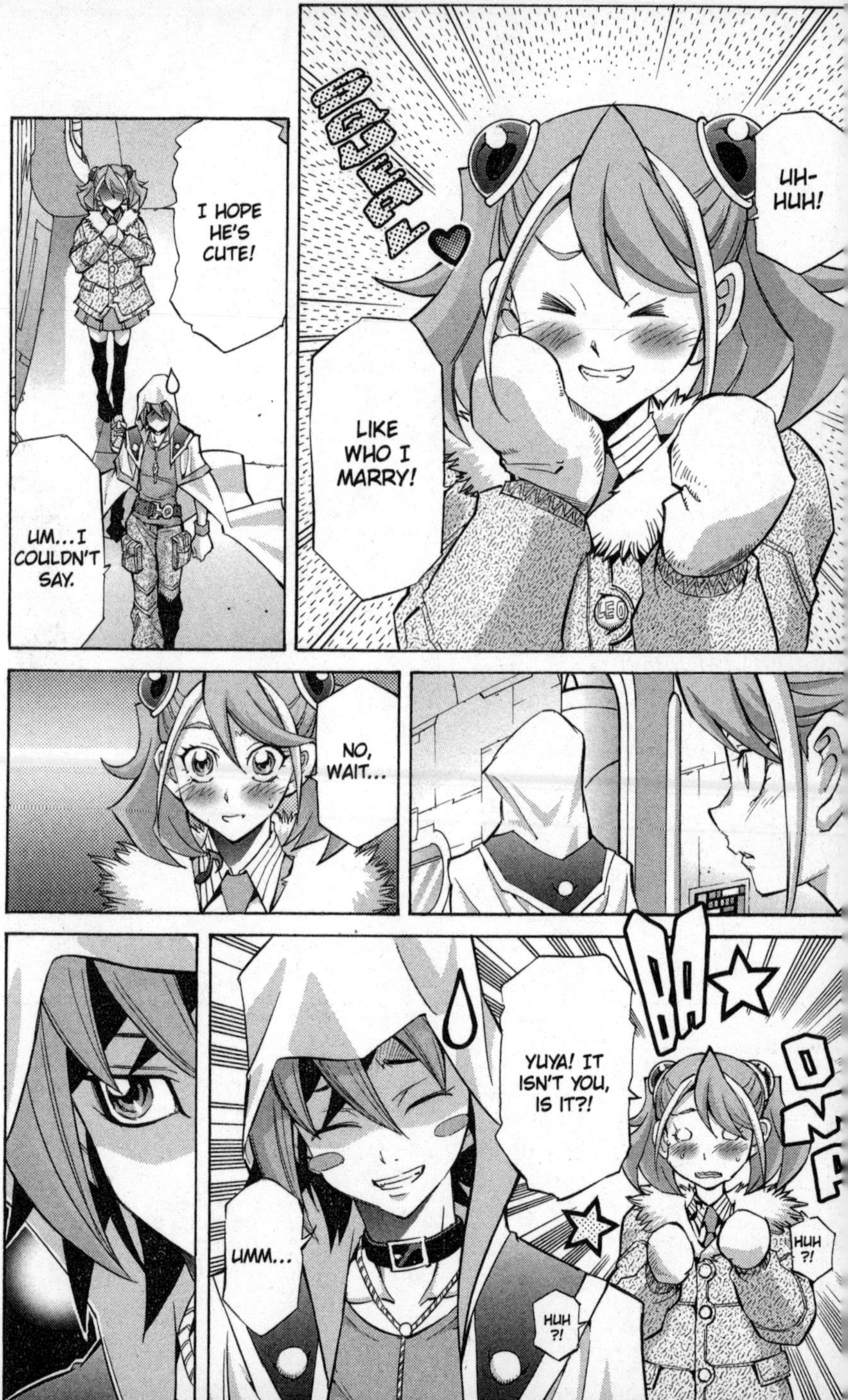
UH-HUH!
LIKE WHO I MARRY!
I HOPE HE'S CUTE!
UM...I COULDN'T SAY.
NO, WAIT...
BA☆
YUYA! IT ISN'T YOU, IS IT?!
HUH?!
HUH?!
UMM...

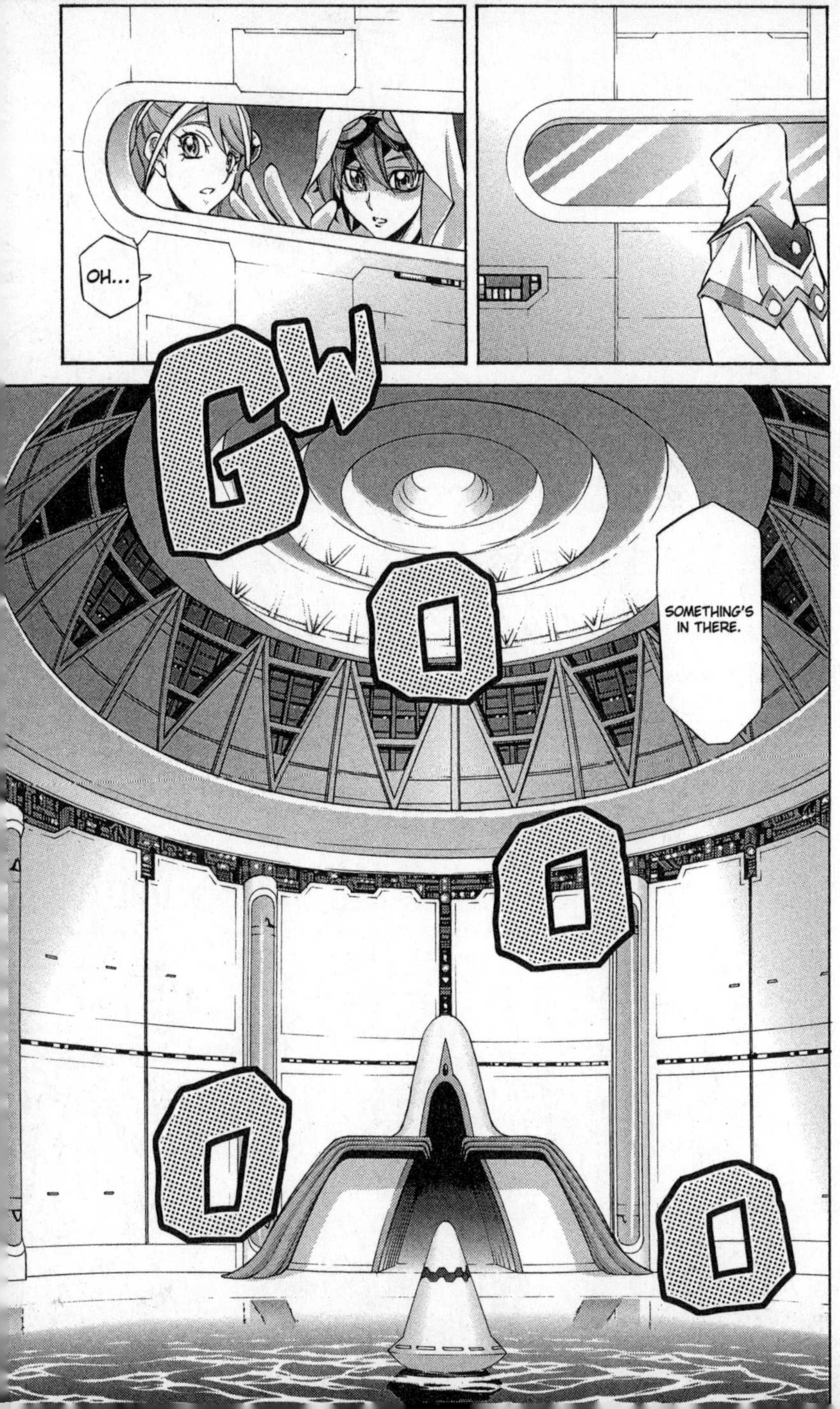
OH...
GWOOOO
SOMETHING'S IN THERE.

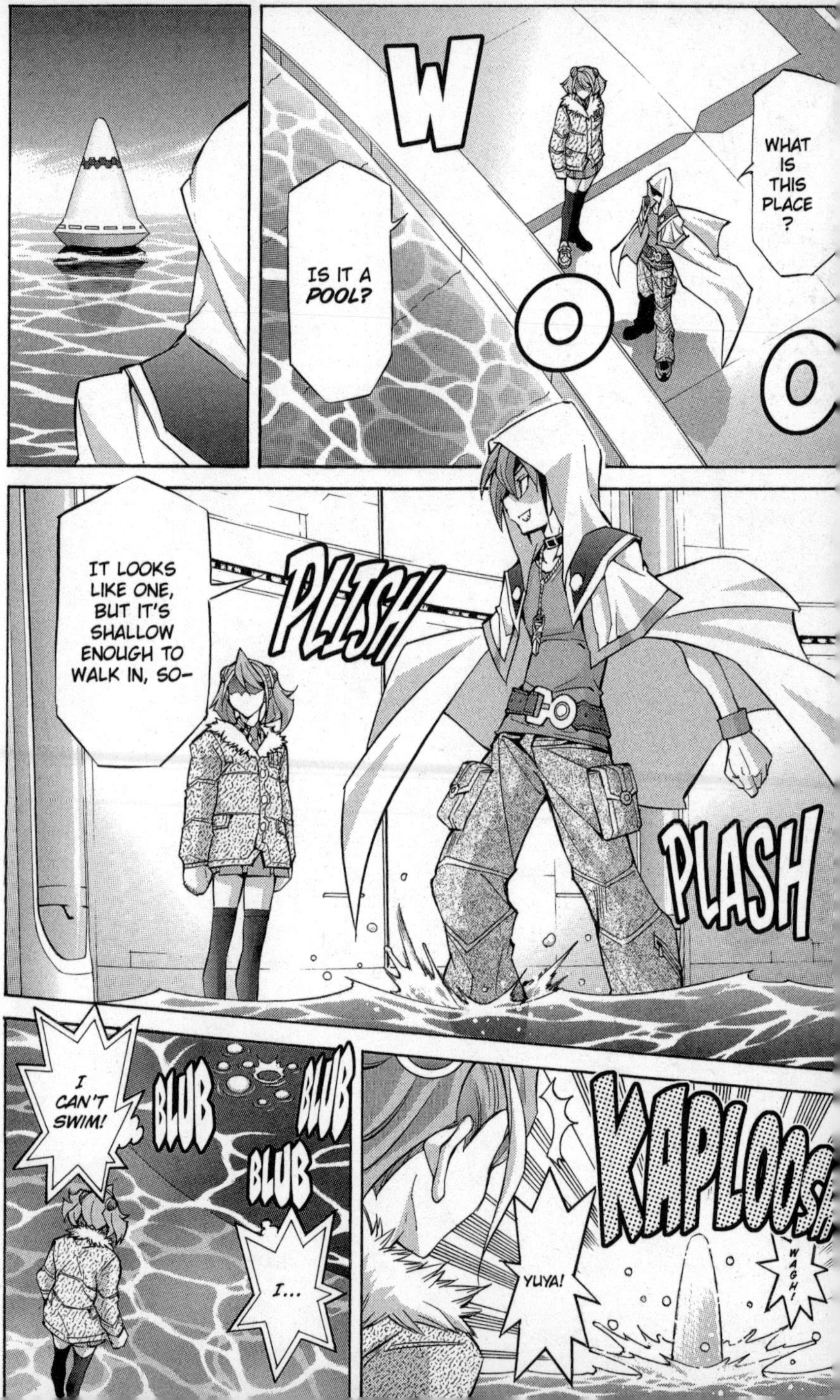
WOO
WHAT IS THIS PLACE?
IS IT A POOL?
IT LOOKS LIKE ONE, BUT IT'S SHALLOW ENOUGH TO WALK IN, SO-
PLISH
PLASH
KAPLOOS
WAGH!
YUYA!
I CAN'T SWIM!
BLUB
BLUB
BLUB
I...

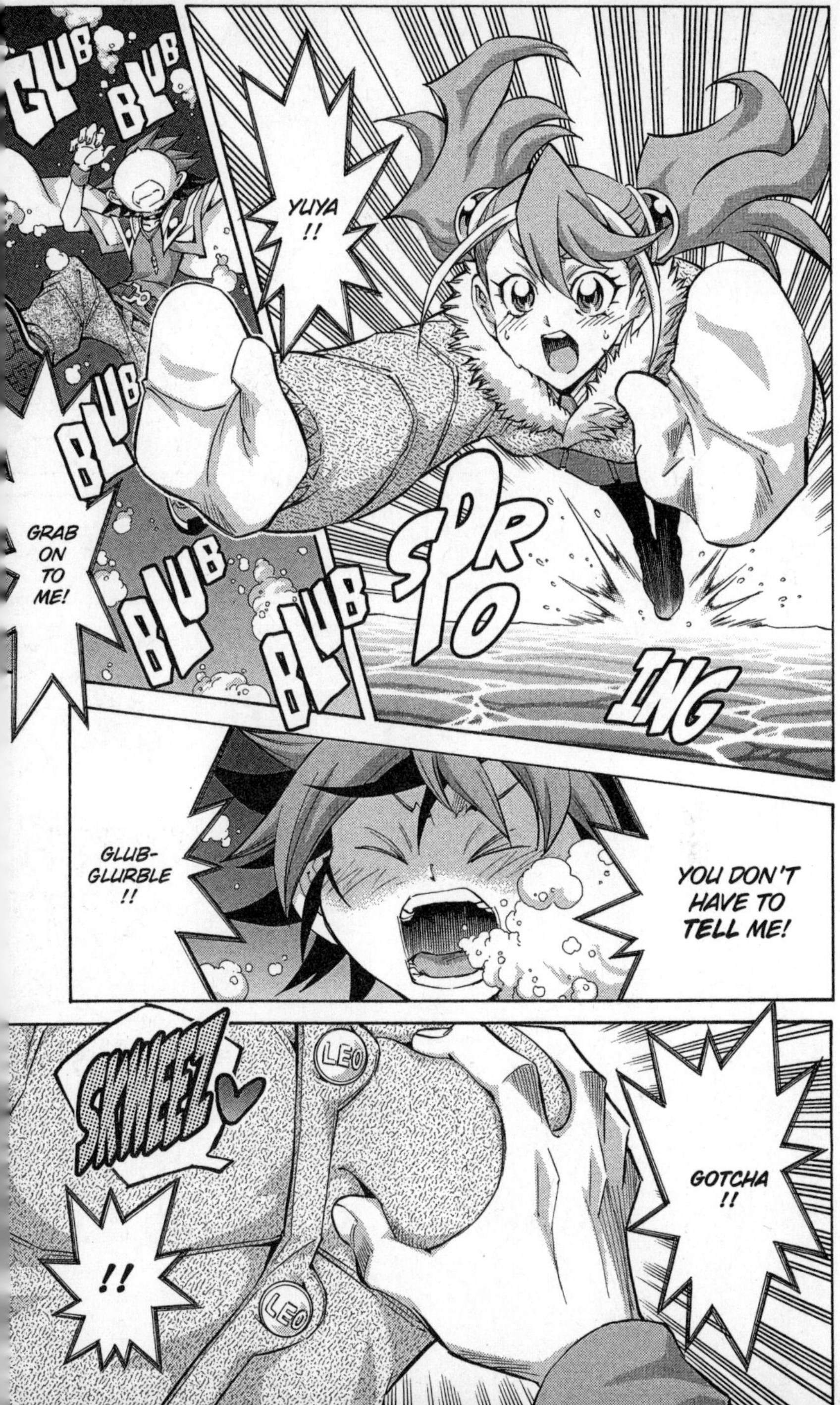
YUYA!!
SPROING
GLUB GLUB
BLUB BLUB
BLUB BLUB
GRAB ON TO ME!
BLUB BLUB
YOU DON'T HAVE TO TELL ME!
GLUB-GLURBLE!!
GOTCHA!!
LEO
SKWEEZ ♥
LEO
!!

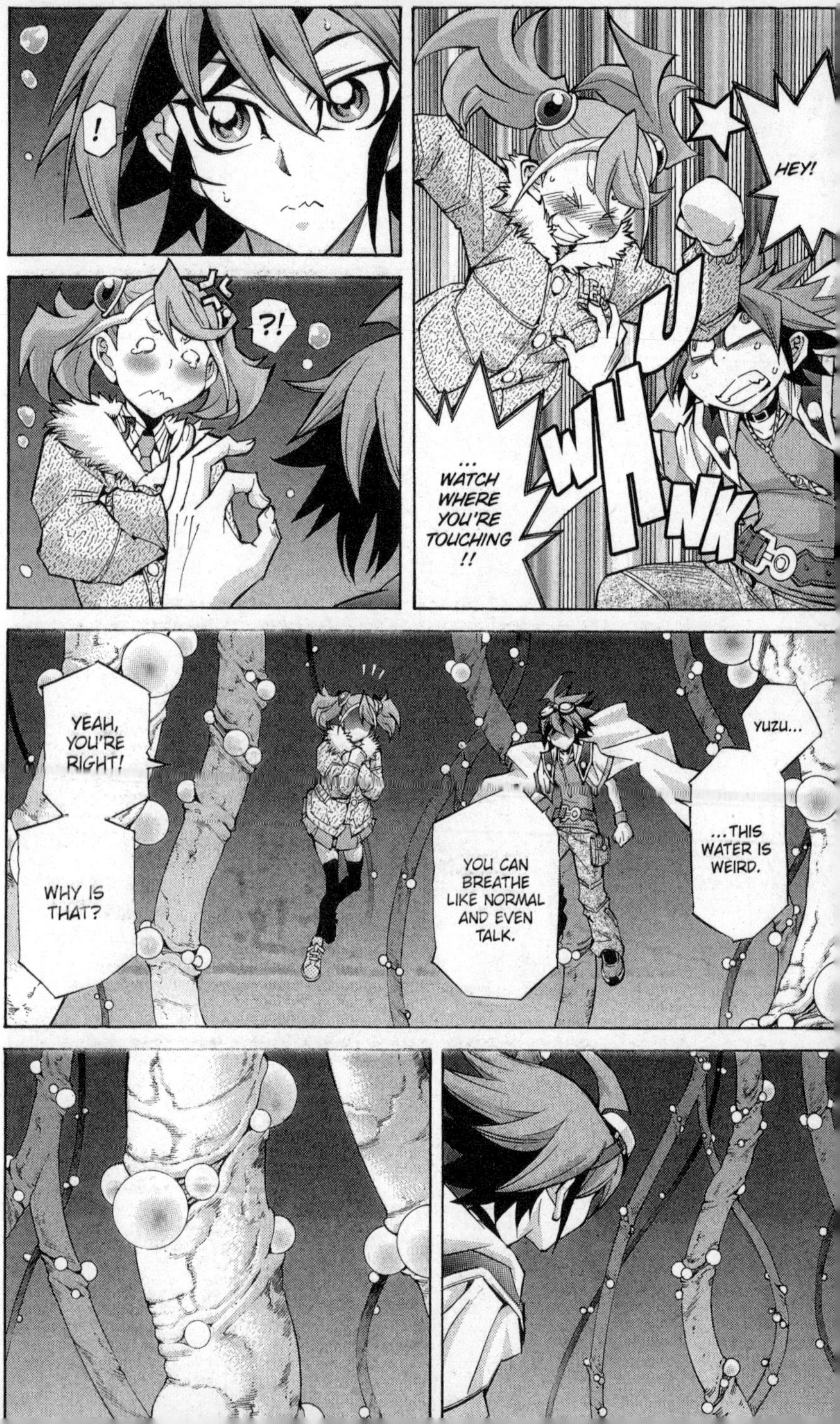
HEY!
WHUNK
...WATCH WHERE YOU'RE TOUCHING!!
!
?!
YUZU...
...THIS WATER IS WEIRD.
YOU CAN BREATHE LIKE NORMAL AND EVEN TALK.
YEAH, YOU'RE RIGHT!
WHY IS THAT?

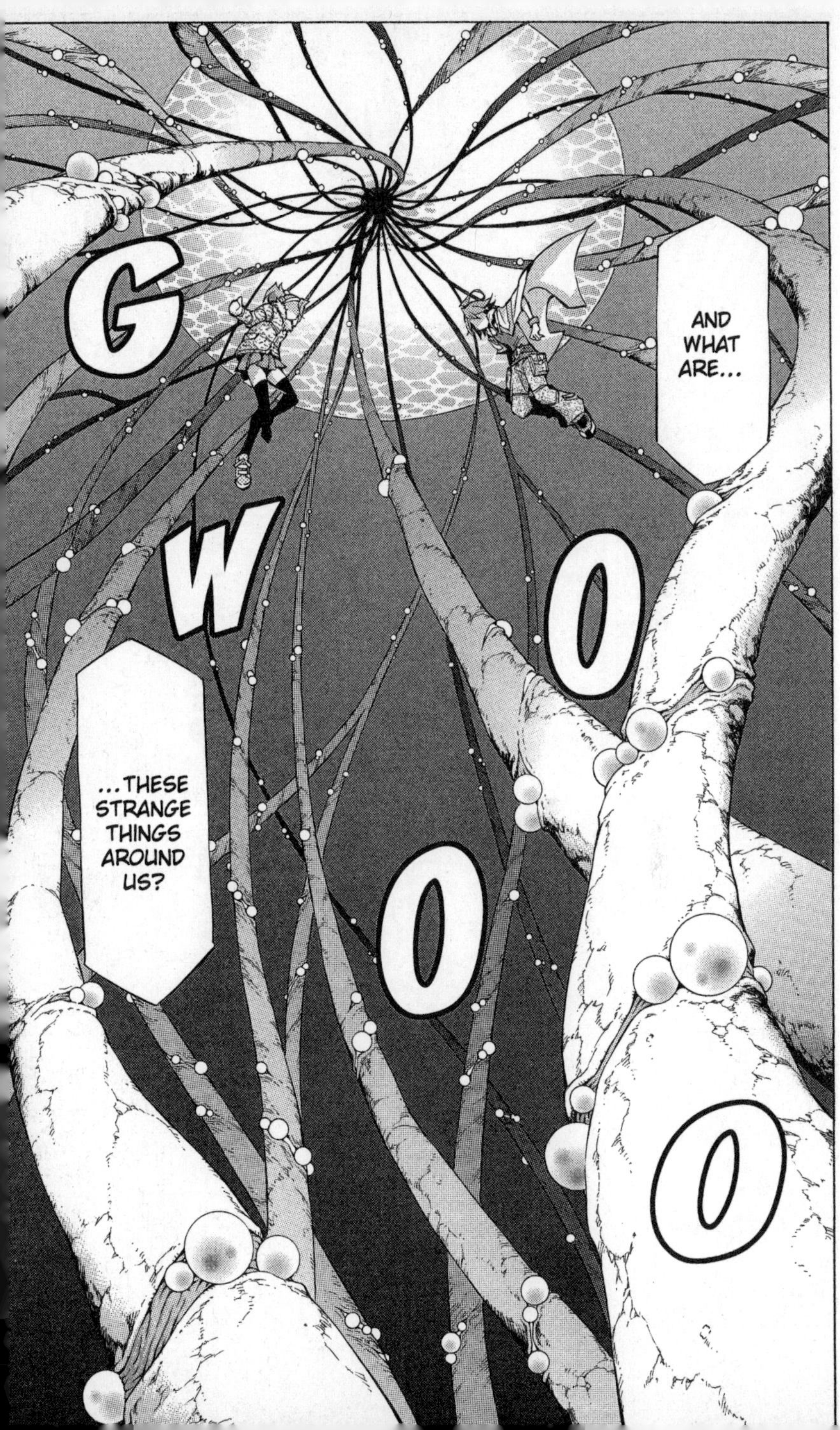
AND WHAT ARE...
GWOOO
...THESE STRANGE THINGS AROUND US?

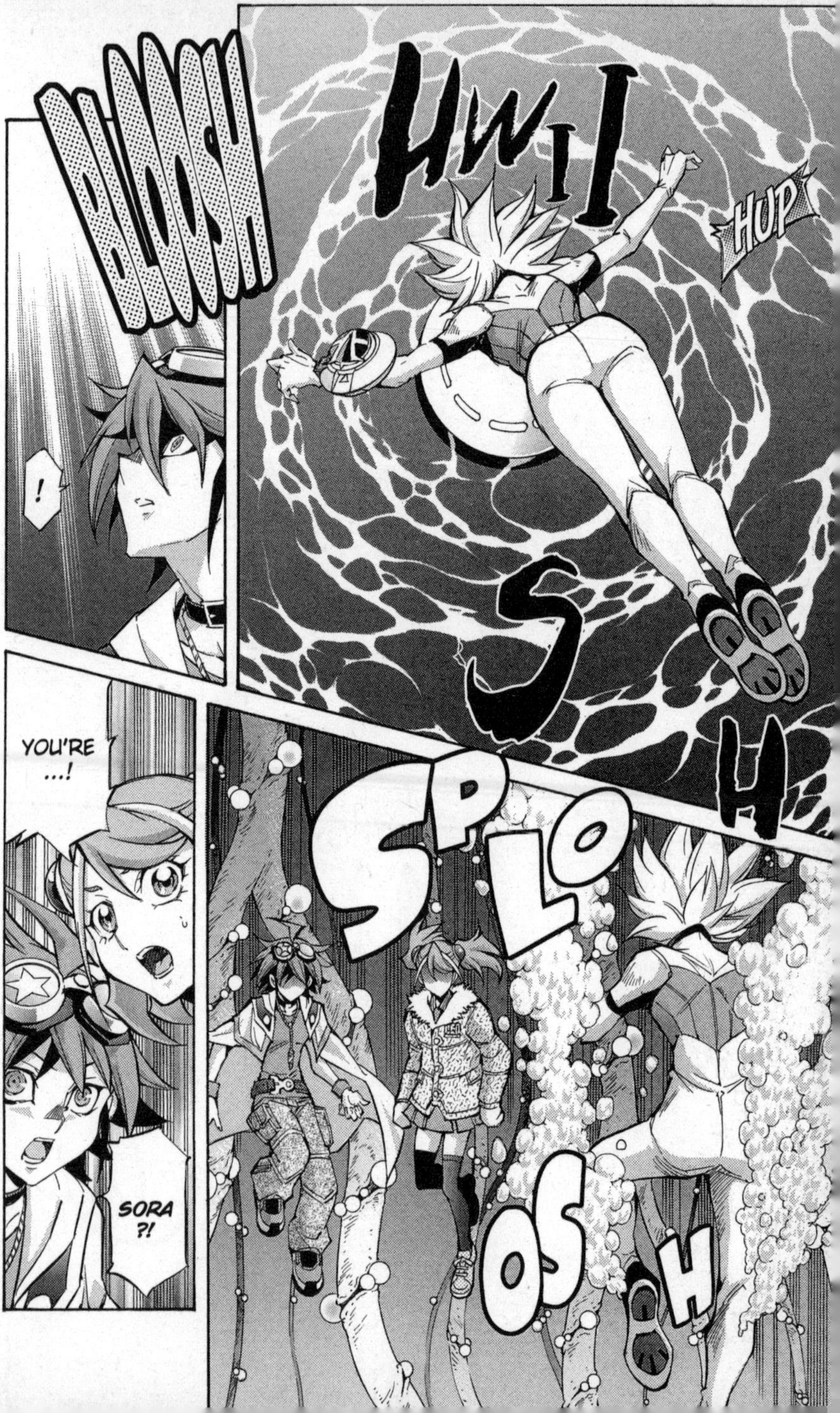

HWII
HUP
SH
BLOOSH
!
SPLOOSH
YOU'RE ...!
SORA ?!

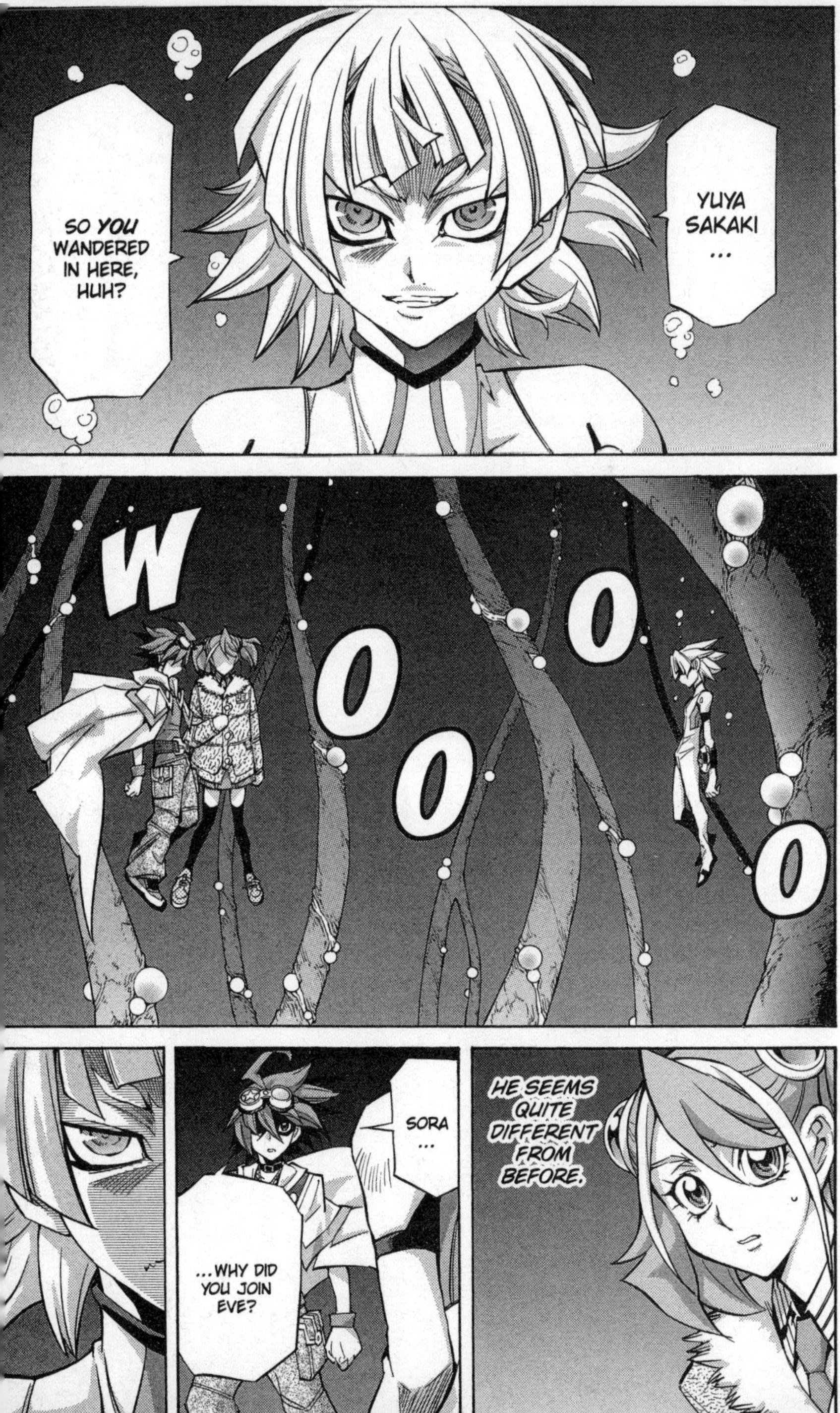
YUYA SAKAKI ...
SO *YOU* WANDERED IN HERE, HUH?
WOOOOO
HE SEEMS QUITE DIFFERENT FROM BEFORE.
SORA ...
...WHY DID YOU JOIN EVE?

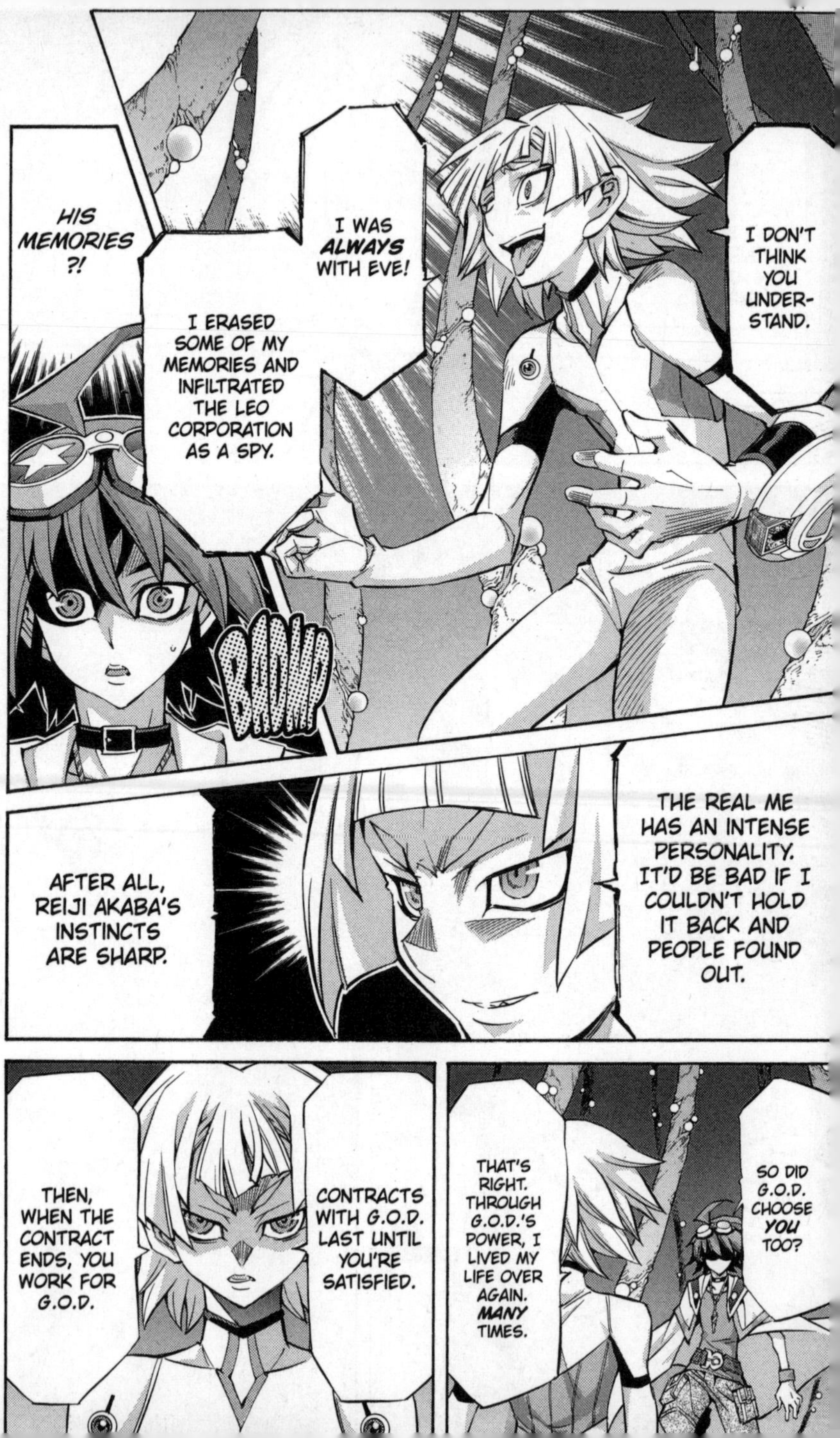
I DON'T THINK YOU UNDERSTAND.
I WAS *ALWAYS* WITH EVE!
I ERASED SOME OF MY MEMORIES AND INFILTRATED THE LEO CORPORATION AS A SPY.
HIS MEMORIES ?!
BADMP
THE REAL ME HAS AN INTENSE PERSONALITY. IT'D BE BAD IF I COULDN'T HOLD IT BACK AND PEOPLE FOUND OUT.
AFTER ALL, REIJI AKABA'S INSTINCTS ARE SHARP.
SO DID G.O.D. CHOOSE *YOU* TOO?
THAT'S RIGHT. THROUGH G.O.D.'S POWER, I LIVED MY LIFE OVER AGAIN. *MANY* TIMES.
CONTRACTS WITH G.O.D. LAST UNTIL YOU'RE SATISFIED.
THEN, WHEN THE CONTRACT ENDS, YOU WORK FOR G.O.D.

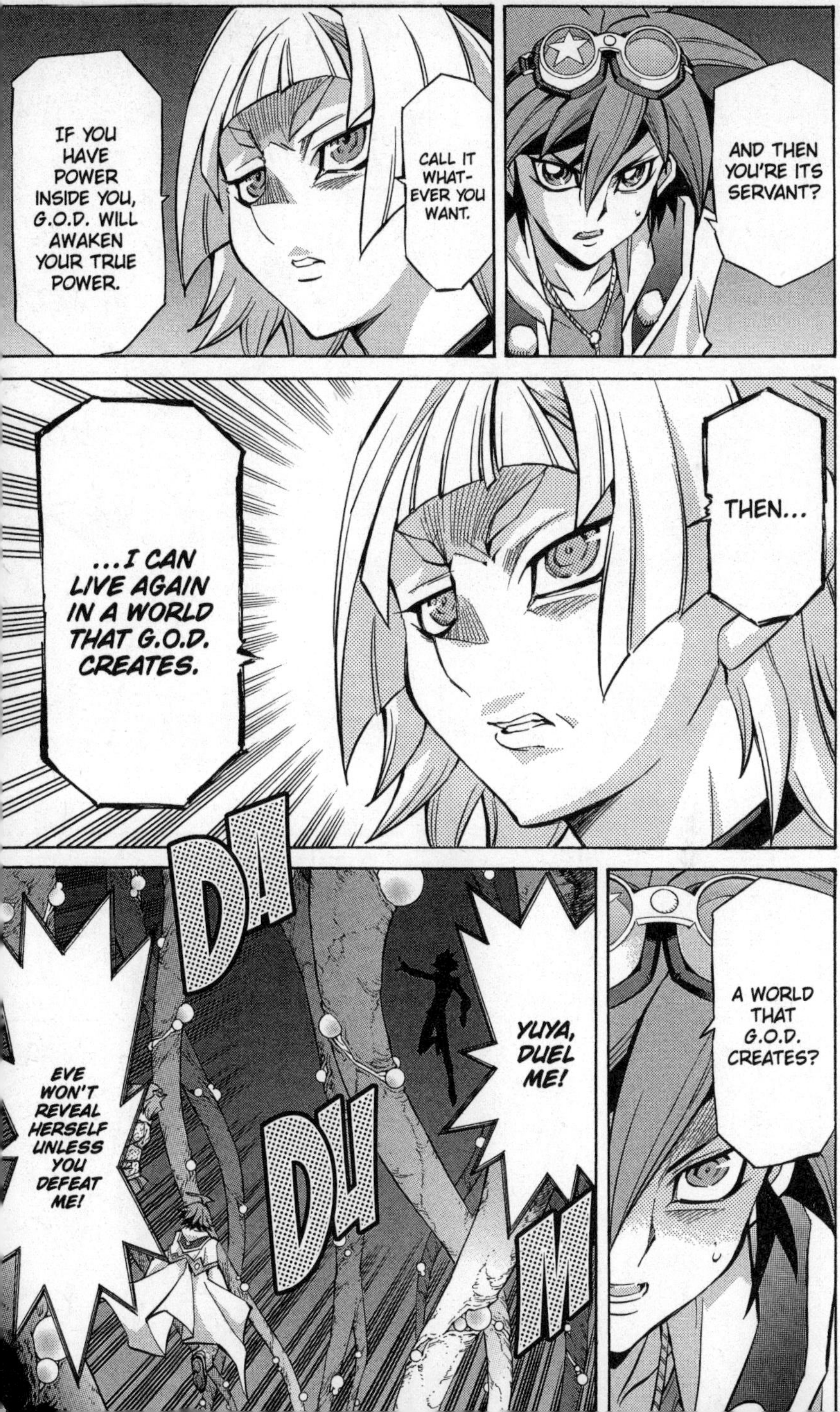

AND THEN YOU'RE ITS SERVANT?
CALL IT WHAT-EVER YOU WANT.
IF YOU HAVE POWER INSIDE YOU, G.O.D. WILL AWAKEN YOUR TRUE POWER.
THEN...
...I CAN LIVE AGAIN IN A WORLD THAT G.O.D. CREATES.
A WORLD THAT G.O.D. CREATES?
DA
YUYA, DUEL ME!
DU
M
EVE WON'T REVEAL HERSELF UNLESS YOU DEFEAT ME!

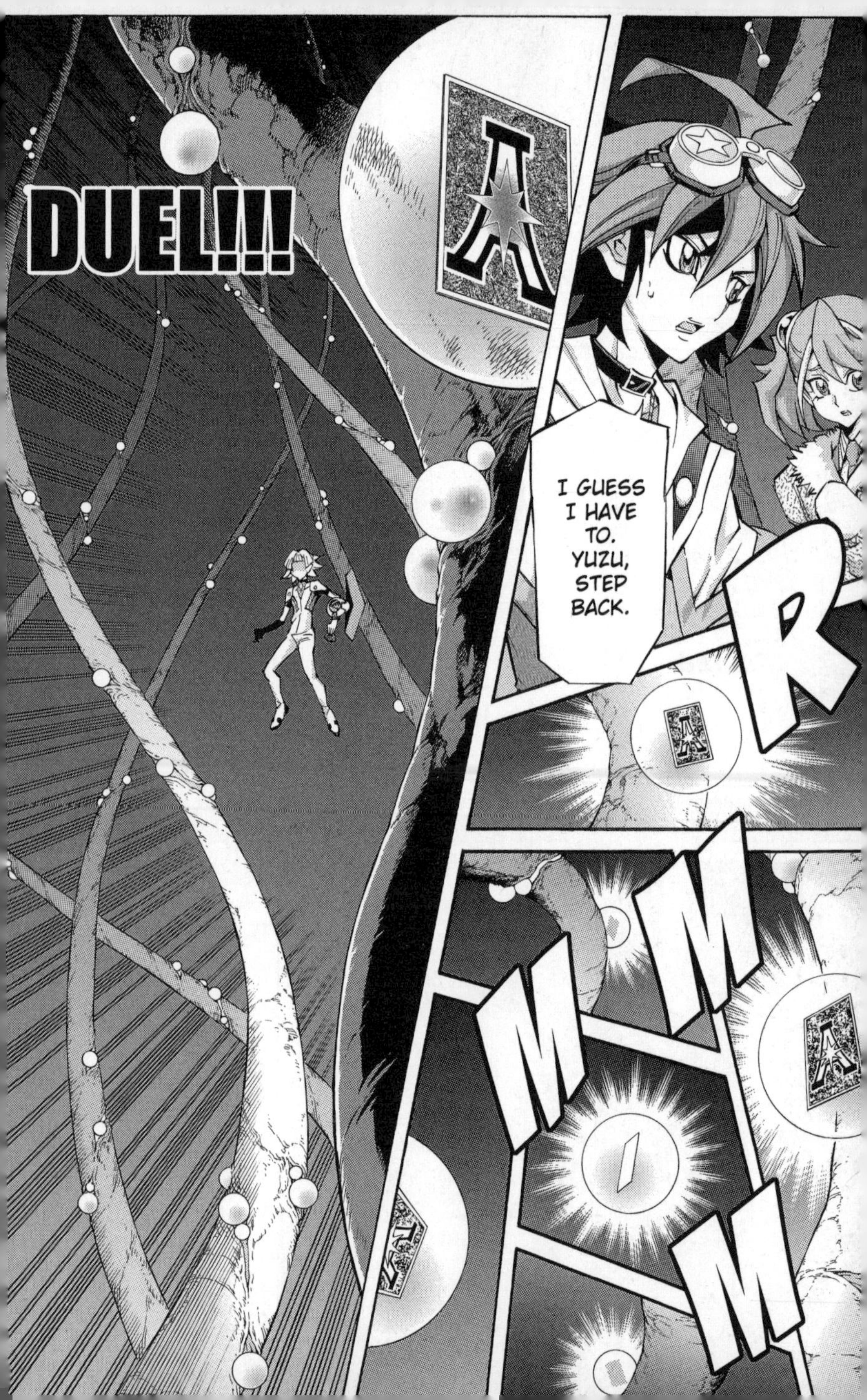
I GUESS I HAVE TO. YUZU, STEP BACK.
RMMMM
DUEL!!!

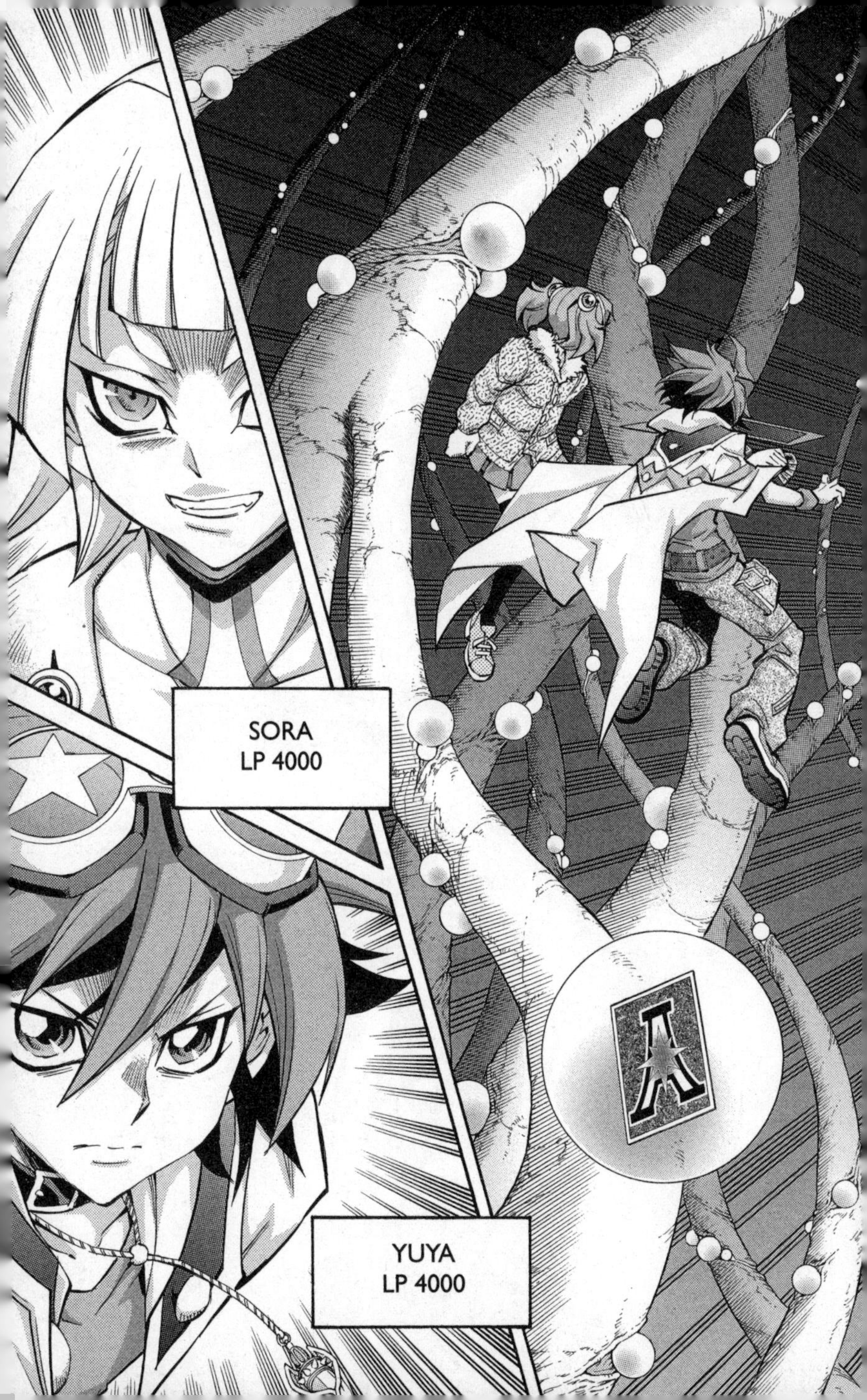
SORA
LP 4000
YUYA
LP 4000

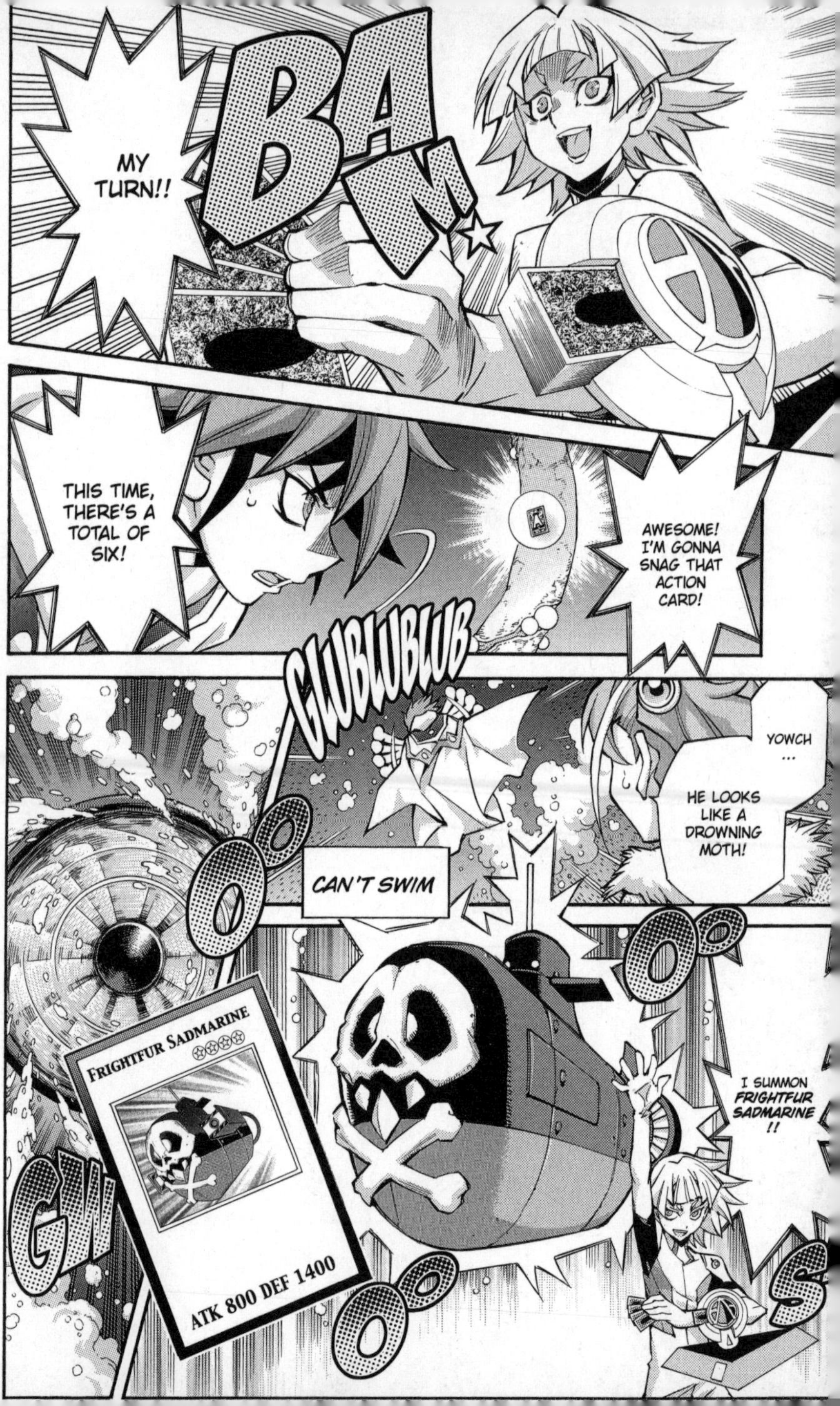
BAM!
MY TURN!!
THIS TIME, THERE'S A TOTAL OF SIX!
AWESOME! I'M GONNA SNAG THAT ACTION CARD!
GLUBLUBLUB
YOWCH ... HE LOOKS LIKE A DROWNING MOTH!
CAN'T SWIM
I SUMMON FRIGHTFUR SADMARINE!!
FRIGHTFUR SADMARINE
ATK 800 DEF 1400
GWOOOOS

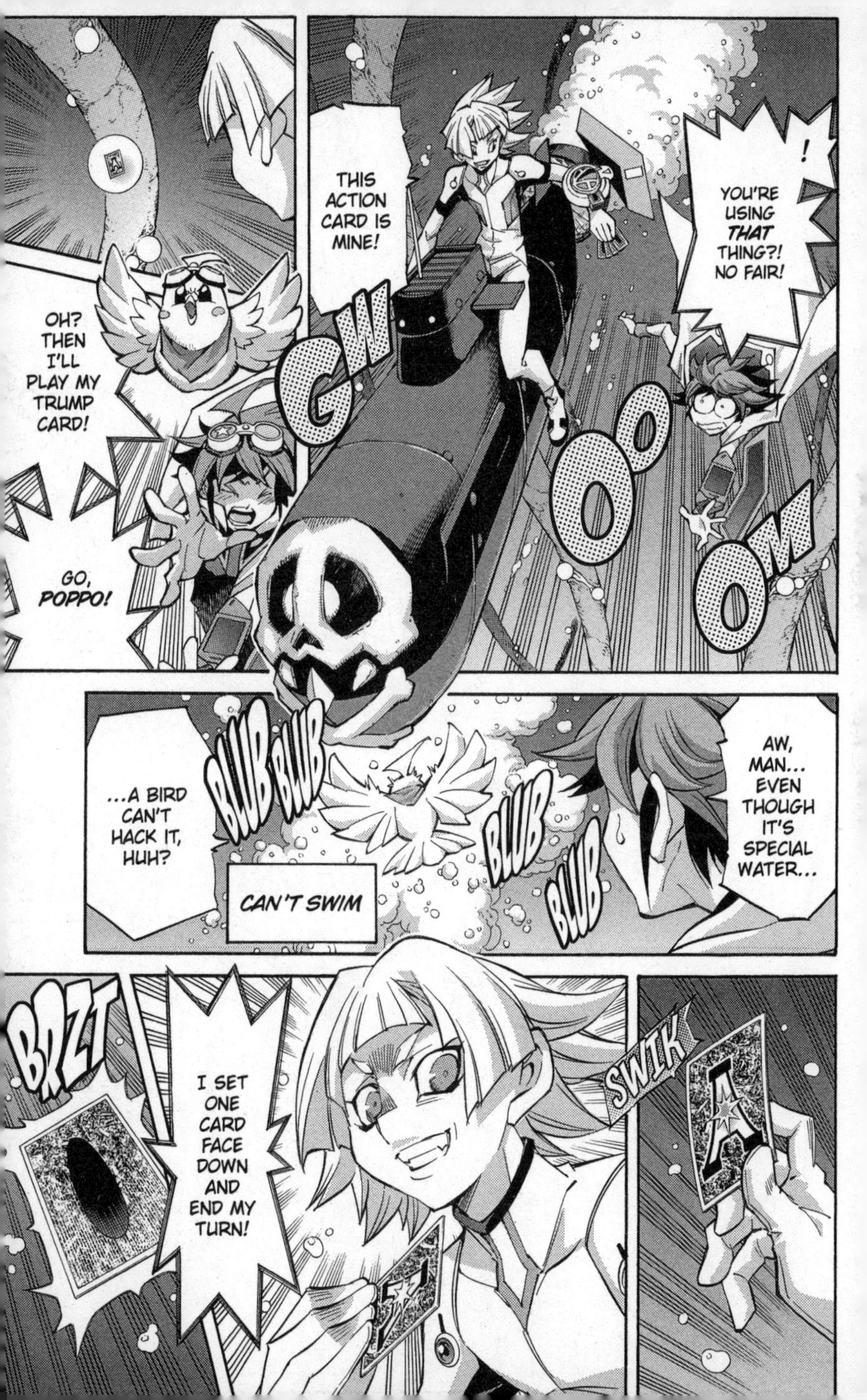
!
YOU'RE USING *THAT* THING?! NO FAIR!
THIS ACTION CARD IS MINE!
GWOOOOM
OH? THEN I'LL PLAY MY TRUMP CARD!
GO, *POPPO!*
AW, MAN... EVEN THOUGH IT'S SPECIAL WATER...
BLUB
BLUB
BLUB BLUB
CAN'T SWIM
...A BIRD CAN'T HACK IT, HUH?
SWIK
I SET ONE CARD FACE DOWN AND END MY TURN!
BRZT

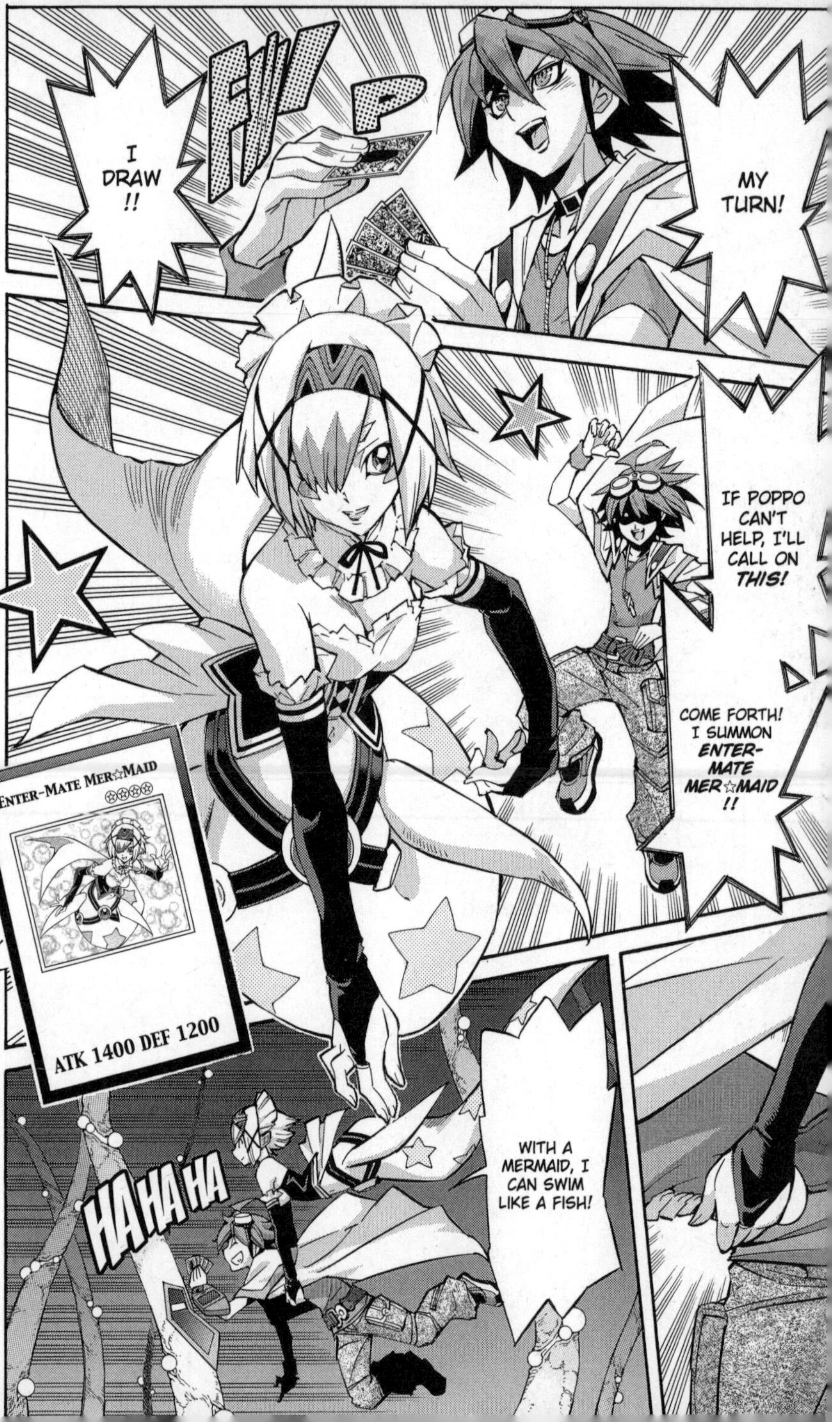
MY TURN!
I DRAW!!
IF POPPO CAN'T HELP, I'LL CALL ON *THIS!*
COME FORTH! I SUMMON *ENTER-MATE MER☆MAID*!!
ENTER-MATE MER☆MAID
ATK 1400 DEF 1200
WITH A MERMAID, I CAN SWIM LIKE A FISH!
HAHAHA

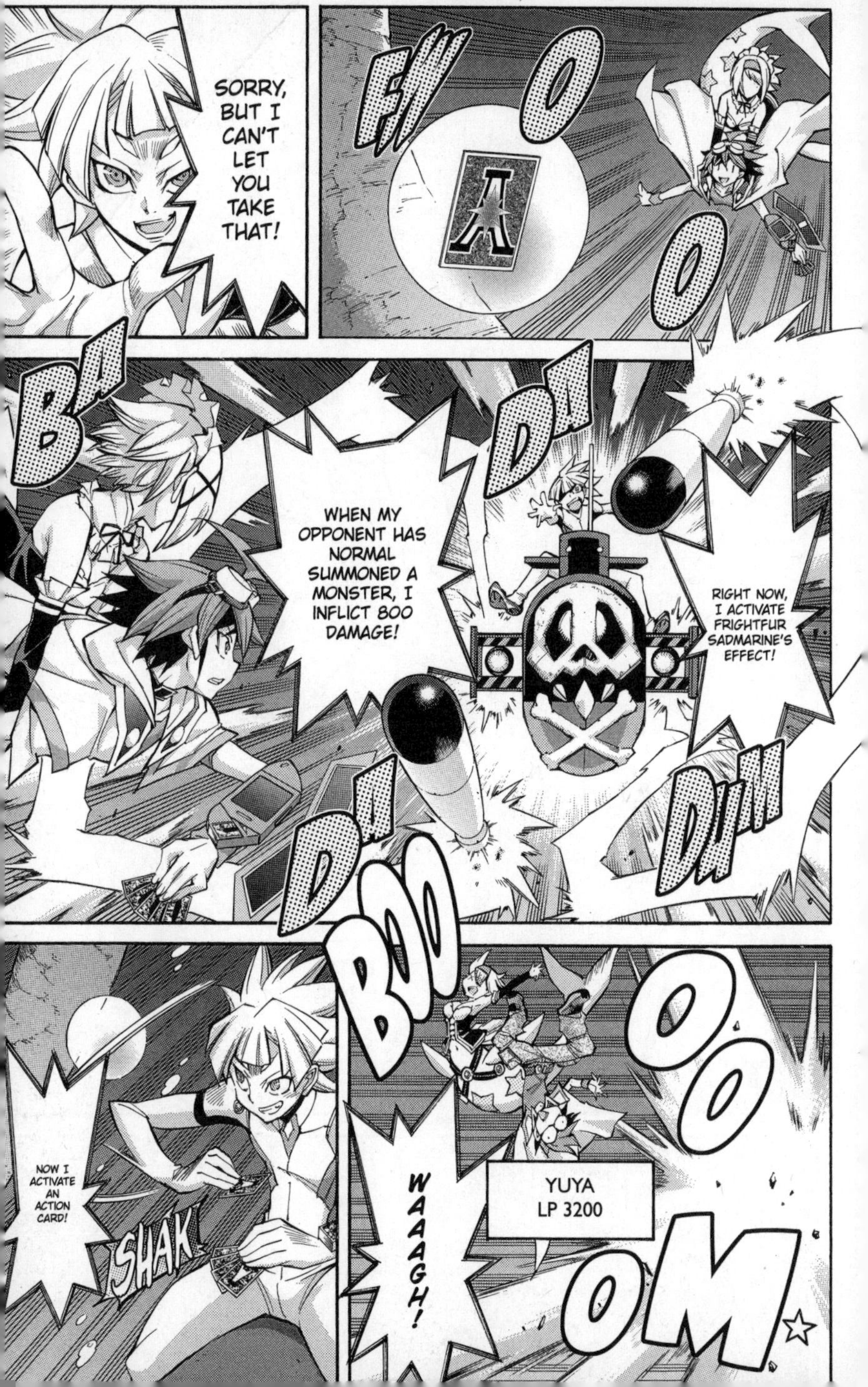
FWOOO
SORRY, BUT I CAN'T LET YOU TAKE THAT!
DA
BA
RIGHT NOW, I ACTIVATE FRIGHTFUR SADMARINE'S EFFECT!
WHEN MY OPPONENT HAS NORMAL SUMMONED A MONSTER, I INFLICT 800 DAMAGE!
DUM
DA
BOOOOOOM
YUYA
LP 3200
WAAAAGH!
NOW I ACTIVATE AN ACTION CARD!
SHAK

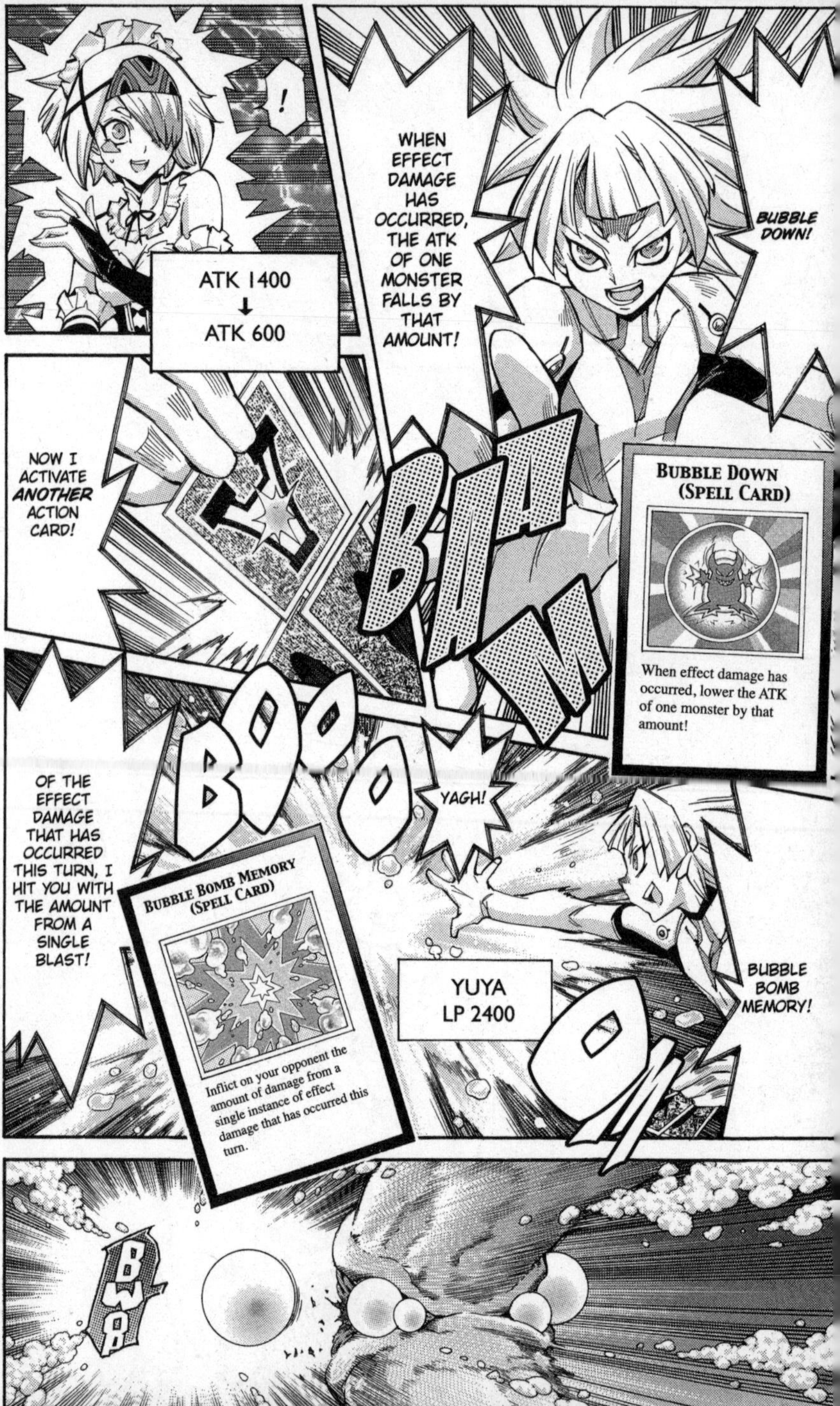
WHEN EFFECT DAMAGE HAS OCCURRED, THE ATK OF ONE MONSTER FALLS BY THAT AMOUNT!
BUBBLE DOWN!
BAM
BUBBLE DOWN (SPELL CARD)
When effect damage has occurred, lower the ATK of one monster by that amount!
!
ATK 1400 → ATK 600
NOW I ACTIVATE ANOTHER ACTION CARD!
BUBBLE BOMB MEMORY!
YAGH!
YUYA LP 2400
BOOOOOM
OF THE EFFECT DAMAGE THAT HAS OCCURRED THIS TURN, I HIT YOU WITH THE AMOUNT FROM A SINGLE BLAST!
BUBBLE BOMB MEMORY (SPELL CARD)
Inflict on your opponent the amount of damage from a single instance of effect damage that has occurred this turn.
BWB

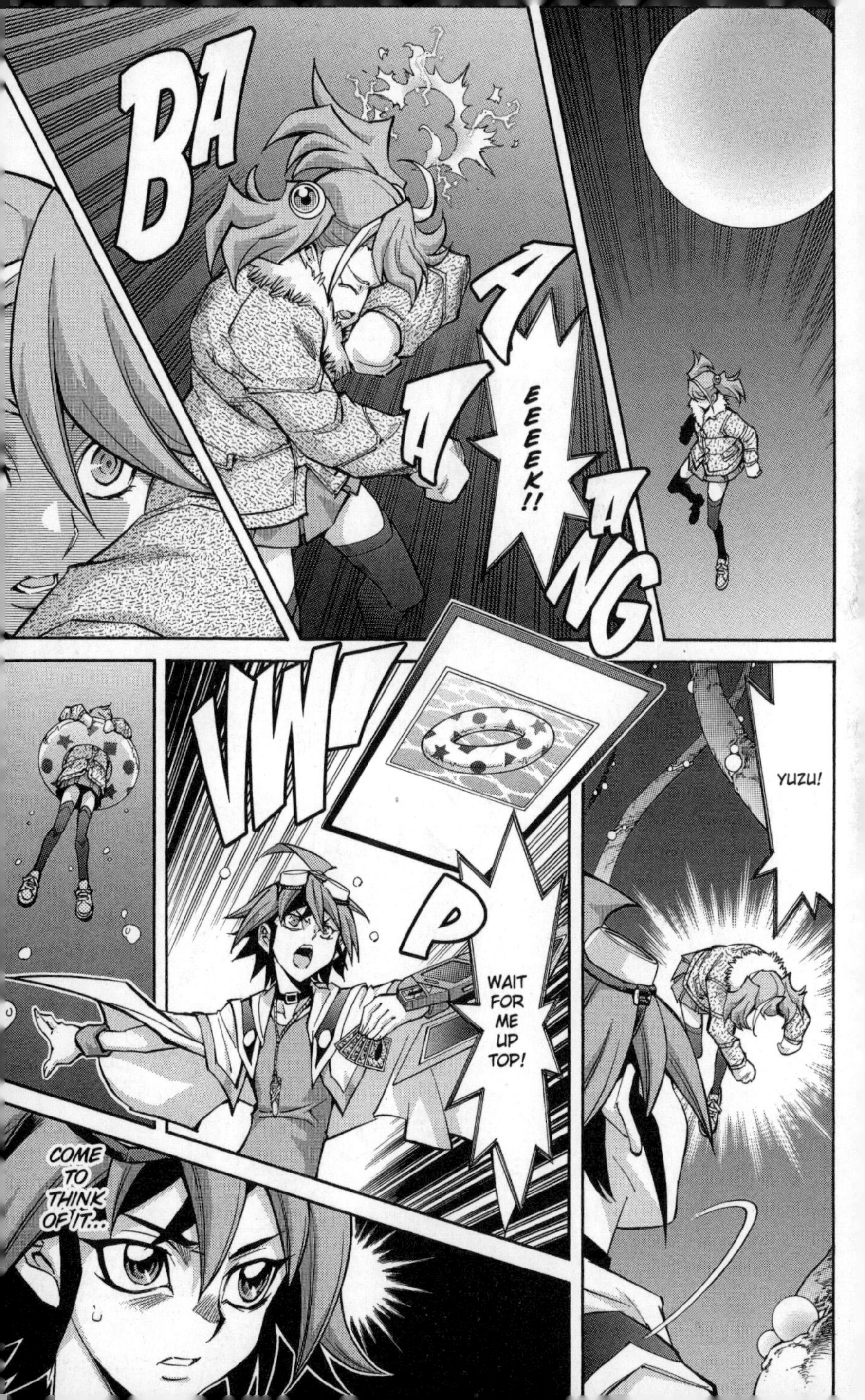
BAAAANG
EEEEK!!
YUZU!
VWP
WAIT FOR ME UP TOP!
COME TO THINK OF IT...

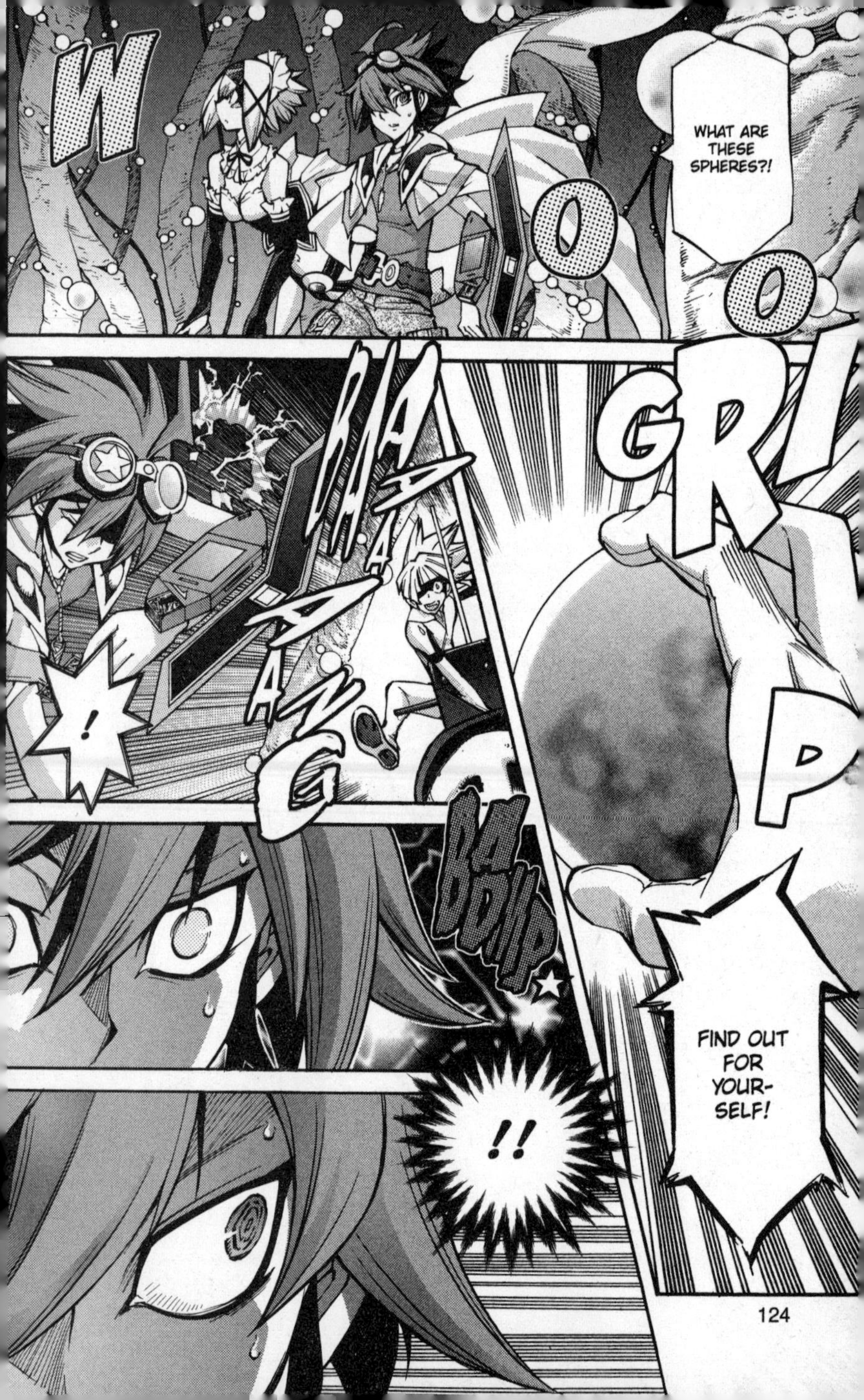
WHAT ARE THESE SPHERES?!
WOO
GRIP
FIND OUT FOR YOUR-SELF!
BAAAAANG
!
BA-BUMP
!!

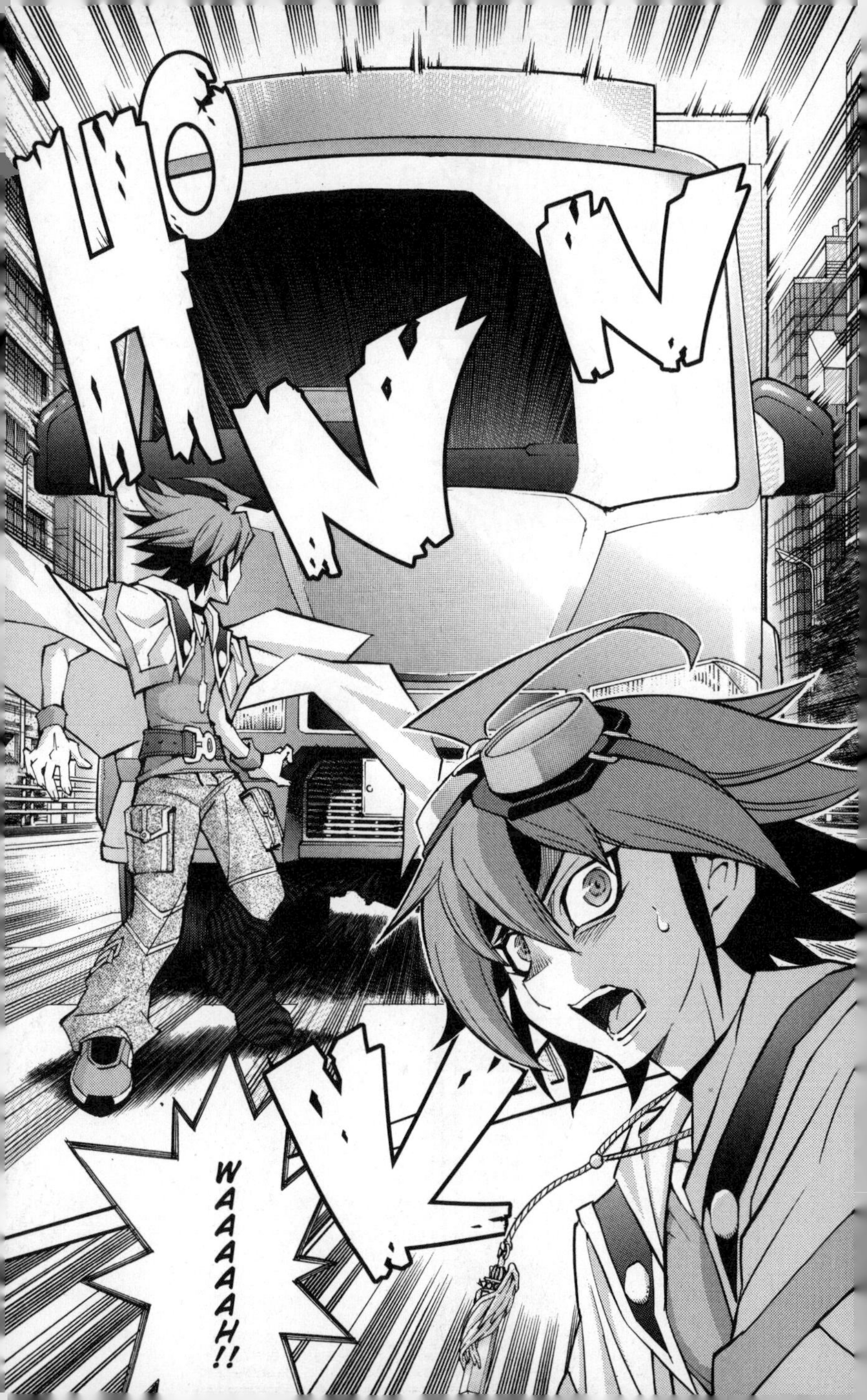
HONNK
WAAAAAAH!!

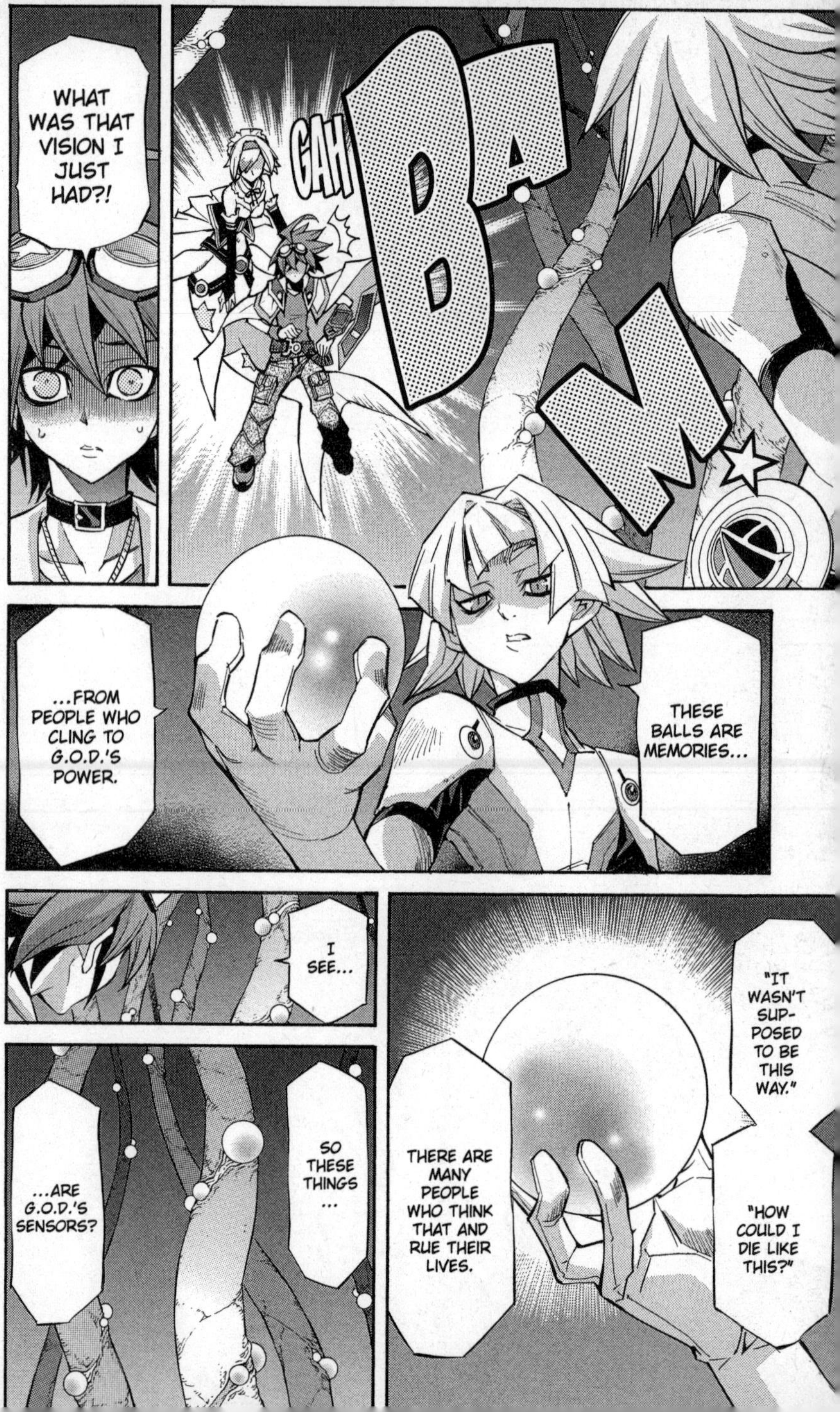
BAM!
GAH
WHAT WAS THAT VISION I JUST HAD?!
THESE BALLS ARE MEMORIES...
...FROM PEOPLE WHO CLING TO G.O.D.'S POWER.
"IT WASN'T SUP-POSED TO BE THIS WAY."
"HOW COULD I DIE LIKE THIS?"
THERE ARE MANY PEOPLE WHO THINK THAT AND RUE THEIR LIVES.
I SEE...
SO THESE THINGS...
...ARE G.O.D.'S SENSORS?

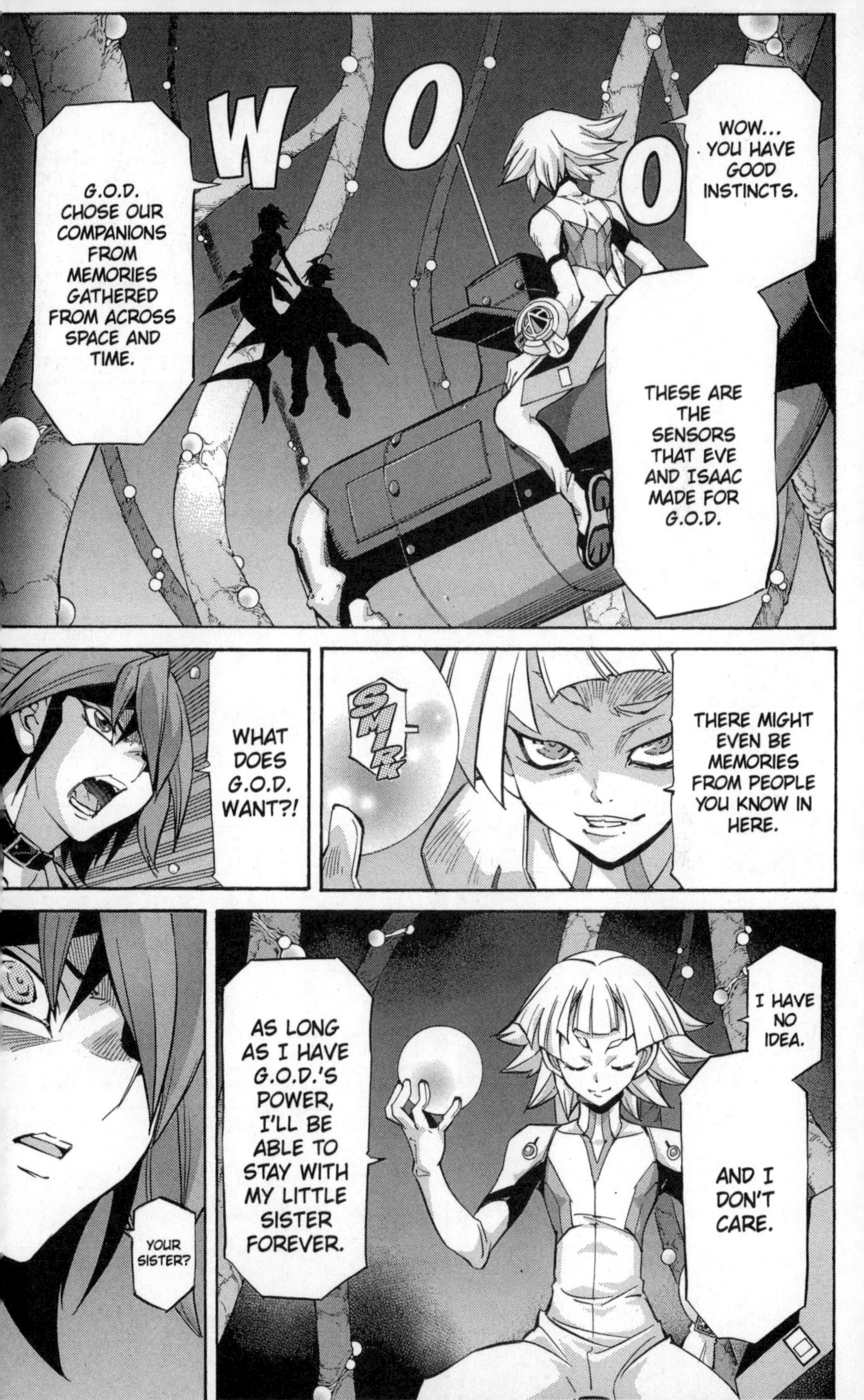
WOW... YOU HAVE GOOD INSTINCTS.
THESE ARE THE SENSORS THAT EVE AND ISAAC MADE FOR G.O.D.
WOO
G.O.D. CHOSE OUR COMPANIONS FROM MEMORIES GATHERED FROM ACROSS SPACE AND TIME.
THERE MIGHT EVEN BE MEMORIES FROM PEOPLE YOU KNOW IN HERE.
SMIRK
WHAT DOES G.O.D. WANT?!
I HAVE NO IDEA.
AND I DON'T CARE.
AS LONG AS I HAVE G.O.D.'S POWER, I'LL BE ABLE TO STAY WITH MY LITTLE SISTER FOREVER.
YOUR SISTER?

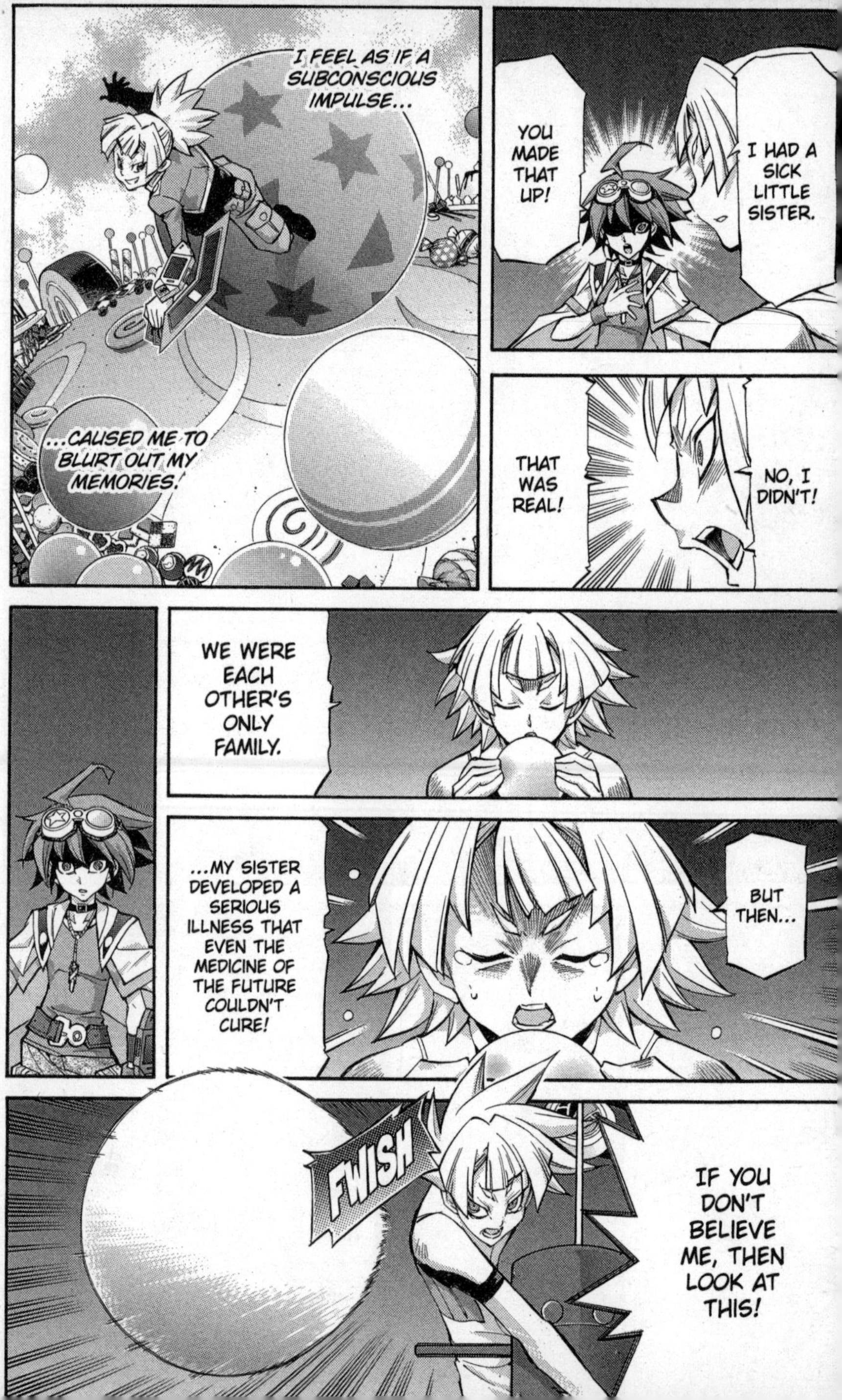
I HAD A SICK LITTLE SISTER.
YOU MADE THAT UP!
NO, I DIDN'T!
THAT WAS REAL!
I FEEL AS IF A SUBCONSCIOUS IMPULSE...
...CAUSED ME TO BLURT OUT MY MEMORIES.
WE WERE EACH OTHER'S ONLY FAMILY.
BUT THEN...
...MY SISTER DEVELOPED A SERIOUS ILLNESS THAT EVEN THE MEDICINE OF THE FUTURE COULDN'T CURE!
IF YOU DON'T BELIEVE ME, THEN LOOK AT THIS!
FWISH

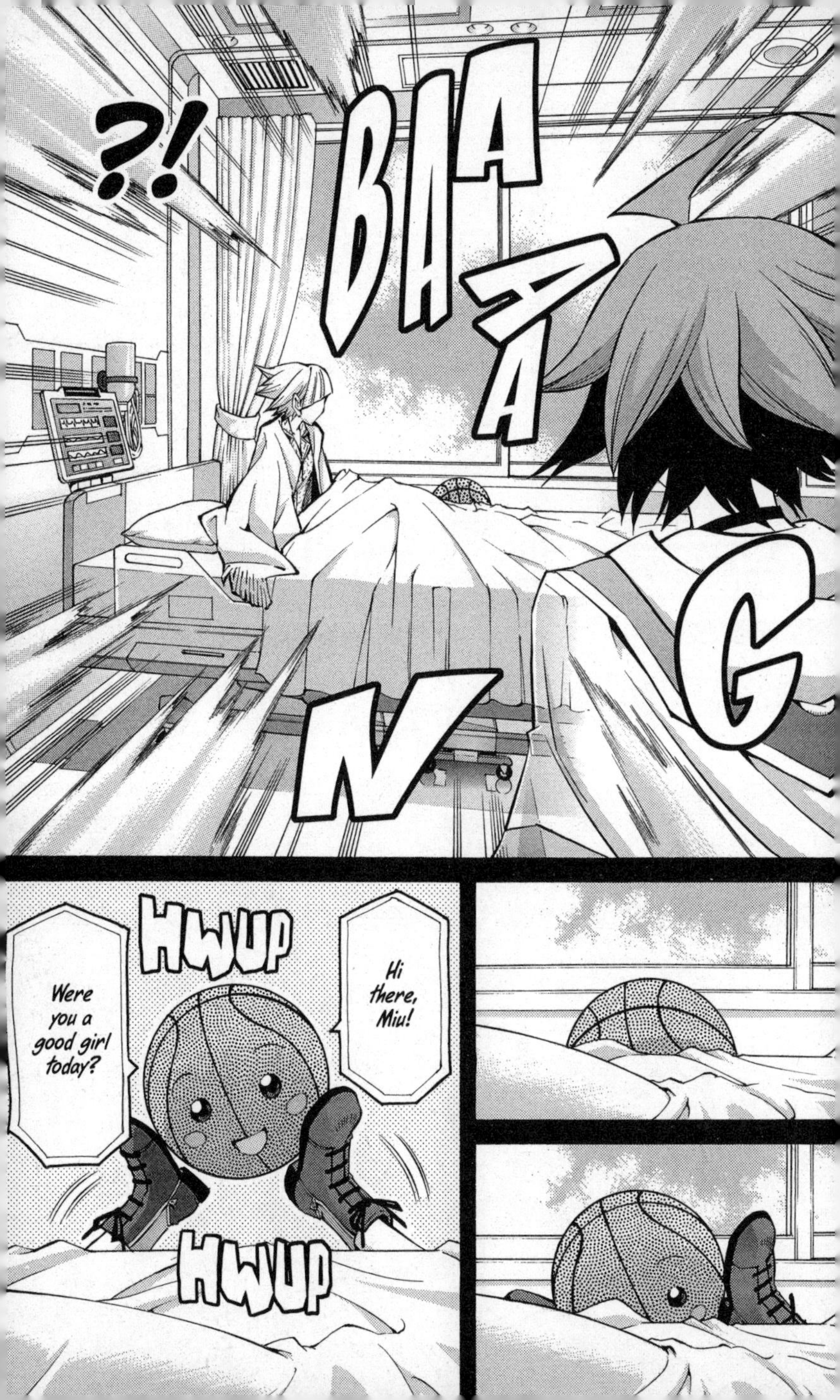
?!
BAAAANG
HWUP
Hi there, Miu!
Were you a good girl today?
HWUP

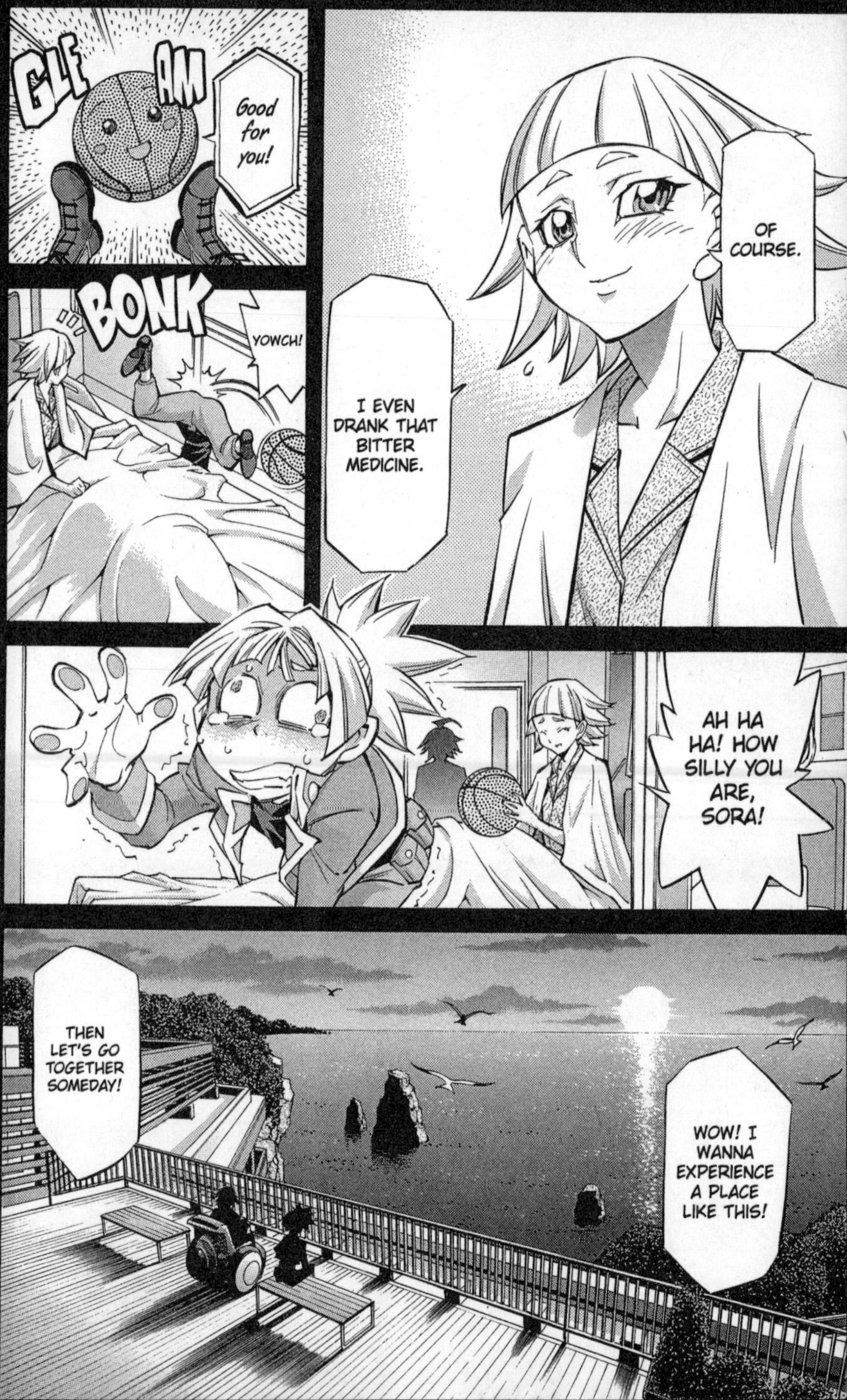

OF COURSE.
I EVEN DRANK THAT BITTER MEDICINE.
GLEAM
Good for you!
BONK
YOWCH!
AH HA HA! HOW SILLY YOU ARE, SORA!
WOW! I WANNA EXPERIENCE A PLACE LIKE THIS!
THEN LET'S GO TOGETHER SOMEDAY!

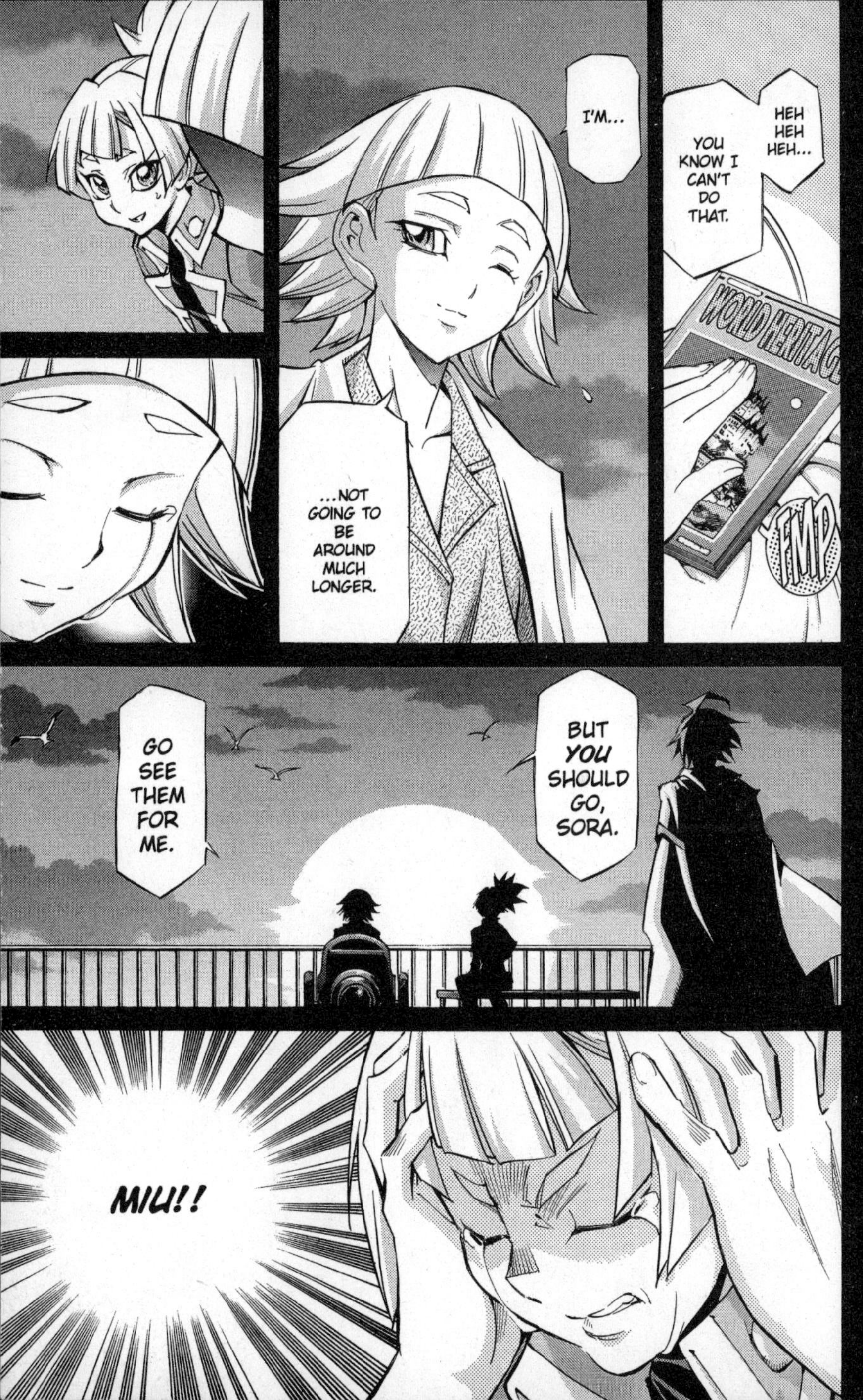
HEH HEH HEH...
YOU KNOW I CAN'T DO THAT.
FMP
I'M...
...NOT GOING TO BE AROUND MUCH LONGER.
BUT *YOU* SHOULD GO, SORA.
GO SEE THEM FOR ME.
MIU!!

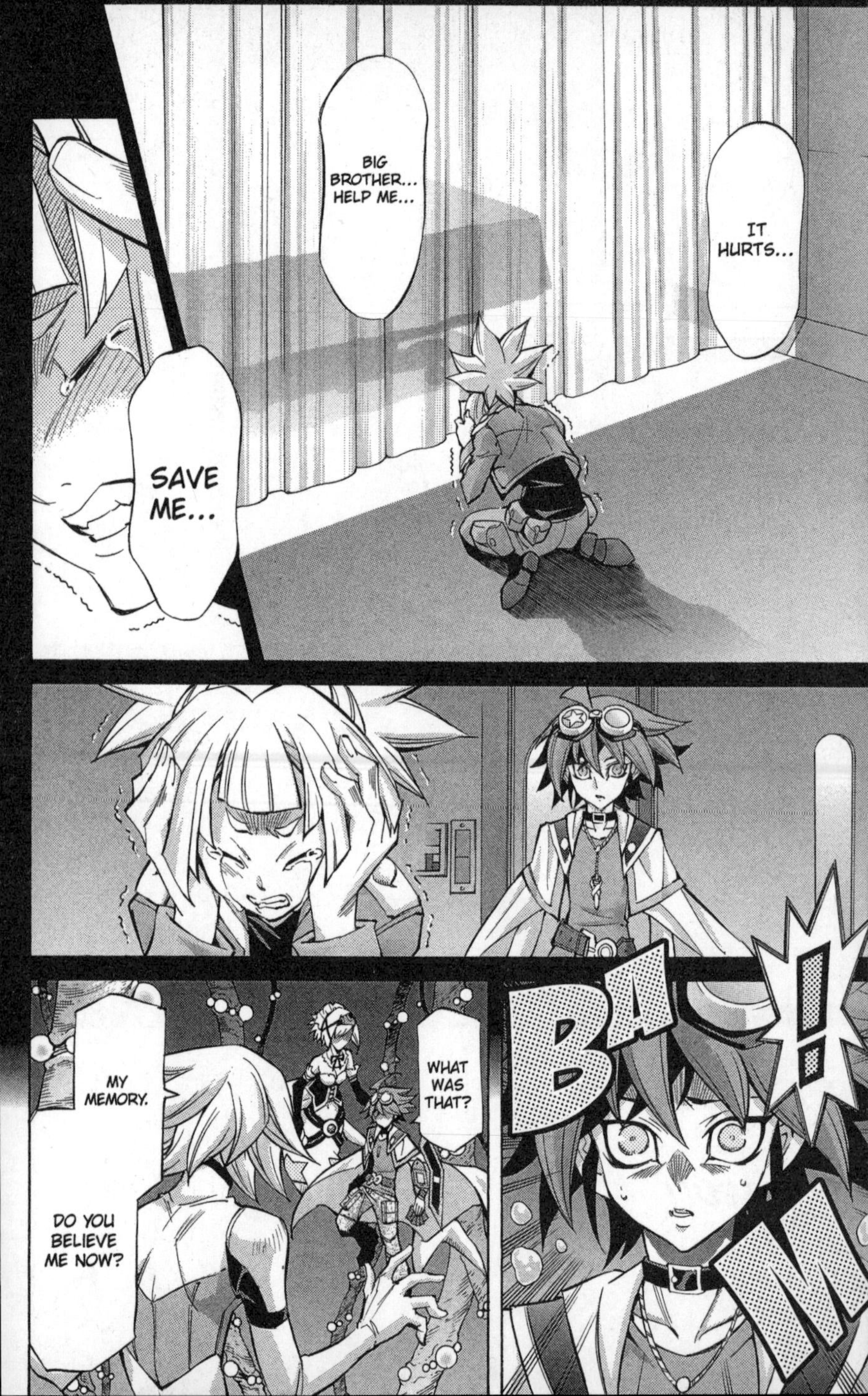
IT HURTS...
BIG BROTHER... HELP ME...
SAVE ME...
BAM!
WHAT WAS THAT?
MY MEMORY.
DO YOU BELIEVE ME NOW?

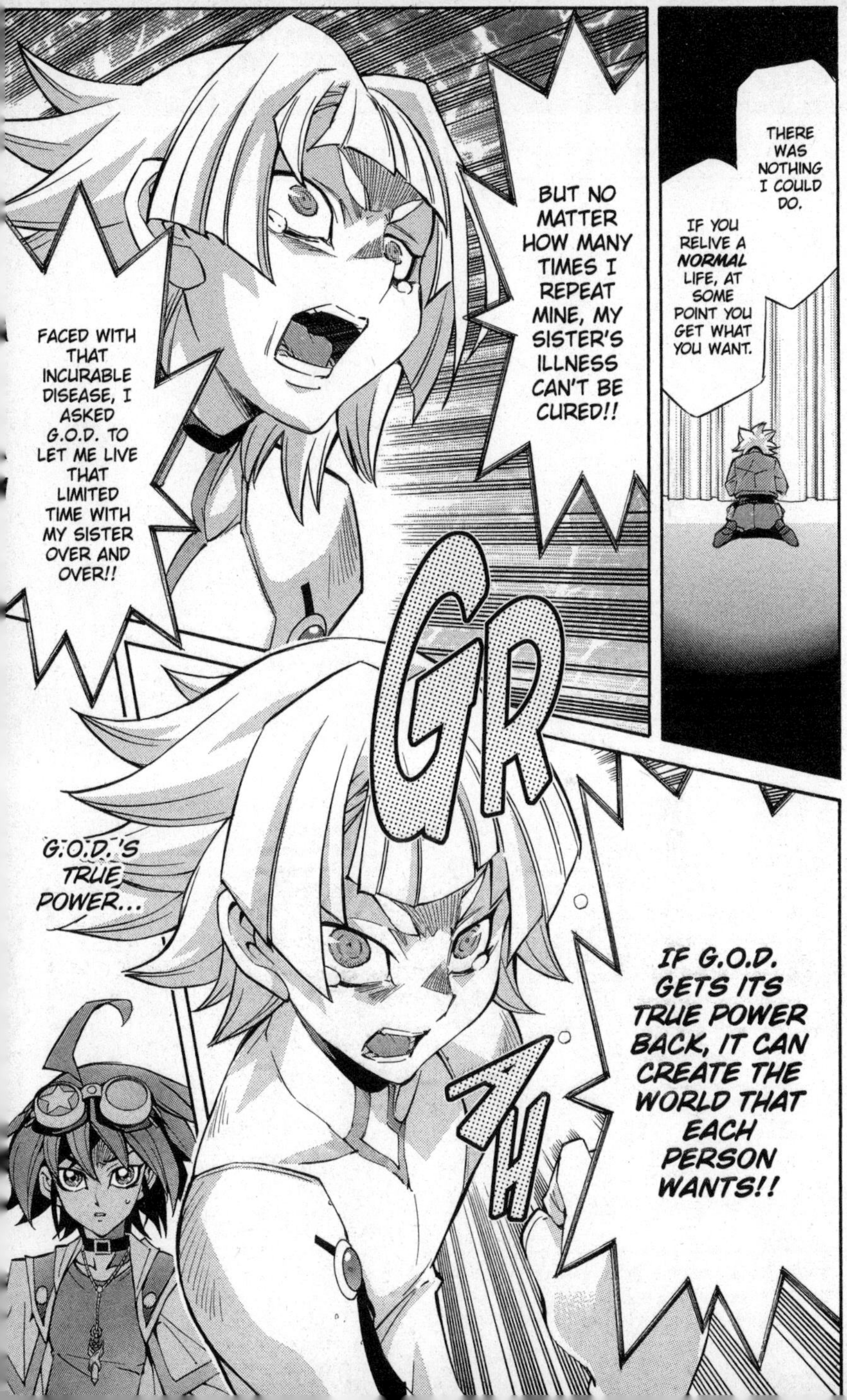
THERE WAS NOTHING I COULD DO.
IF YOU RELIVE A **NORMAL** LIFE, AT SOME POINT YOU GET WHAT YOU WANT.
BUT NO MATTER HOW MANY TIMES I REPEAT MINE, MY SISTER'S ILLNESS CAN'T BE CURED!!
FACED WITH THAT INCURABLE DISEASE, I ASKED G.O.D. TO LET ME LIVE THAT LIMITED TIME WITH MY SISTER OVER AND OVER!!
GRAH
IF G.O.D. GETS ITS TRUE POWER BACK, IT CAN CREATE THE WORLD THAT EACH PERSON WANTS!!
G.O.D.'S TRUE POWER...

STARVING VENEMY LETHAL DOSE DRAGON

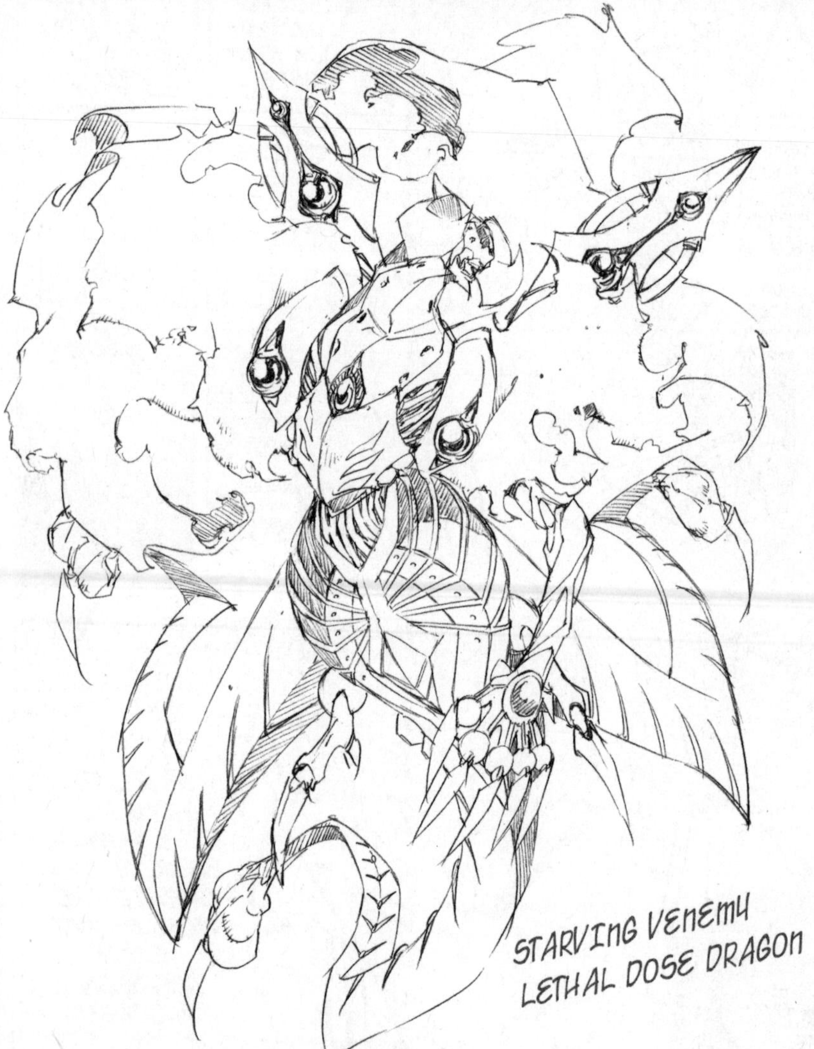
STARVING VENEMY
LETHAL DOSE DRAGON

Yuri's ultimate dragon gives his opponents lethal doses of venom! The poison capsules on its tail and its spreading, plant like wings beckon the enemy to death!

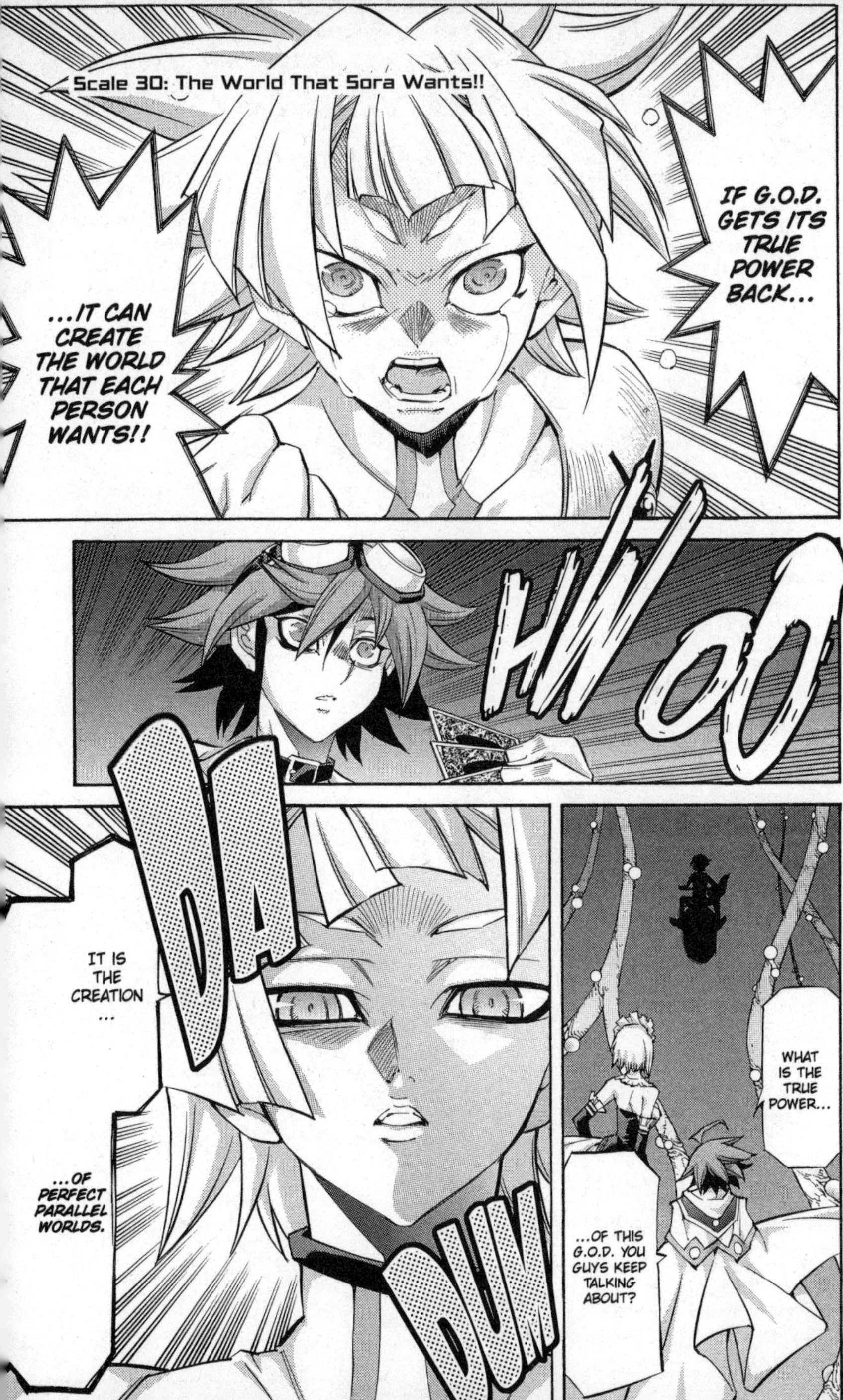
Scale 30: The World That Sora Wants!!
IF G.O.D. GETS ITS TRUE POWER BACK...
...IT CAN CREATE THE WORLD THAT EACH PERSON WANTS!!
HWOO
WHAT IS THE TRUE POWER...
...OF THIS G.O.D. YOU GUYS KEEP TALKING ABOUT?
DA
DUM
IT IS THE CREATION...
...OF PERFECT PARALLEL WORLDS.

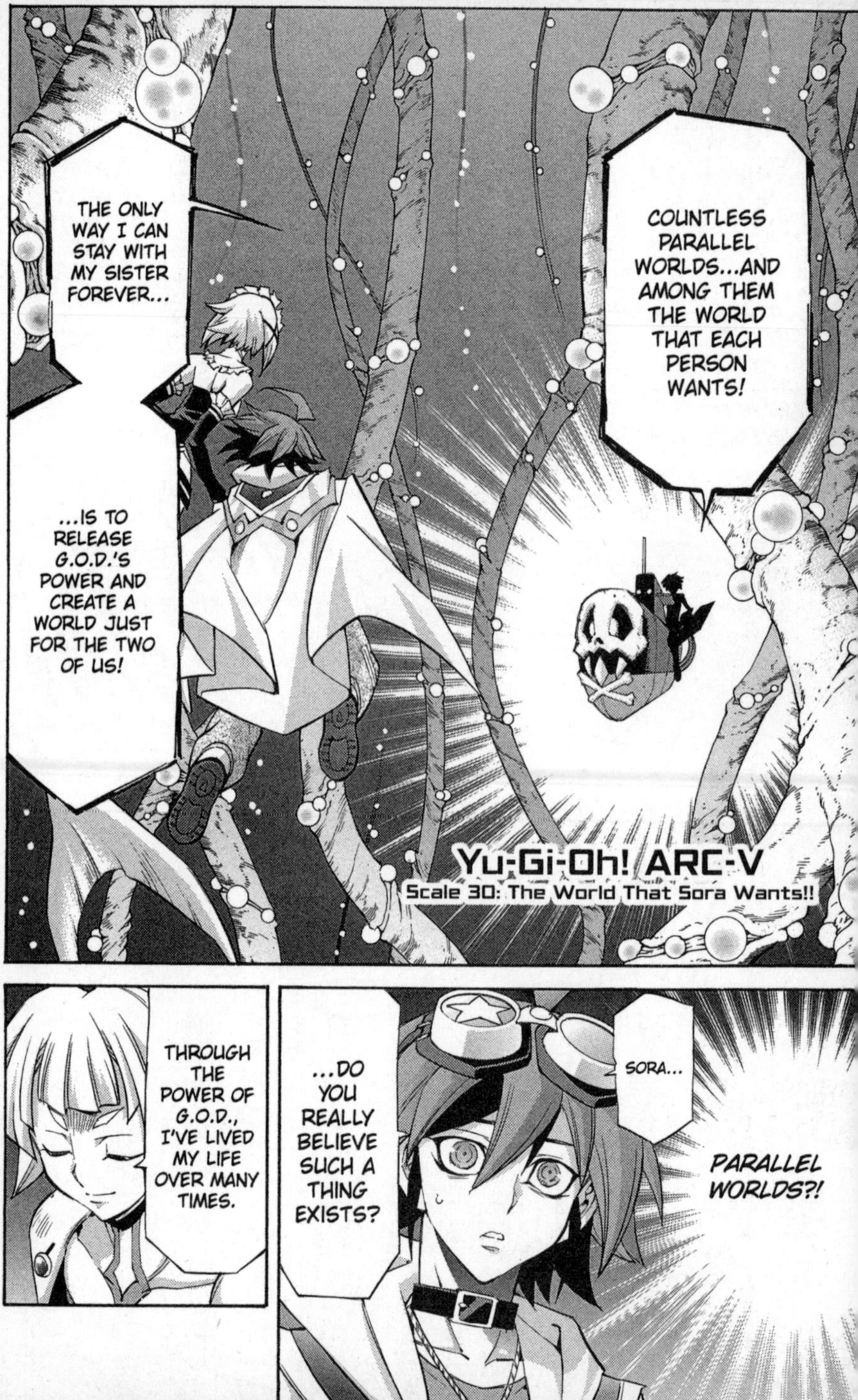
COUNTLESS PARALLEL WORLDS...AND AMONG THEM THE WORLD THAT EACH PERSON WANTS!
THE ONLY WAY I CAN STAY WITH MY SISTER FOREVER...
...IS TO RELEASE G.O.D.'S POWER AND CREATE A WORLD JUST FOR THE TWO OF US!
Yu-Gi-Oh! ARC-V
Scale 30: The World That Sora Wants!!
SORA...
PARALLEL WORLDS?!
...DO YOU REALLY BELIEVE SUCH A THING EXISTS?
THROUGH THE POWER OF G.O.D., I'VE LIVED MY LIFE OVER MANY TIMES.

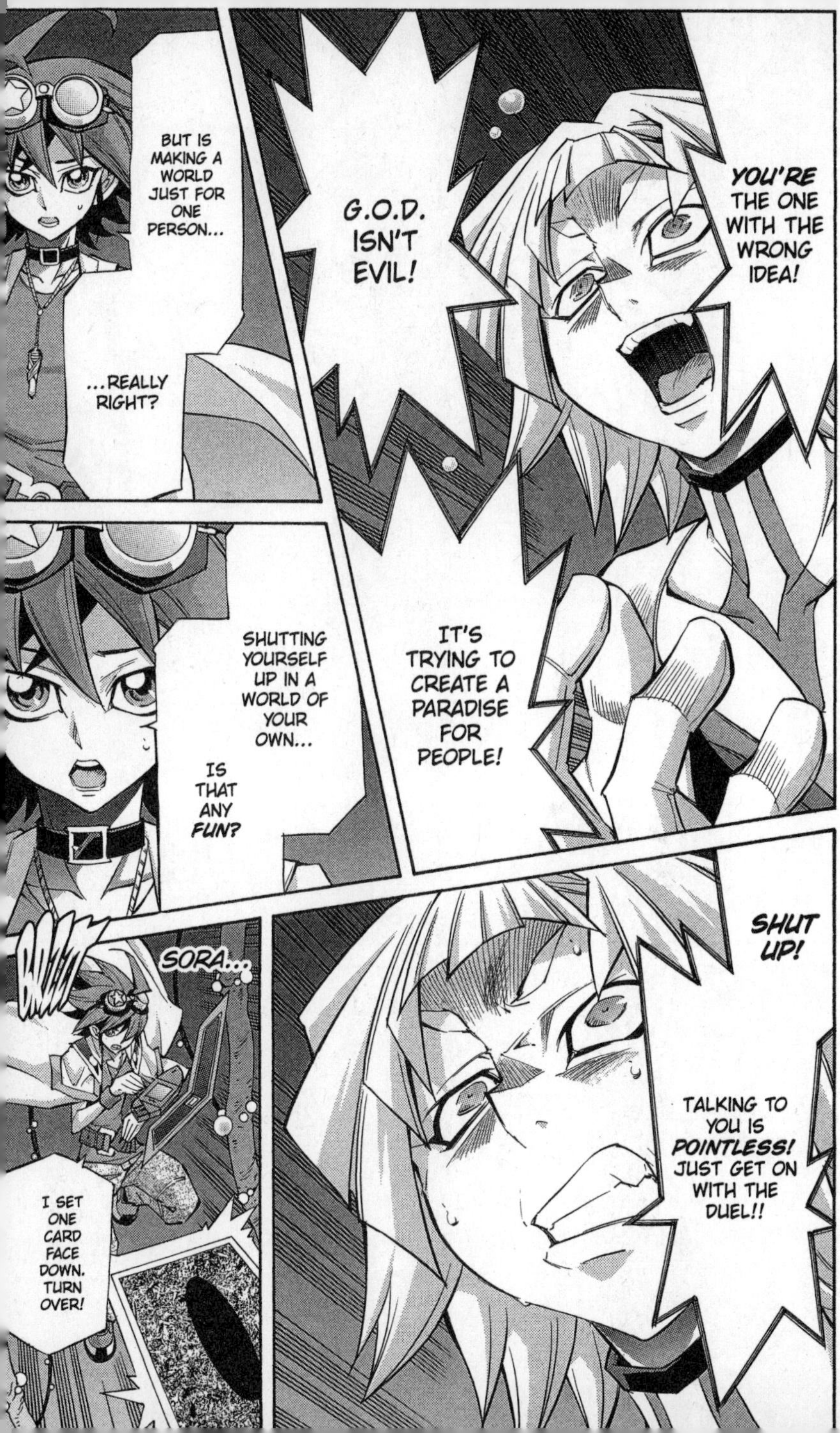
YOU'RE THE ONE WITH THE WRONG IDEA!
G.O.D. ISN'T EVIL!
IT'S TRYING TO CREATE A PARADISE FOR PEOPLE!
BUT IS MAKING A WORLD JUST FOR ONE PERSON...
...REALLY RIGHT?
SHUTTING YOURSELF UP IN A WORLD OF YOUR OWN...
IS THAT ANY FUN?
SHUT UP!
TALKING TO YOU IS POINTLESS! JUST GET ON WITH THE DUEL!!
SORA...
I SET ONE CARD FACE DOWN. TURN OVER!

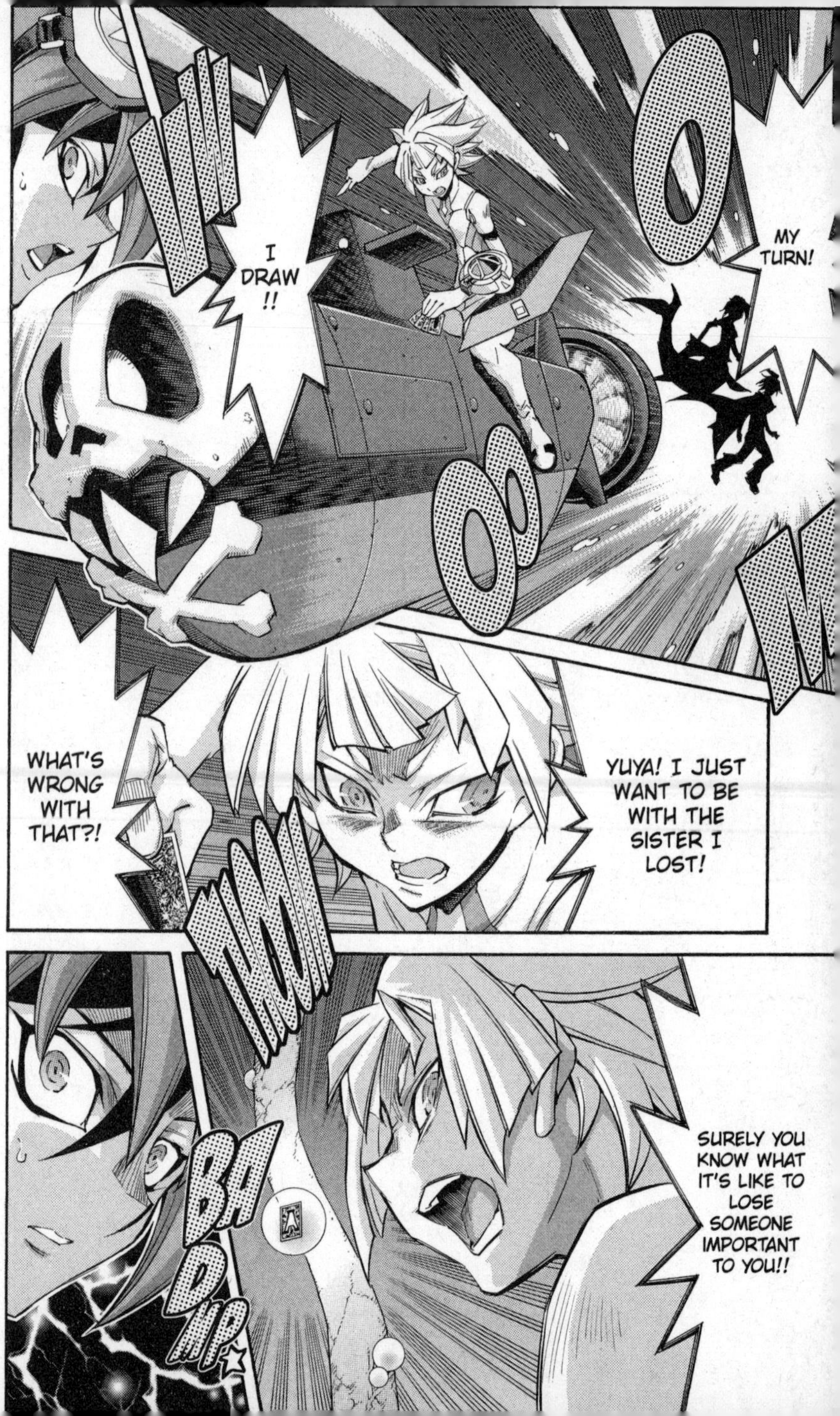
MY TURN!
I DRAW!!
YUYA! I JUST WANT TO BE WITH THE SISTER I LOST!
WHAT'S WRONG WITH THAT?!
SURELY YOU KNOW WHAT IT'S LIKE TO LOSE SOMEONE IMPORTANT TO YOU!!
BA DMP

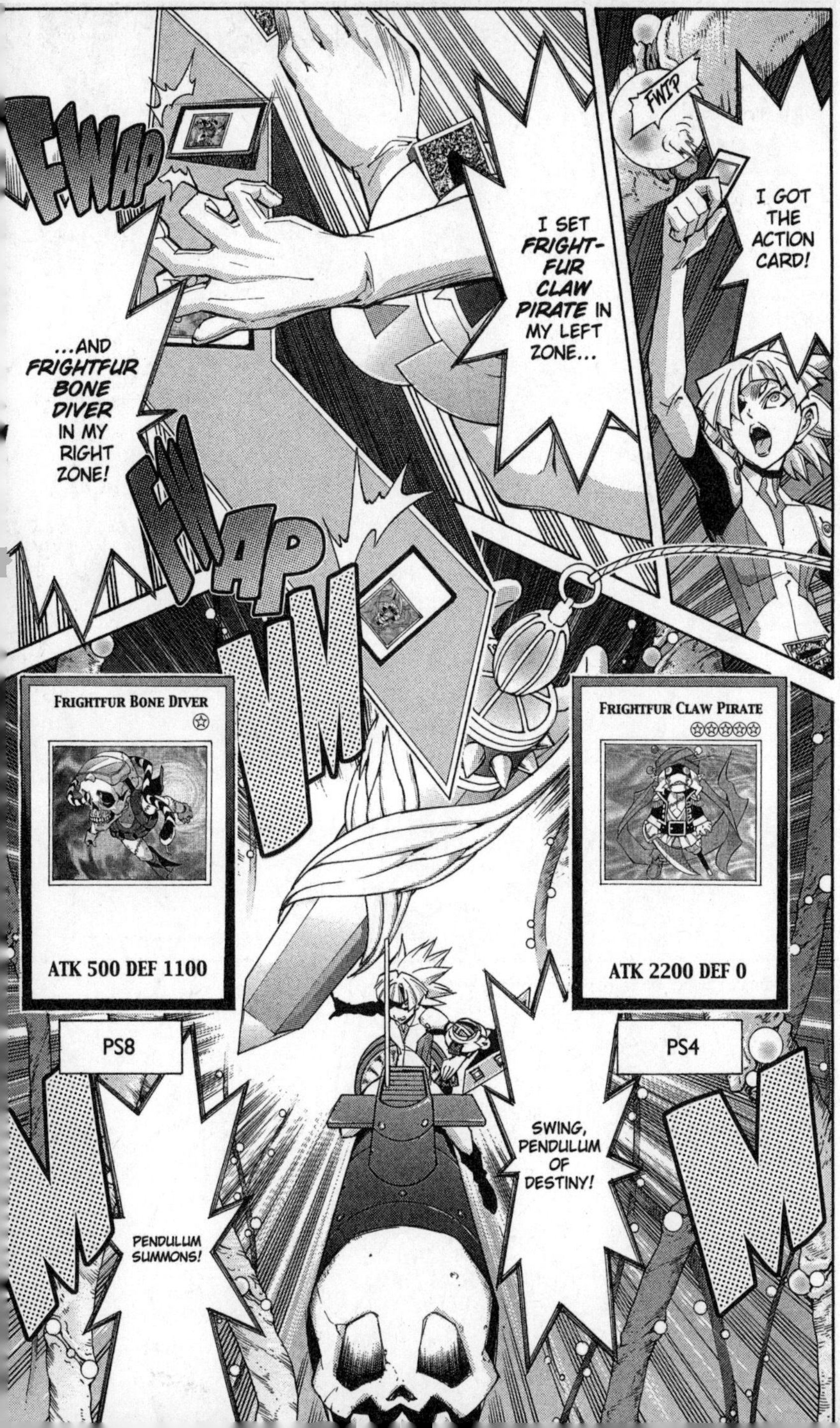
FWIP
I GOT THE ACTION CARD!
FWAP
I SET FRIGHTFUR CLAW PIRATE IN MY LEFT ZONE...
...AND FRIGHTFUR BONE DIVER IN MY RIGHT ZONE!
FWAP
FRIGHTFUR CLAW PIRATE
ATK 2200 DEF 0
PS4
FRIGHTFUR BONE DIVER
ATK 500 DEF 1100
PS8
SWING, PENDULUM OF DESTINY!
PENDULUM SUMMONS!

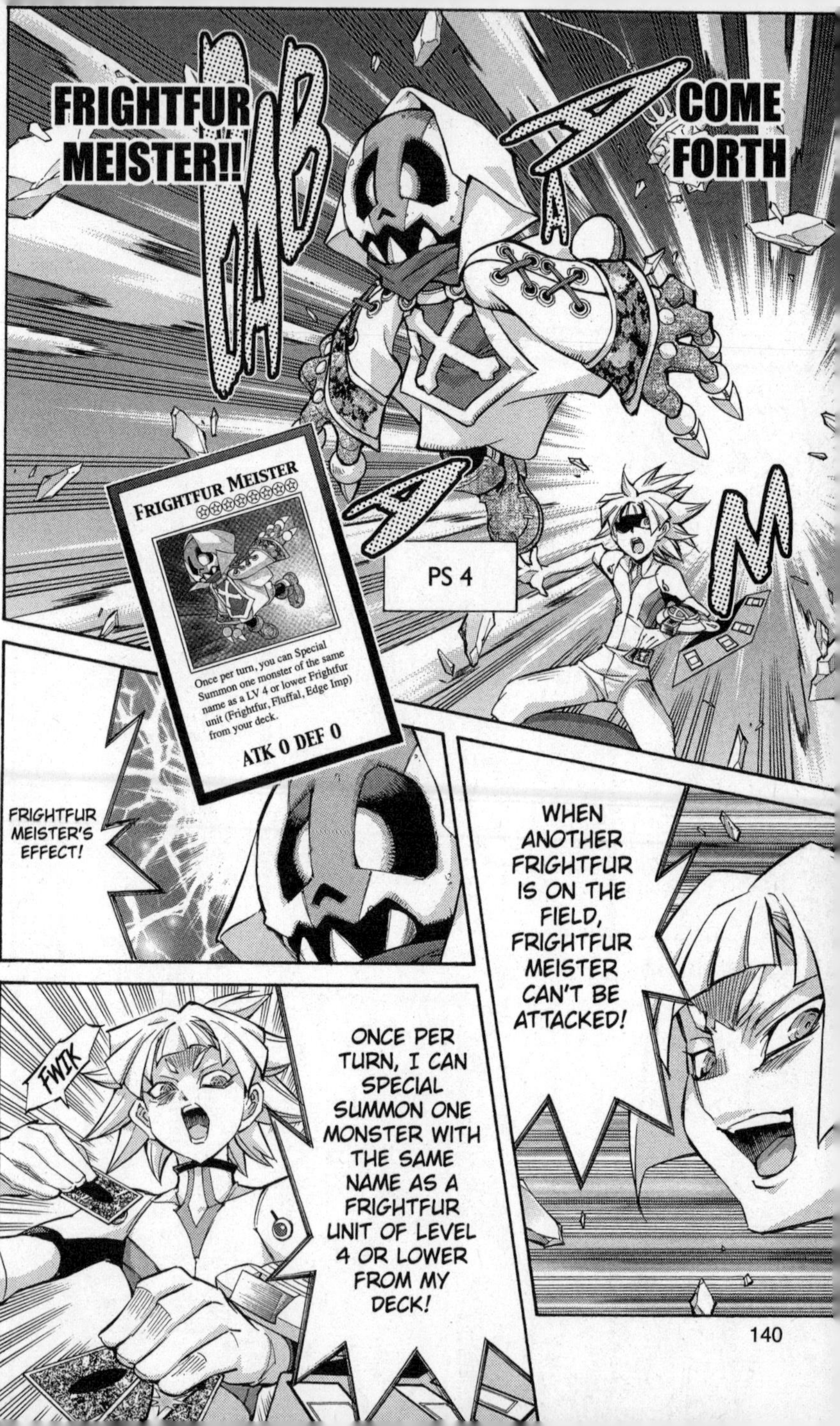
COME FORTH
FRIGHTFUR MEISTER!!
DABAAM
PS 4
FRIGHTFUR MEISTER
Once per turn, you can Special Summon one monster of the same name as a LV 4 or lower Frightfur unit (Frightfur, Fluffal, Edge Imp) from your deck.
ATK 0 DEF 0
WHEN ANOTHER FRIGHTFUR IS ON THE FIELD, FRIGHTFUR MEISTER CAN'T BE ATTACKED!
FRIGHTFUR MEISTER'S EFFECT!
ONCE PER TURN, I CAN SPECIAL SUMMON ONE MONSTER WITH THE SAME NAME AS A FRIGHTFUR UNIT OF LEVEL 4 OR LOWER FROM MY DECK!
FWIK

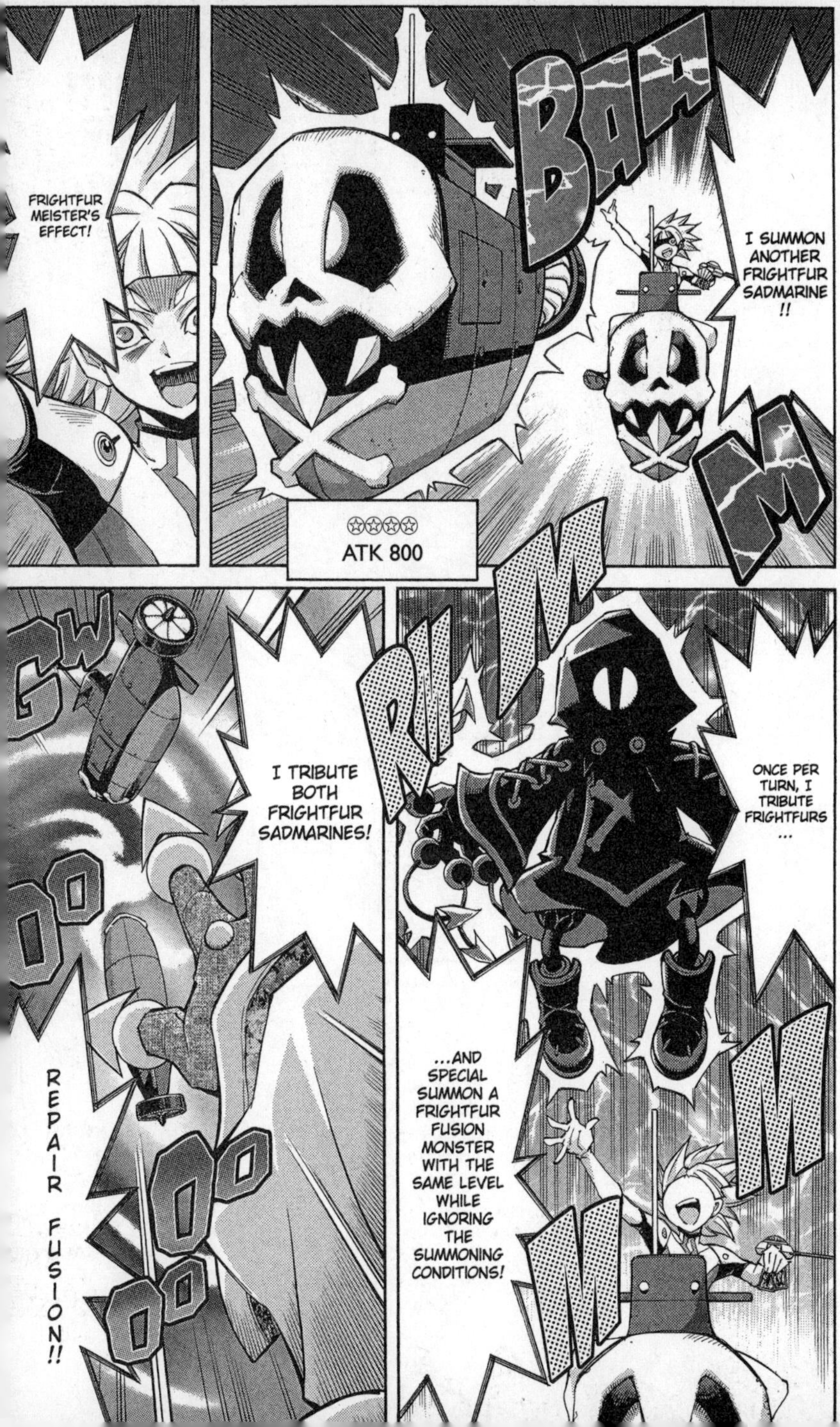
BAAM
I SUMMON ANOTHER FRIGHTFUR SADMARINE!!
ATK 800
FRIGHTFUR MEISTER'S EFFECT!
ONCE PER TURN, I TRIBUTE FRIGHTFURS...
RMMM
...AND SPECIAL SUMMON A FRIGHTFUR FUSION MONSTER WITH THE SAME LEVEL WHILE IGNORING THE SUMMONING CONDITIONS!
MMM
I TRIBUTE BOTH FRIGHTFUR SADMARINES!
GWOOO
REPAIR FUSION!!

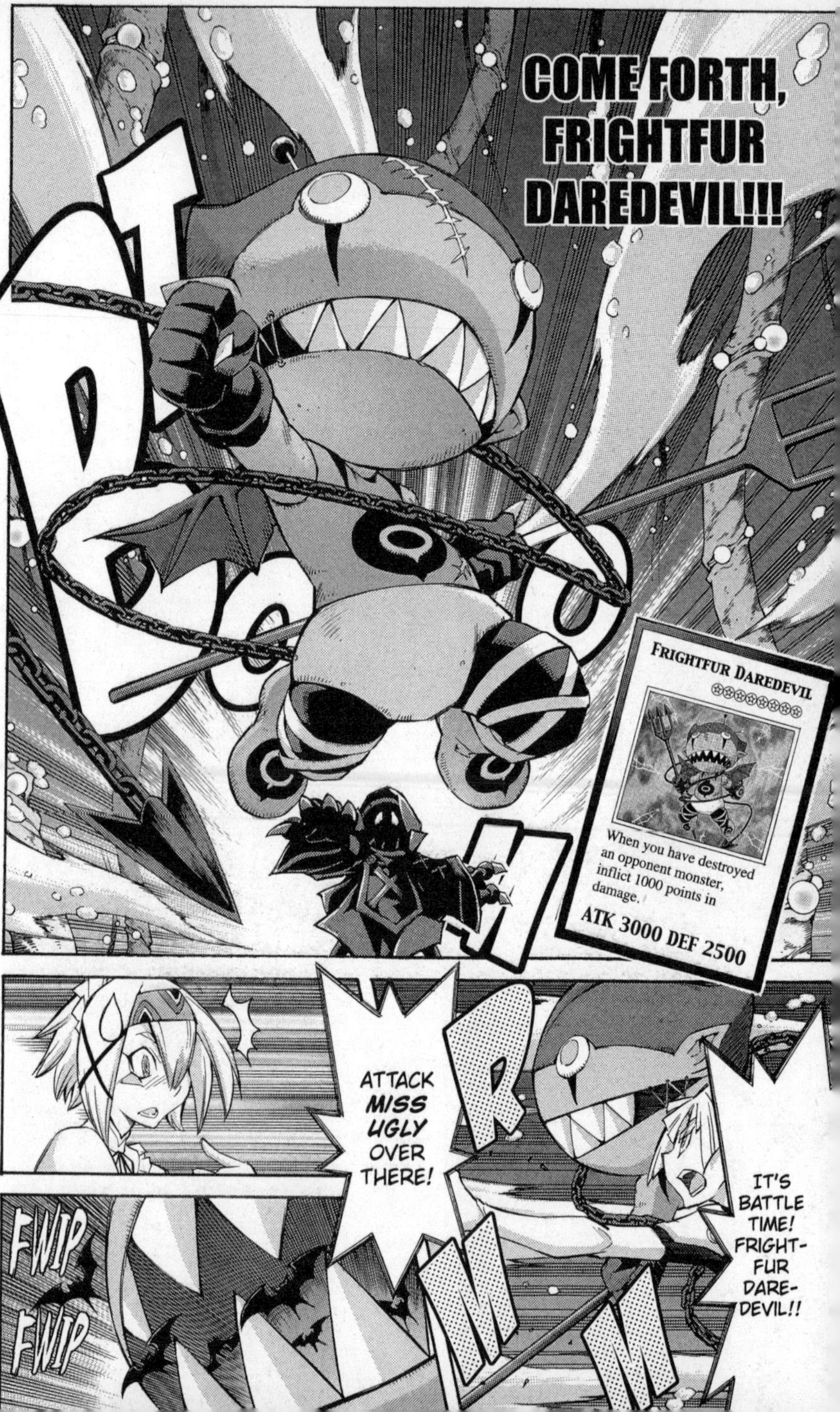
COME FORTH, FRIGHTFUR DAREDEVIL!!!
FRIGHTFUR DAREDEVIL
When you have destroyed an opponent monster, inflict 1000 points in damage.
ATK 3000 DEF 2500
IT'S BATTLE TIME! FRIGHT-FUR DARE-DEVIL!!
ATTACK MISS UGLY OVER THERE!
FWIP
FWIP

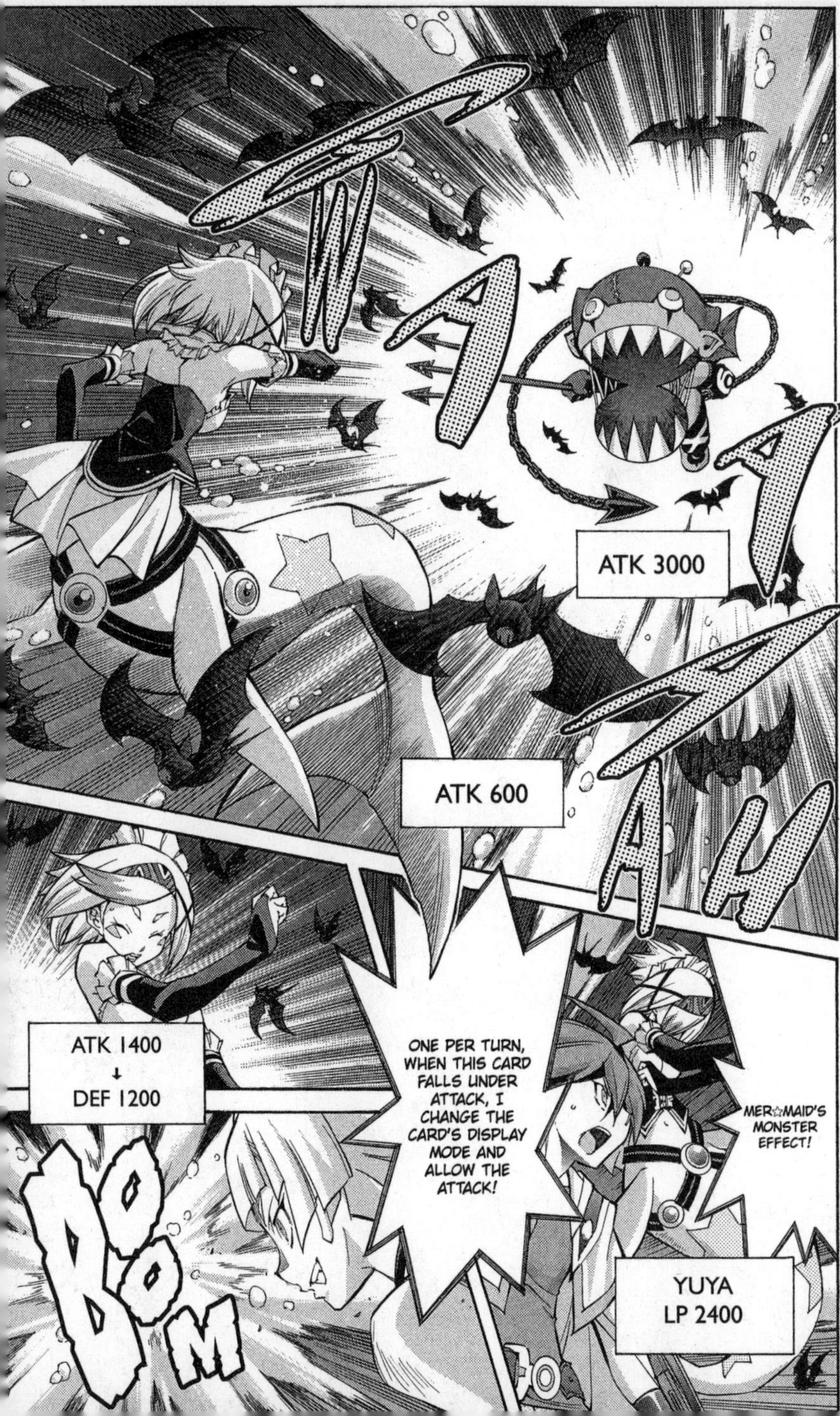
TWAAAAH
ATK 3000
ATK 600
MER☆MAID'S MONSTER EFFECT!
YUYA
LP 2400
ONE PER TURN, WHEN THIS CARD FALLS UNDER ATTACK, I CHANGE THE CARD'S DISPLAY MODE AND ALLOW THE ATTACK!
ATK 1400
↓
DEF 1200
BOOM

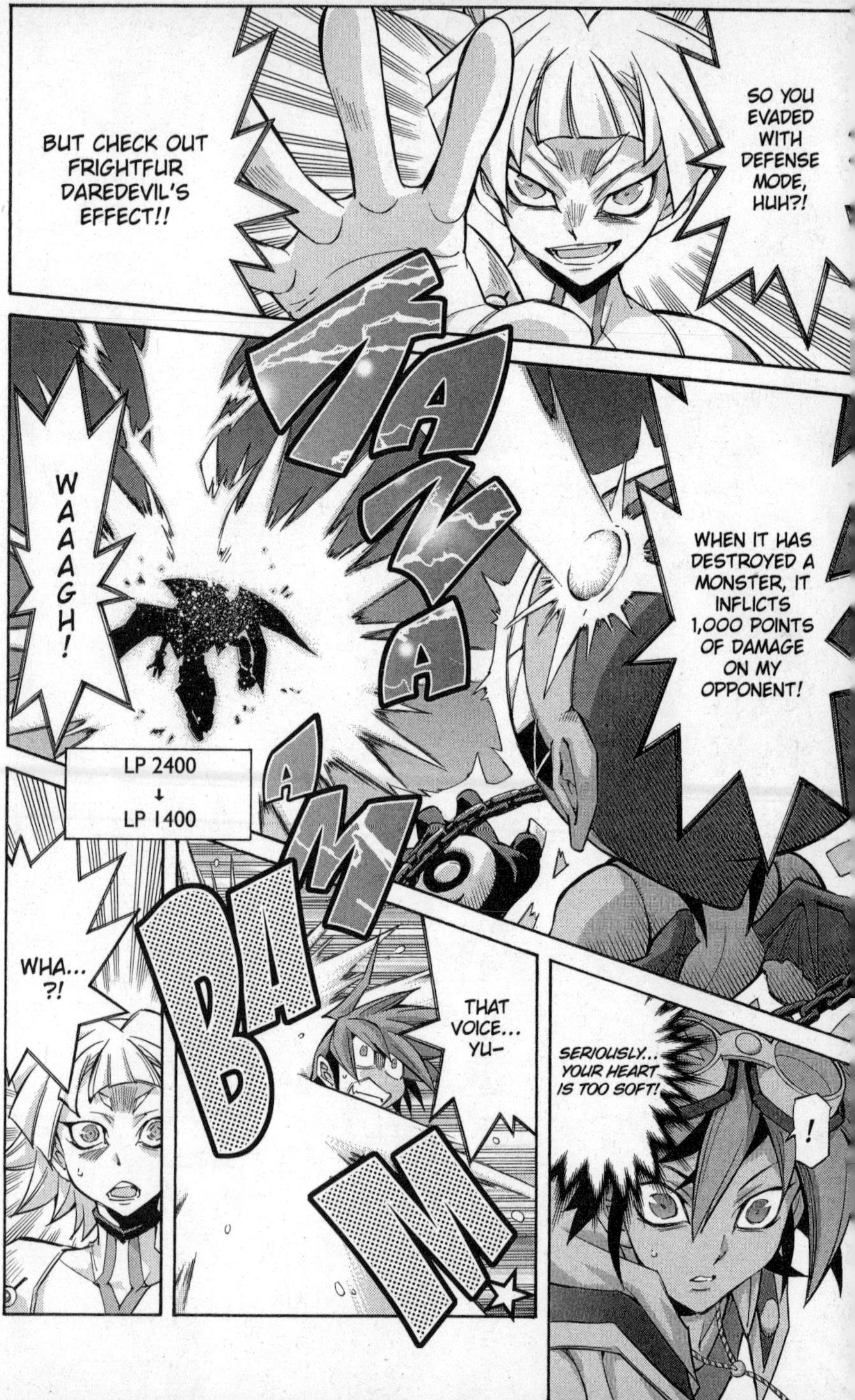
SO YOU EVADED WITH DEFENSE MODE, HUH?!
BUT CHECK OUT FRIGHTFUR DAREDEVIL'S EFFECT!!
WHEN IT HAS DESTROYED A MONSTER, IT INFLICTS 1,000 POINTS OF DAMAGE ON MY OPPONENT!
WAAAAGH!
LP 2400 ↓ LP 1400
!
SERIOUSLY... YOUR HEART IS TOO SOFT!
THAT VOICE... YU-
WHA... ?!

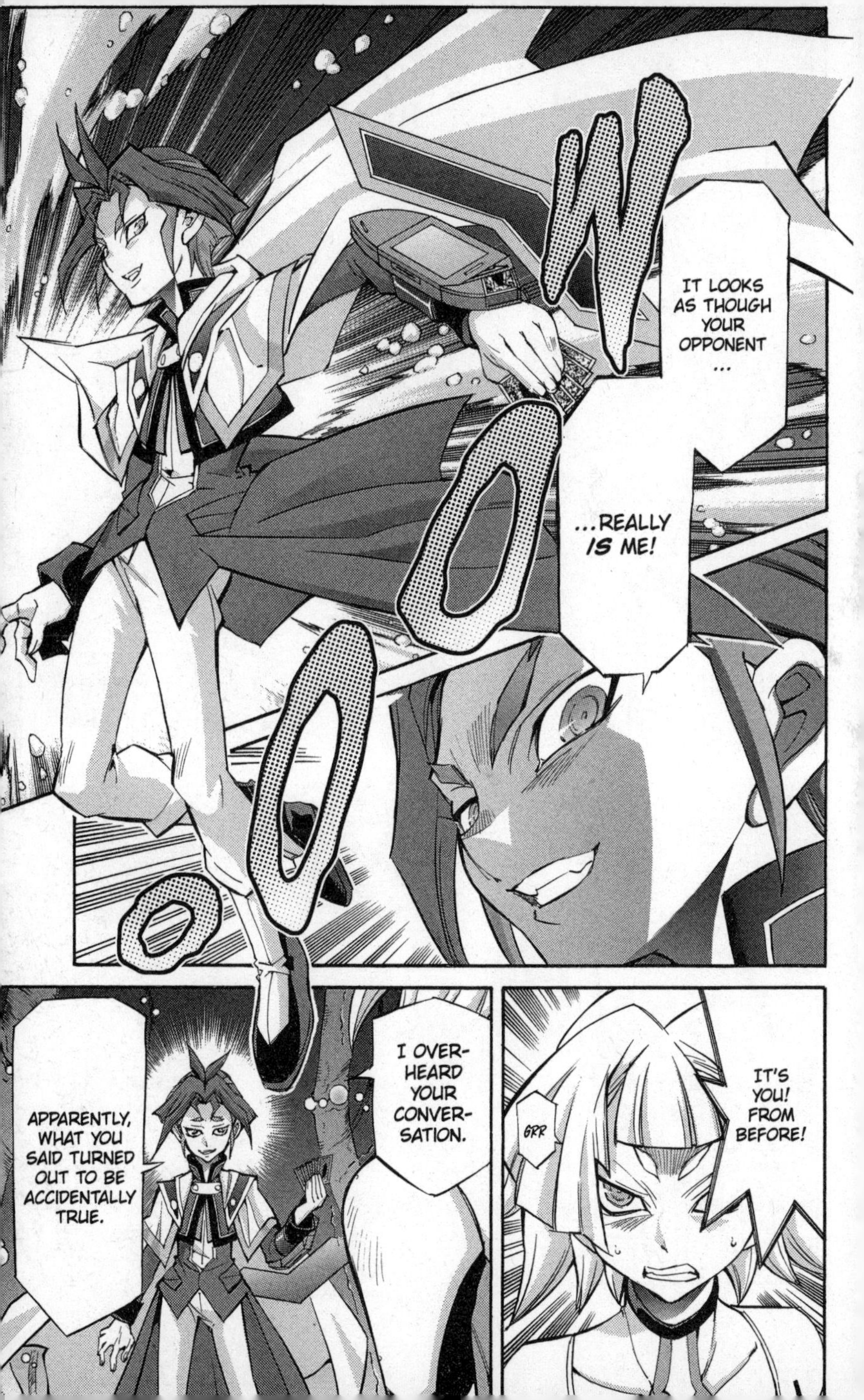
WOOO
IT LOOKS AS THOUGH YOUR OPPONENT ...
...REALLY *IS* ME!
IT'S YOU! FROM BEFORE!
GRR
I OVER-HEARD YOUR CONVER-SATION.
APPARENTLY, WHAT YOU SAID TURNED OUT TO BE ACCIDENTALLY TRUE.

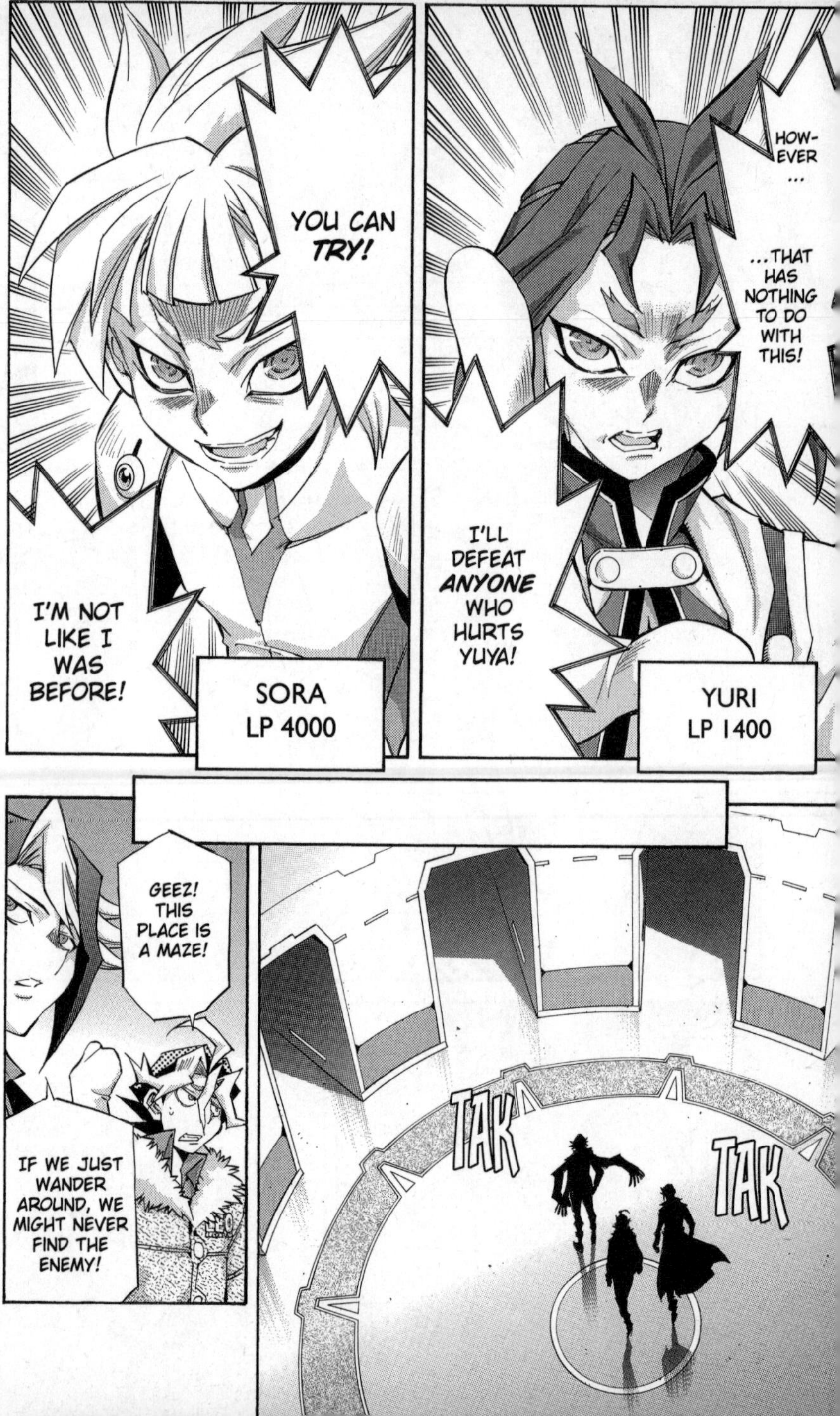
HOW-EVER...
...THAT HAS NOTHING TO DO WITH THIS!
I'LL DEFEAT *ANYONE* WHO HURTS YUYA!
YURI
LP 1400
YOU CAN *TRY!*
I'M NOT LIKE I WAS BEFORE!
SORA
LP 4000
TAK
TAK
GEEZ! THIS PLACE IS A MAZE!
IF WE JUST WANDER AROUND, WE MIGHT NEVER FIND THE ENEMY!

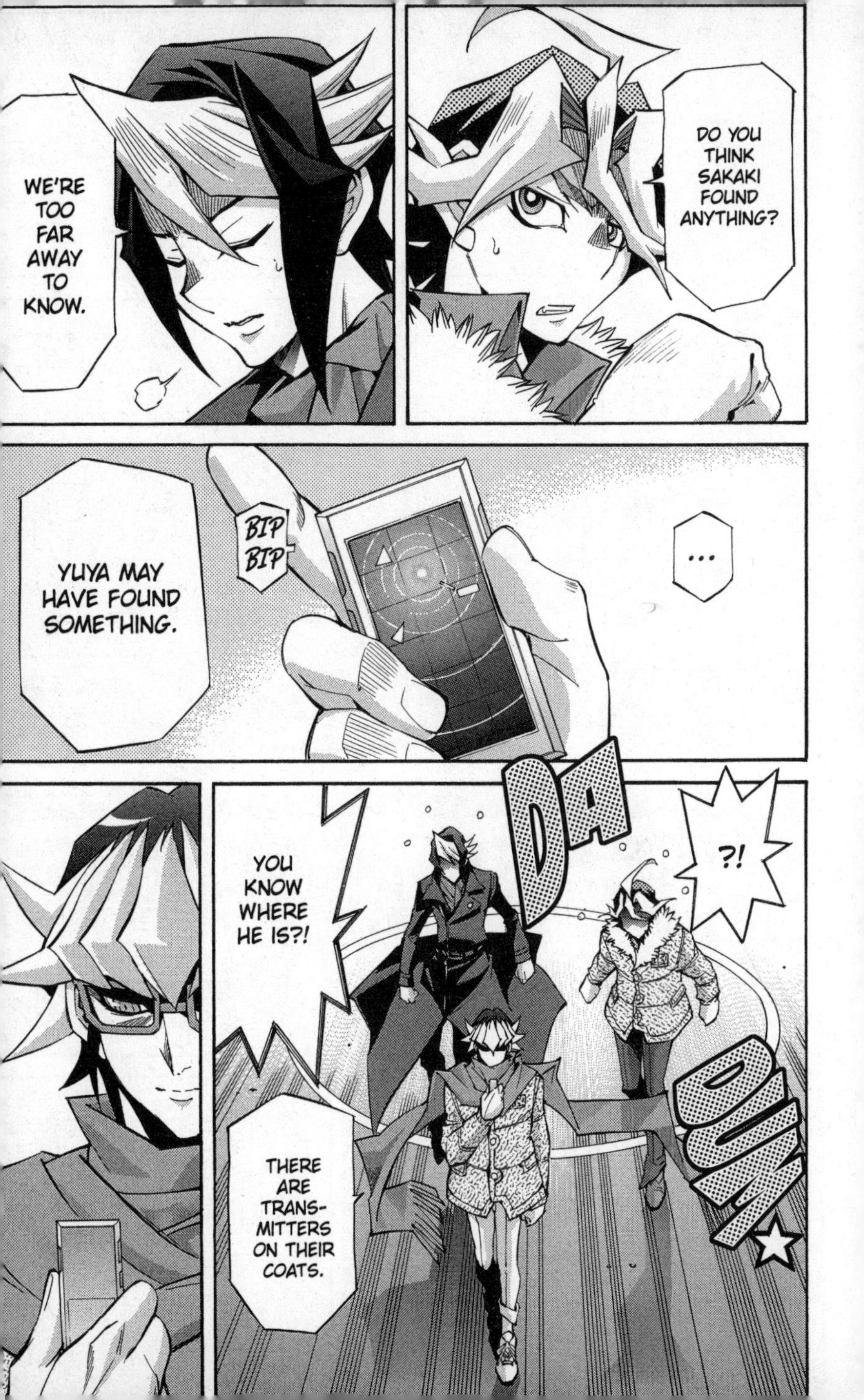
DO YOU THINK SAKAKI FOUND ANYTHING?
WE'RE TOO FAR AWAY TO KNOW.
...
BIP BIP
YUYA MAY HAVE FOUND SOMETHING.
?!
DA
DUN
YOU KNOW WHERE HE IS?!
THERE ARE TRANS-MITTERS ON THEIR COATS.

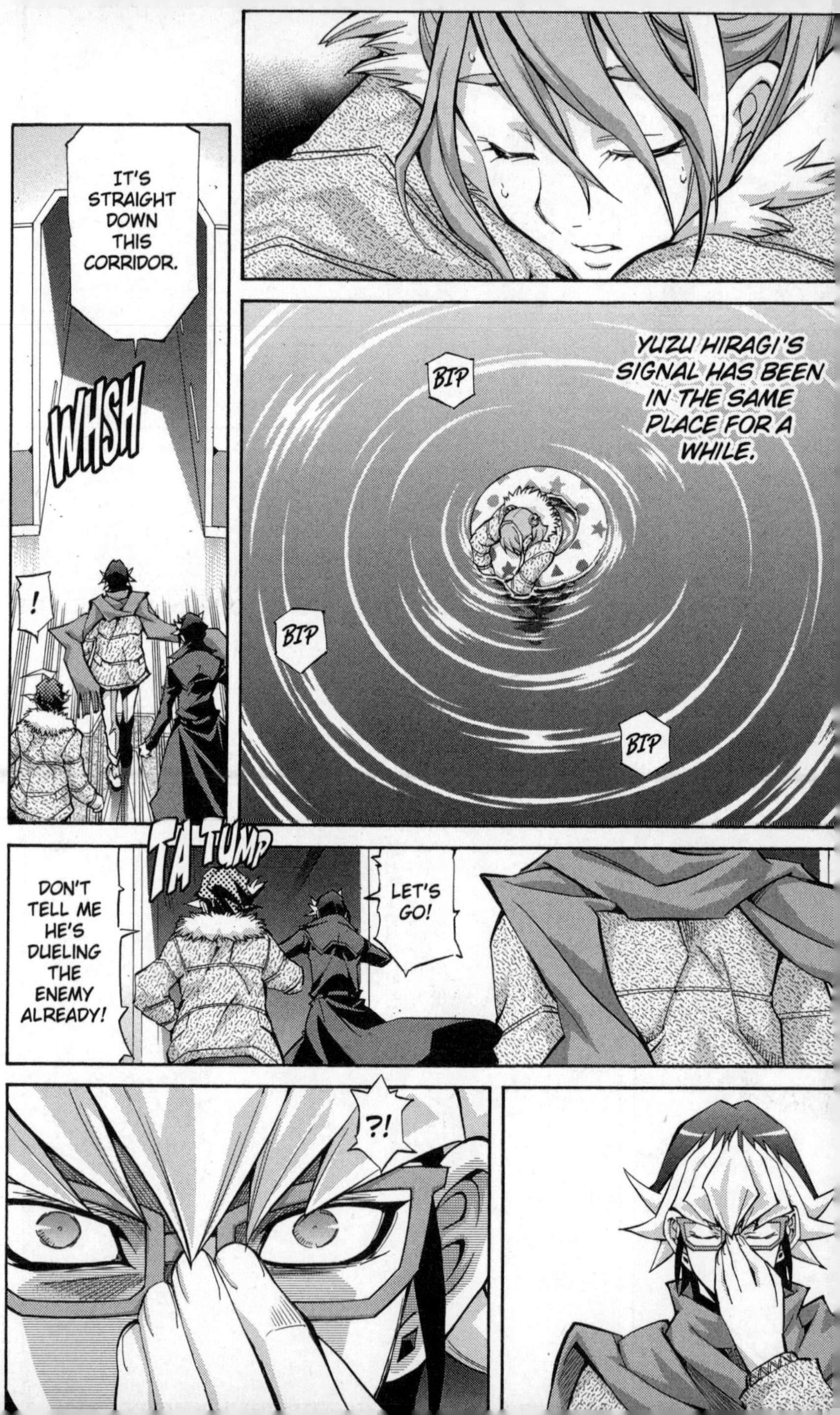
YUZU HIRAGI'S SIGNAL HAS BEEN IN THE SAME PLACE FOR A WHILE.
BIP
BIP
BIP
IT'S STRAIGHT DOWN THIS CORRIDOR.
WHSH
!
LET'S GO!
TA TUMP
DON'T TELL ME HE'S DUELING THE ENEMY ALREADY!
?!

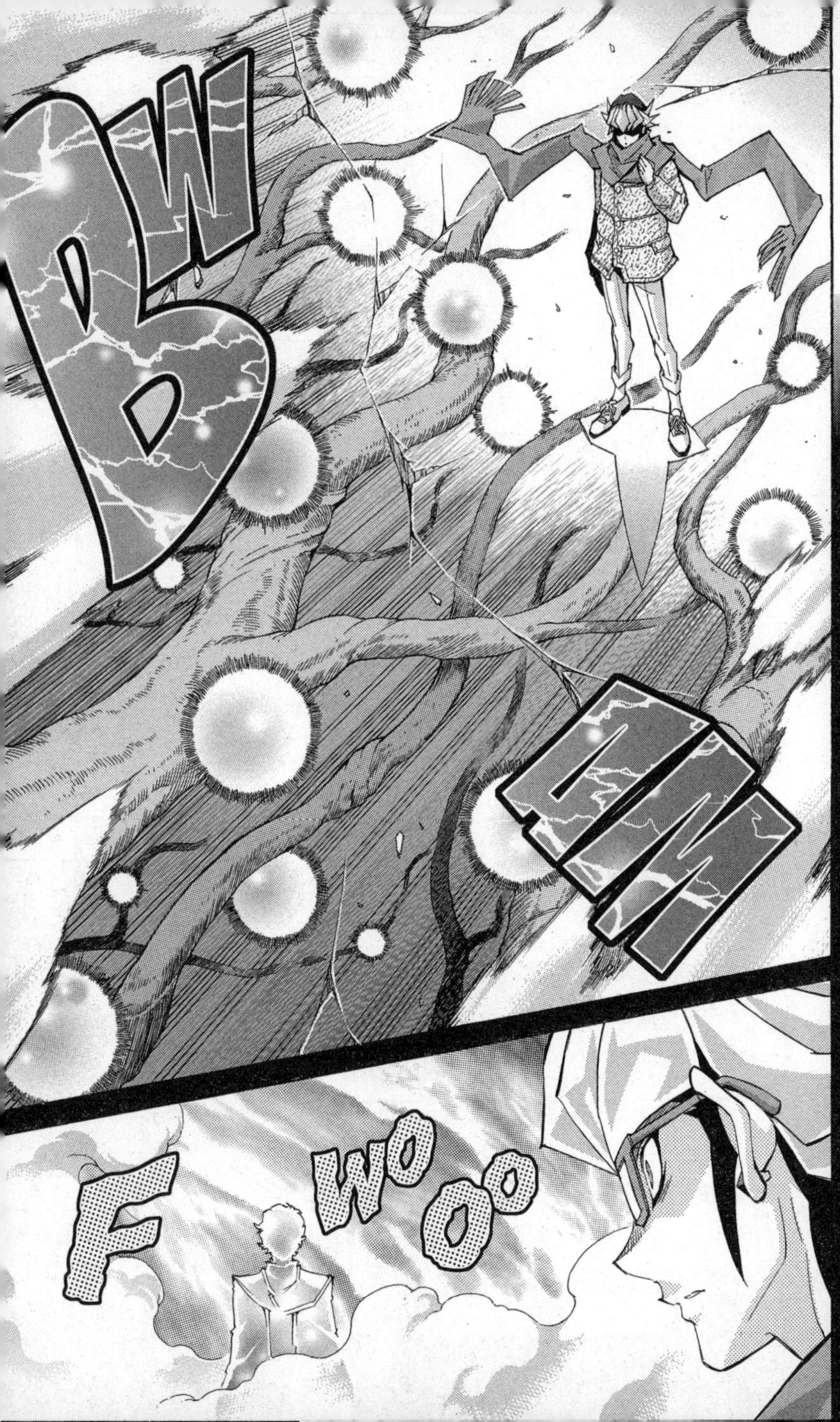
FWOOO

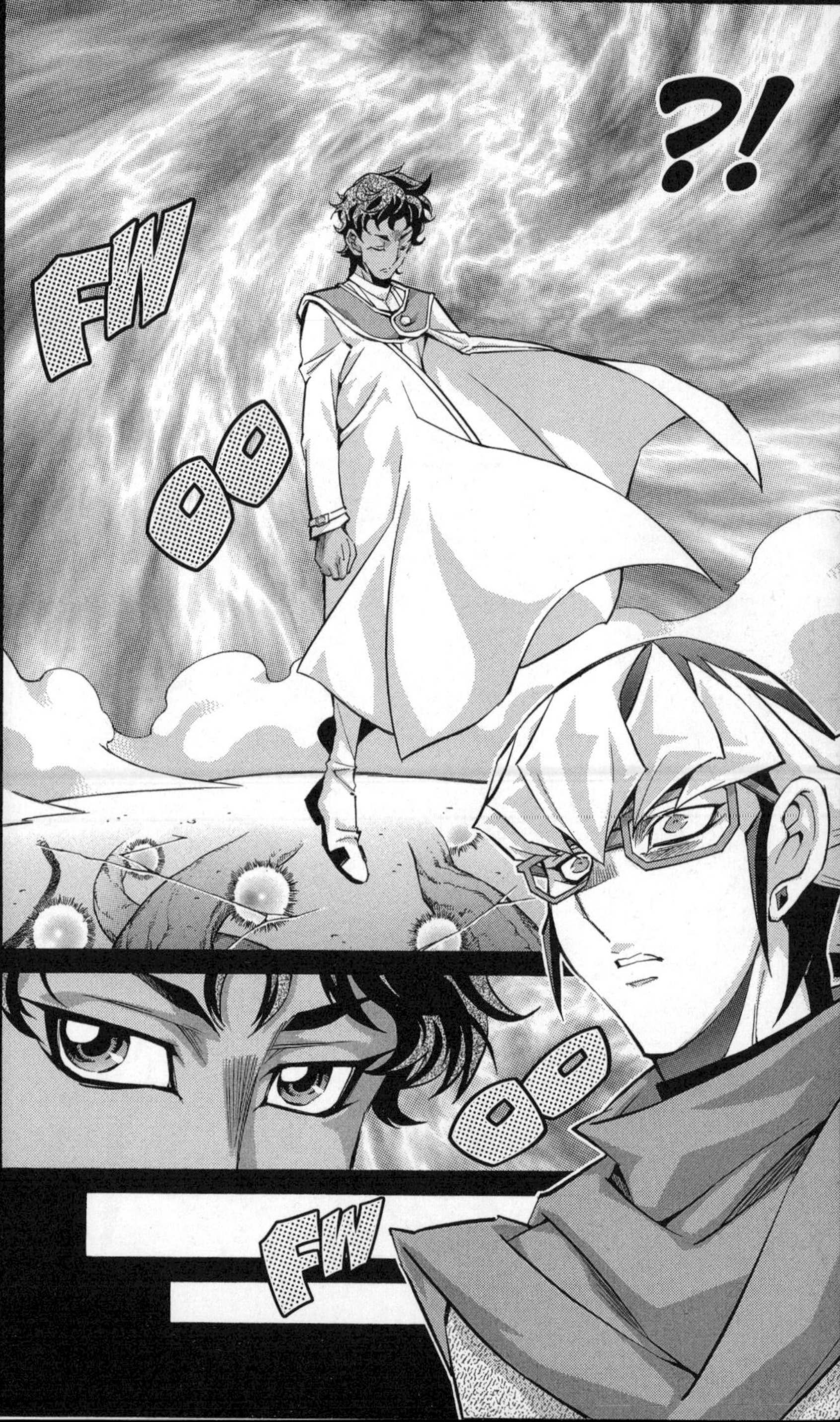
?!
FWOO
OO
FW

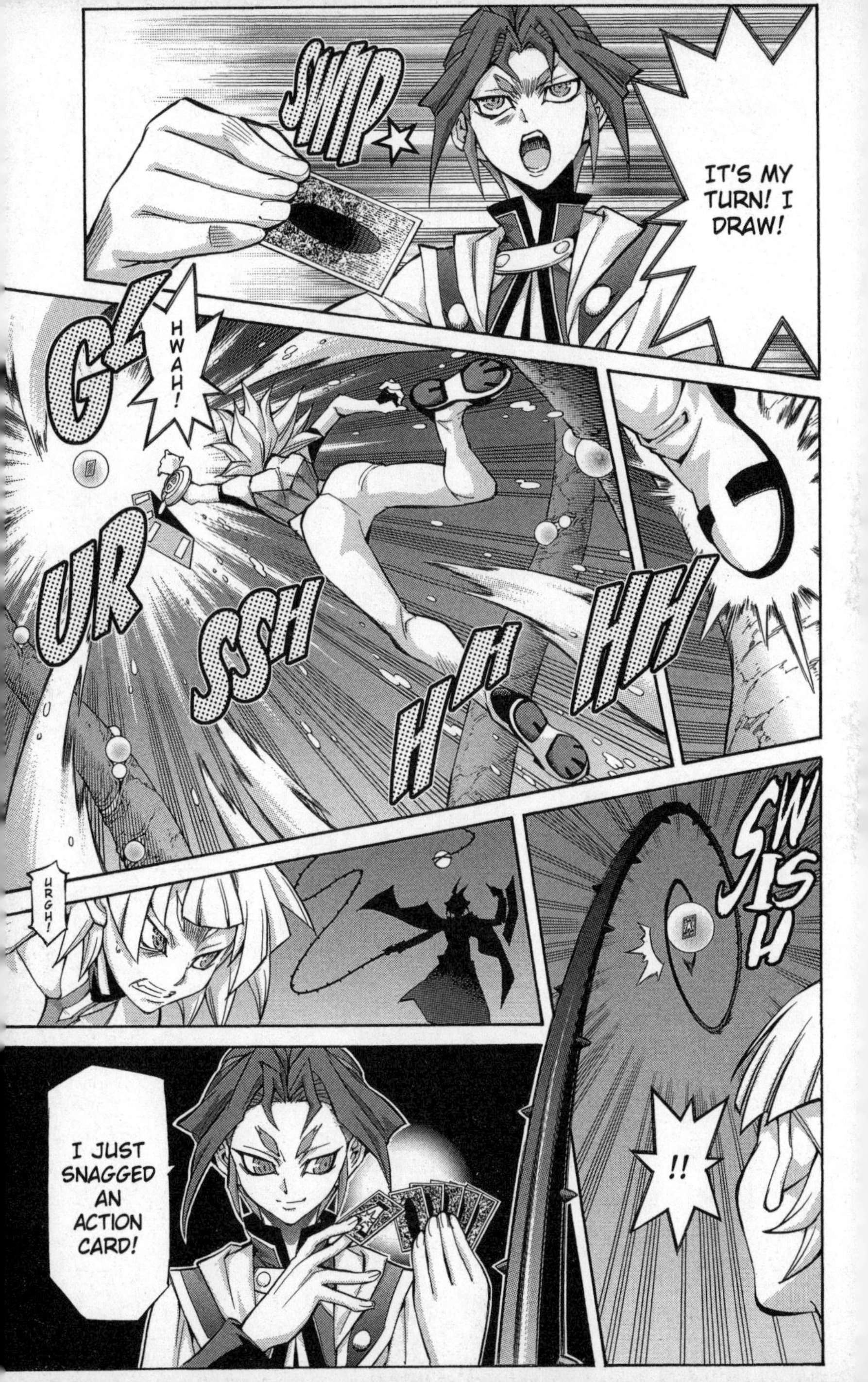

IT'S MY TURN! I DRAW!
SWIP
HWAH!
GUR
SSH
HHHH
SWISH
URGH!
!!
I JUST SNAGGED AN ACTION CARD!

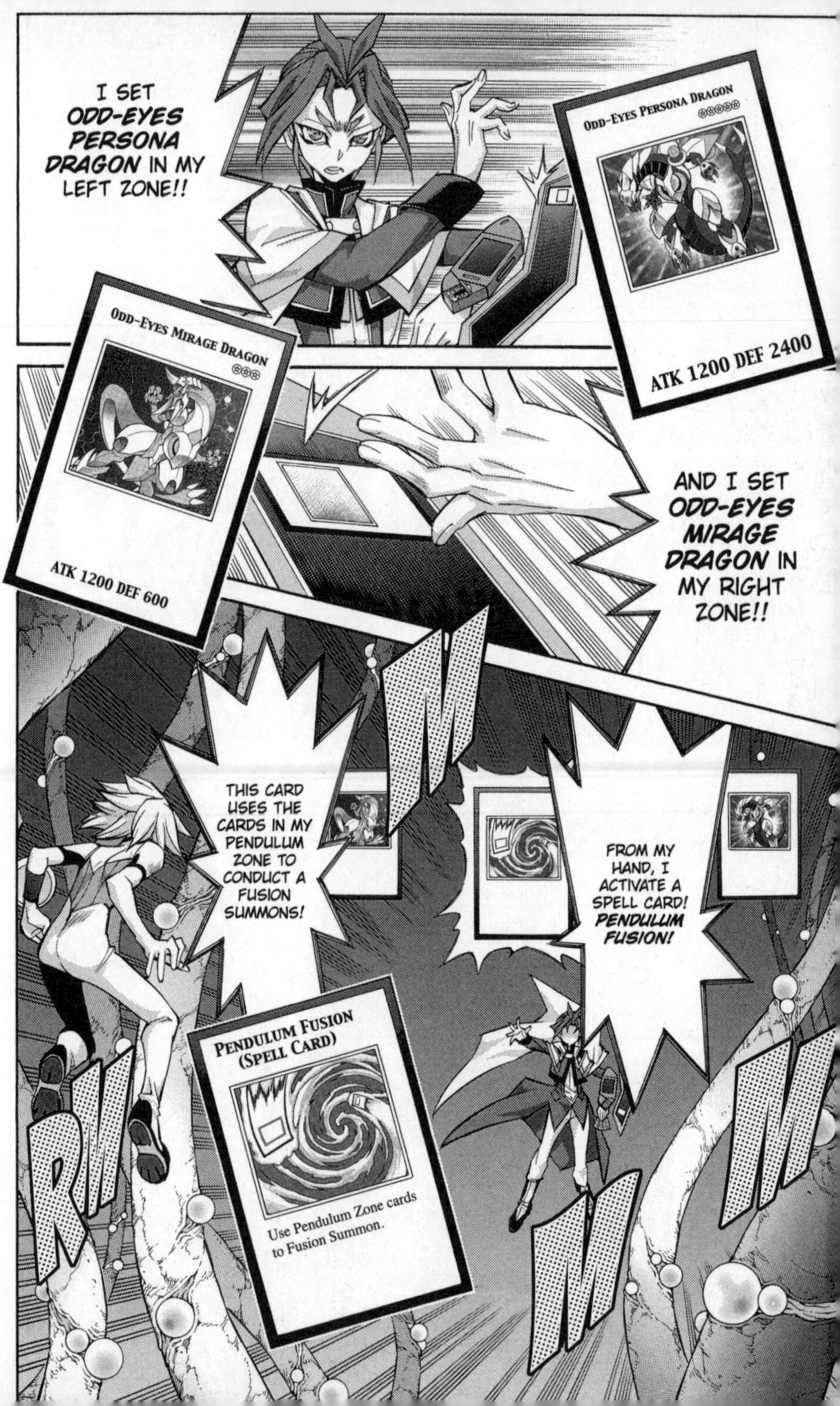

ODD-EYES PERSONA DRAGON
ATK 1200 DEF 2400
I SET ODD-EYES PERSONA DRAGON IN MY LEFT ZONE!!
AND I SET ODD-EYES MIRAGE DRAGON IN MY RIGHT ZONE!!
ODD-EYES MIRAGE DRAGON
ATK 1200 DEF 600
FROM MY HAND, I ACTIVATE A SPELL CARD! PENDULUM FUSION!
THIS CARD USES THE CARDS IN MY PENDULUM ZONE TO CONDUCT A FUSION SUMMONS!
PENDULUM FUSION (SPELL CARD)
Use Pendulum Zone cards to Fusion Summon.

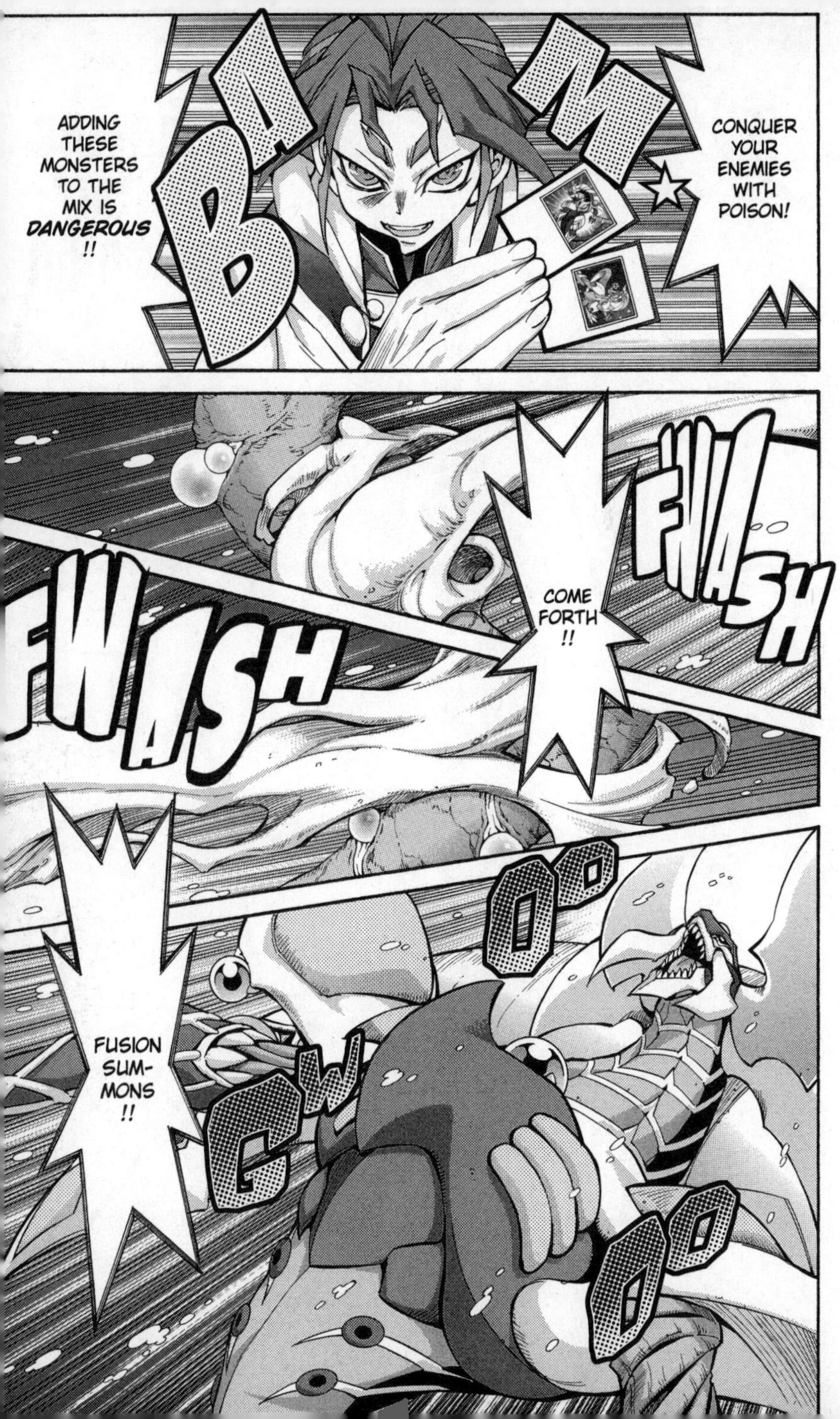
CONQUER YOUR ENEMIES WITH POISON!
BAM
ADDING THESE MONSTERS TO THE MIX IS DANGEROUS!!
FWASH
COME FORTH!!
FWASH
OOO
FUSION SUMMONS!!
GW
OOO

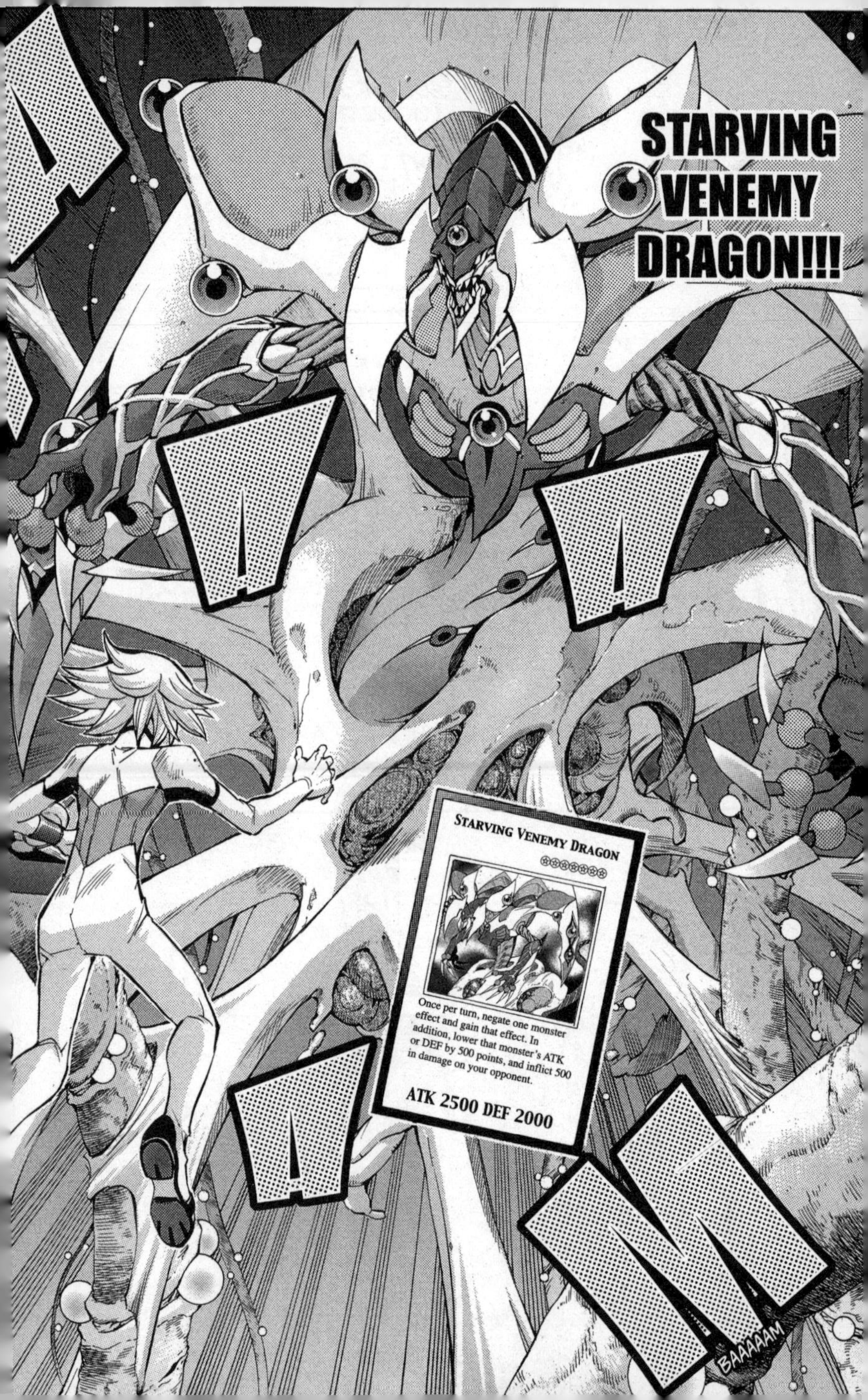
STARVING VENEMY DRAGON!!!
STARVING VENEMY DRAGON
Once per turn, negate one monster effect and gain that effect. In addition, lower that monster's ATK or DEF by 500 points, and inflict 500 in damage on your opponent.
ATK 2500 DEF 2000
BAAAAAM

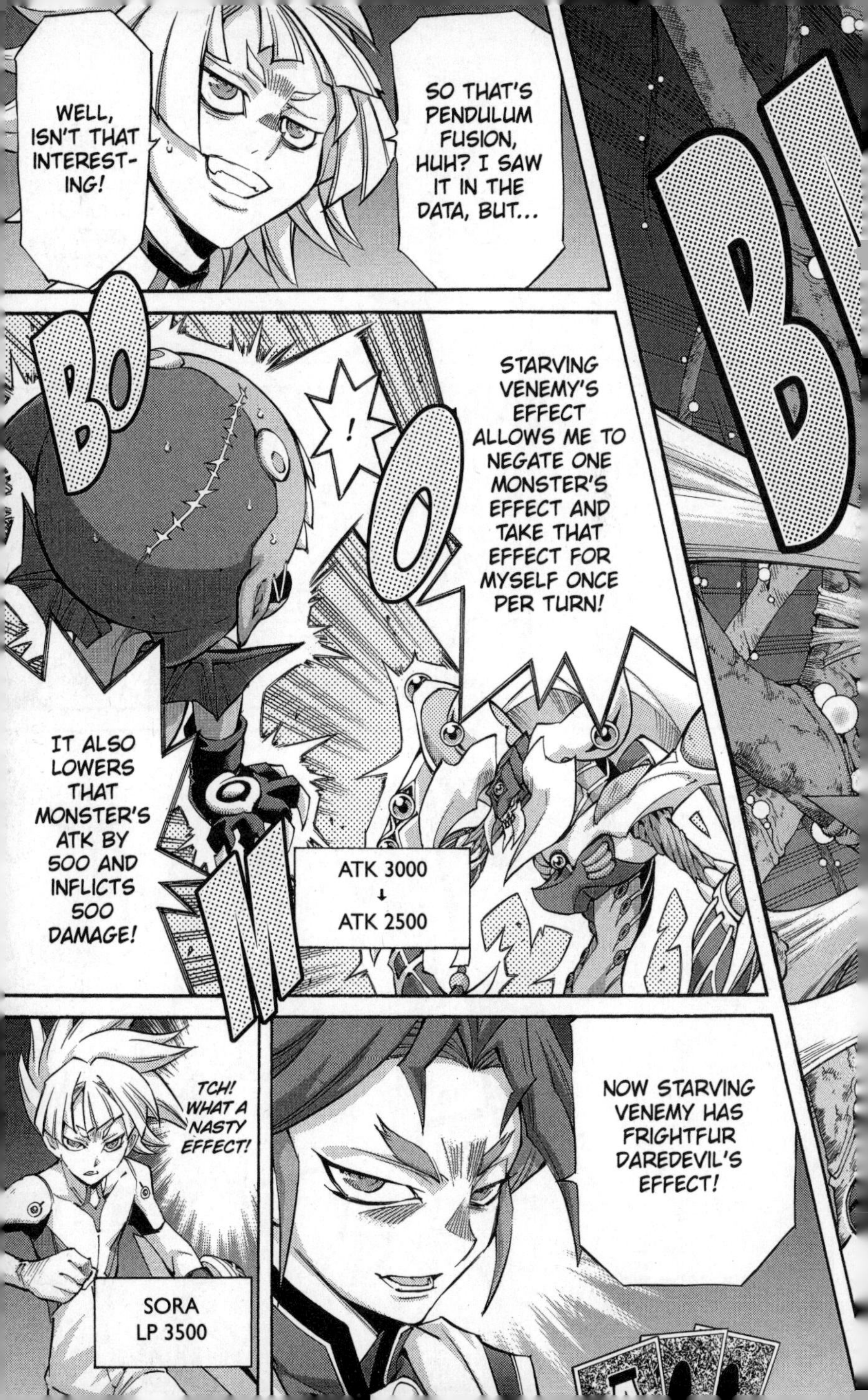
SO THAT'S PENDULUM FUSION, HUH? I SAW IT IN THE DATA, BUT...
WELL, ISN'T THAT INTEREST-ING!
STARVING VENEMY'S EFFECT ALLOWS ME TO NEGATE ONE MONSTER'S EFFECT AND TAKE THAT EFFECT FOR MYSELF ONCE PER TURN!
!
BOOM
IT ALSO LOWERS THAT MONSTER'S ATK BY 500 AND INFLICTS 500 DAMAGE!
ATK 3000 ↓ ATK 2500
NOW STARVING VENEMY HAS FRIGHTFUR DAREDEVIL'S EFFECT!
TCH! WHAT A NASTY EFFECT!
SORA LP 3500

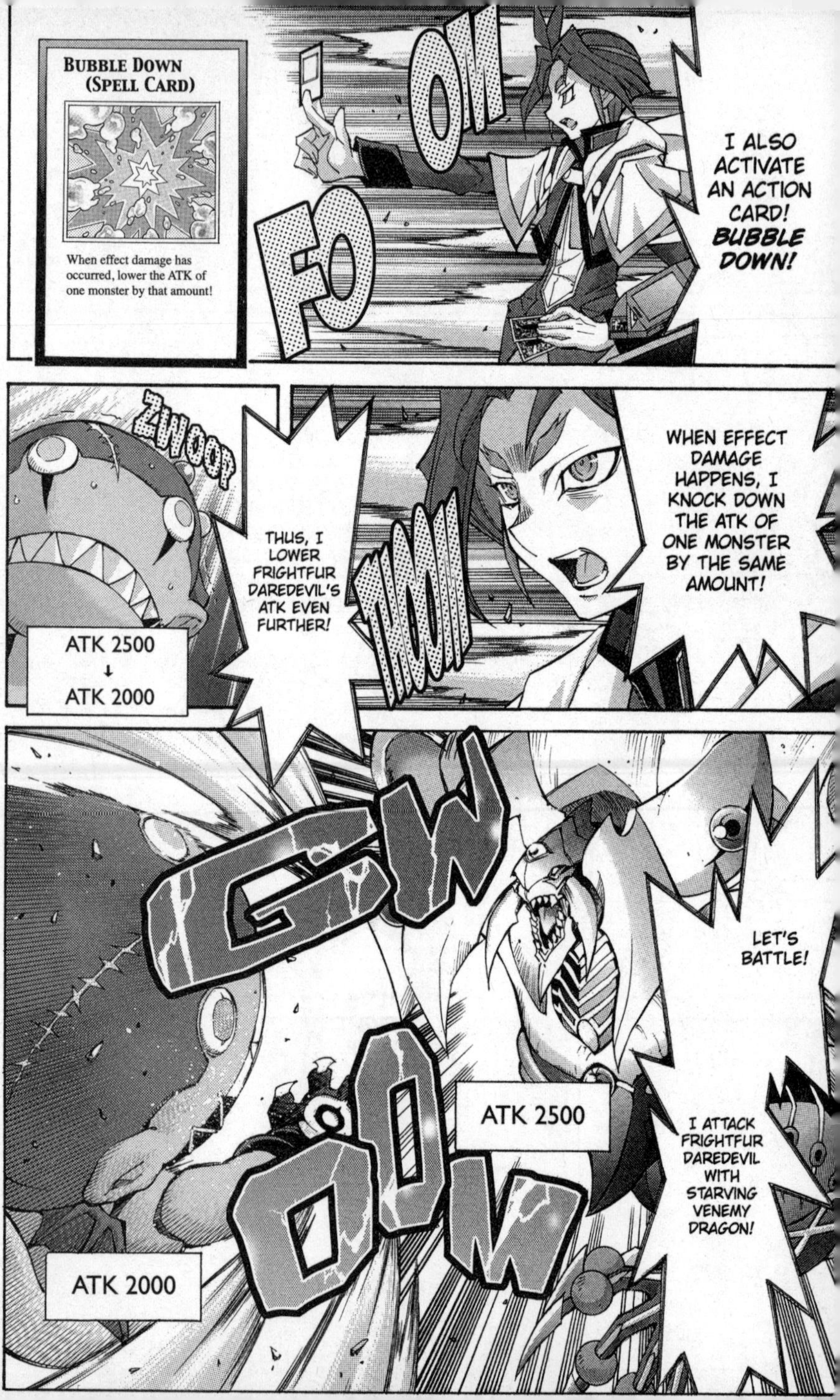
I ALSO ACTIVATE AN ACTION CARD! **BUBBLE DOWN!**
FOOM
BUBBLE DOWN (SPELL CARD)
When effect damage has occurred, lower the ATK of one monster by that amount!
WHEN EFFECT DAMAGE HAPPENS, I KNOCK DOWN THE ATK OF ONE MONSTER BY THE SAME AMOUNT!
THOOM
ZWOOP
THUS, I LOWER FRIGHTFUR DAREDEVIL'S ATK EVEN FURTHER!
ATK 2500
↓
ATK 2000
LET'S BATTLE!
I ATTACK FRIGHTFUR DAREDEVIL WITH STARVING VENEMY DRAGON!
ATK 2500
GOW
OOOW
ATK 2000

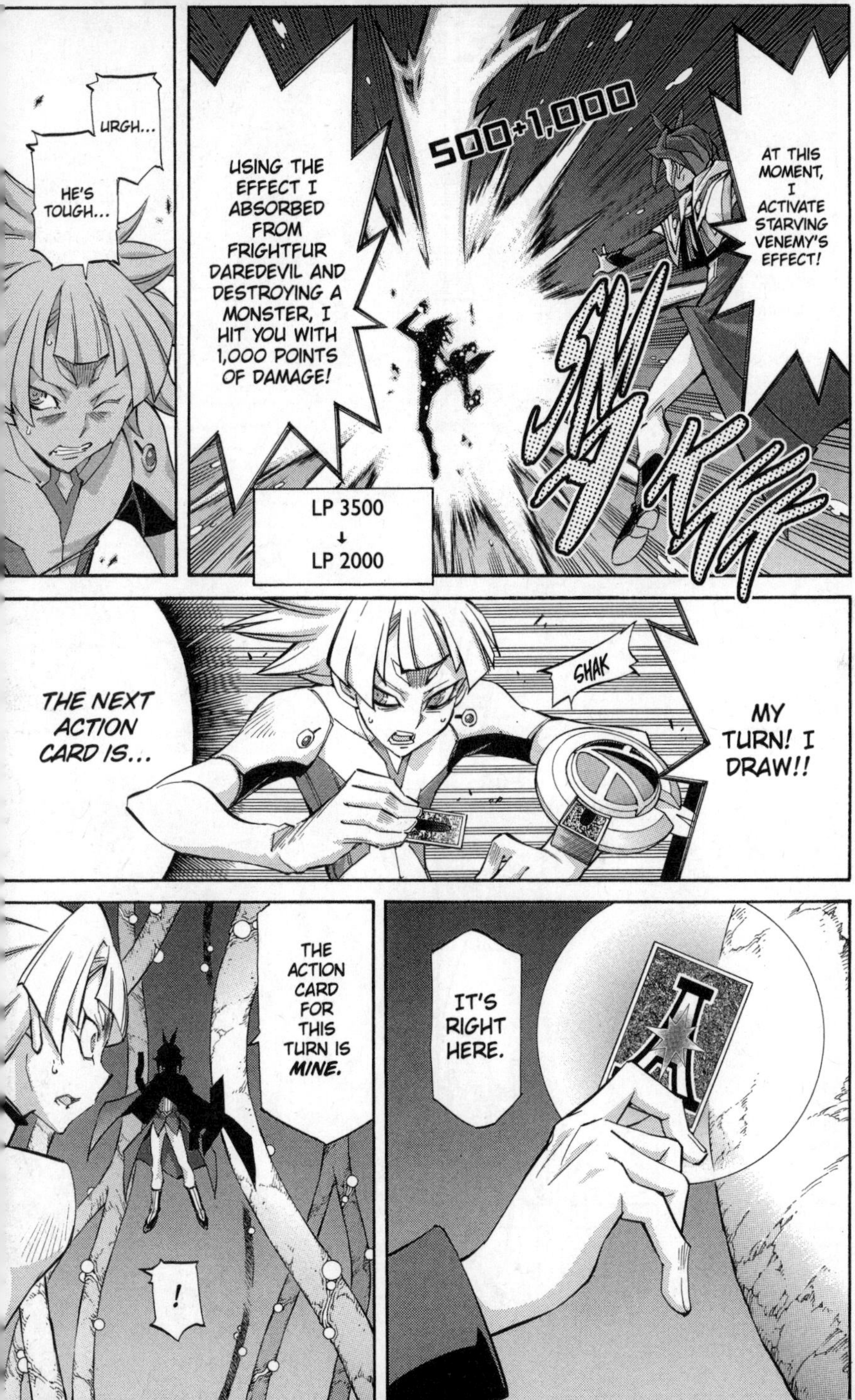
AT THIS MOMENT, I ACTIVATE STARVING VENEMY'S EFFECT!
500+1,000
USING THE EFFECT I ABSORBED FROM FRIGHTFUR DAREDEVIL AND DESTROYING A MONSTER, I HIT YOU WITH 1,000 POINTS OF DAMAGE!
LP 3500 ↓ LP 2000
URGH...
HE'S TOUGH...
MY TURN! I DRAW!!
SHAK
THE NEXT ACTION CARD IS...
IT'S RIGHT HERE.
THE ACTION CARD FOR THIS TURN IS *MINE.*
!

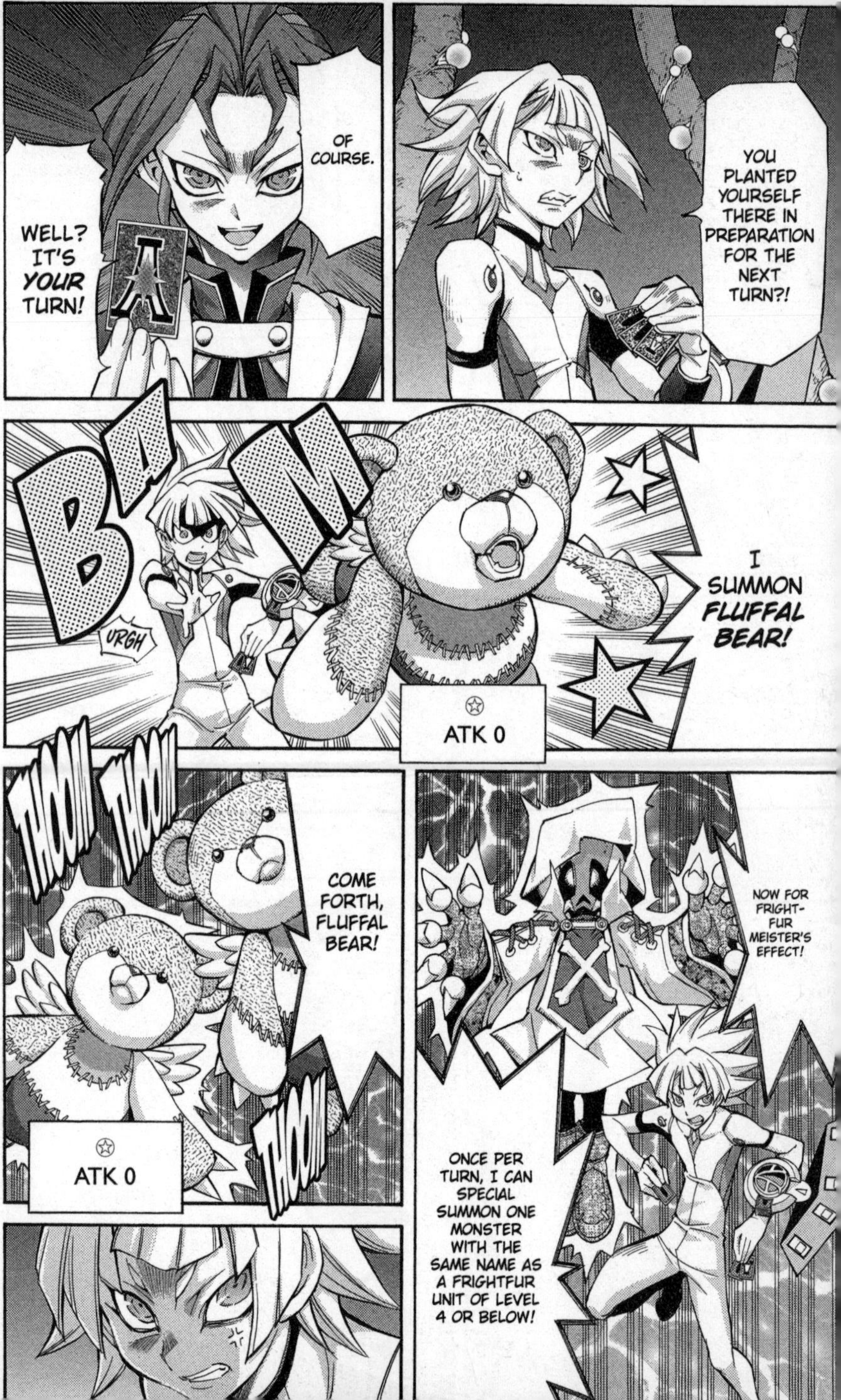
YOU PLANTED YOURSELF THERE IN PREPARATION FOR THE NEXT TURN?!
OF COURSE.
WELL? IT'S *YOUR* TURN!
I SUMMON *FLUFFAL BEAR!*
BAM
URGH
ATK 0
NOW FOR FRIGHT-FUR MEISTER'S EFFECT!
ONCE PER TURN, I CAN SPECIAL SUMMON ONE MONSTER WITH THE SAME NAME AS A FRIGHTFUR UNIT OF LEVEL 4 OR BELOW!
THOOM
THOOM
COME FORTH, FLUFFAL BEAR!
ATK 0
THOOM

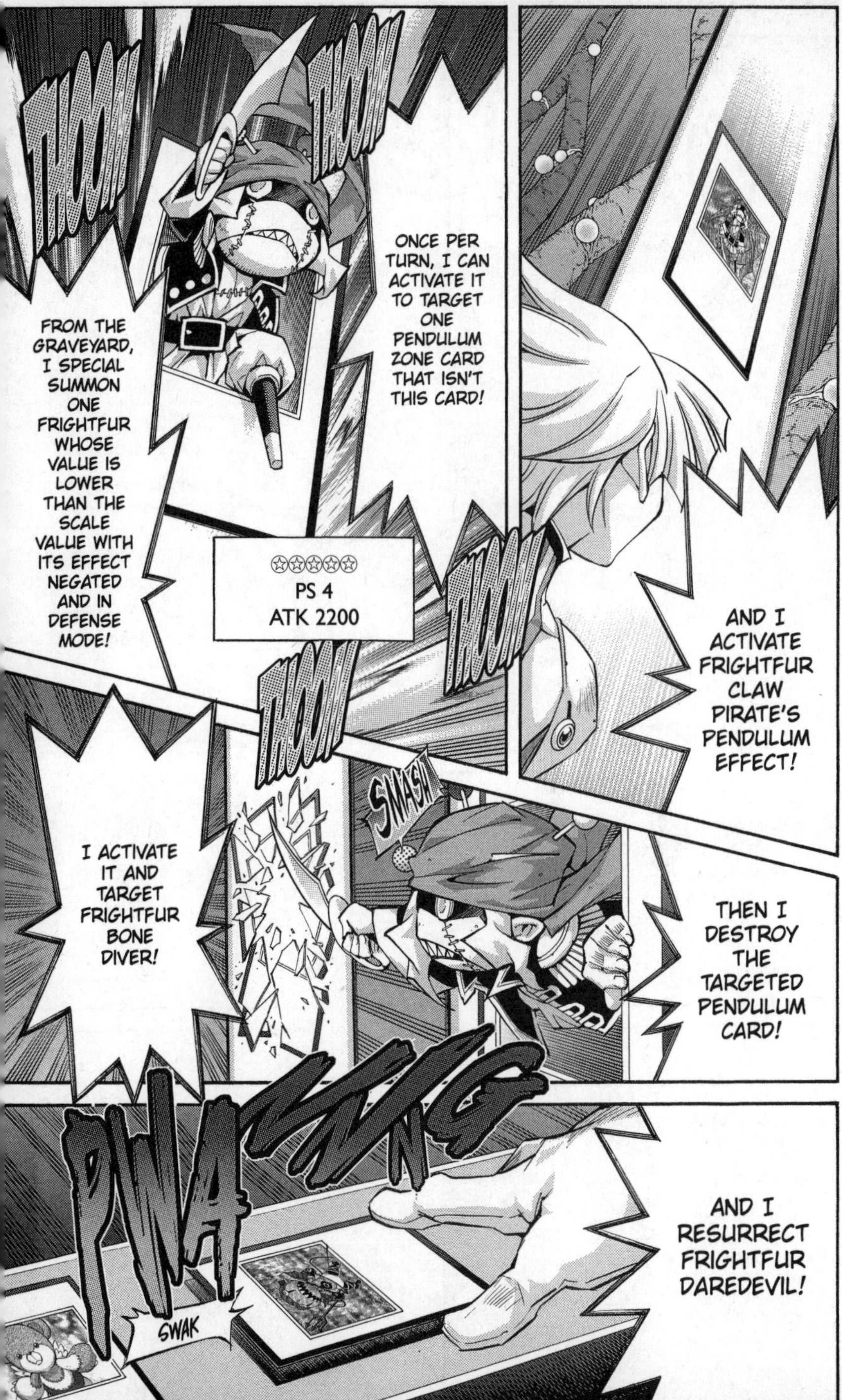
AND I ACTIVATE FRIGHTFUR CLAW PIRATE'S PENDULUM EFFECT!
THOOM
THOOM
THOOM
ONCE PER TURN, I CAN ACTIVATE IT TO TARGET ONE PENDULUM ZONE CARD THAT ISN'T THIS CARD!
FROM THE GRAVEYARD, I SPECIAL SUMMON ONE FRIGHTFUR WHOSE VALUE IS LOWER THAN THE SCALE VALUE WITH ITS EFFECT NEGATED AND IN DEFENSE MODE!
☆☆☆☆☆
PS 4
ATK 2200
THOOM
SMASH
I ACTIVATE IT AND TARGET FRIGHTFUR BONE DIVER!
THEN I DESTROY THE TARGETED PENDULUM CARD!
AND I RESURRECT FRIGHTFUR DAREDEVIL!
PWAANNNG
SWAK

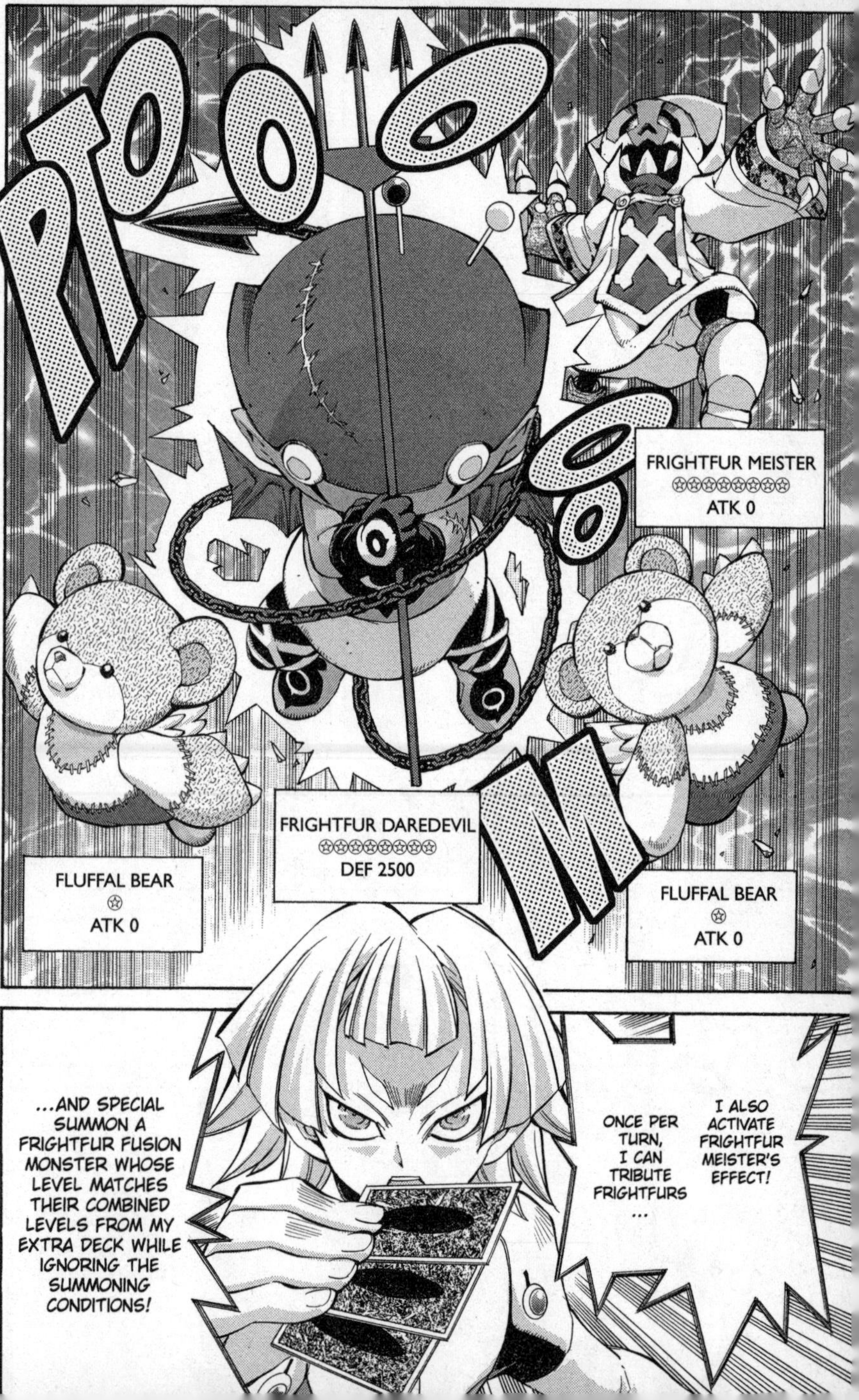
PTOOOOOM
FRIGHTFUR MEISTER
ATK 0
FLUFFAL BEAR
ATK 0
FRIGHTFUR DAREDEVIL
DEF 2500
FLUFFAL BEAR
ATK 0
I ALSO ACTIVATE FRIGHTFUR MEISTER'S EFFECT!
ONCE PER TURN, I CAN TRIBUTE FRIGHTFURS...
...AND SPECIAL SUMMON A FRIGHTFUR FUSION MONSTER WHOSE LEVEL MATCHES THEIR COMBINED LEVELS FROM MY EXTRA DECK WHILE IGNORING THE SUMMONING CONDITIONS!

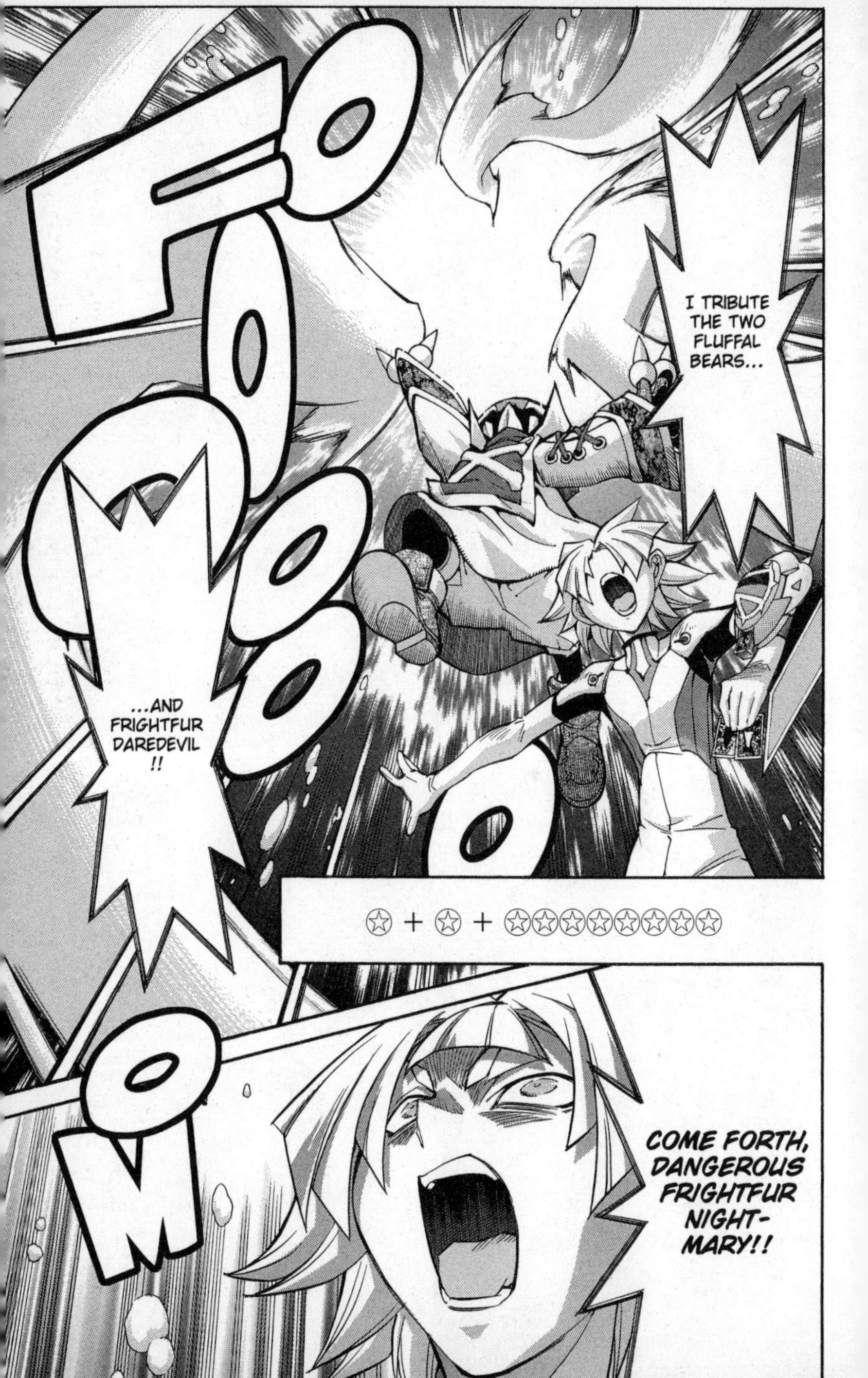
I TRIBUTE THE TWO FLUFFAL BEARS...
...AND FRIGHTFUR DAREDEVIL!!
FOOOOOOM
☆ + ☆ + ☆☆☆☆☆☆☆☆
COME FORTH, DANGEROUS FRIGHTFUR NIGHT-MARY!!

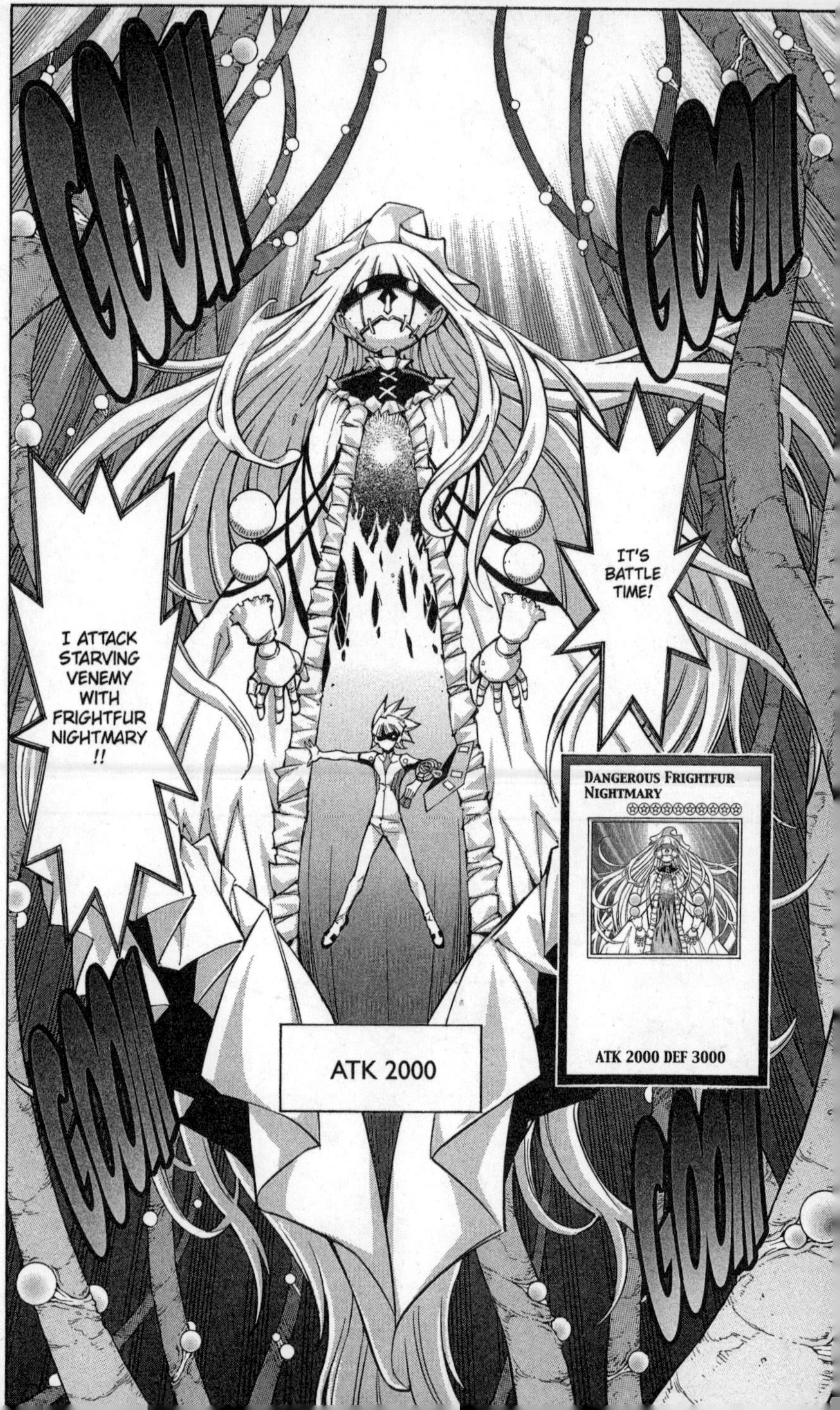
IT'S BATTLE TIME!
I ATTACK STARVING VENEMY WITH FRIGHTFUR NIGHTMARY!!
DANGEROUS FRIGHTFUR NIGHTMARY
ATK 2000 DEF 3000
ATK 2000

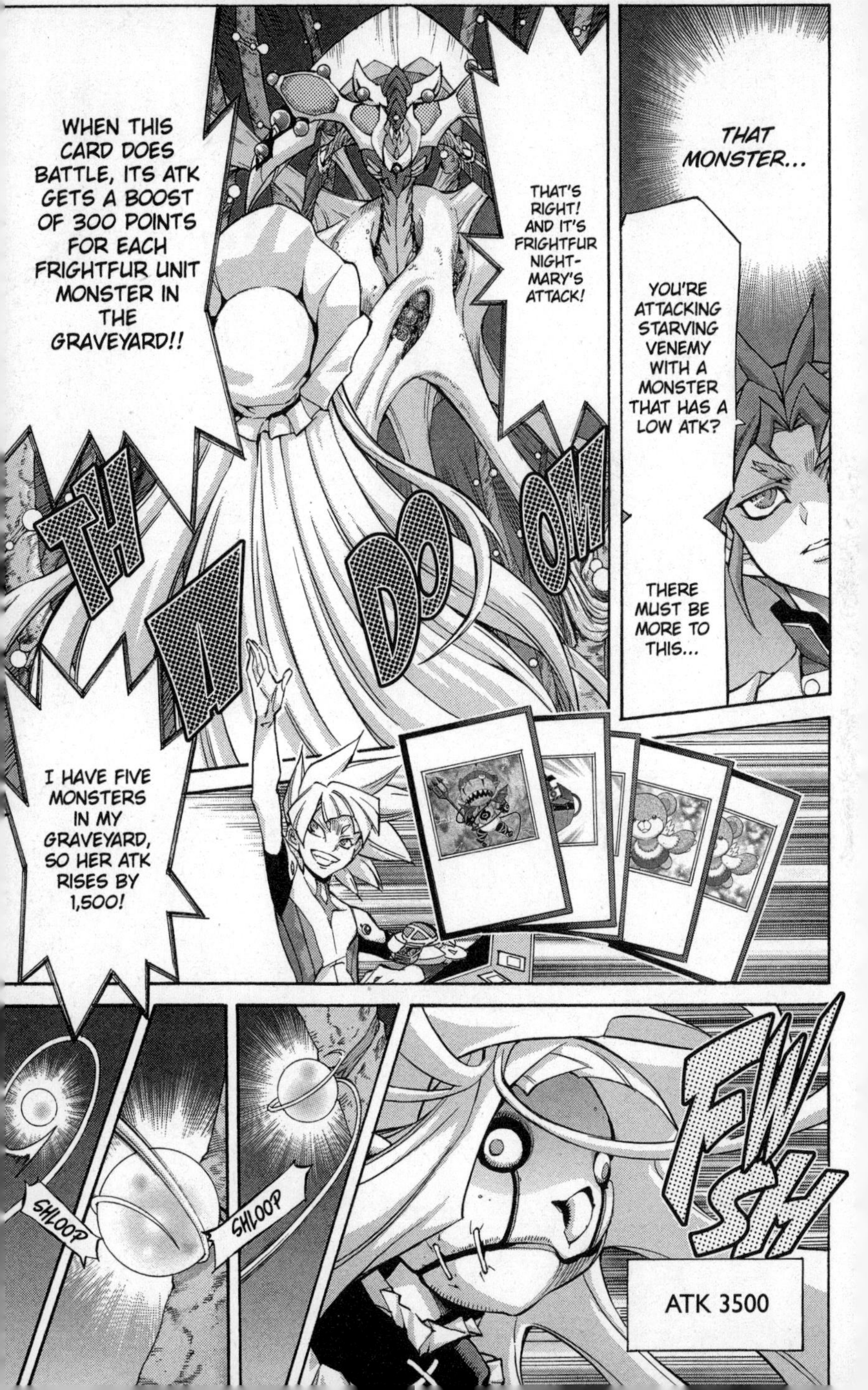

THAT MONSTER...
YOU'RE ATTACKING STARVING VENEMY WITH A MONSTER THAT HAS A LOW ATK?
THERE MUST BE MORE TO THIS...
THAT'S RIGHT! AND IT'S FRIGHTFUR NIGHT-MARY'S ATTACK!
WHEN THIS CARD DOES BATTLE, ITS ATK GETS A BOOST OF 300 POINTS FOR EACH FRIGHTFUR UNIT MONSTER IN THE GRAVEYARD!!
THOOM
I HAVE FIVE MONSTERS IN MY GRAVEYARD, SO HER ATK RISES BY 1,500!
FWISH
ATK 3500
SHLOOP
SHLOOP

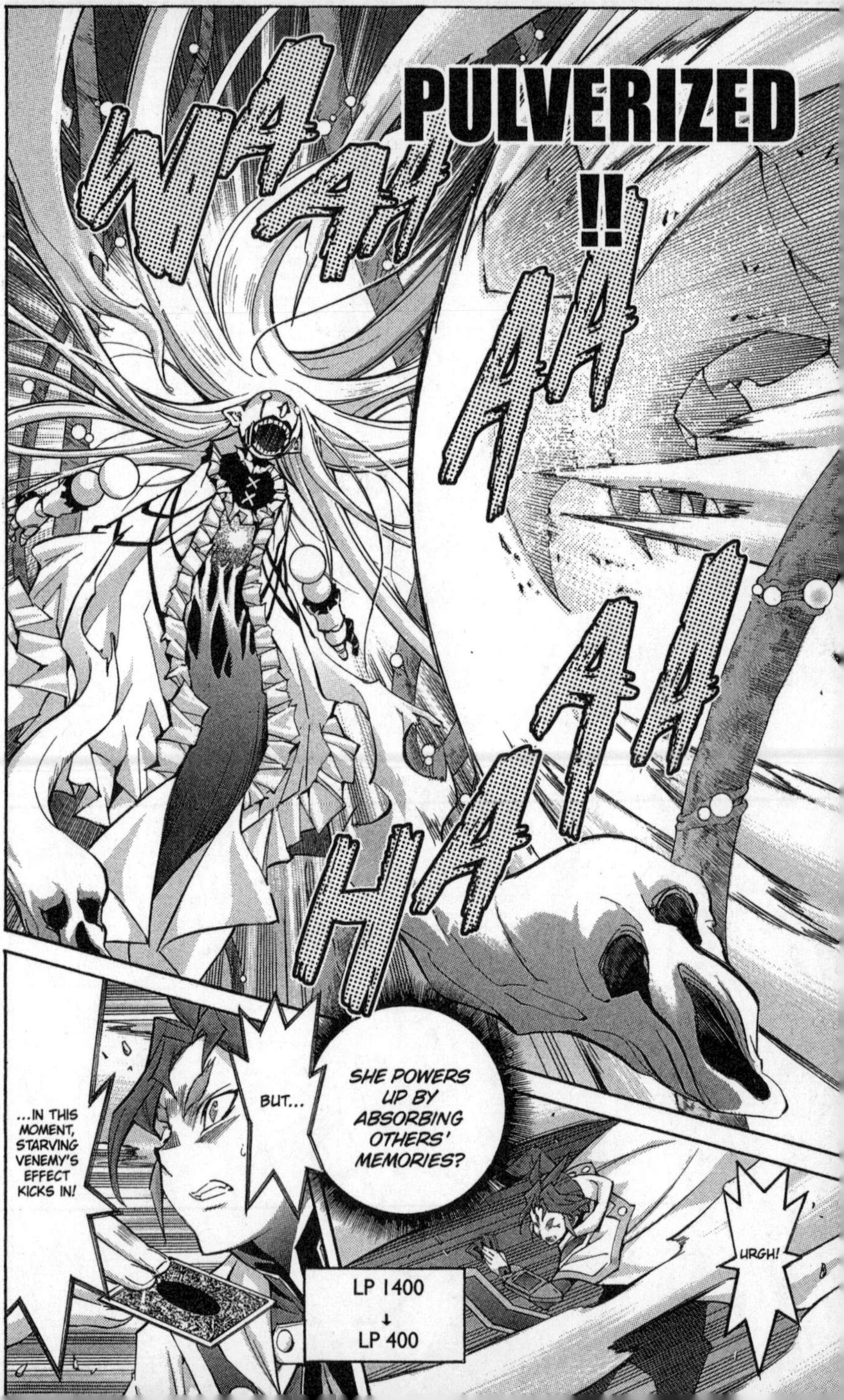
PULVERIZED!!
WAAAAAAAAH
URGH!
LP 1400 ↓ LP 400
BUT...
SHE POWERS UP BY ABSORBING OTHERS' MEMORIES?
...IN THIS MOMENT, STARVING VENEMY'S EFFECT KICKS IN!

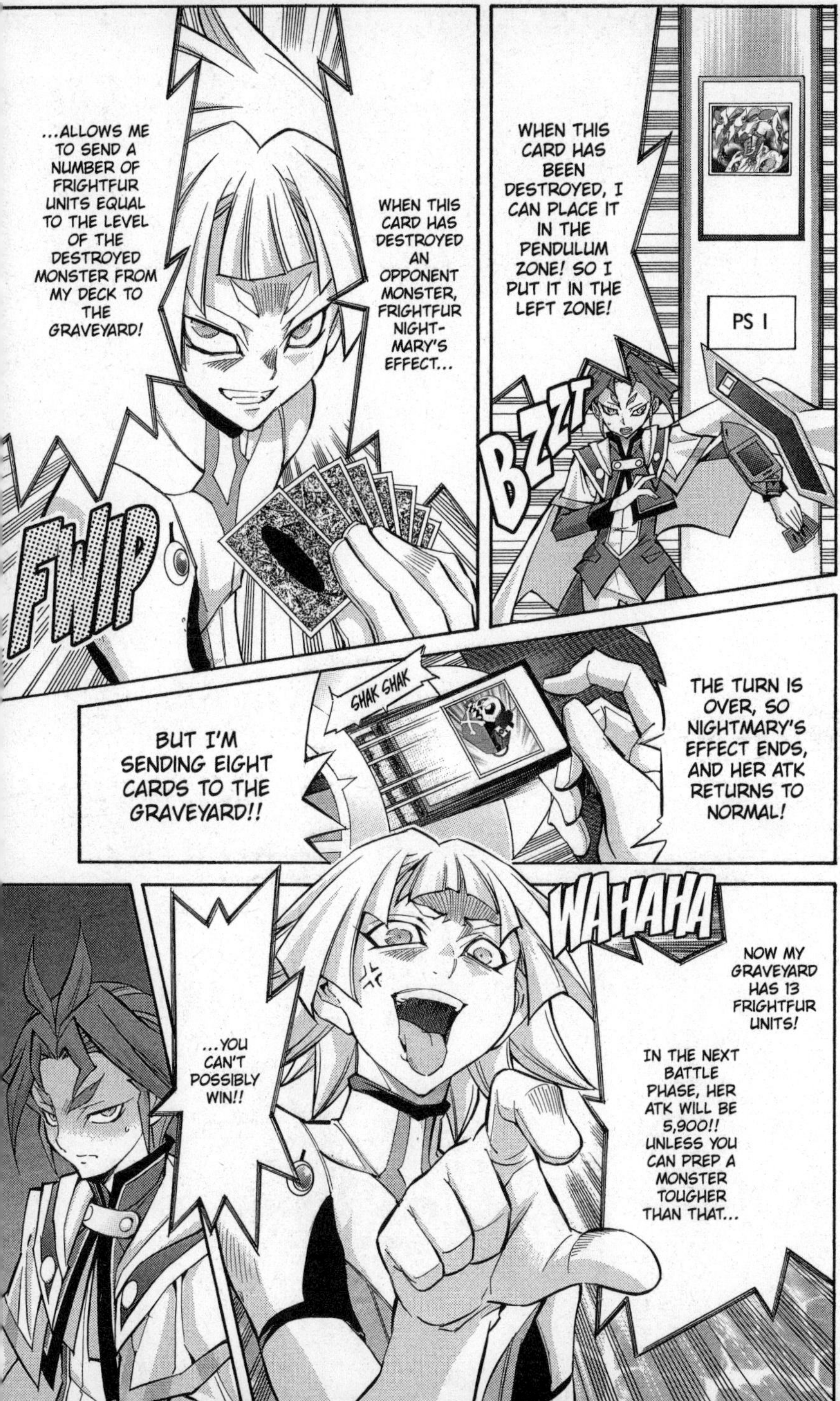
WHEN THIS CARD HAS BEEN DESTROYED, I CAN PLACE IT IN THE PENDULUM ZONE! SO I PUT IT IN THE LEFT ZONE!
PS 1
BZZZT
WHEN THIS CARD HAS DESTROYED AN OPPONENT MONSTER, FRIGHTFUR NIGHT-MARY'S EFFECT...
...ALLOWS ME TO SEND A NUMBER OF FRIGHTFUR UNITS EQUAL TO THE LEVEL OF THE DESTROYED MONSTER FROM MY DECK TO THE GRAVEYARD!
FWIP
THE TURN IS OVER, SO NIGHTMARY'S EFFECT ENDS, AND HER ATK RETURNS TO NORMAL!
SHAK SHAK
BUT I'M SENDING EIGHT CARDS TO THE GRAVEYARD!!
WAHAHA
NOW MY GRAVEYARD HAS 13 FRIGHTFUR UNITS!
IN THE NEXT BATTLE PHASE, HER ATK WILL BE 5,900!! UNLESS YOU CAN PREP A MONSTER TOUGHER THAN THAT...
...YOU CAN'T POSSIBLY WIN!!

Yu-Gi-Oh! ARC-V

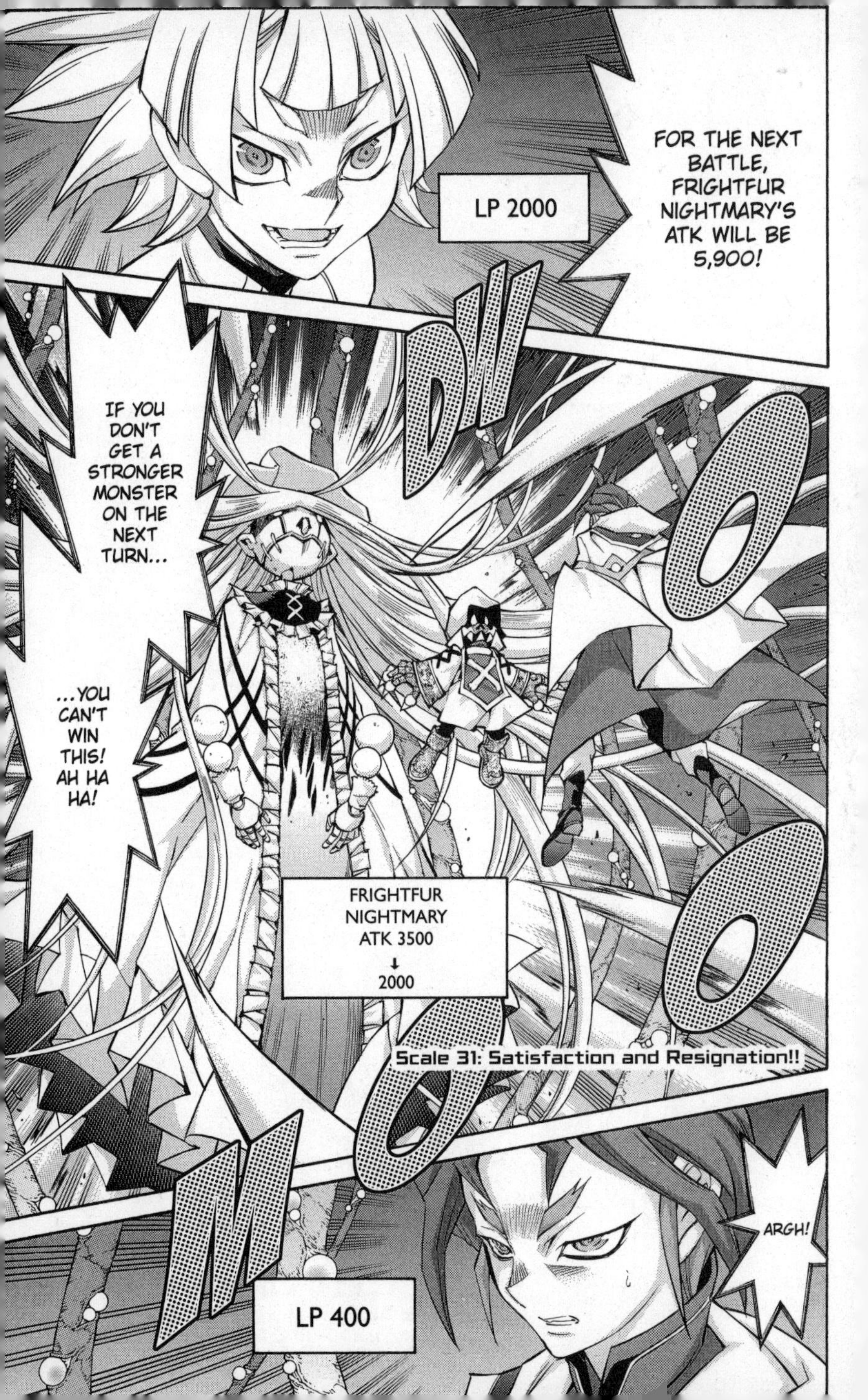

FOR THE NEXT BATTLE, FRIGHTFUR NIGHTMARY'S ATK WILL BE 5,900!
LP 2000
DOOOM
IF YOU DON'T GET A STRONGER MONSTER ON THE NEXT TURN...
...YOU CAN'T WIN THIS! AH HA HA!
FRIGHTFUR NIGHTMARY ATK 3500 ↓ 2000
Scale 31: Satisfaction and Resignation!!
ARGH!
LP 400

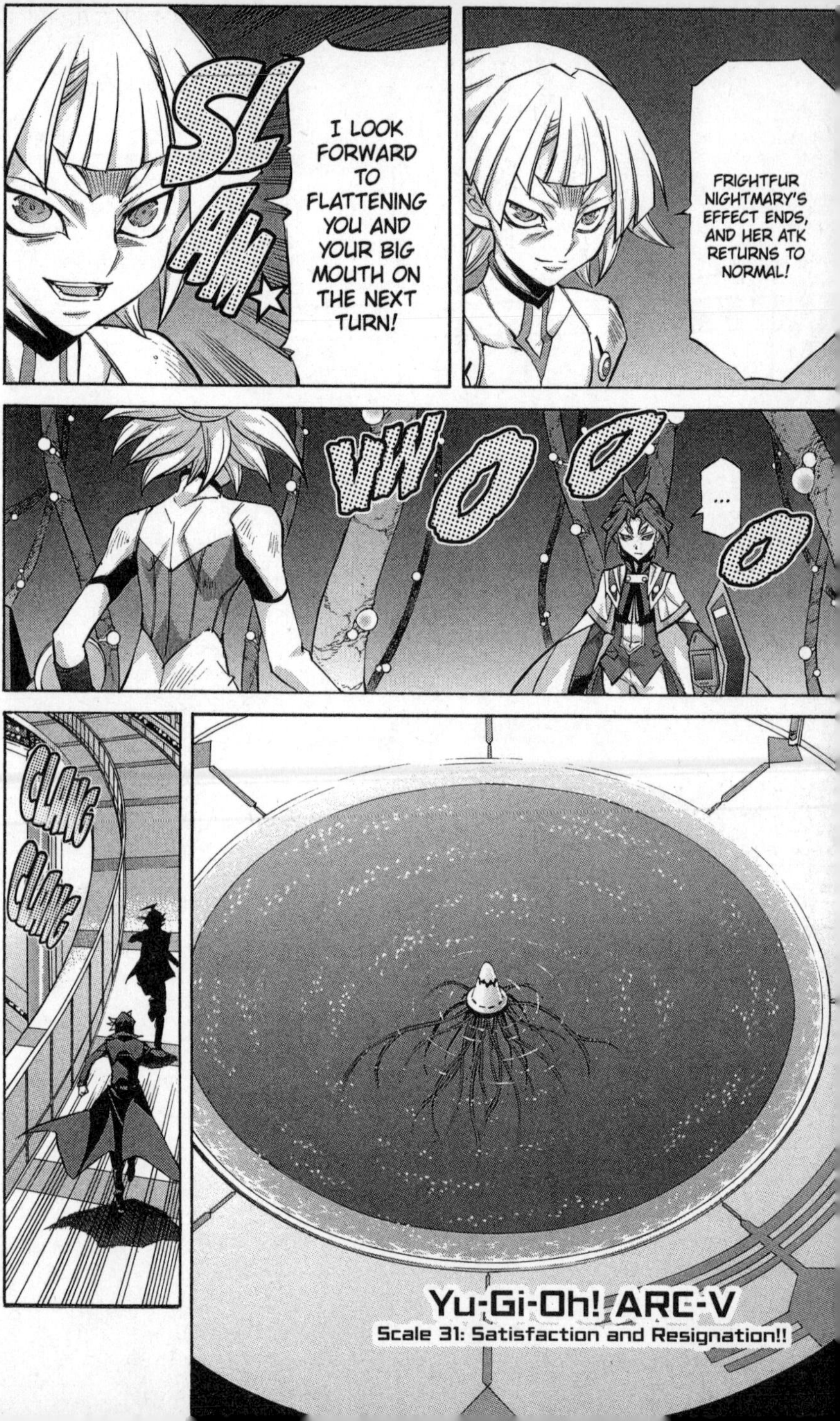
FRIGHTFUR NIGHTMARY'S EFFECT ENDS, AND HER ATK RETURNS TO NORMAL!
SLAM☆
I LOOK FORWARD TO FLATTENING YOU AND YOUR BIG MOUTH ON THE NEXT TURN!
...
VWOOOO
Yu-Gi-Oh! ARC-V
Scale 31: Satisfaction and Resignation!!
CLANG
CLANG

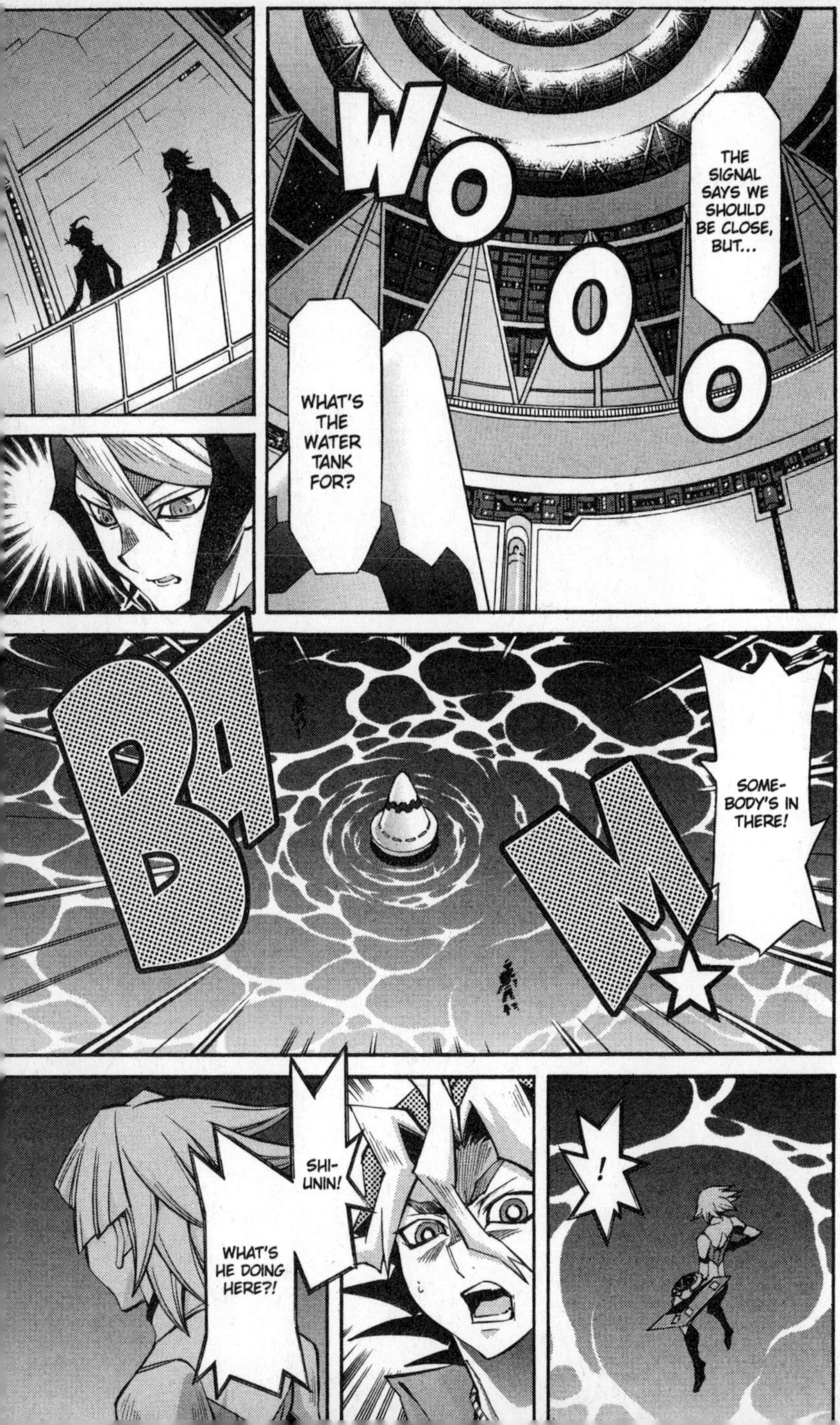
THE SIGNAL SAYS WE SHOULD BE CLOSE, BUT...
WOOOO
WHAT'S THE WATER TANK FOR?
SOMEBODY'S IN THERE!
BAM
!
SHI-UNIN!
WHAT'S HE DOING HERE?!

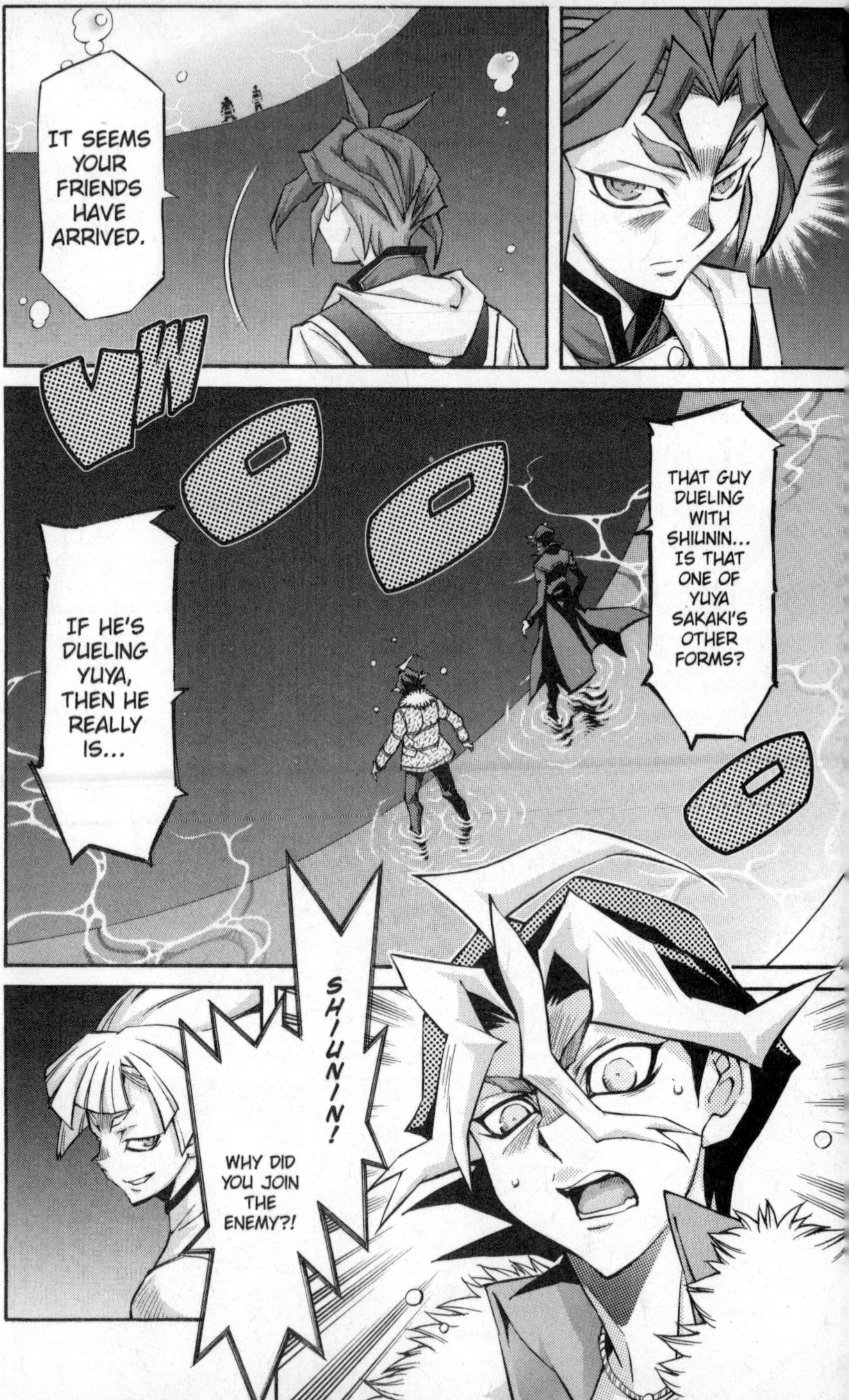
IT SEEMS YOUR FRIENDS HAVE ARRIVED.
VVW
THAT GUY DUELING WITH SHIUNIN... IS THAT ONE OF YUYA SAKAKI'S OTHER FORMS?
IF HE'S DUELING YUYA, THEN HE REALLY IS...
SHIUNIN!
WHY DID YOU JOIN THE ENEMY?!

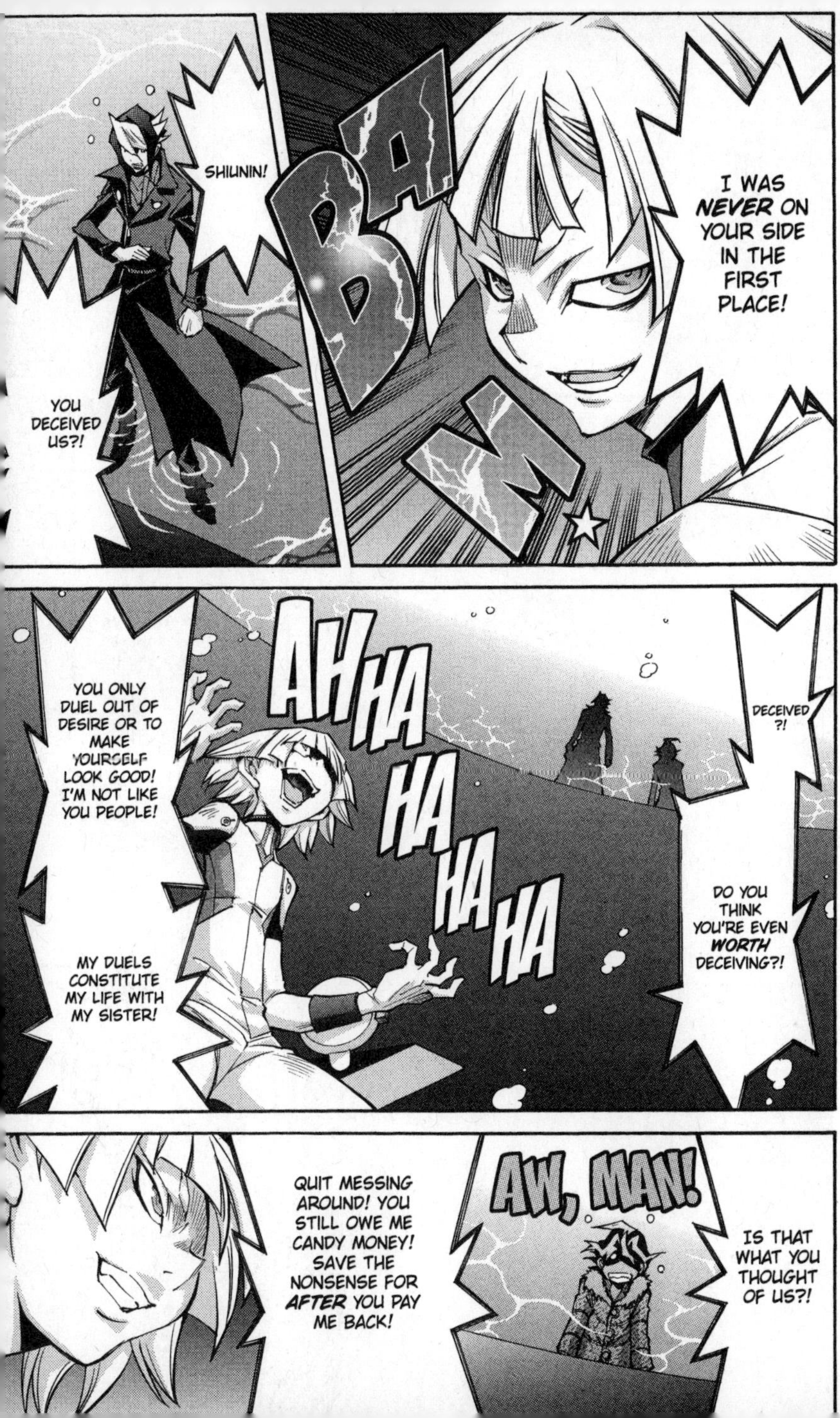

BAM☆
I WAS NEVER ON YOUR SIDE IN THE FIRST PLACE!
SHIUNIN!
YOU DECEIVED US?!
DECEIVED?!
DO YOU THINK YOU'RE EVEN WORTH DECEIVING?!
AHHAHAHAHAHA
YOU ONLY DUEL OUT OF DESIRE OR TO MAKE YOURSELF LOOK GOOD! I'M NOT LIKE YOU PEOPLE!
MY DUELS CONSTITUTE MY LIFE WITH MY SISTER!
AW, MAN!
IS THAT WHAT YOU THOUGHT OF US?!
QUIT MESSING AROUND! YOU STILL OWE ME CANDY MONEY! SAVE THE NONSENSE FOR AFTER YOU PAY ME BACK!

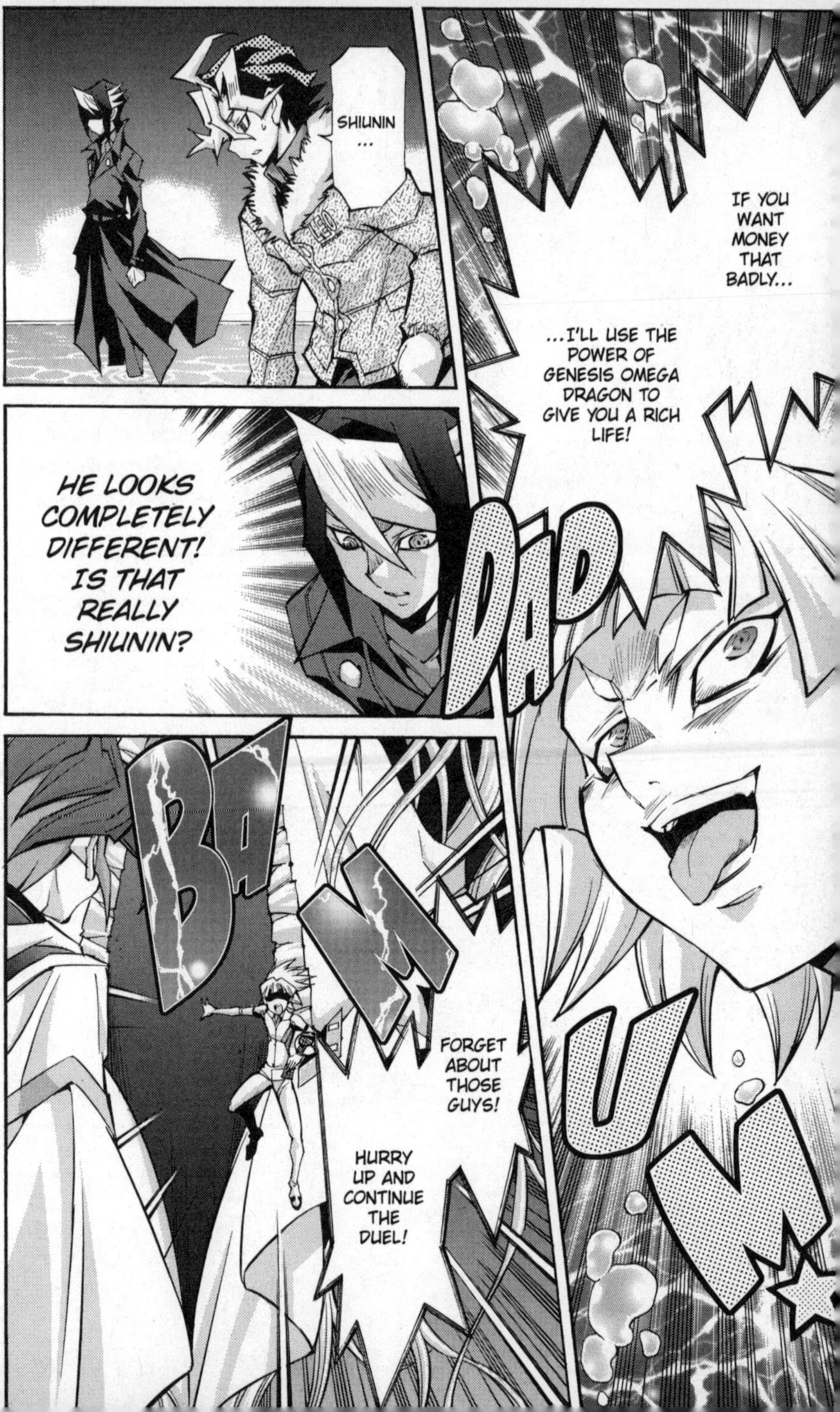
IF YOU WANT MONEY THAT BADLY...
...I'LL USE THE POWER OF GENESIS OMEGA DRAGON TO GIVE YOU A RICH LIFE!
DADUM
SHIUNIN ...
HE LOOKS COMPLETELY DIFFERENT! IS THAT REALLY SHIUNIN?
BAM
FORGET ABOUT THOSE GUYS!
HURRY UP AND CONTINUE THE DUEL!

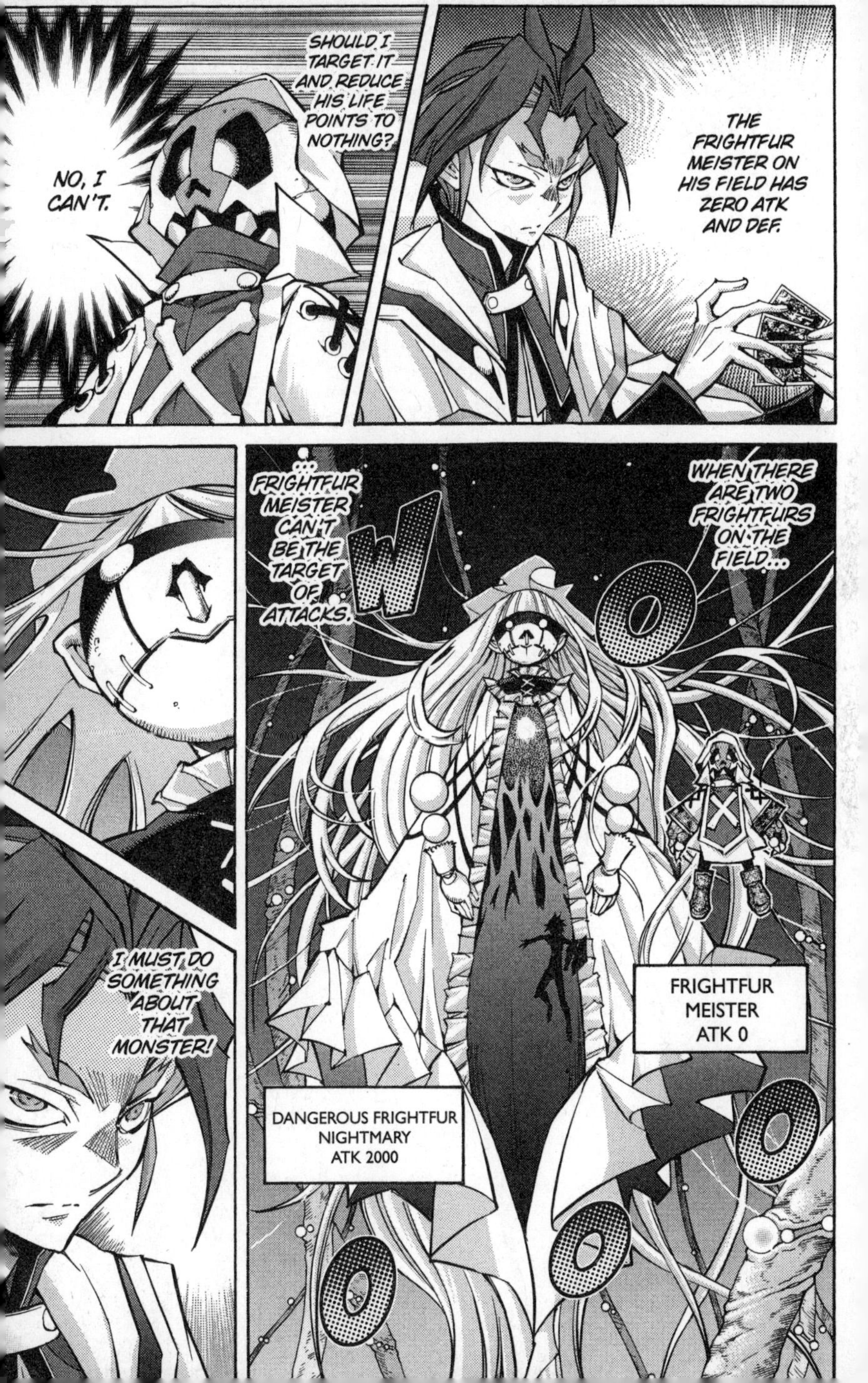
THE FRIGHTFUR MEISTER ON HIS FIELD HAS ZERO ATK AND DEF.
SHOULD I TARGET IT AND REDUCE HIS LIFE POINTS TO NOTHING?
NO, I CAN'T.
WHEN THERE ARE TWO FRIGHTFURS ON THE FIELD...
...FRIGHTFUR MEISTER CAN'T BE THE TARGET OF ATTACKS.
FRIGHTFUR MEISTER ATK 0
DANGEROUS FRIGHTFUR NIGHTMARY ATK 2000
I MUST DO SOMETHING ABOUT THAT MONSTER!

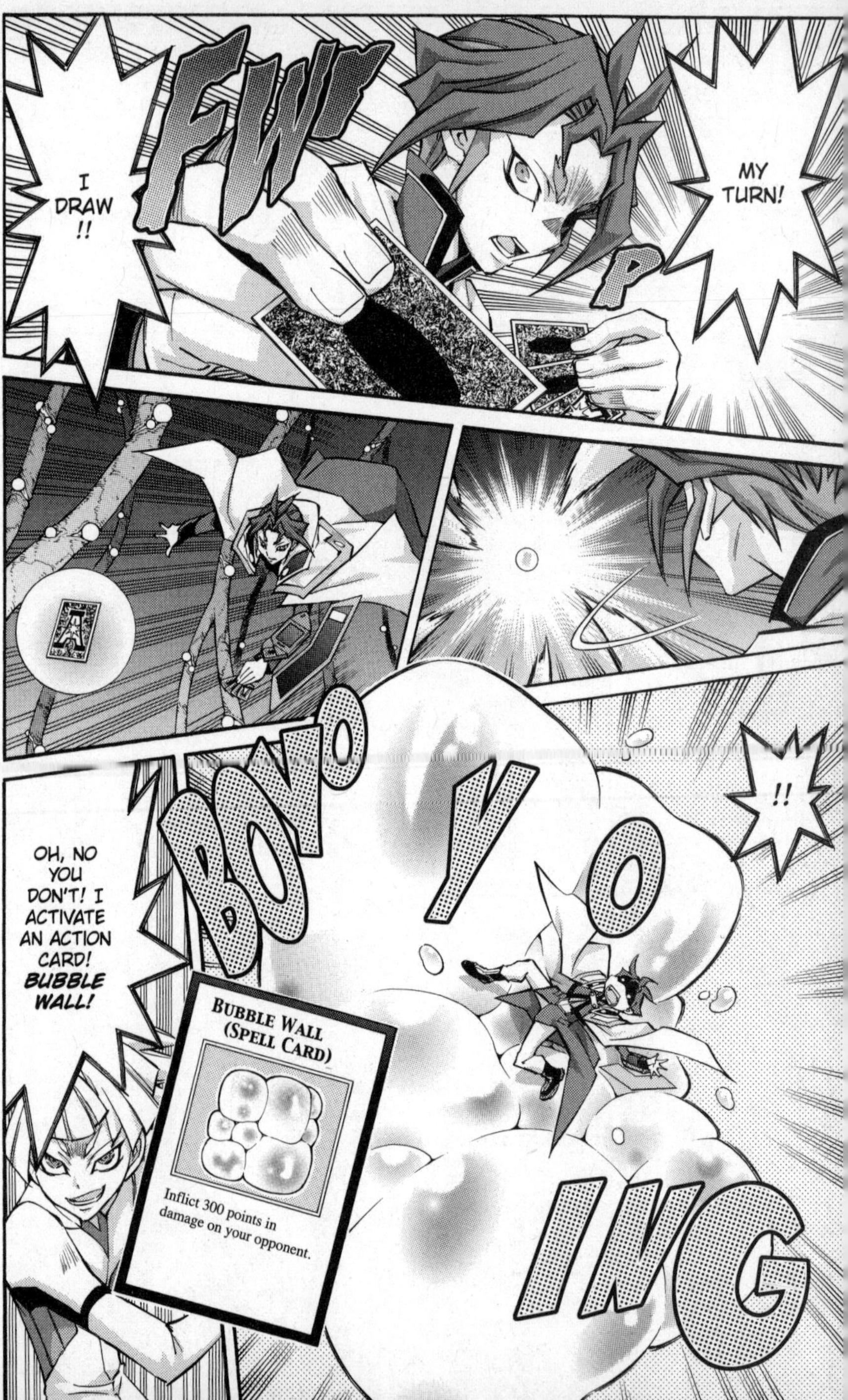
MY TURN!
I DRAW!!
!!
BOYOING
OH, NO YOU DON'T! I ACTIVATE AN ACTION CARD! BUBBLE WALL!
BUBBLE WALL (SPELL CARD)
Inflict 300 points in damage on your opponent.

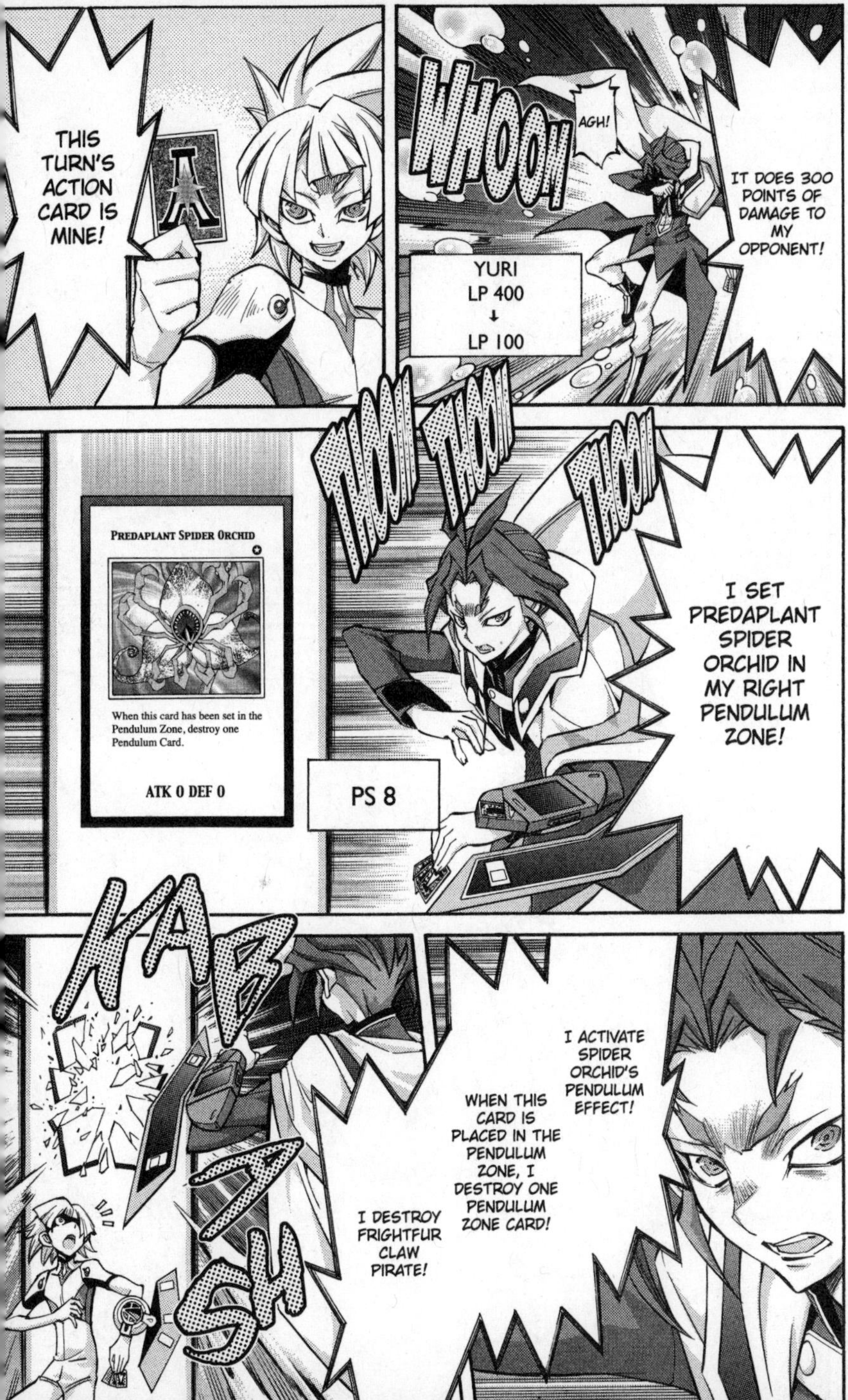
WHOOM
AGH!
IT DOES 300 POINTS OF DAMAGE TO MY OPPONENT!
YURI LP 400 ↓ LP 100
THIS TURN'S ACTION CARD IS MINE!
THOOM THOOM THOOM
I SET PREDAPLANT SPIDER ORCHID IN MY RIGHT PENDULUM ZONE!
PREDAPLANT SPIDER ORCHID
When this card has been set in the Pendulum Zone, destroy one Pendulum Card.
ATK 0 DEF 0
PS 8
I ACTIVATE SPIDER ORCHID'S PENDULUM EFFECT!
WHEN THIS CARD IS PLACED IN THE PENDULUM ZONE, I DESTROY ONE PENDULUM ZONE CARD!
I DESTROY FRIGHTFUR CLAW PIRATE!
KABASH

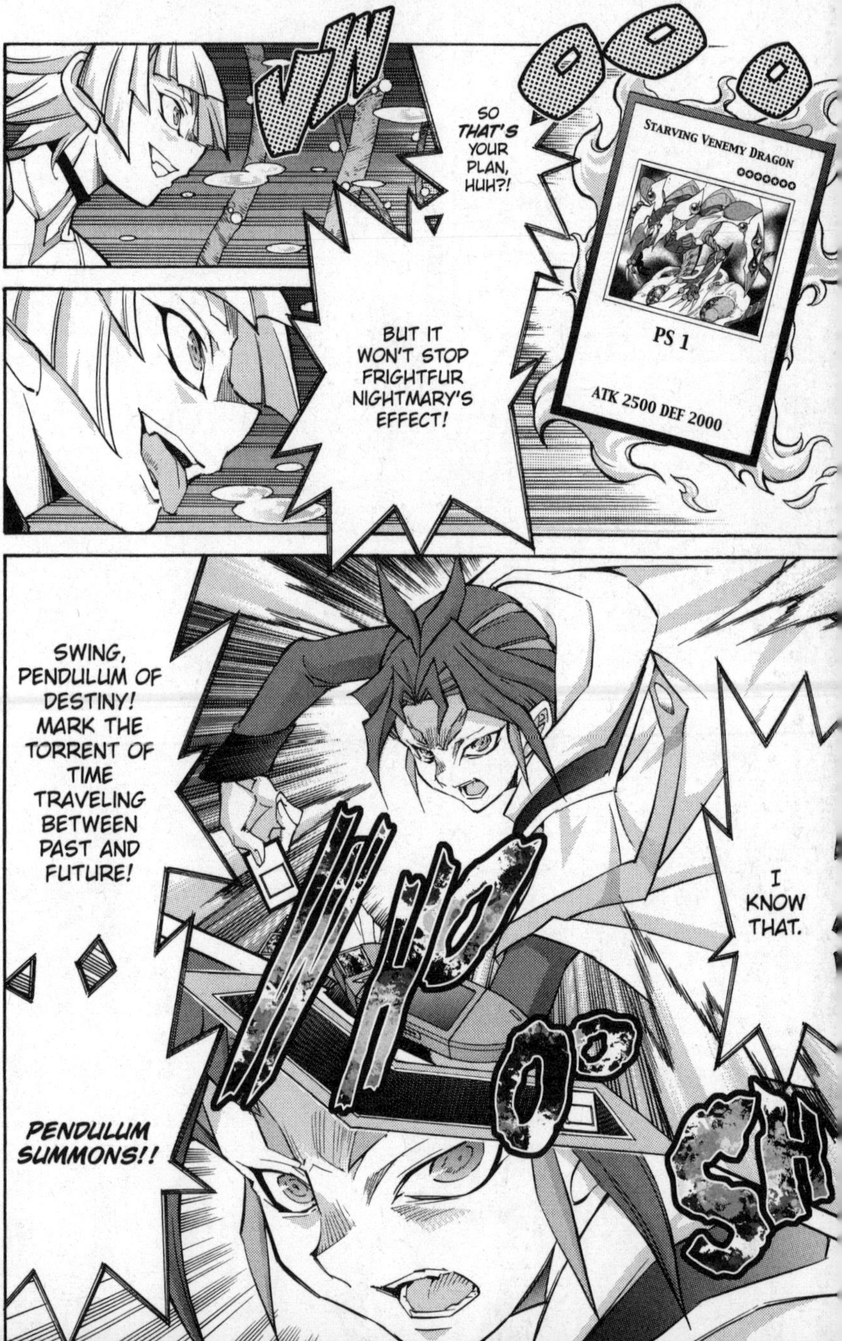
STARVING VENEMY DRAGON
PS 1
ATK 2500 DEF 2000
SO THAT'S YOUR PLAN, HUH?!
BUT IT WON'T STOP FRIGHTFUR NIGHTMARY'S EFFECT!
I KNOW THAT.
SWING, PENDULUM OF DESTINY! MARK THE TORRENT OF TIME TRAVELING BETWEEN PAST AND FUTURE!
PENDULUM SUMMONS!!

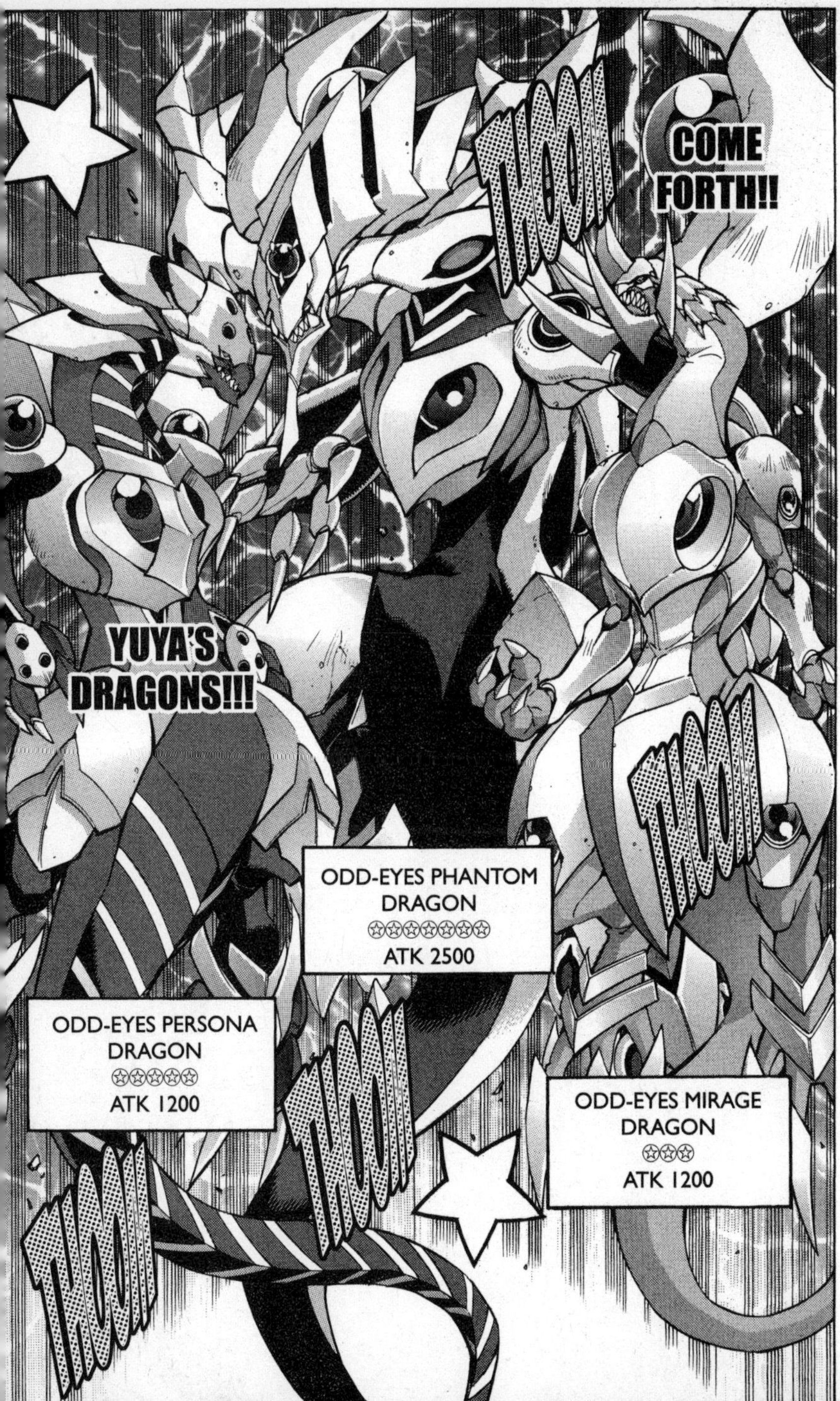
COME FORTH!!
THOOM!!
YUYA'S DRAGONS!!!
THOOM!!
ODD-EYES PHANTOM DRAGON
☆☆☆☆☆☆☆☆
ATK 2500
ODD-EYES MIRAGE DRAGON
☆☆☆
ATK 1200
ODD-EYES PERSONA DRAGON
☆☆☆☆☆
ATK 1200
THOOM!!
THOOM!!

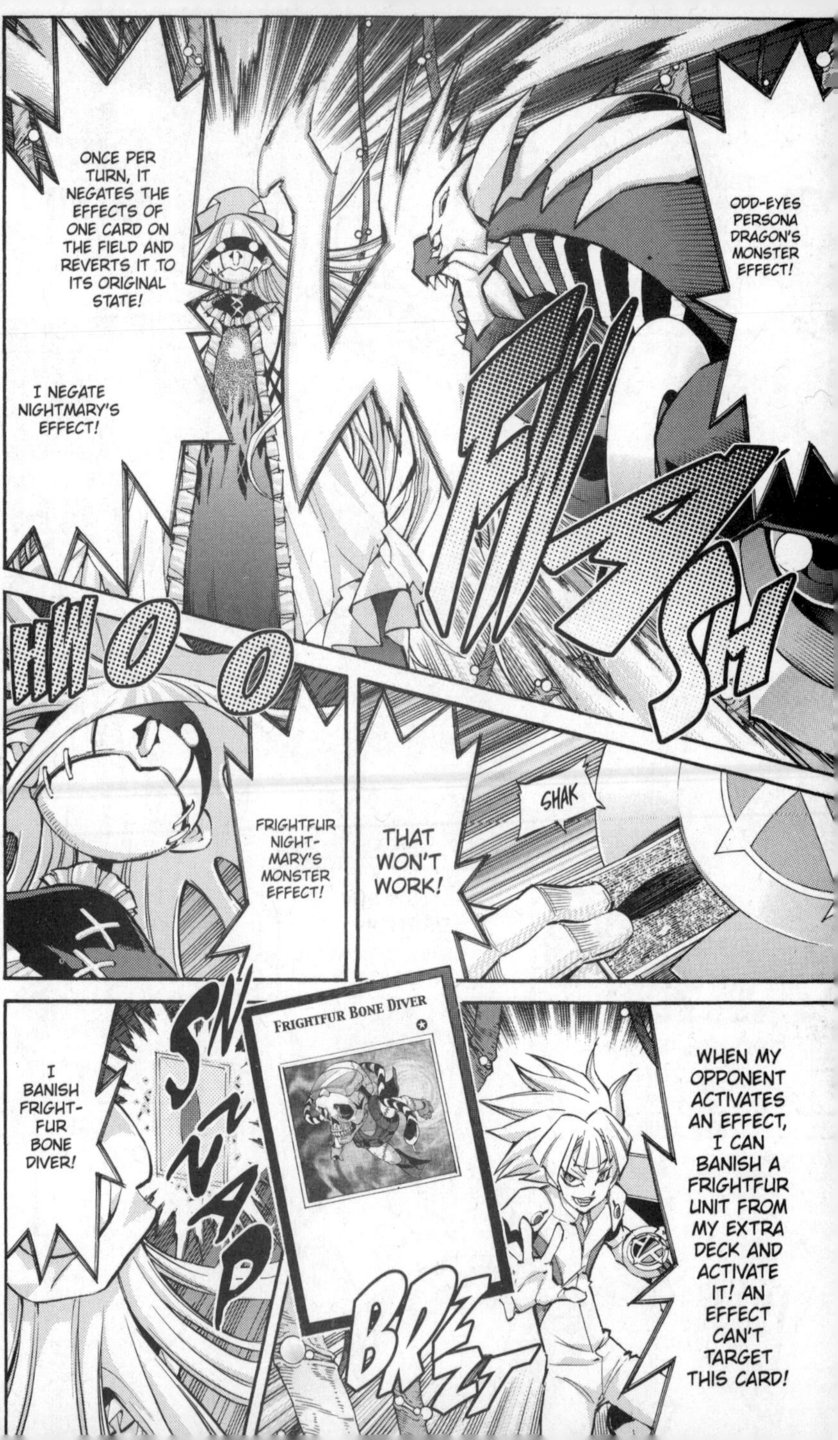
ODD-EYES PERSONA DRAGON'S MONSTER EFFECT!
ONCE PER TURN, IT NEGATES THE EFFECTS OF ONE CARD ON THE FIELD AND REVERTS IT TO ITS ORIGINAL STATE!
I NEGATE NIGHTMARY'S EFFECT!
SHAK
THAT WON'T WORK!
FRIGHTFUR NIGHT-MARY'S MONSTER EFFECT!
WHEN MY OPPONENT ACTIVATES AN EFFECT, I CAN BANISH A FRIGHTFUR UNIT FROM MY EXTRA DECK AND ACTIVATE IT! AN EFFECT CAN'T TARGET THIS CARD!
FRIGHTFUR BONE DIVER
I BANISH FRIGHT-FUR BONE DIVER!

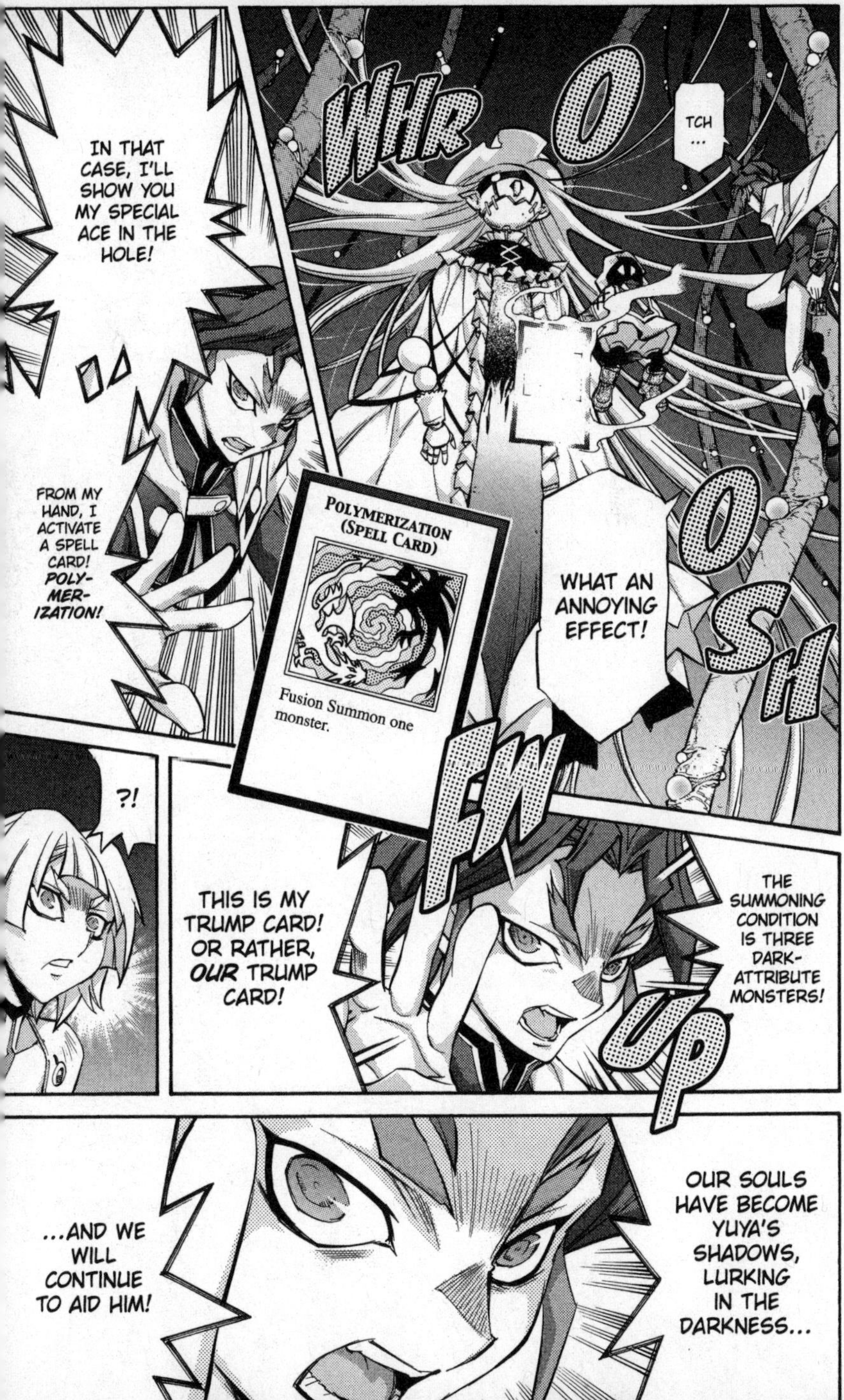

TCH ...
WHAT AN ANNOYING EFFECT!
WHRO OOSH
IN THAT CASE, I'LL SHOW YOU MY SPECIAL ACE IN THE HOLE!
FROM MY HAND, I ACTIVATE A SPELL CARD! POLYMERIZATION!
POLYMERIZATION (SPELL CARD)
Fusion Summon one monster.
THE SUMMONING CONDITION IS THREE DARK-ATTRIBUTE MONSTERS!
THIS IS MY TRUMP CARD! OR RATHER, OUR TRUMP CARD!
FWUP
?!
OUR SOULS HAVE BECOME YUYA'S SHADOWS, LURKING IN THE DARKNESS...
...AND WE WILL CONTINUE TO AID HIM!

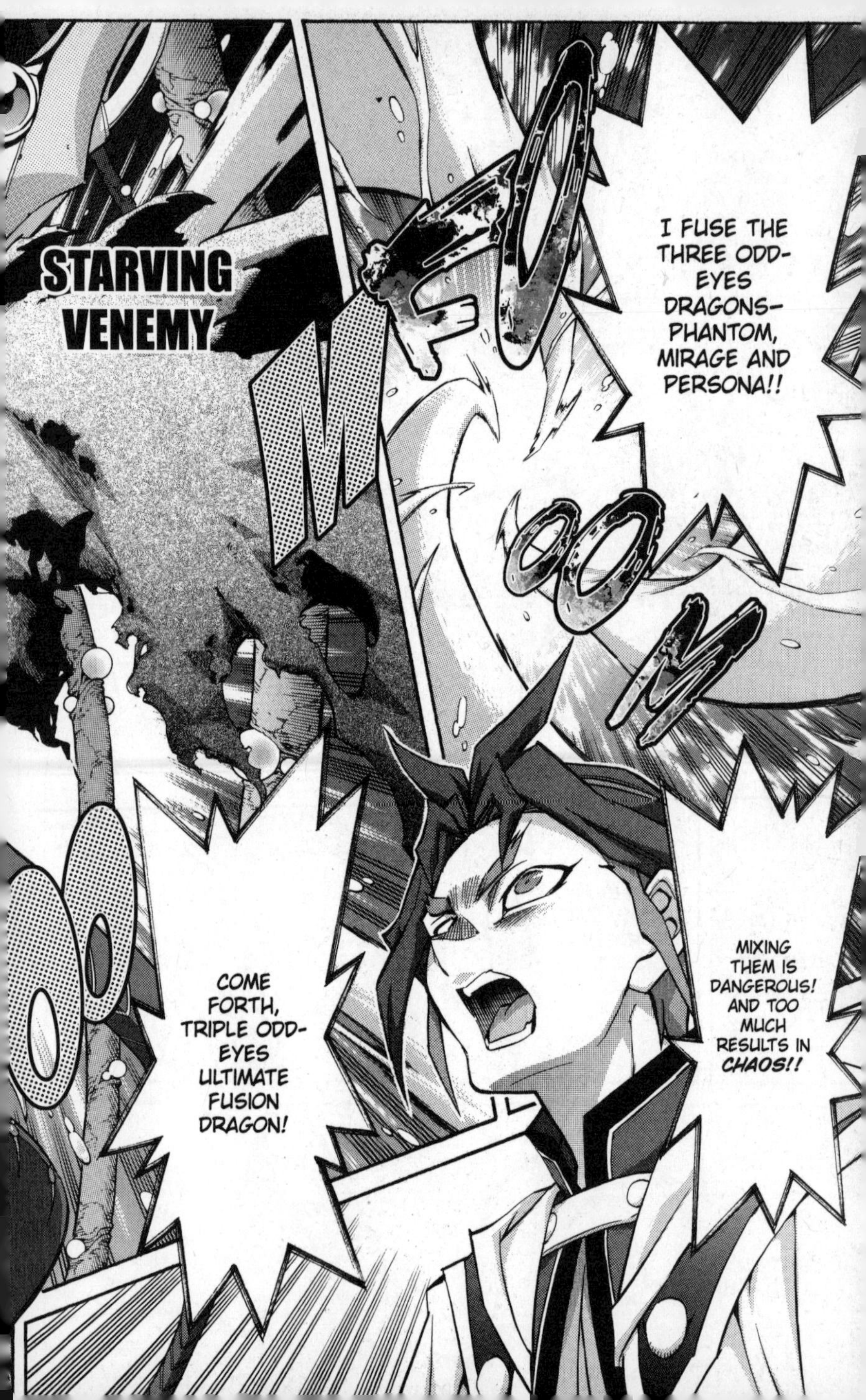
I FUSE THE THREE ODD-EYES DRAGONS—PHANTOM, MIRAGE AND PERSONA!!
FOOM
STARVING VENEMY
MIXING THEM IS DANGEROUS! AND TOO MUCH RESULTS IN *CHAOS!!*
COME FORTH, TRIPLE ODD-EYES ULTIMATE FUSION DRAGON!

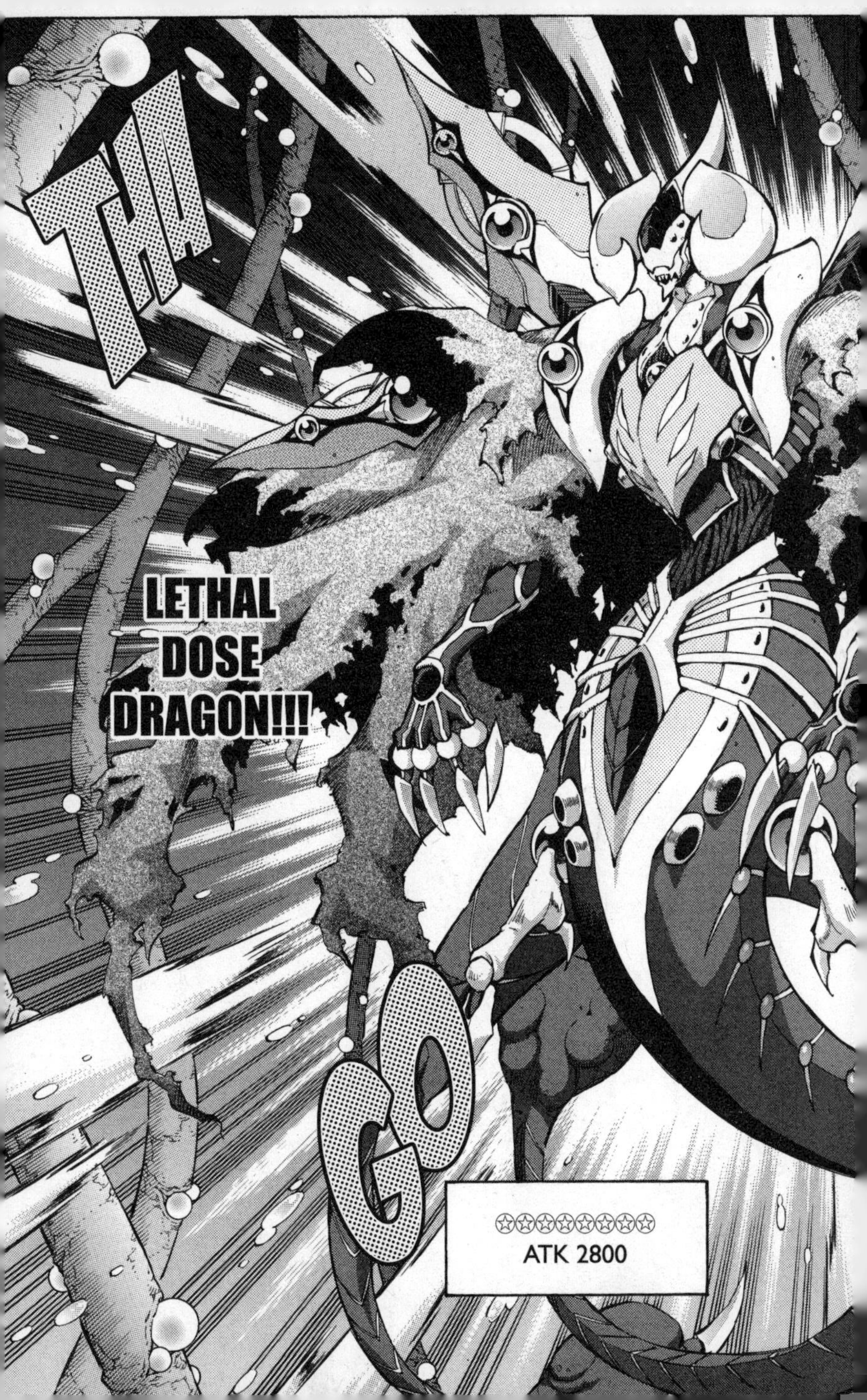
THA
LETHAL DOSE DRAGON!!!
GO
ATK 2800

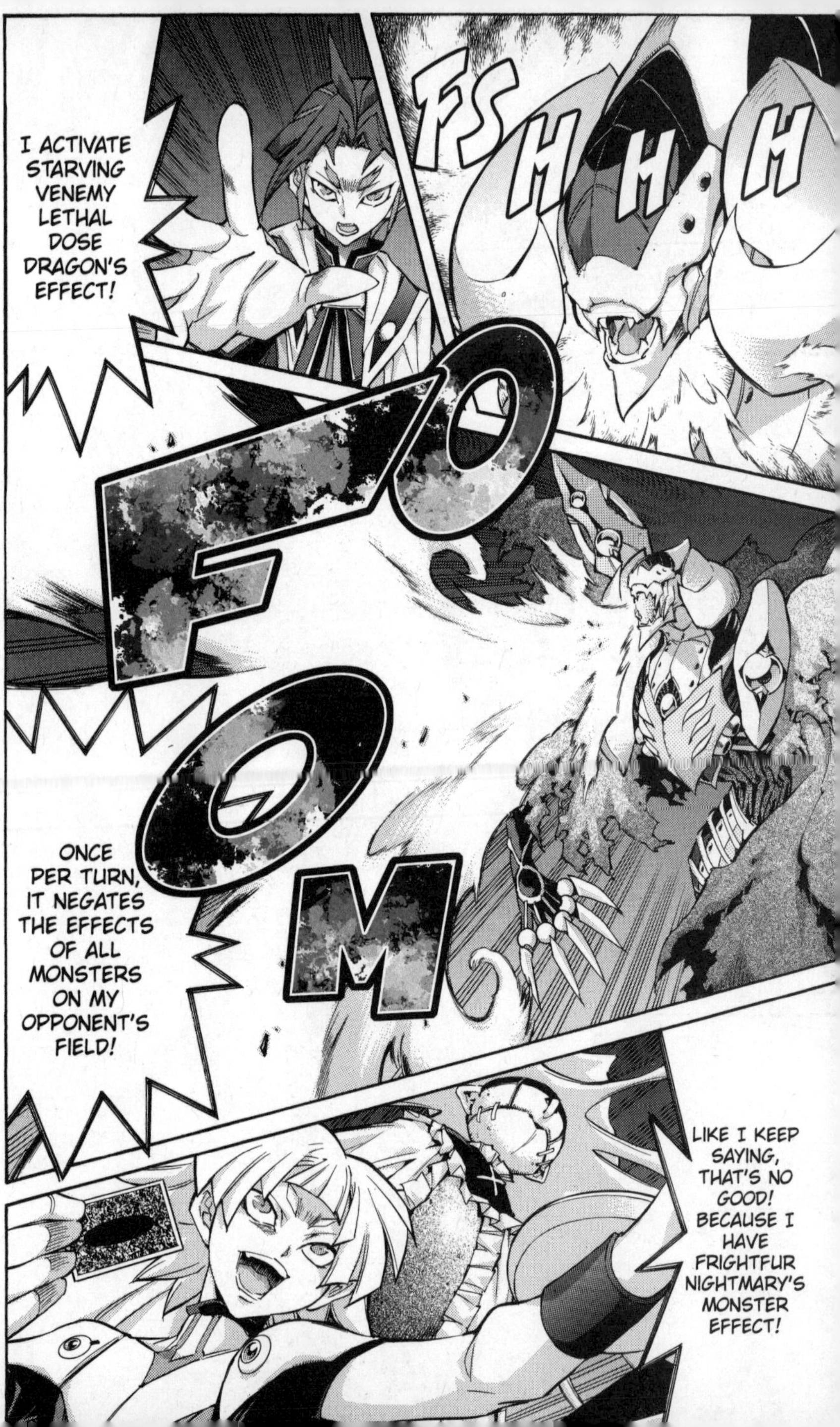
FSHHHH
I ACTIVATE STARVING VENEMY LETHAL DOSE DRAGON'S EFFECT!
FOOM
ONCE PER TURN, IT NEGATES THE EFFECTS OF ALL MONSTERS ON MY OPPONENT'S FIELD!
LIKE I KEEP SAYING, THAT'S NO GOOD! BECAUSE I HAVE FRIGHTFUR NIGHTMARY'S MONSTER EFFECT!

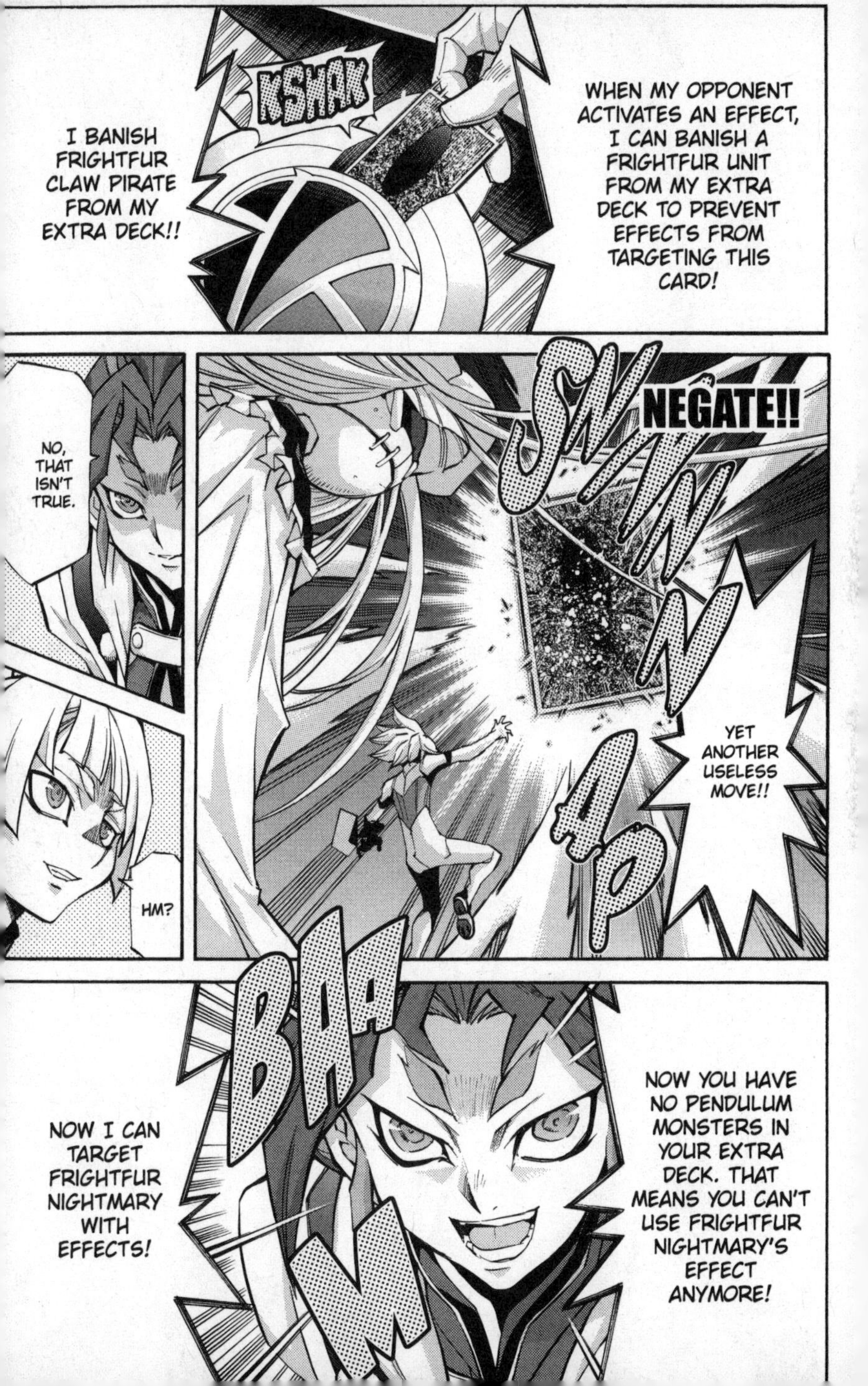
WHEN MY OPPONENT ACTIVATES AN EFFECT, I CAN BANISH A FRIGHTFUR UNIT FROM MY EXTRA DECK TO PREVENT EFFECTS FROM TARGETING THIS CARD!
KSHAK
I BANISH FRIGHTFUR CLAW PIRATE FROM MY EXTRA DECK!!
SWAAAP
NEGATE!!
YET ANOTHER USELESS MOVE!!
NO, THAT ISN'T TRUE.
HM?
NOW YOU HAVE NO PENDULUM MONSTERS IN YOUR EXTRA DECK. THAT MEANS YOU CAN'T USE FRIGHTFUR NIGHTMARY'S EFFECT ANYMORE!
BAAM
NOW I CAN TARGET FRIGHTFUR NIGHTMARY WITH EFFECTS!

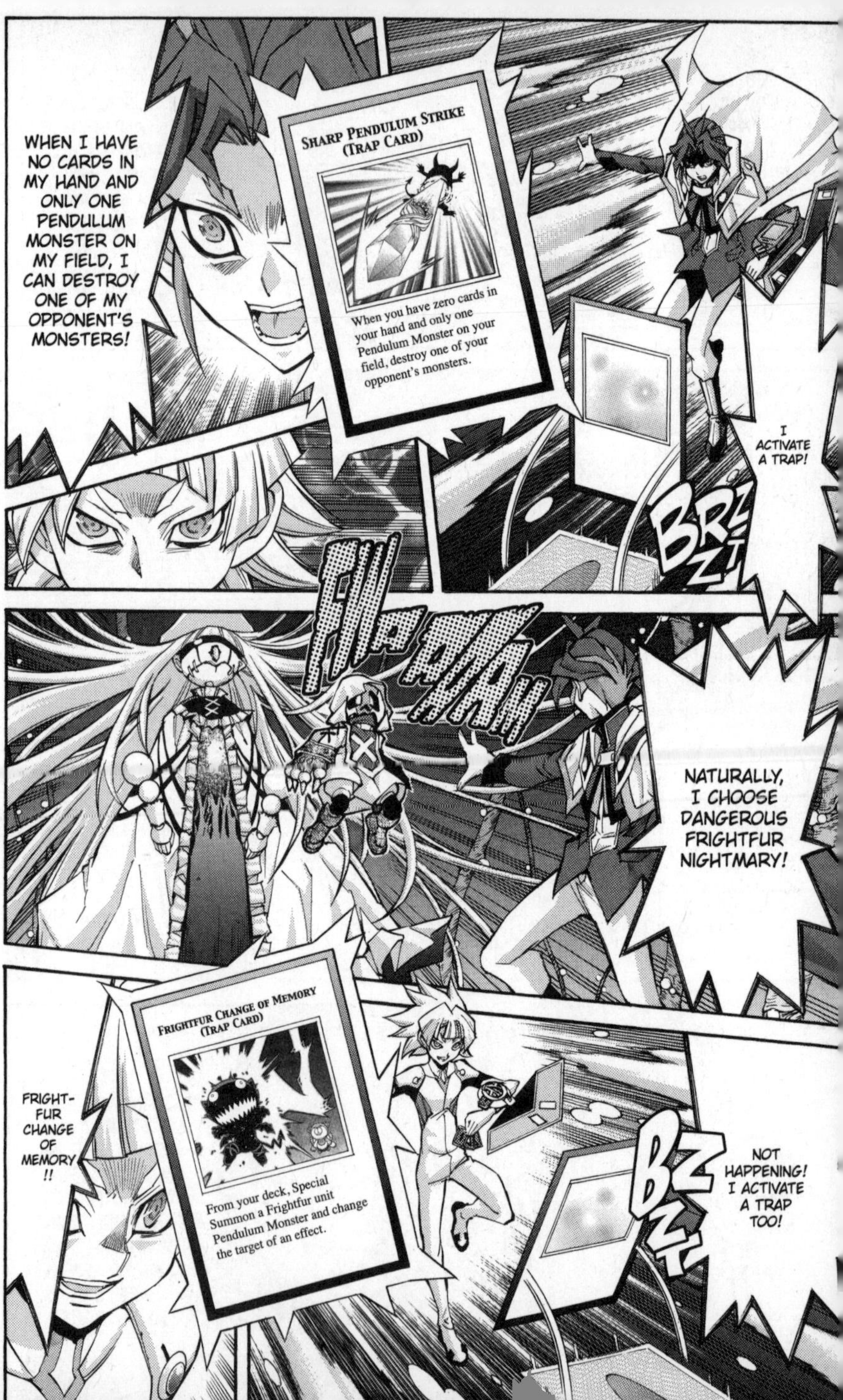
I ACTIVATE A TRAP!
BRZZT
WHEN I HAVE NO CARDS IN MY HAND AND ONLY ONE PENDULUM MONSTER ON MY FIELD, I CAN DESTROY ONE OF MY OPPONENT'S MONSTERS!
SHARP PENDULUM STRIKE (TRAP CARD)
When you have zero cards in your hand and only one Pendulum Monster on your field, destroy one of your opponent's monsters.
NATURALLY, I CHOOSE DANGEROUS FRIGHTFUR NIGHTMARY!
NOT HAPPENING! I ACTIVATE A TRAP TOO!
BZZT
FRIGHTFUR CHANGE OF MEMORY (TRAP CARD)
From your deck, Special Summon a Frightfur unit Pendulum Monster and change the target of an effect.
FRIGHT-FUR CHANGE OF MEMORY!!

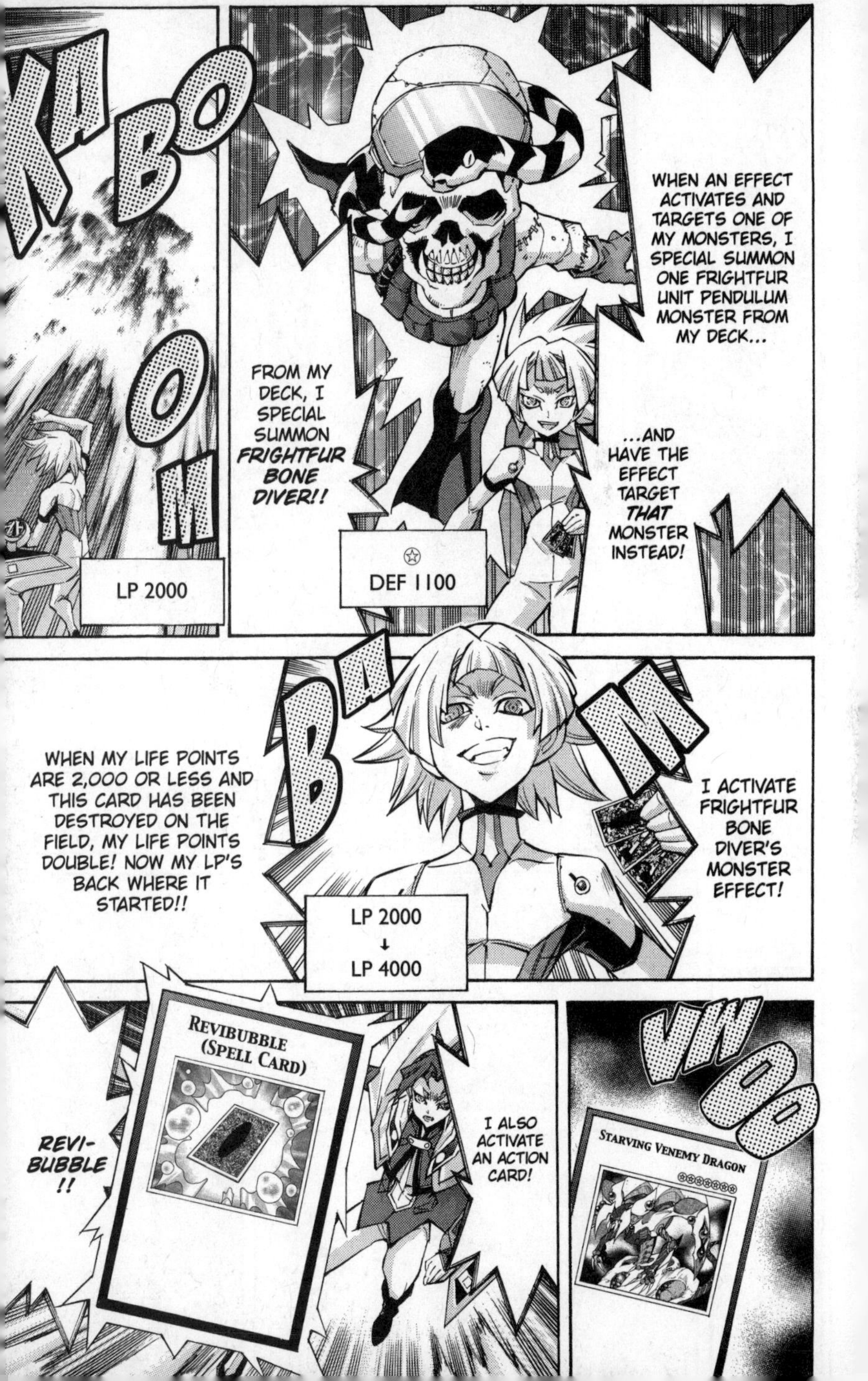

WHEN AN EFFECT ACTIVATES AND TARGETS ONE OF MY MONSTERS, I SPECIAL SUMMON ONE FRIGHTFUR UNIT PENDULUM MONSTER FROM MY DECK...
...AND HAVE THE EFFECT TARGET *THAT* MONSTER INSTEAD!
FROM MY DECK, I SPECIAL SUMMON *FRIGHTFUR BONE DIVER!!*
DEF 1100
KABOOM
LP 2000
I ACTIVATE FRIGHTFUR BONE DIVER'S MONSTER EFFECT!
BAM
WHEN MY LIFE POINTS ARE 2,000 OR LESS AND THIS CARD HAS BEEN DESTROYED ON THE FIELD, MY LIFE POINTS DOUBLE! NOW MY LP'S BACK WHERE IT STARTED!!
LP 2000 ↓ LP 4000
VWOOO
STARVING VENEMY DRAGON
I ALSO ACTIVATE AN ACTION CARD!
REVIBUBBLE (SPELL CARD)
REVI-BUBBLE!!

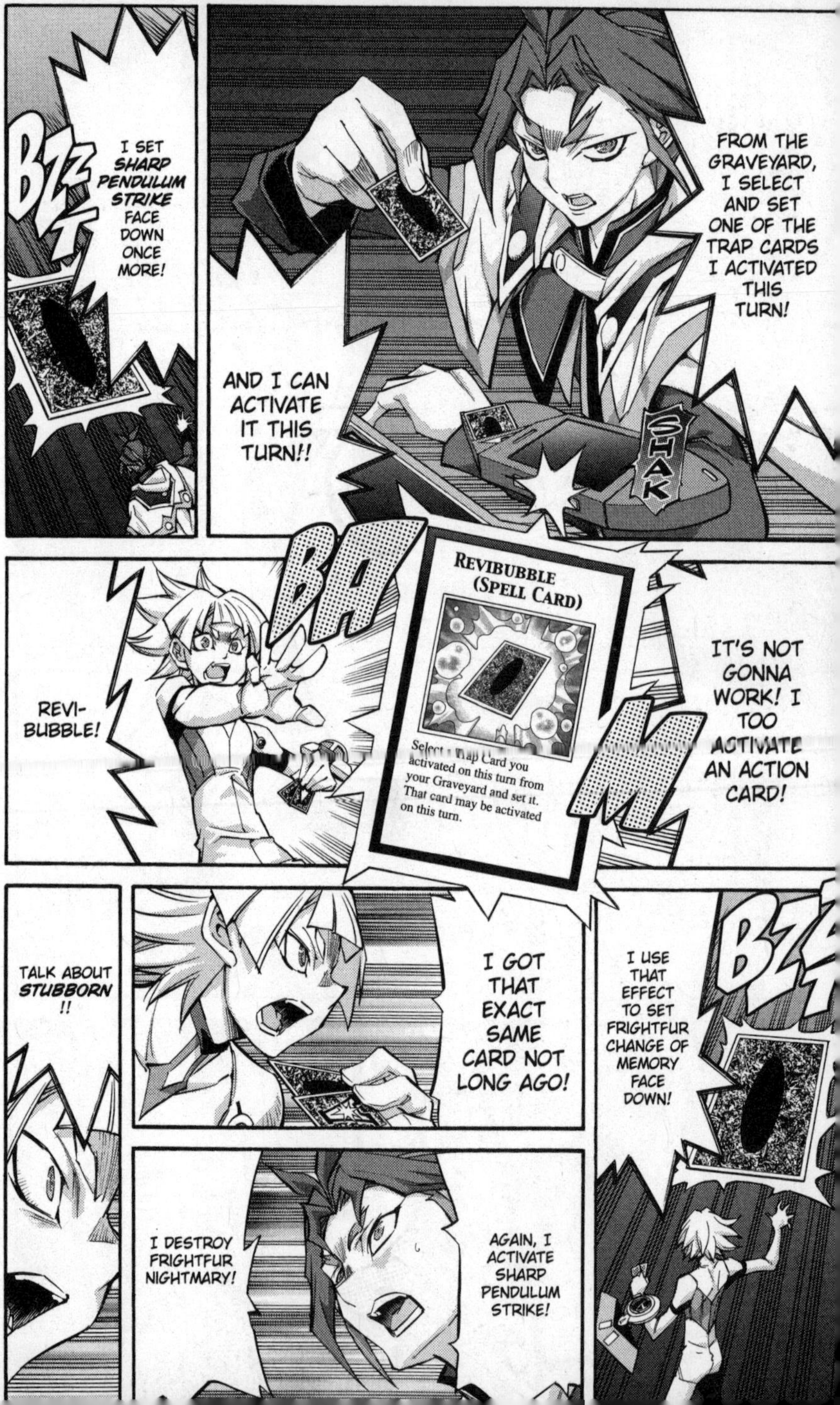
FROM THE GRAVEYARD, I SELECT AND SET ONE OF THE TRAP CARDS I ACTIVATED THIS TURN!
SHAK
AND I CAN ACTIVATE IT THIS TURN!!
BZZT
I SET *SHARP PENDULUM STRIKE* FACE DOWN ONCE MORE!
IT'S NOT GONNA WORK! I TOO ACTIVATE AN ACTION CARD!
REVIBUBBLE (SPELL CARD)
Select a Trap Card you activated on this turn from your Graveyard and set it. That card may be activated on this turn.
BAM
REVI-BUBBLE!
BZ
I USE THAT EFFECT TO SET FRIGHTFUR CHANGE OF MEMORY FACE DOWN!
I GOT THAT EXACT SAME CARD NOT LONG AGO!
AGAIN, I ACTIVATE SHARP PENDULUM STRIKE!
I DESTROY FRIGHTFUR NIGHTMARY!
TALK ABOUT *STUBBORN* !!

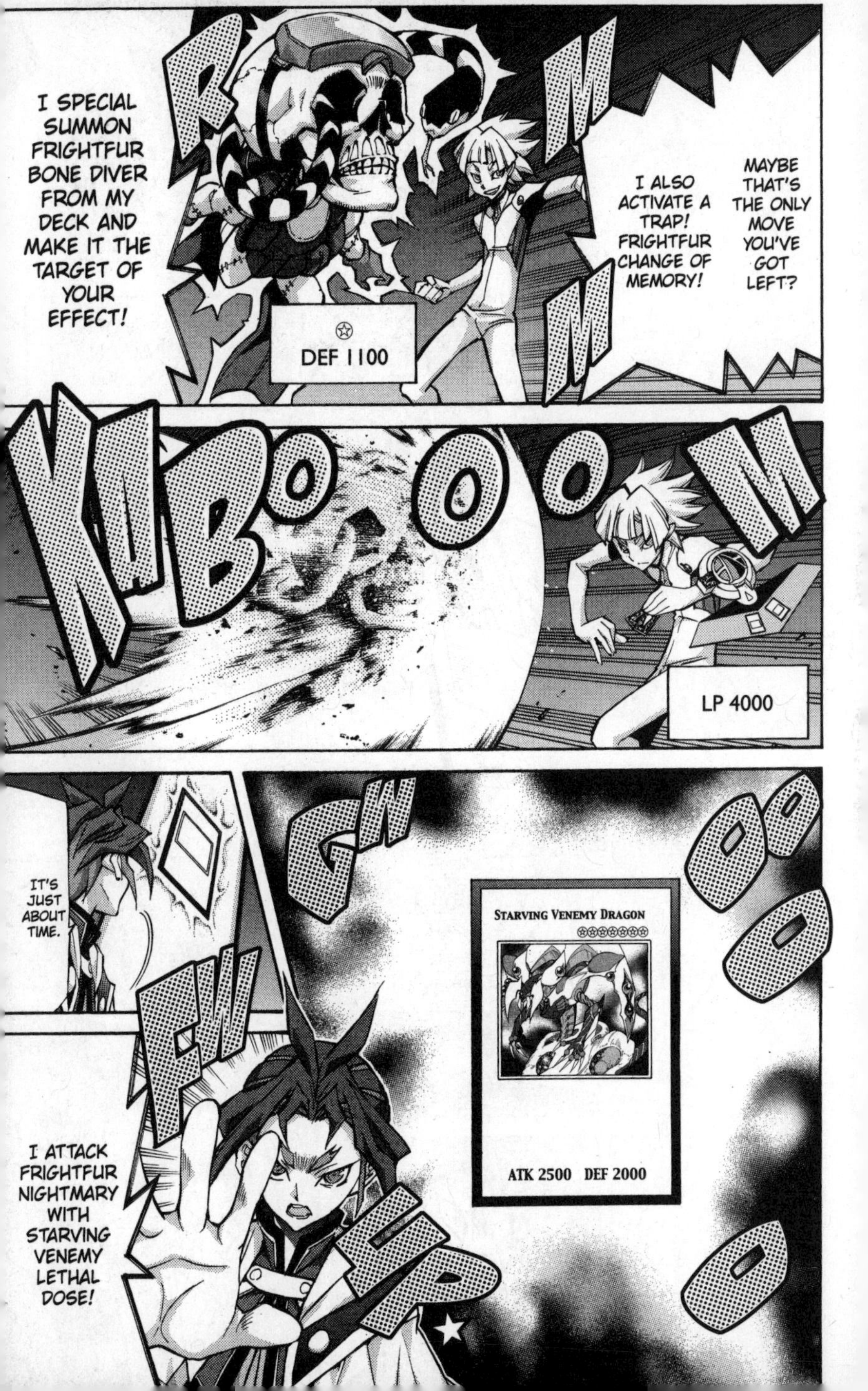
MAYBE THAT'S THE ONLY MOVE YOU'VE GOT LEFT?
I ALSO ACTIVATE A TRAP! FRIGHTFUR CHANGE OF MEMORY!
I SPECIAL SUMMON FRIGHTFUR BONE DIVER FROM MY DECK AND MAKE IT THE TARGET OF YOUR EFFECT!
DEF 1100
LP 4000
STARVING VENEMY DRAGON
ATK 2500 DEF 2000
IT'S JUST ABOUT TIME.
I ATTACK FRIGHTFUR NIGHTMARY WITH STARVING VENEMY LETHAL DOSE!

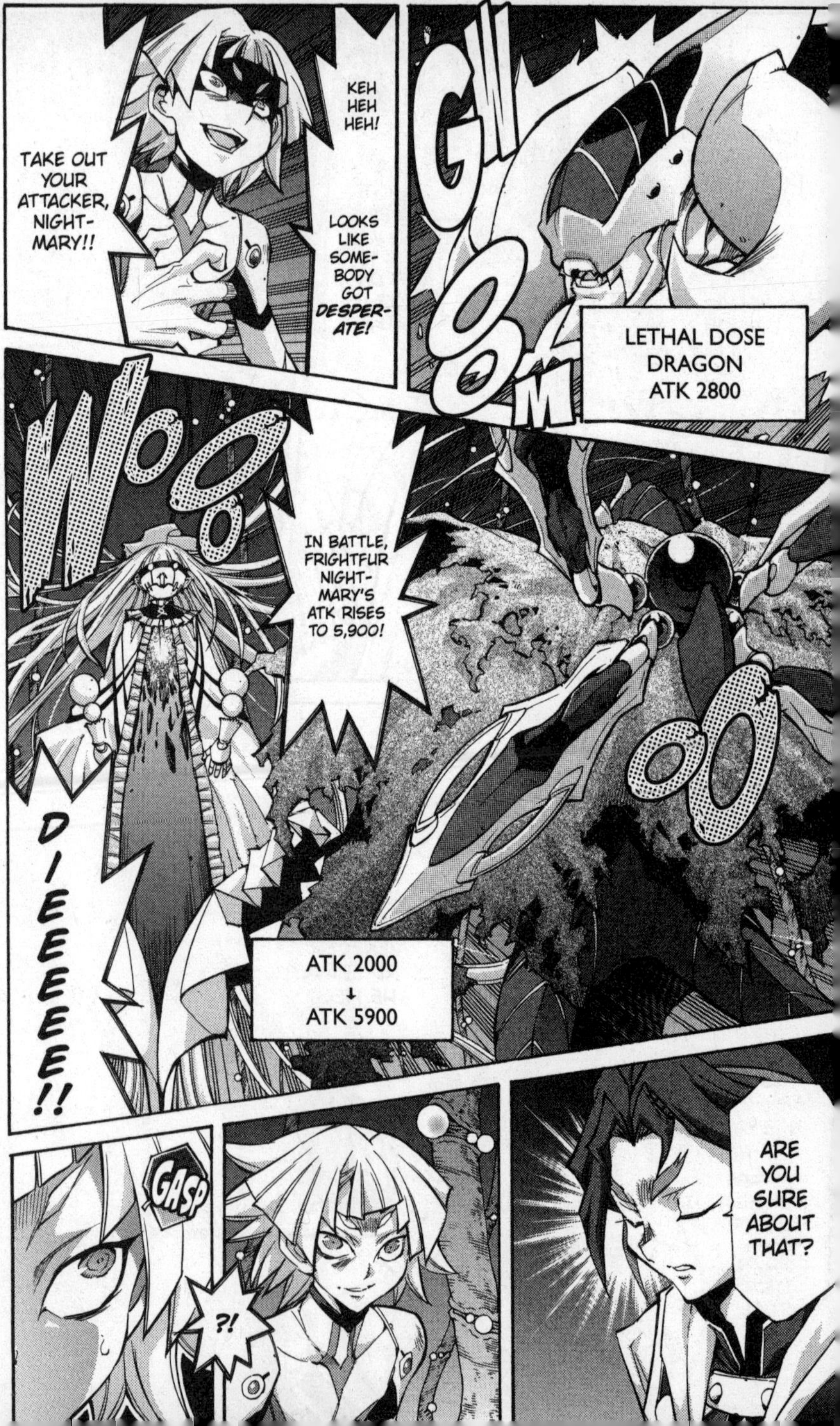
GWOOOM
LETHAL DOSE DRAGON ATK 2800
KEH HEH HEH!
LOOKS LIKE SOMEBODY GOT DESPERATE!
TAKE OUT YOUR ATTACKER, NIGHTMARY!!
WOOOOO
IN BATTLE, FRIGHTFUR NIGHTMARY'S ATK RISES TO 5,900!
ATK 2000 ↓ ATK 5900
DIEEEEEE!!
ARE YOU SURE ABOUT THAT?
GASP
?!

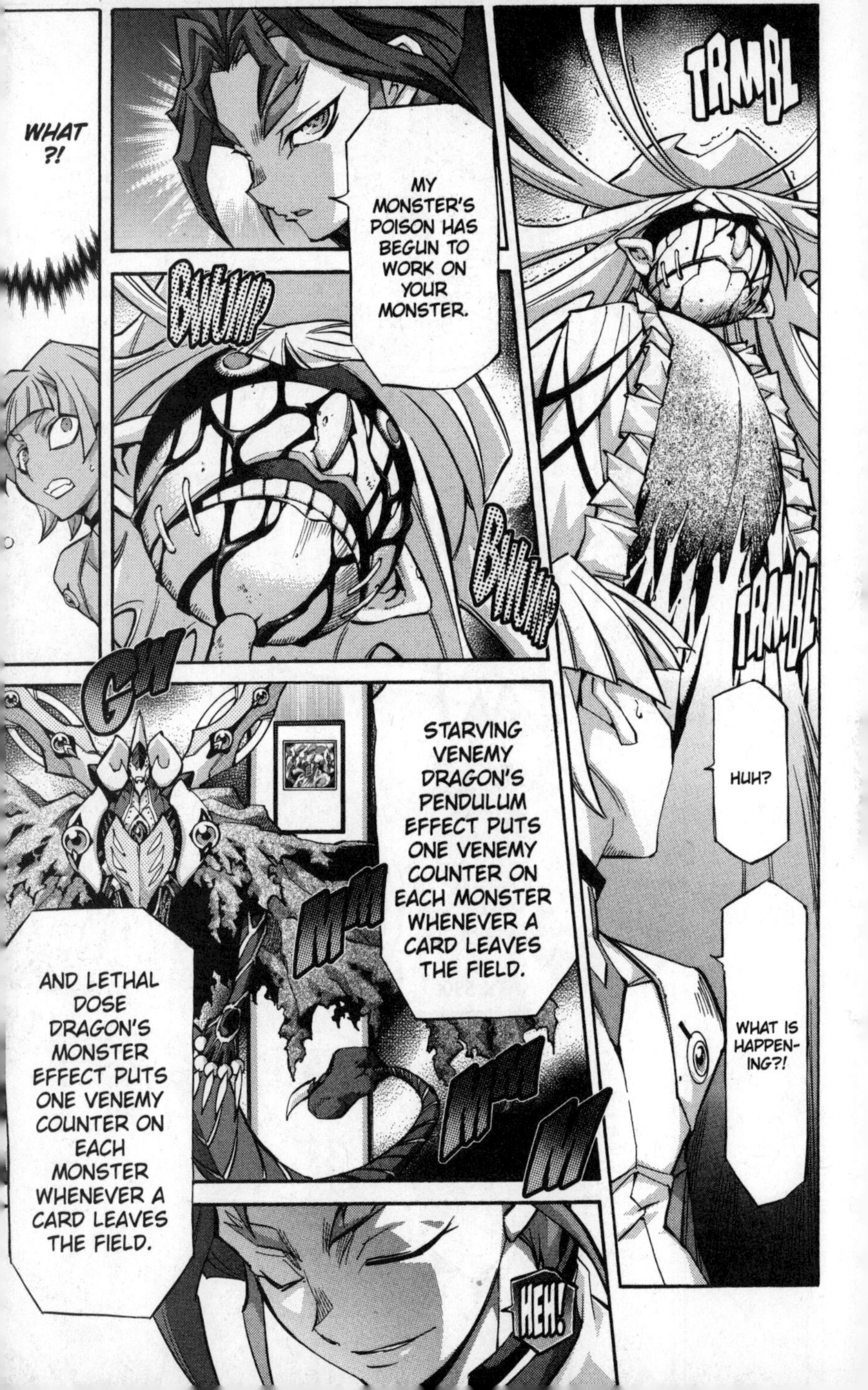
TRMBL
TRMBL
HUH?
WHAT IS HAPPENING?!
MY MONSTER'S POISON HAS BEGUN TO WORK ON YOUR MONSTER.
WHAT ?!
STARVING VENEMY DRAGON'S PENDULUM EFFECT PUTS ONE VENEMY COUNTER ON EACH MONSTER WHENEVER A CARD LEAVES THE FIELD.
AND LETHAL DOSE DRAGON'S MONSTER EFFECT PUTS ONE VENEMY COUNTER ON EACH MONSTER WHENEVER A CARD LEAVES THE FIELD.
HEH!

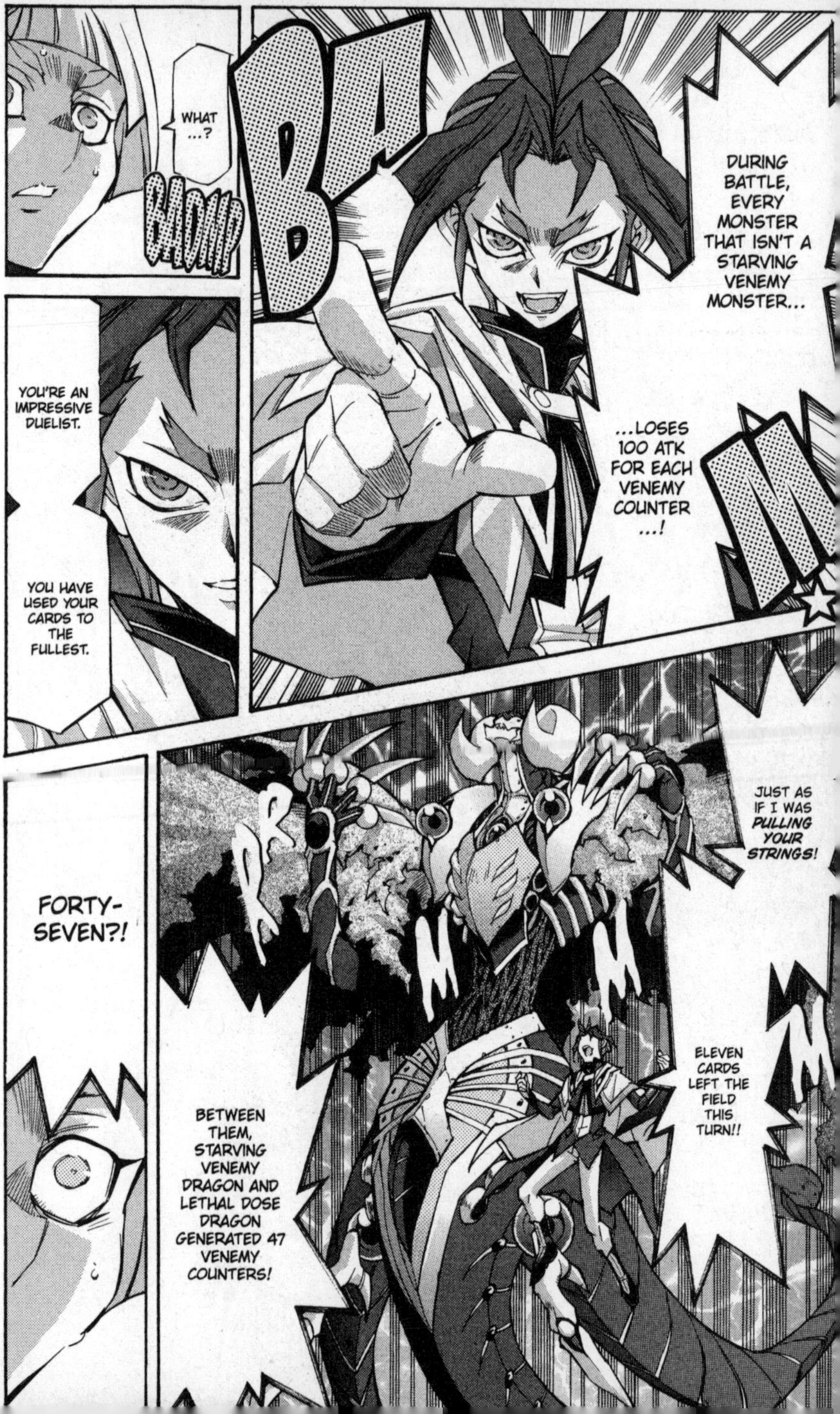
DURING BATTLE, EVERY MONSTER THAT ISN'T A STARVING VENEMY MONSTER...
BA
...LOSES 100 ATK FOR EACH VENEMY COUNTER ...!
WHAT ...?
BADUMP
YOU'RE AN IMPRESSIVE DUELIST.
YOU HAVE USED YOUR CARDS TO THE FULLEST.
JUST AS IF I WAS *PULLING YOUR STRINGS!*
ELEVEN CARDS LEFT THE FIELD THIS TURN!!
BETWEEN THEM, STARVING VENEMY DRAGON AND LETHAL DOSE DRAGON GENERATED 47 VENEMY COUNTERS!
FORTY-SEVEN?!

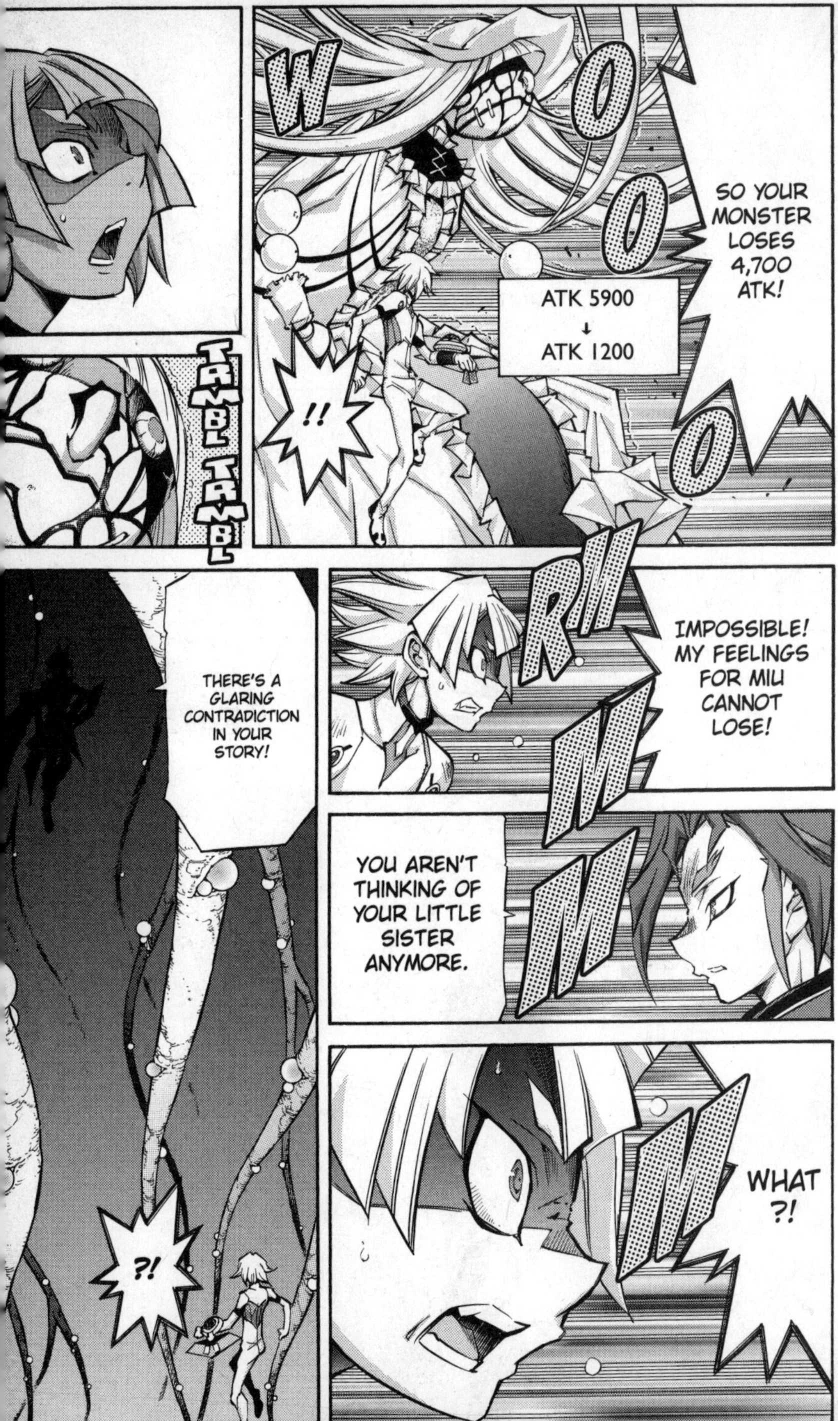
SO YOUR MONSTER LOSES 4,700 ATK!
WOOOO
ATK 5900 ↓ ATK 1200
!!
TRAMBL TRAMBL
IMPOSSIBLE! MY FEELINGS FOR MIU CANNOT LOSE!
RMMMM
YOU AREN'T THINKING OF YOUR LITTLE SISTER ANYMORE.
WHAT?!
THERE'S A GLARING CONTRADICTION IN YOUR STORY!
?!

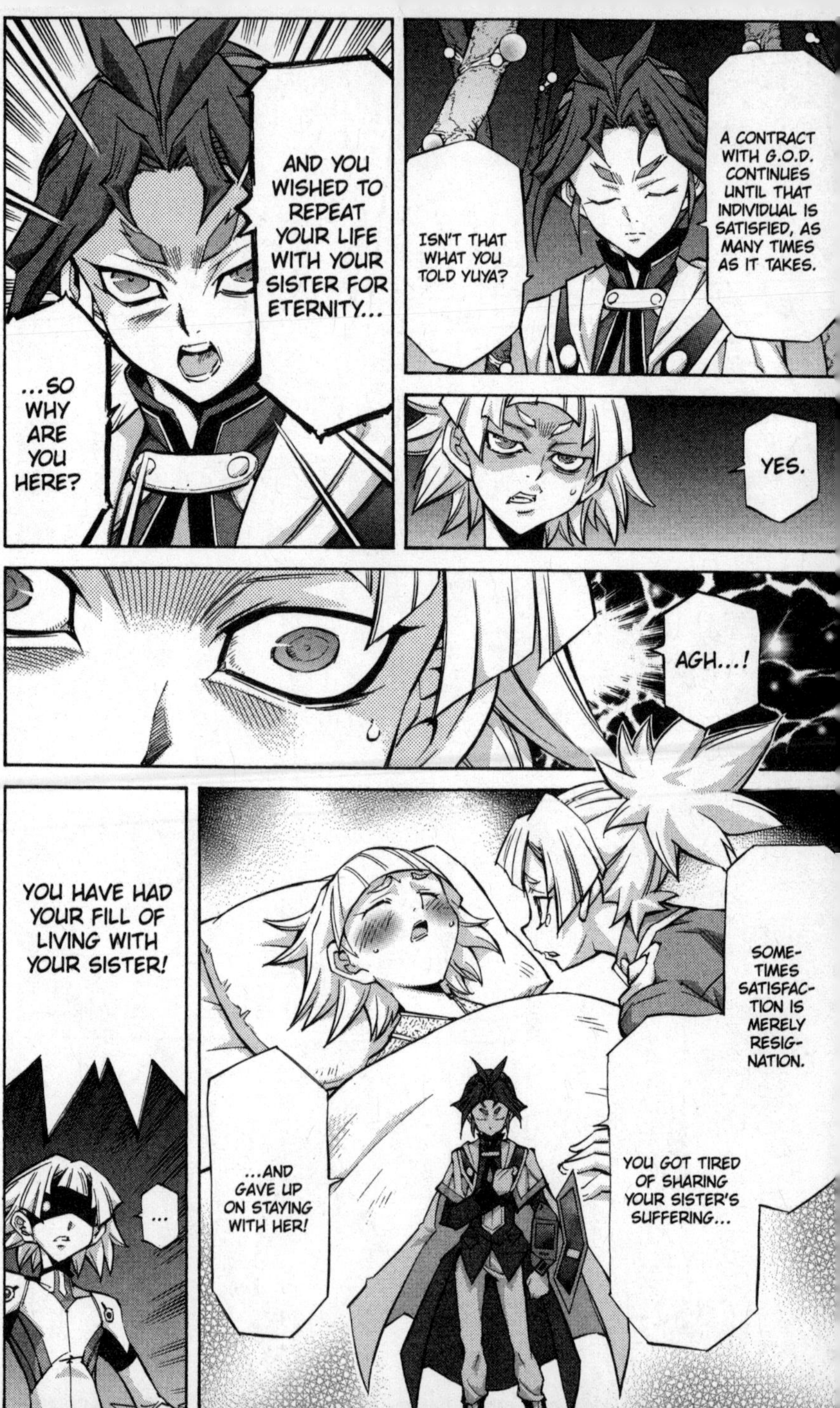
A CONTRACT WITH G.O.D. CONTINUES UNTIL THAT INDIVIDUAL IS SATISFIED, AS MANY TIMES AS IT TAKES.
ISN'T THAT WHAT YOU TOLD YUYA?
YES.
AND YOU WISHED TO REPEAT YOUR LIFE WITH YOUR SISTER FOR ETERNITY...
...SO WHY ARE YOU HERE?
AGH...!
SOMETIMES SATISFACTION IS MERELY RESIGNATION.
YOU GOT TIRED OF SHARING YOUR SISTER'S SUFFERING...
...AND GAVE UP ON STAYING WITH HER!
YOU HAVE HAD YOUR FILL OF LIVING WITH YOUR SISTER!
...

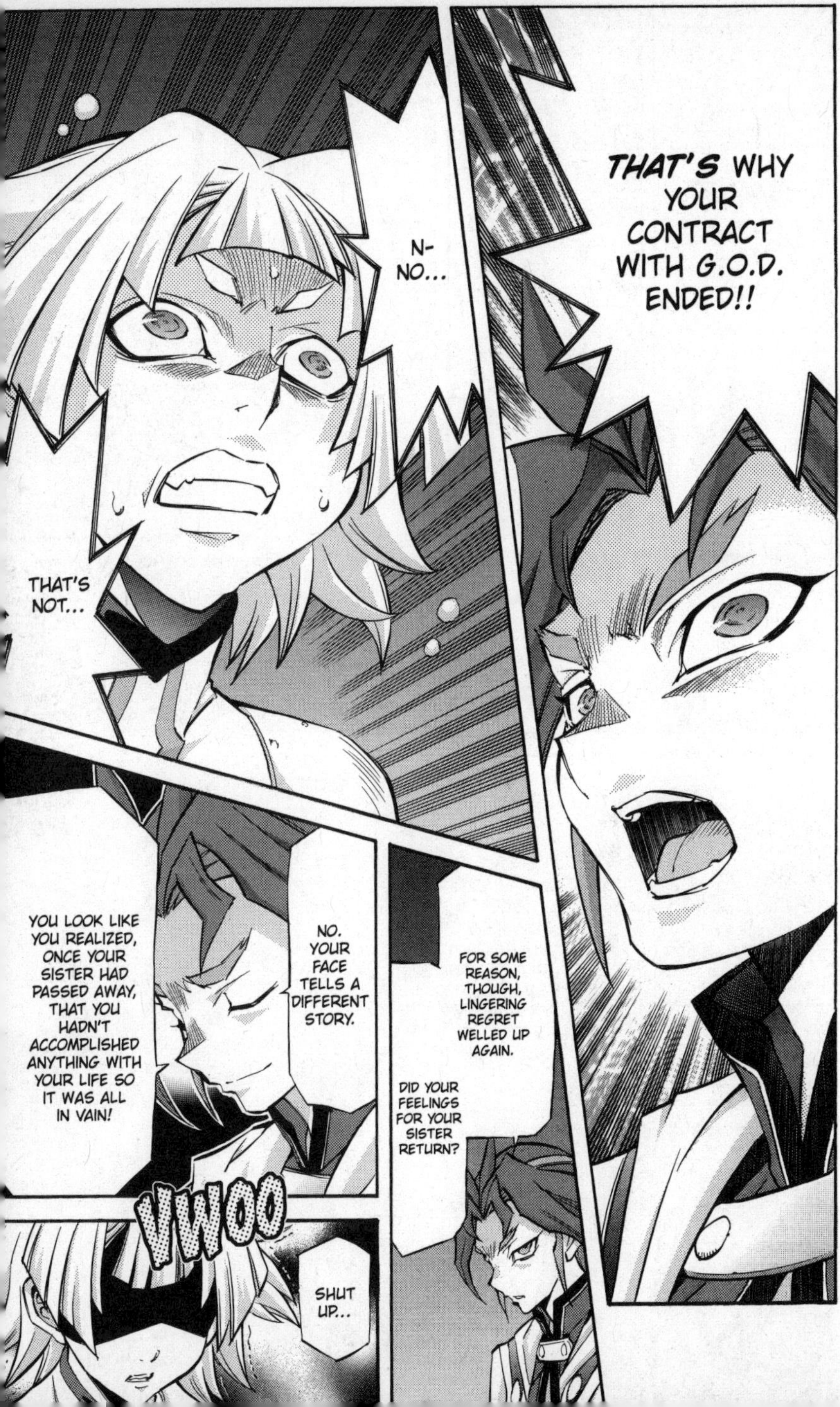
THAT'S WHY YOUR CONTRACT WITH G.O.D. ENDED!!
N-NO...
THAT'S NOT...
FOR SOME REASON, THOUGH, LINGERING REGRET WELLED UP AGAIN.
DID YOUR FEELINGS FOR YOUR SISTER RETURN?
NO. YOUR FACE TELLS A DIFFERENT STORY.
YOU LOOK LIKE YOU REALIZED, ONCE YOUR SISTER HAD PASSED AWAY, THAT YOU HADN'T ACCOMPLISHED ANYTHING WITH YOUR LIFE SO IT WAS ALL IN VAIN!
VWOO
SHUT UP...

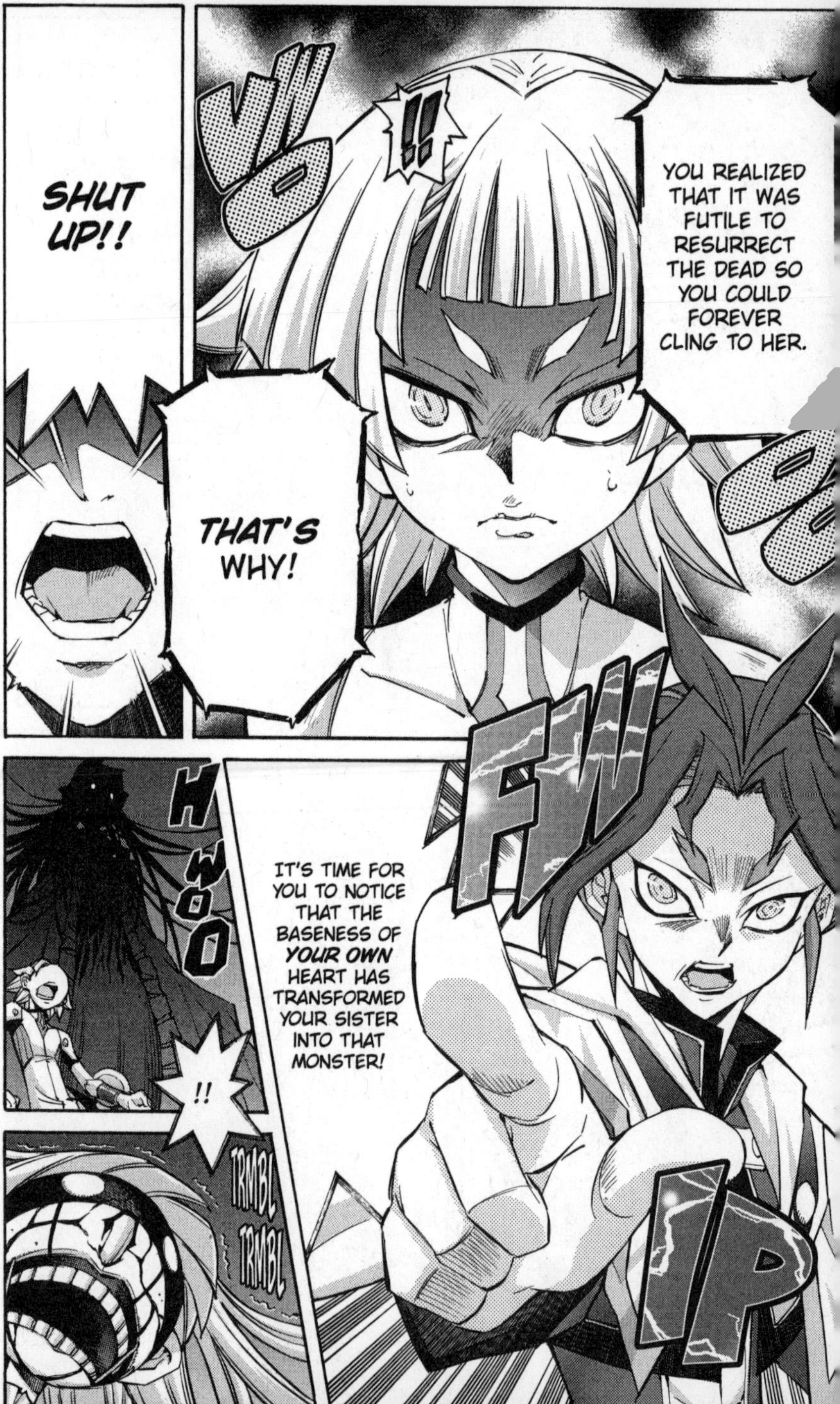
YOU REALIZED THAT IT WAS FUTILE TO RESURRECT THE DEAD SO YOU COULD FOREVER CLING TO HER.
!!
THAT'S WHY!
SHUT UP!!
FWIP
IT'S TIME FOR YOU TO NOTICE THAT THE BASENESS OF ***YOUR OWN*** HEART HAS TRANSFORMED YOUR SISTER INTO THAT MONSTER!
HWOO
!!
TRMBL TRMBL

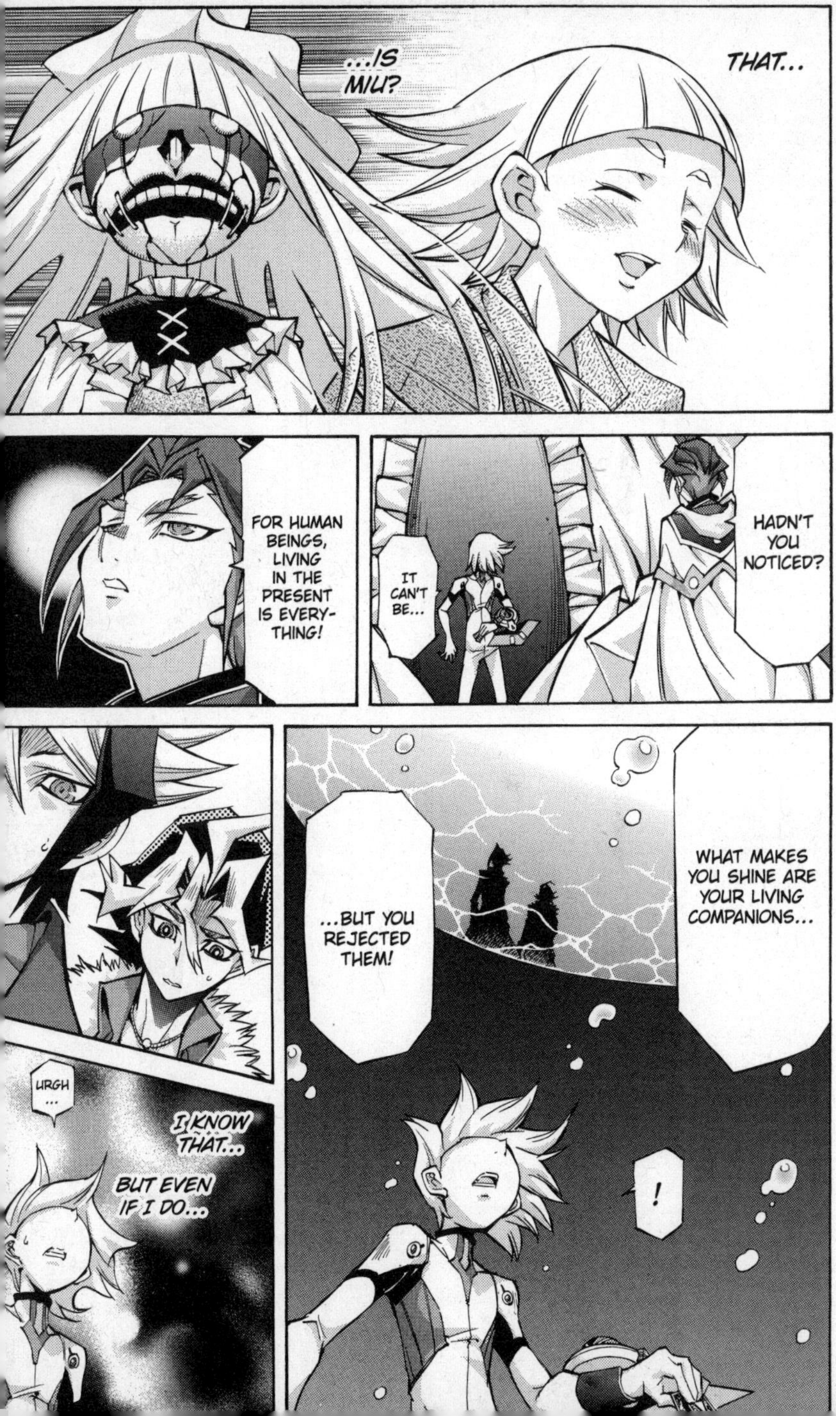
THAT...
...IS MIU?
HADN'T YOU NOTICED?
IT CAN'T BE...
FOR HUMAN BEINGS, LIVING IN THE PRESENT IS EVERYTHING!
WHAT MAKES YOU SHINE ARE YOUR LIVING COMPANIONS...
...BUT YOU REJECTED THEM!
!
URGH ...
I KNOW THAT...
BUT EVEN IF I DO...

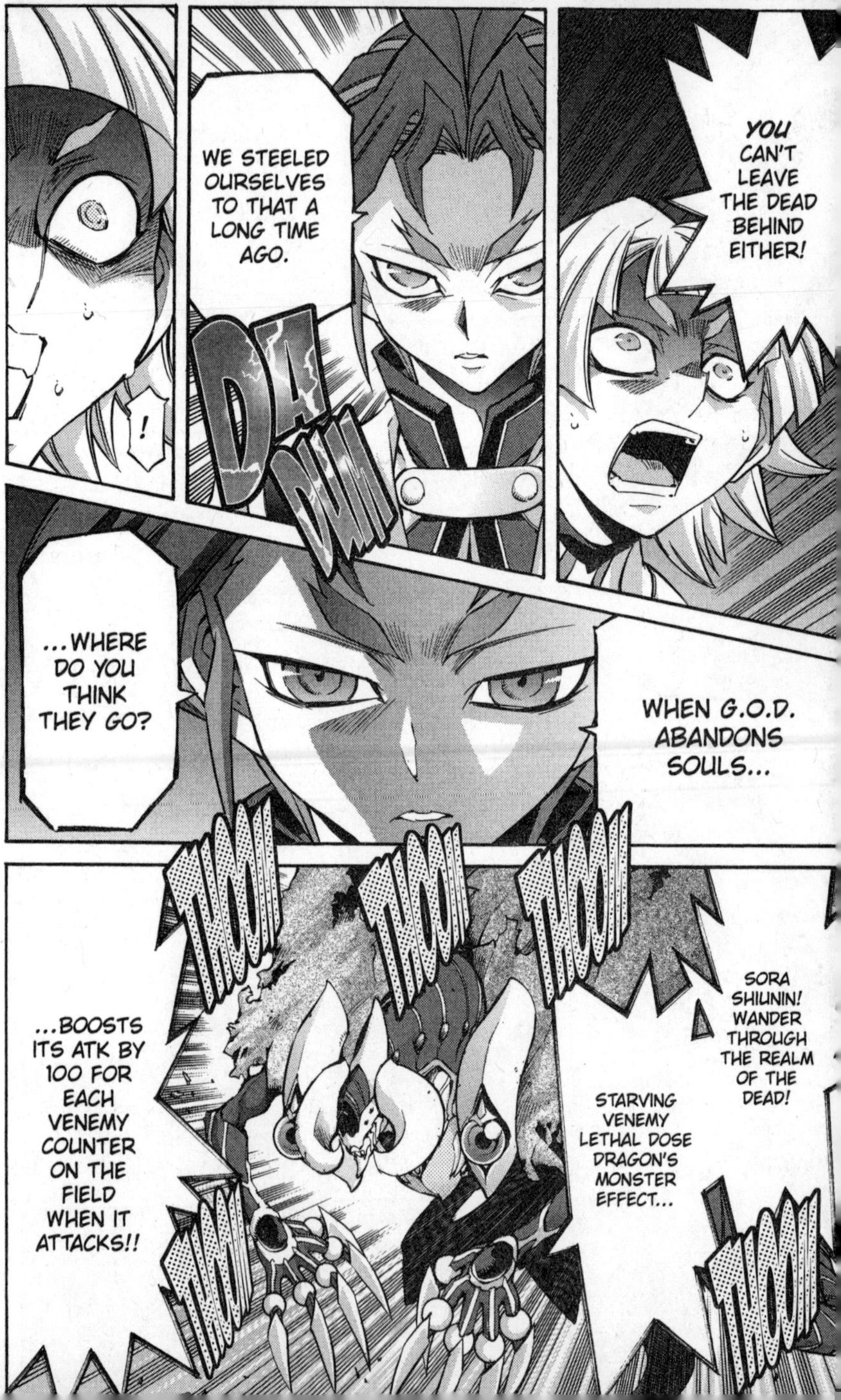
YOU CAN'T LEAVE THE DEAD BEHIND EITHER!
WE STEELED OURSELVES TO THAT A LONG TIME AGO.
!
WHEN G.O.D. ABANDONS SOULS...
...WHERE DO YOU THINK THEY GO?
THOOM!!
THOOM!!
THOOM!!
SORA SHIUNIN! WANDER THROUGH THE REALM OF THE DEAD!
STARVING VENEMY LETHAL DOSE DRAGON'S MONSTER EFFECT...
...BOOSTS ITS ATK BY 100 FOR EACH VENEMY COUNTER ON THE FIELD WHEN IT ATTACKS!!
THOOM!!
THOOM!!

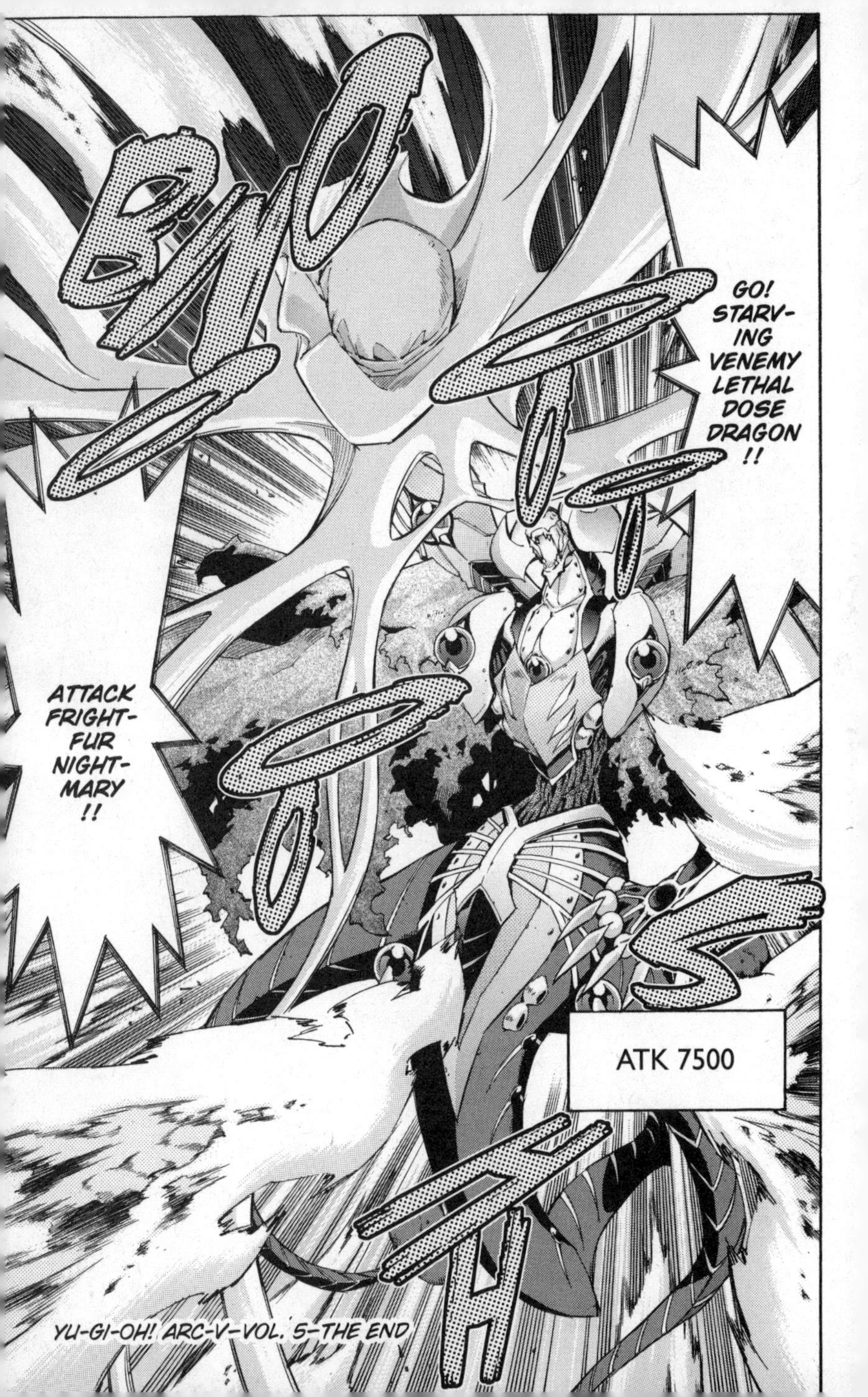
GO! STARV-ING VENEMY LETHAL DOSE DRAGON!!
ATTACK FRIGHT-FUR NIGHT-MARY!!
ATK 7500
YU-GI-OH! ARC-V—VOL. 5—THE END

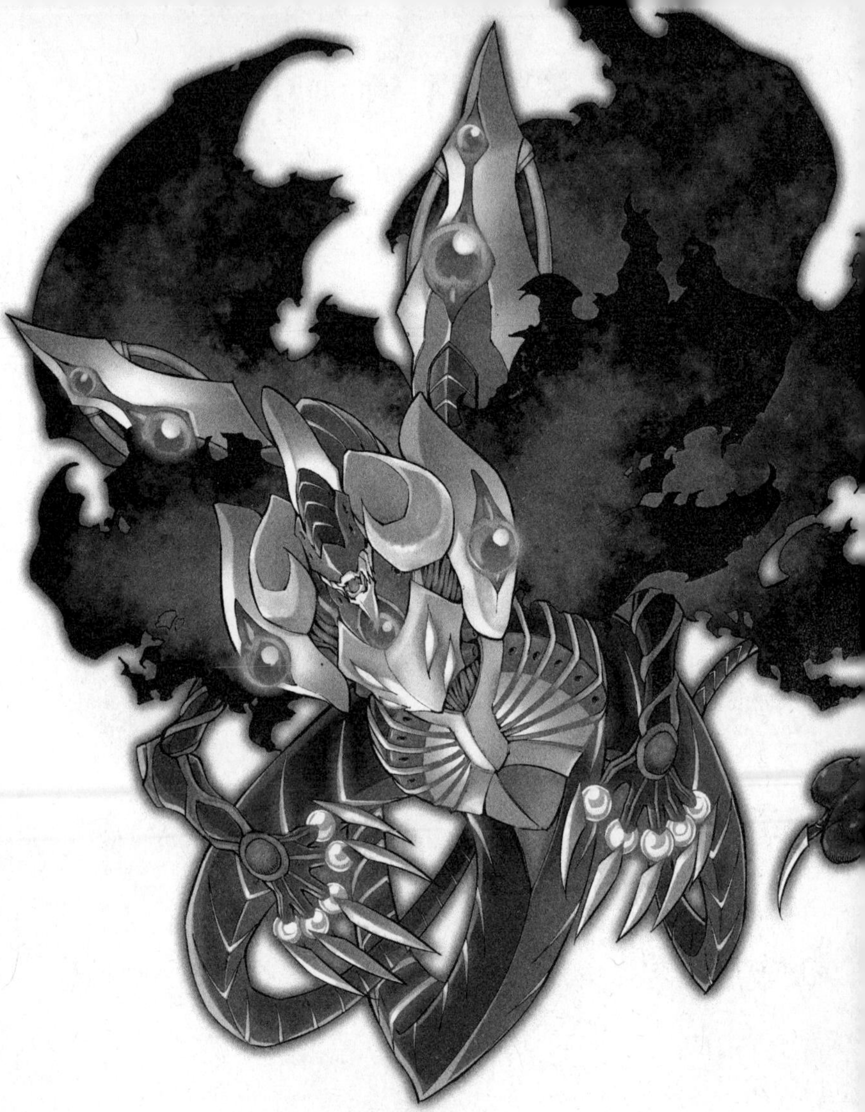

Staff	Junya Uchino Kazuo Ochiai
Coloring	Toru Shimizu
Editing	Takahiko Aikawa
Support	Gallop Wedge Holdings

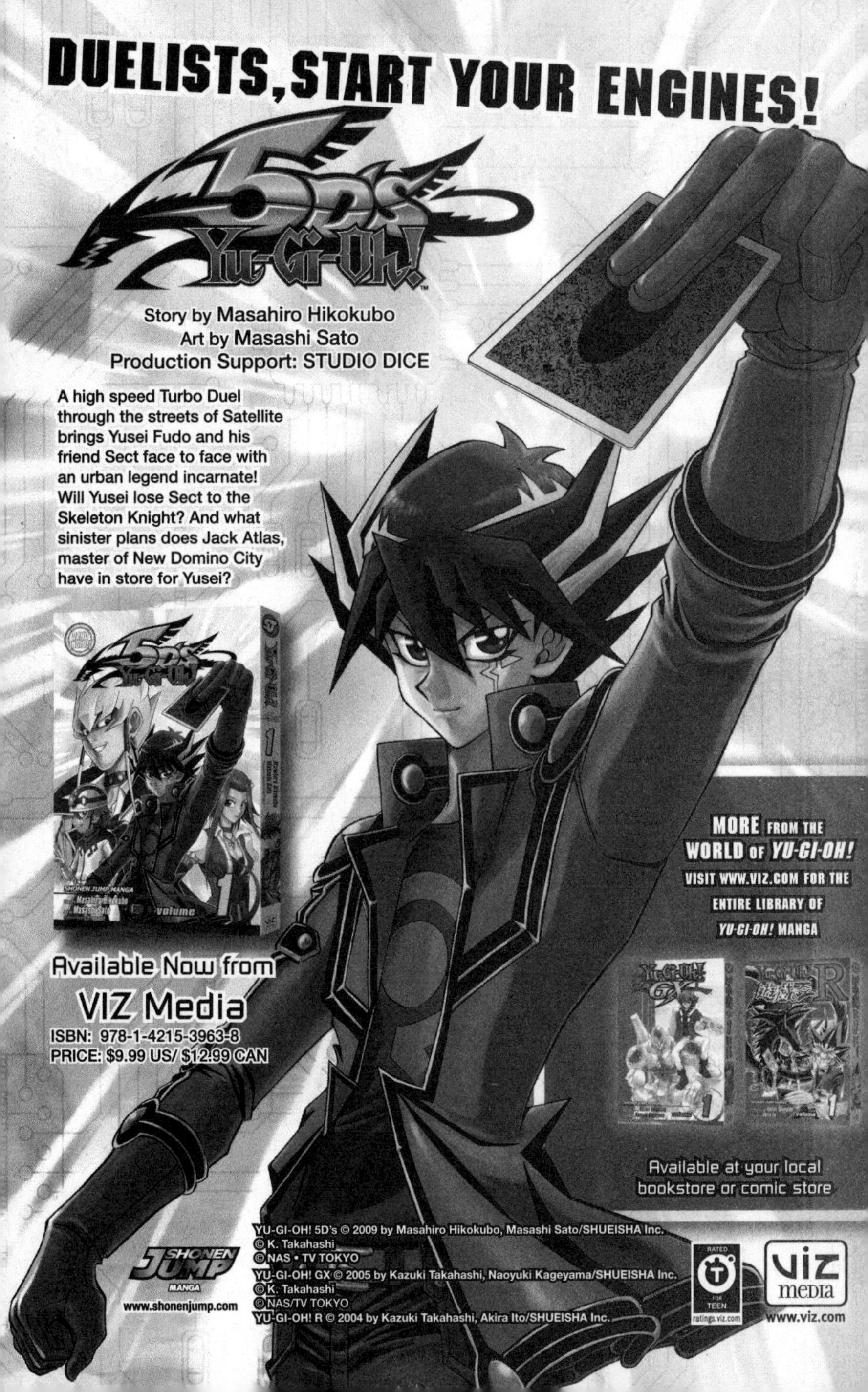
DUELISTS, START YOUR ENGINES!
5D's YU-GI-OH!
Story by Masahiro Hikokubo
Art by Masashi Sato
Production Support: STUDIO DICE
A high speed Turbo Duel through the streets of Satellite brings Yusei Fudo and his friend Sect face to face with an urban legend incarnate! Will Yusei lose Sect to the Skeleton Knight? And what sinister plans does Jack Atlas, master of New Domino City have in store for Yusei?
Available Now from
VIZ Media
ISBN: 978-1-4215-3963-8
PRICE: $9.99 US/ $12.99 CAN
MORE FROM THE WORLD OF YU-GI-OH!
VISIT WWW.VIZ.COM FOR THE ENTIRE LIBRARY OF YU-GI-OH! MANGA
Available at your local bookstore or comic store
SHONEN JUMP MANGA
www.shonenjump.com
YU-GI-OH! 5D's © 2009 by Masahiro Hikokubo, Masashi Sato/SHUEISHA Inc.
© K. Takahashi
© NAS • TV TOKYO
YU-GI-OH! GX © 2005 by Kazuki Takahashi, Naoyuki Kageyama/SHUEISHA Inc.
© K. Takahashi
© NAS/TV TOKYO
YU-GI-OH! R © 2004 by Kazuki Takahashi, Akira Ito/SHUEISHA Inc.
RATED T FOR TEEN
ratings.viz.com
VIZ media
www.viz.com

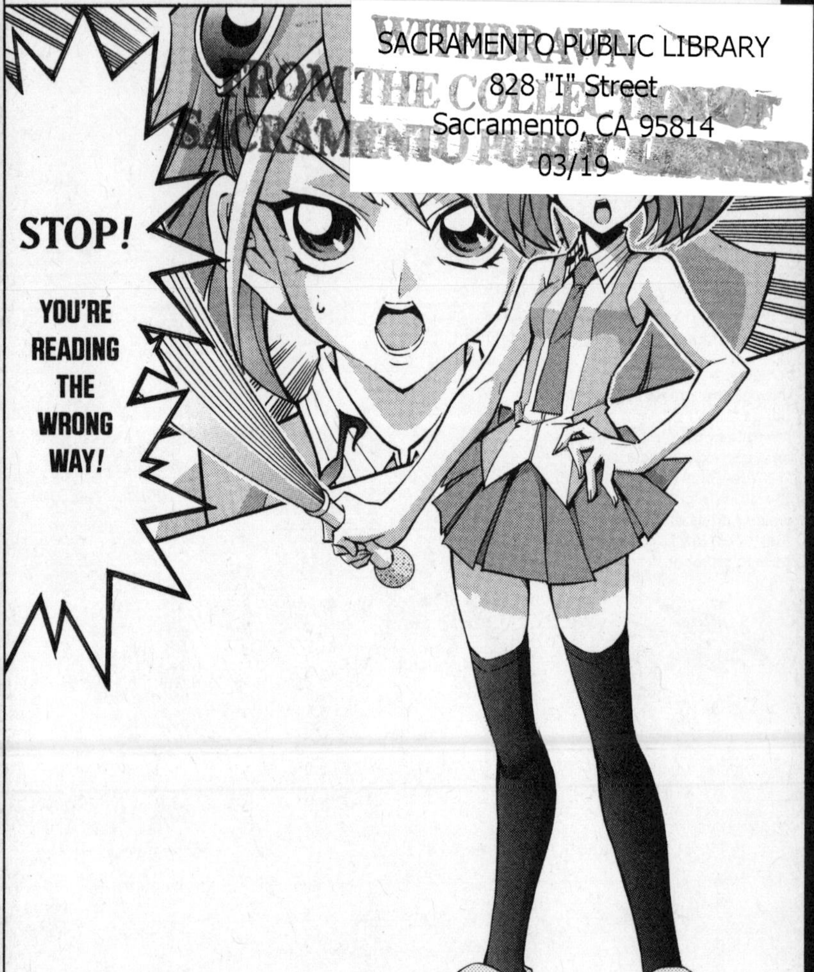
STOP!
YOU'RE READING THE WRONG WAY!

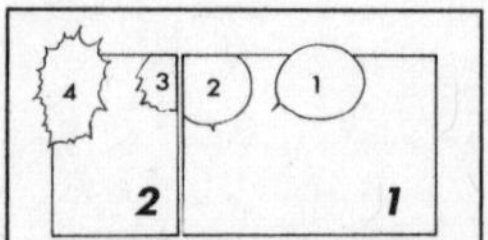

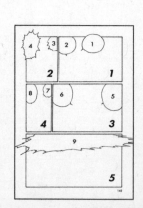

Yu-Gi-Oh! ARC-V

reads from right to left, starting in the upper-right corner. Japanese is read from right to left, meaning that action, sound effects and word-balloon order are completely reversed from English order.